W9-DGT-183

THE THERAPIST AS A PERSON

Life Crises, Life Choices, Life Experiences,
and Their Effects on Treatment

Relational Perspectives Book Series

Stephen A. Mitchell and Lewis Aron
Series Editors

THE THERAPIST AS A PERSON

Life Crises, Life Choices, Life Experiences,
and Their Effects on Treatment

edited by

Barbara Gerson

THE ANALYTIC PRESS

1996   Hillsdale, NJ   London

Published by
   The Analytic Press, Inc.
   Editorial Offices:
   101 West Street
   Hillsdale, New Jersey 07642

Library of Congress Cataloging-in-Publication Data

The therapist as a person : life crises, life choices, life
experiences, and their effects on treatment / Barbara Gerson, editor
      p.   cm. — (Relational perspectives book series : v. 6)
   Includes bibliographical references and index.
   ISBN 0-88163-178-7
   1. Psychotherapists—Psychology.   2. Psychotherapist and patient.
I. Gerson, Barbara. II. Series.
   RC480.5.G476 1996
   616.89'14'023—dc20   96-27077
                                                                  CIP

Printed in the United States of America
10 9 8 7 6 5 4 3 2 1

To Ken and Molly, with love

CONTENTS

Contributors

Claire Basescu, Ph.D., Faculty and Supervisor, William Alanson White Institute; Associate Editor, *Contemporary Psychoanalysis.*

Mark J. Blechner, Ph.D., Supervisor of Psychotherapy, Faculty, and Founder and Director of the HIV Clinical Service, William Alanson White Institute; Director of Curriculum, Supervisor, and Faculty, Manhattan Institute for Psychoanalysis.

Jane B. Burka, Ph.D., Psychologist, Psychotherapy Institute, Berkeley, CA; coauthor with L. M. Yuen of *Procrastination: Why You Do It and What to Do About It.*

Barbara Chasen, Ph.D., Private practice, New York City.

Michael A. Civin, Ph.D., Associate Clinical Professor, Derner Institute of Advanced Psychological Studies, Adelphi University; Director of Clinical Training, Baldwin Community House, Baldwin, NY; Private practice, Sea Cliff, NY.

Sue N. Elkind, Ph.D., Dean of Candidates, Psychoanalytic Institute of Northern California (PINC); Private practice in Consultation and Psychoanalytic Psychotherapy, Orinda CA.

Jesse D. Geller, Ph.D., Adjunct Faculty and Member, Psychoanalytic Center of California; Private practice.

Barbara Gerson, Ph.D. (editor), Associate Professor, Ferkauf Graduate School of Psychology, Yeshiva University; Private practice, Manhattan.

Lynn Leibowitz, Ph.D., Supervisor, New York University Postdoctoral Program in Psychotherapy and Psychoanalysis; Private practice, New York City.

Karen L. Lombardi, Ph.D., Associate Professor, Derner Institute of Advanced Psychological Studies, Adelphi University; Faculty, Postdoctoral Programs in Psychoanalysis and Psychotherapy, Derner Institute, Adelphi University.

Eric M. Mendelsohn, Ph.D., Faculty and Supervisor, National Institute for the Psychotherapies; Faculty, Connecticut Psychoanalytic Psychotherapy Center.

Stephen A. Mitchell, Ph.D., Training and Supervising Analyst, William Alanson White Institute; Faculty, New York University Postdoctoral Program in Psychotherapy and Psychoanalysis; Editor, *Psychoanalytic Dialogues.*

Andrew P. Morrison, M.D., Assistant Clinical Professor of Psychiatry, Harvard Medical School; Faculties, Boston Psychoanalytic Society and Institute and Massachusetts Institute for Psychoanalysis.

Naomi Rucker, Ph.D., Supervising and Training Analyst, Institute of Contemporary Psychoanalysis, Los Angeles; Core Faculty, California School of Professional Psychology, San Diego.

Peter J. Schlachet, Ph.D., Senior Staff Member and Supervisor, Postgraduate Center for Mental Health, New York.

B. F. Stevens (pseudonym), Licensed psychologist in private practice in the Northeast.

Helen May Strauss, Ph.D., Field Supervisor and cofounder, Graduate School of Applied and Professional Psychology, Rutgers University; Faculty, Institute for Psychoanalysis and Psychotherapy of New Jersey.

Susan C. Warshaw, Ed.D., Supervisor, New York University Postdoctoral Program in Psychotherapy and Psychoanalysis; Associate Professor, Ferkauf Graduate School of Psychology, Yeshiva University.

Acknowledgments

I am grateful to a circle of friends and colleagues who contributed in various ways to this book. I am appreciative of the support from colleagues at Ferkauf Graduate School—Abraham Givner, Joyce Weil, Louise Silverstein, Susan Warshaw, Barbara Melamed—and am particularly grateful for their belief in the importance of this book in its early, fragile stages.

I am also very appreciative of the encouragement and ideas from Beatrice Beebe, Jonathan Cobb, and Sandra Lee.

My deepest thanks to my buddies, editors, and supporters throughout the years—Barbara Breslau, Sharon Kozberg, and Martin Rock. Thanks for listening to yet another "issue," reading yet another draft, and for always being interested in this book with me.

Thanks to Stephen Mitchell, who provided thoughtful, honest, and tactful help as well as a reassuring presence. Thanks also to Nancy Liguori at The Analytic Press for her patient, steady, and knowledgeable guidance.

My gratitude to Leon Lurie and Chaim Shatan, for being there for me in life. And to my parents, for having encouraged me to follow my own paths.

And, most of all, thanks to Ken Pearlman, who inspired me by example to create. Thanks for your unique perspectives and humor. It's a treat to share the rocky roads with you.

Introduction

This book is about the effects of central life crises and identity concerns of therapists on their work as therapists. It is an exploration into the once publically silenced question of how our professional selves are touched by our personal selves. The intent is to show how we make clinical use of what we have fashioned from our life encounters as children and as adults. Personal struggles with crises or with certain aspects of identity (particularly those of the body-self) sometimes enhance, sometimes limit, but always affect our clinical work. This book presents a mosaic of voices; the authors speak about the impact of key circumstances in their lives on the conduct and tone of therapy with their patients.

The idea for this book developed in a highly personal context. I became taken with the topic after I experienced an unexpected and traumatic late pregnancy loss (see Chapter 4 of this book). I sadly put away my growing collection of articles on the effects of the analyst's pregnancy on treatment, entered a period in which there was room for no literature, and emerged much later cherishing a smaller selection of articles by analysts coping with crises equivalent in impact, if not in specifics, to mine.

The articles I found most comforting and useful (Schoolman, 1988; Lazar, 1990; Morrison, 1990) felt like conversations with very thoughtful friends who opened up their lives, personal and analytic, in unusual and profound ways. I found myself wanting and needing more such personal and clinically specific discussions. I was fortunate to have friends and colleagues with whom I could talk over what I was experiencing, and a few who would talk over what they were experiencing. I hoped, in creating this book, to provide a place for thoughtful clinicians to talk to others about the ways they think and work amidst and with their struggles. So this book is, for me, what we hope our patients will find from their analyses with us—some positive legacy from pain and something to offer others from the struggle.

ANALYST–PATIENT INTERACTION

This book fits within ongoing theoretical discussions about the use of the analyst's "subjectivity" with patients. As patients (including ourselves as patients) know, their therapist's personality, style, and world view do make a difference to the treatment. Patients who have had more than one analyst can also point out significant differences in the treatments related, in part, to the analyst. There is widespread acceptance now of the belief . that analytic interaction resembles all other interactions as a relationship between two people, each of whom contributes to the twosome.

Each analyst's work is unique, affected by the analyst's "values, assumptions, and psychological idiosyncracies" (Renik, 1993, p. 553), by their "own dynamics, passions, ideas and general subjectivity" (Mitchell, 1995, p. 65), and by their "experiences and personal development" (Winnicott, 1949, p. 195). The analyst's individuality is seen as integral to the analytic process, becoming intermixed with the patient's dynamics. The analyst is now seen as positioned inside the therapy. His/her reactions to each patient are viewed not as problematic, but as inevitable (Aron, 1992; Hoffman, 1992) or even as providing the central leverage for movement (Bollas, 1989; Ehrenberg, 1992).

Countertransference has become broadened by the concept of "subjectivity." The analyst's feelings and reactions to patients are no longer regarded as manifestations of the analyst's pathology, or as unresolved residues from historical relationships in need of further analytic scrutiny. Nor are they thought to be helpful guides in illuminating the picture of the patient, an idea that implies that there is but one picture of a person. Rather, our reactions are essential and necessary aspects of who we are; reacting personally is all we can do. We have no choice but to be who we are, as therapists as well as in our other roles.

Levenson, writing since the 1960s about the role of the analyst as a participant observer, emphasized that the analyst can only respond to a patient "authentically," by which he meant that the analyst can respond only by being "in touch . . . with one's experience of the situation" (1991, p. 108). The therapist's understanding of the patient and the patient's history is thus relative, and there is no one truth (Levenson, 1991; Aron, 1992; Hoffman, 1992; Renik, 1993). As Renik (1993) said, an analyst cannot minimize his or her personal involvement and subjectivity. Instead, he recommends that we be more forthcoming about our reactions, so that our patients will be able to deal with our subjectivity more openly.

There is no objective reality or truth in understanding the patient's story; in addition, the analyst can never know fully or objectively the meaning of his or her behavior (Hoffman, 1992). This implies again that it is impossible to avoid what has traditionally been referred to as countertransference. In speaking about how the analyst decides to do or say something, Hoffman says, "The actions occur largely as an immediate expression of a myriad of considerations within the analyst's 'unformulated experience' . . . the very fact that the analyst's subjectivity is implicated on multiple levels brings with it a measure of uncertainty about the meaning and wisdom of whatever he or she may choose to say or do" (1992, p. 294). Hoffman discusses the "special kind of authenticity" (p. 297) that follows when therapists maintain a questioning and open attitude about their own participation with patients.

Self-disclosure, then, is an unavoidable and omnipresent element of treatment, and analytic anonymity a myth (Ferenczi, 1988; Greenberg,

1995). There are significant differences in what each analyst reveals by choice, but all of us reveal much about ourselves by chance, as well as by our conscious and unconscious choices about the structure of our practices. Our thinking about the facts or feelings that we reveal deliberately, though, is informative and shows the many ways that we try to best serve our patients' interests. Some (for example, Maroda, 1991; Ehrenberg, 1992, 1995) rely heavily on their feelings with patients and share them easily. Others (for example, Davies, 1994) may reveal a very intimate feeling for a specific therapeutic purpose. Ferenczi (1988), of course, went furthest in self-disclosure in his "mutual analyses" when he revealed even free associations to patients. In contrast, some argue that it may be an appropriate choice not to answer what appears to be a straightforward question, in order to advance the analytic process (for example, Greenberg, 1995). Our factual self-disclosures also vary according to life circumstances and in response to variations in our feelings with different patients at different points in the treatment process (Stricker and Fisher, 1990).

In this book, questions about the effects of the analyst's subjectivity as a result of pressing life crises and identity concerns of the body-self (i.e., about body size, ethnicity, sexual orientation, age) on all aspects of interaction will be considered. The detailed clinical inquiries presented in each chapter are intended to enliven and deepen our understanding of the general questions of how our lives affect our interactions with patients. Patient–therapist boundaries, transferences and countertransferences, interpretations, resistances from both patient and therapist, therapist empathy, overinvolvement, underinvolvement, and values will be addressed throughout the book. The question of self-disclosure runs throughout these discussions.

Crises of all kinds—past, present, and ongoing—heighten the often silent background influence of therapists' lives and personalities on interactions with patients and thus can provide a new perspective on how interactions may operate. In addition, crises may deepen one's views and reactions to the central existential dilemmas of therapy and life, such as freedom, responsibility, will, courage, choice, or limitation. As a result, new patterns of feeling and thinking may appear in the intimate work with patients, providing new leverage for movement for both patient and therapist.

CURRENT LIFE CRISES OF THERAPISTS

Nearly fifty years ago, Fromm-Reichmann (1950) cautioned therapists to neither underestimate nor overestimate the importance of "intercurrent events," such as a death, marriage, childbirth, or divorce, in their lives. She encouraged therapists not to evade acknowledging their life crises if patients notice some change, to reassure patients of one's competence to continue the work, and to take time off if necessary. She concluded,

"These suggestions may suffice to facilitate the psychiatrist's orientation to the problem of his attitude to patients with regard to intercurrent events in his life" (1950, p. 213). We now acknowledge that such practical, down-to-earth advice is merely the beginning of how we can deal with personal crises.

The inevitability of physical changes in the analyst initially propelled many analytically oriented clinicians to pay attention to their life crises at work. Pregnancy became the first area to be widely discussed (Hannett, 1949; Lax, 1969; Barbanel, 1980). Perhaps it was easiest to acknowledge the effects of pregnancy, since it is a nonstigmatized physical intrusion and belongs to the world of women, who are accorded cultural sanction for personal expression. Discussions of the impact of physical illnesses soon followed (Weinberg, 1988; Schwartz and Silver, 1990). By now, there is a substantial and always increasing literature about both pregnancy and illness (Fenster, Phillips, and Rapoport, 1986; Penn, 1986; Imber, 1990; Grunebaum, 1993; Sayres Van Niel, 1993). Singer's early article on the effects of his wife's illness and death is unique because it is about a crisis that is not necessarily visible (Singer, 1971). Although there have been some other discussions of deaths of loved ones (Givelbar and Simon, 1981; Colson, 1995), these are relatively rare.

The question of analysts' self-disclosure of the facts of their physical health was the prime question in much of the literature, with concern for transference changes in the face of decreased anonymity. Generally, as I discuss in more detail in my chapter, orientation to self-disclosure varies in accordance with the analyst's overall theoretical orientation, although increased self-disclosure seems to be the norm at times of physical changes. Colson (1995) notes, however, the generally sparse information on the details of analysts' subjective experience of their illnesses, at the cost, he says, "of examining how the hopes, disappointments, and sufferings that are at the heart of being seriously ill and fearing for one's life affect the analytic work" (p. 460).

There has been some attention to the consequences of life crises on the vicissitudes of treatment, apart from questions about self-disclosure. Much of the focus has been on minimizing potential negative impacts. Even those who have been receptive to and positive about the useful-ness of countertransference for therapeutic work have cautioned us about possible negative effects of life crises. Witenberg (1979), for example, presents the case of an analyst whose fears of heart disease interfered with work with a patient with heart problems. He also talks about the negative impact of his own unresolved residues from the death of a younger brother when he was six years old, indicating the lasting effects of a past crisis.

In contrast, Singer (1971) noted the unexpected positive effect of his crisis on some of his patients, and other such life-enhancing effects have been discussed by others since then (Lazar, 1990; Durban, Lazar, and Ofer, 1993; Colson, 1995). However, some underlying feeling of regret for our humanness still pokes through, even as we are more open about our humanness. Gold, in her introduction to a contemporary book about therapists' lives, says, "Although many patients . . . see their therapist as omnipotent and therefore, problem free, this is . . . *unfortunately,* not an accurate perception" (Gold, 1993, p. ix, italics added).

There are, of course, many adult life crises in addition to the generally joyful crisis of pregnancy and the frightening crisis of illness that analysts, like all adults, are likely to encounter. Many of these crises are included in this book, with the hope of presenting a fuller picture of the realities of our work.

Most traumatic are the deaths of loved ones, a topic only minimally addressed in prior literature. Death of one's child is, as Barbara Chasen says in her chapter, "the unutterably unthinkable." In writing about the death of her twelve-year-old son, who was struck by a car, Chasen generously shares with us, in journal-like form, how she and her patients have survived. Eric Mendelsohn writes about the death of his eleven-month-old daughter, who suffered from severe heart disease and who had bravely become, as Mendelsohn puts it, "a person among people" even in the face of her serious illness. It is painful to read both their chapters, and also strengthening, as we are shown how a broken heart, in Chasen's terms, and grief and love, as a patient of Mendelsohn's observed, can be shared, endured, and "used" by patients and therapist.

Andrew Morrison discusses the death of his wife, also an analyst, who had written beautifully herself about her life-threatening illness (Morrison, 1990). In his current chapter, Morrison focuses on the difficulties of working at a time when one's own "self-state" becomes "destabilized." He presents issues of denial, anger, guilt, grief, dependency, and vulnerability operating in both patients and therapist when his wife died. Morrison bravely reveals his differing reactions with women and men patients and hypothesizes about the meaning of his and his patients' gender-specific reactions.

A visible late pregnancy loss, a death of a different sort, turns a joyful experience around in a moment, as both therapist and patients suddenly confront vulnerability, the harshness of fate, and fears of destruction. My original article (Gerson, 1994) on my pregnancy loss is Chapter 4 of this book. As I observe in the chapter, this highly disruptive crisis became a focal point around which some patients and I confronted analytic issues that had become mutually intense and emotionally charged. I discuss several patients with whom struggles intensified following my loss, as well as patients with other problems around intimacy. My patients and I found new ways of being with each other, as Chasen and Mendelsohn also found with their patients after their losses.

There are several possible resolutions to the problems encountered in trying to have a child. As infertility problems increase and medical technology extends our options, and our anxiety, about the ways to conceive babies, we are confronted with many choices if biological parenthood is not an option. Lynn Leibowitz writes about her decision not to have children after infertility problems. She discusses the evolution in her thinking about the nature of therapeutic relationships, with her childlessness as a focus. To illustrate this evolution, she describes her answers to patients' questions about whether she has children. From her chapter, we can begin to appreciate some of the complexities of self-disclosure, and we can see how Leibowitz has grappled with the uncertain and unknown aspects of countertransference. The theoretical ideas of the social-constructivist view of analysis are brought to life as Leibowitz shares her thinking about what she has seen about herself through her patients' reactions.

Michael Civin and Karen Lombardi write what they learned about their relationships with patients when they had to suddenly announce their departure to adopt their daughter Chloë. As in Leibowitz's chapter, the complexities of self-disclosure become evident as Civin and Lombardi observe the differences in what they disclosed to various patients. We are able to see how even the self-disclosure of facts is colored by and reflects subtle aspects of the therapist–patient relationship, often difficult to perceive or acknowledge. Both Civin and Lombardi find their views of their patients, of themselves, and of the analytic dyad broadened and deepened as a result of the adoption and its overflow into their treatments.

Parenthood itself is, as Claire Basescu writes, an "ongoing crisis," usually with much happiness associated with it and always potentially anxiety provoking. Parenthood is also a powerful subject for both therapist and patients; in her chapter, Basescu explores how children "in the therapist's head and heart" enter into the therapeutic relationship. She discusses themes that are integral to the realities of parenthood; she talks, for example, about her vulnerability as a parent, her concerns of having a "parentcentric" bias and her envy of a woman patient who has chosen a different path in the career/mothering thicket than she has. Her chapter points out how the therapist's values, life-styles, and choices may interact with patients' values, styles, and choices. She gives clinical reality to Thompson's (1956) idea that the totality of the analyst, including the analyst's values about central issues, influences the work.

Jesse Geller reflects on being a parent to a child born profoundly deaf. Geller's thinking, working, and way of being were profoundly altered by what started out as a shattering experience for him and his family. Learning to communicate with Jenny and to help Jenny become the "highly intelligent, creative young woman" she now is, impressed upon Geller the importance of "authenticity of communication" and the sharp effects of feeling misunderstood. Being Jenny's father helped Geller understand the role of pity in therapy and in grief. He speaks with originality of the positive meaning of pity and of the intermixing of pity, sympathy, compassion, and empathy.

Divorce, unlike crises that are "blows of fate," is a crisis for which the therapist may feel responsible and which may bring a sense of failure and stigma, as Peter Schlachet points out. It is also a crisis that can evoke deep reactions from patients, given the importance of a committed relationship as a culturally sanctioned value. Schlachet cogently discusses his choice not to disclose his divorce to his patients. He relates how, despite this choice, his divorce affected his patients in both group and individual therapy, thereby pointing out the intricate communication between therapist and patient. Through Schlachet's presentations of the carry-over of his divorce to his patients' own relationships, we are again able to see how patients can make use of our life situations to help themselves.

Sue Elkind writes about the trauma of being an analytic patient in crisis and finding that her analyst could not help her. Her grief at the therapeutic stalemate compounded her grief about her life crisis. Elkind shares some of what she learned from her long process of understanding and working through the "therapeutic impasse" (with another analyst) and how the failed therapy affected her work as a therapist both at that time and in the years since then. Part of her resolution has been the development of a specialty as a consultant for patients and therapists "in serious, unresolvable impasses." Her experiences with the failed treatment remind us of the necessity of using one's life experiences and feelings about patients for their benefit only and not for ours.

CHILDHOOD LIFE CRISES AND IDENTITY CONCERNS OF THERAPISTS

Our past crises become part of our histories and our backgrounds; life crises ultimately shape and become part of our personalities. They contribute to the formation of our values and orientations to the world and inform our work. Similarly, our identities, particularly aspects of our body-self with which we have struggled, color our world view and our reactions to our patients' assumptions and views. Recently, Sue Shapiro (1993) has urged therapists to write their "background stories" more often, so that "it would be easier for all of us (i.e., therapists) to explore our prejudices" (p. 378). With greater mutual self-disclosure within the profession, we could explore our "subjectivity" more easily.

A small group of recent publications look in more detail at the ways in which unchangeable aspects of an analyst's subjectivity affect the vicissitudes of treatment. Gruenthal (1993) and Hirsch (1993) talk about the effects of their gender and age on their work, and Eissler (1993) discusses the impact of aging. Leary (1995) describes the influence of her race and ethnicity with three patients, concluding that the bodily and social–historical meanings of race and ethnicity in each dyad need to be understood. She makes the often-overlooked point that race often plays a role in treatment, whether the therapist and patient are of the same or different races. Isay (1991) explores the meaning to his patients of his homosexuality and how this has affected the work with both homosexual and heterosexual patients. Jacobs (1991) discusses transference–countertransference "enactments" with patients that reflect his background and real-life events. He views these enactments as essential and as "indispensable guides" in analytic work, thereby indicating the usefulness of our early experiences and personalities.

There are six chapters in this book that continue the tradition of these self-exploratory journeys. B. F. Stevens and Susan Warshaw write about traumas they experienced growing up and the influence of their traumas on their clinical approaches. Stevens was sexually violated by her older brother for a ten-year period. She writes about her work with two sexually abused patients, showing the themes she has become sensitized to from her own abuse. The chapter gives a moving and disturbing account of the indelible consequences of sexual abuse. In her chapter, Stevens shows how she works conscientiously to use her similarities and differences from her patients to promote their growth. Stevens chose to write under a pseudonym, alerting us to the sensitivity of the material and of the concern of being stigmatized or judged if "known" so fully.

Warshaw's father died suddenly when she was thirteen years old, leaving her and her family emotionally bereft and financially anxious. Warshaw talks about her own work to "reestablish stability, to integrate, to compensate for and move beyond this powerfully traumatic experience." She presents her view of the role of the therapist with traumatized patients and discusses the longing for the idealized therapist/parent that traumatized patients carry. Her presentations—of a child whose father died when the patient was two and of an adult whose family was disrupted by the trauma of having a handicapped child—show how Warshaw understands and relates to others in trauma.

Mark Blechner, Naomi Rucker, and Jane Burka write about identity concerns with which they have struggled. They discuss core aspects of their body-identities, defining parts of who they are, which individualize and ultimately strengthen them. Feeling different from a cultural norm has forced their values into sharper perspective and has profoundly colored their clinical work. Blechner writes about his long process of coming out to reveal his homosexuality to other psychologists and to his patients. He discusses the inhibiting and dangerous effects of prejudice and the binds that secrecy impose. Disclosure to his patients, homosexual and hetero-sexual, has been one of the consequences, at times intentional and at times inevitable, of Blechner's increased openness in the community. We are able to appreciate disclosure as one aspect of the larger process of self-definition and self-valuation.

As the only child of a biracial couple, Rucker grew up in the era of the 1950s and early 1960s, when difference was even less accepted than it is now. She writes about her search to appreciate her differentness and to accept the accompanying "quiet loneliness and sorrow that never fully go away." In her work, she is sensitively attuned to the conflicts and solutions of her patients who are coping with their differences. She presents a patient trying to come to terms with being Filipino in the American culture and what happened when the patient inadvertently learned about Rucker's mixed racial background. We learn about two patients who feel different because of special talents and about a patient who grew up in a foreign culture. Rucker shows how the intimate connection in therapy develops most fully when the therapist uses her own experiences authen-tically and when both similarity and difference are acknowledged.

Jane Burka discusses an issue that does not require factual disclosure; she writes about the effects of being an overweight therapist in our culture, which equates excessive weight with unattractiveness and pathology. She expands our ideas of the body and shows how the unconscious of both the therapist and patient create dynamics around the body. She discusses the creation of a body "that represents the shared unconscious life of the therapist/patient pair." Burka shows us some of the reactions she and her patients have to each other's bodies and some of the complex construc-tions formed together. We come to appreciate how a body exists as part of a relationship.

Finally, Helen Strauss writes about an identity issue that we all hope we will face—the experience of being an elder analyst. At the age of eighty, Strauss talks about the gradual experience of becoming an elder analyst and the changes that aging brings in transferences and counter-transferences. She writes about her growing ease in using her life expe-riences with her patients. She discusses a sense of urgency about time, as well as a sense of time continuing. As she welcomes change in her own life, she helps her patients welcome it into their lives. Her chapter reminds us of the continuity and changes in the issues of growth, loss, sexuality, and cross-generational identifications.

CONCLUSION

Therapy is an encounter between two people. This book shows the pain, the beauty, and the power possible when therapist and patient meet each other in unpredictable ways. Healing and growth develop from the explo-rations and the struggles of the encounter.

REFERENCES

Aron, L. (1992), Interpretation as expression of the analyst's subjectivity. *Psychoanal. Dial.,* 2:475–507.

Barbanel, L. (1980), The therapist's pregnancy. In: *Psychological Aspects of Pregnancy, Birthing and Bonding,* ed. B. L. Blum. New York: Human Sciences Press, pp. 232–246.

Bollas, C. (1989), *Forces of Destiny: Psychoanalysis and Human Idiom.* London: Free Association Books.

Colson, D. B. (1995), An analyst's multiple losses: Countertransference and other reactions. *Contemp. Psychoanal.,* 31:459–478.

Davies, J. M. (1994), Love in the afternoon: A relational reconsideration of desire and dread in the countertransference. *Psychoanal. Dial.,* 4:153–170.

Durban, J., Lazar, R. & Ofer, G. (1993), The cracked container, the containing crack: Chronic illness—Its effect on the therapist and the therapeutic process. *Internat. J. Psycho-Anal.,* 74:705–713.

Ehrenberg, D. (1992), *The Intimate Edge: Extending the Reach of Psychoanalytic Interaction.* New York: Norton.

———(1995), Self-disclosure: Therapeutic tool or indulgence? *Contemp. Psychoanal.,* 31:213–228.

Eissler, K. (1993), On possible effects of aging on the practice of psychoanalysis: An essay. *Psychoanal. Inq.,* 13:316–332.

Fenster, S., Phillips, S. & Rapoport, E. (1986), *The Therapist's Pregnancy.* Hillsdale, NJ: The Analytic Press.

Ferenczi, S. (1988), *The Clinical Diary of Sandor Ferenczi,* ed. J. Dupont. Cambridge, MA: Harvard University Press.

Fromm-Reichmann, F. (1950), *Principles of Intensive Psychotherapy.* Chicago: The University of Chicago Press.

Gerson, B. F. (1994), An analyst's pregnancy loss and its effect on treatment: Disruption and growth. *Psychoanal. Dial.,* 4:1–18.

Givelbar, F. & Simon, B. (1981), A death in the life of a therapist and its impact on therapy. *Psychiatry,* 44:141–149.

Gold, J. H. (1993), Introduction, In: *Beyond Transference: When the Therapist's Real Life Intrudes,* ed. J. H. Gold & J. C. Nemiah. Washington, DC: American Psychiatric Press, pp. ix–xii.

Greenberg, J. (1995), Self-disclosure: Is it psychoanalytic? *Contemp. Psychoanal.,* 31:193–205.

Gruenthal, R. (1993), The patient's transference experience of the analyst's gender: Projection, factuality, interpretation or construction. *Psychoanal. Dial.,* 3:323–341.

Grunebaum, H. (1993), The vulnerable therapist: On being ill or injured. In: *Beyond Transference: When the Therapist's Real Life Intrudes,* ed. J. H. Gold & J. C. Nemiah. Washington, DC: American Psychiatric Press, pp. 21–50.

Hannett, F. (1949), Transference reactions to an event in the life of the analyst. *Psychoanal. Rev.,* 36:69–81.

Hirsch, I. (1993), Countertransference enactments and some issues related to external factors in the analyst's life. *Psychoanal. Dial.,* 3:343–365.

Hoffman, I. Z. (1992), Some practical implications of a social-constructivist view of the psychoanalytic situation. *Psychoanal. Dial.,* 2:287–304.

Imber, R. (1990), The avoidance of countertransference awareness in a pregnant analyst. *Contemp. Psychoanal.,* 26:223–236.

Isay, R. A. (1991), The homosexual analyst: Clinical considerations. *The Psychoanalytic Study of the Child,* 46:199–216. New Haven, CT: Yale University Press.

Jacobs, T. J. (1991), *The Use of the Self: Countertransference and Communication in the Analytic Situation.* Madison, CT: International Universities Press.

Lax, R. (1969), Some considerations about transference and countertransference manifestations evoked by the analyst's pregnancy. *Internat. J. Psycho-Anal.*, 50:363–372.

Lazar, S. (1990), Patients' responses to pregnancy and miscarriage in the analyst. In: *Illness in the Analyst*, ed. H. J. Schwartz & A. L. Silver. Madison, CT: International Universities Press, pp. 199–226.

Leary, K. (1995), "Interpreting in the dark": Race and ethnicity in psychoanalytic psychotherapy. *Psychoanal. Psychol.*, 12:127–140.

Levenson, E. A. (1991), *The Purloined Self: Interpersonal Perspectives in Psychoanalysis.* New York: Contemporary Psychoanalysis Books.

Maroda, K. J. (1991), *The Power of Countertransference: Innovations in Analytic Technique.* New York: Wiley.

Mitchell, S. A. (1995), Interaction in the Kleinian and interpersonal traditions. *Contemp. Psychoanal.*, 31:65–91.

Morrison, A. L. (1990), Doing psychotherapy while living with a life-threatening illness. In: *Illness in the Analyst*, ed. H. J. Schwartz & A. L. Silver. Madison, CT: International Universities Press, pp. 227–250.

Penn, L. (1986), The pregnant therapist: Transference and countertransference issues. In: *Psychoanalysis and Women*, ed. J. L. Alpert. Hillsdale, NJ: The Analytic Press, pp. 287–315.

Renik, O. (1993), Analytic interactions: Conceptualizing technique in light of the analyst's irreducible subjectivity. *Psychoanal. Quart.*, 62:553–571.

Sayres Van Niel, M. (1993), Pregnancy: The obvious and evocative real event in a therapist's life. In: *Beyond Transference: When the Therapist's Real Life Intrudes*, ed. J. H. Gold & J. C. Nemiah. Washington, DC: American Psychiatric Press, pp. 125–140.

Schoolman, J. (1988), Remission: An experiential account. *Prof. Psychol. Res. Pract.*, 19:426–432.

Schwartz, H. J. & Silver, A. L., eds. (1990), *Illness in the Analyst*. Madison, CT: International Universities Press.

Shapiro, S. A. (1993), Gender-role stereotypes and clinical process: Commentary on papers by Gruenthal and Hirsch. *Psychoanal. Dial.*, 3:371–387.

Singer, E. (1971), The patient aids the analyst: Some clinical and theoretical considerations. In: *In the Name of Life*, ed. B. Landis & E. S. Tauber. New York: Holt Rinehart & Winston, pp. 56–68.

Stricker, G. & Fisher, M., eds. (1990), *Self-Disclosure in the Therapeutic Relationship.* New York: Plenum Press.

Thompson. C. (1956), The role of the analyst's personality in therapy. *Amer. J. Psychother.*, 10:347–359.

Weinberg, H. (1988), Illness and the working analyst. *Contemp. Psychoanal.*, 24:452–461.

Winnicott, D. (1949), Hate in the countertransference. In: *Through Paediatrics to Psycho-Analysis.* New York: Basic Books, 1958, pp. 194–203. Reprinted from *Internat. J. Psycho-Anal.*, 30:69–75.

Witenberg, E. (1979), The inner experience of the psychoanalyst. In: *Countertransference*, ed. L. Epstein & A. H. Feiner. New York: Aronson, pp. 45–57.

I

Current Life Crises of Therapists

1

Death of a Psychoanalyst's Child

BARBARA CHASEN

I only know that summer
sang in me
a little while, that in me
sings no more.

Edna St. Vincent Millay

Let me comfort you, let me weep with you in your bottomless sorrow, let me sob, let me grieve for you in your endless mourning, let me wail, let me clasp you in my arms, let me rock wordlessly back and forth in your dreadful pain.

A patient's sympathy note

The unutterably unthinkable has happened. My twelve-year-old son, my only child, whom I had longed for for years, was killed. We were walking on a country road after a concert, he behind me, when he was struck by a car driven by a sixteen-year-old who had been driving six weeks. It was September 5, 1993, Labor Day weekend. We were looking forward to returning home to New York City the next day, after a five-week vacation in our country house in the Berkshires. Shaun had just been proudly graduated from the Rodeph Sholom Day School and was accepted for seventh grade at Dalton. He had a new girlfriend, Debbie, eleven, whom he had met that July at Camp Eisner. He was singing in the Metropolitan Opera Children's Chorus, and I had had the joy of seeing him in six operas, one with Pavarotti himself, on the stage of the great

Metropolitan Opera. He had just earned his yellow belt in Karate. His artwork was exceptional. His comic collection was extraordinary. He wanted to be a surgeon and would have been. He was handsome, smart as can be, and full of life.

Yet, in one minute he was dead, and my life was totally shattered. In the hospital when they told me he was brain dead, I realized with horror that, instead of his Bar Mitzvah, I would be arranging his funeral. Now, three and a half months since that tragic, that unspeakable day, I weep every day. I cannot believe he is dead. I cannot accept he is dead. It cannot be that I will never see him again, won't ever touch him again, or watch him grow, or have grandchildren. The fact that he is not here to live his life, to love and be loved, to achieve, to enjoy, to give—for him—is too painful to even speak about. I think about death a great deal. It comforts me to think that I could be near him in the earth.

Called to the hospital by the local Rabbi,[1] the Associate Rabbi[2] of our New York City temple and Shaun's school happened to be in the Berkshires that fateful Labor Day weekend. They were with me for hours after Shaun was killed. There was no time to contact a psychology colleague, so my Rabbi was the one I asked to call my patients, whom I had been planning to resume seeing in two days. He told them there was a "death in the family" and that I would contact them as soon as I could. I had debated whether to tell my patients that it was my son but decided that it was more humane not to shock them without being available to them. Most of my patients sent cordial sympathy cards, but it was obvious that early on they did not know specifically who had died. When the obituary notice appeared and some patients realized it was my child, several of them sent much more deeply felt cards.

Hundreds of people, many of them colleagues from the NYU Postdoctoral Program and the NYU School Psychology Program, came to the funeral. Parents themselves, they were traumatized by what had happened; they told me it was their worst nightmare. During Shiva (the traditional Jewish week of mourning), my colleagues visited and gently suggested going back to work as soon as possible, saying it would help. By the Monday following the week of Shiva, counting my five-week vacation, I had been gone from my patients seven weeks.

THOUGHTS ABOUT RETURNING TO WORK

I planned to resume seeing my patients exactly two weeks after Shaun was killed. Taking medication, it was going to be an experiment, as I

---

[1] Rabbi Dennis Ross, Temple Anshe Emunim, Pittsfield, Massachusetts.*

[2] Rabbi Aaron Pankin, Temple Rodeph Sholom, New York City.*

*I am profoundly grateful to you both.

could not imagine how I would be able to function. Visions of going on disability appeared. Yet, on a practical level, there were bills to pay. Also, now that I no longer had my son to care for, I could not imagine what I would do all day long without work. Even with work, there seemed to be endless time for crying and grief. I do not think I thought about my patients' needs for me, and if I did, I am sure I felt that I did not have much, if anything, to give.

Yet amazingly, amazingly, I was able to concentrate. Traditionally in my work, I am not particularly self-revealing, preferring a more "neutral" analytic stance. But I had decided that, if asked who had died, given the enormity of the trauma for me, I would not respond with, "What is your fantasy?" I knew I would answer each patient, though I felt I would not tell those who did not ask. Several of my patients were astute enough to realize that the mourning period had extended two weeks instead of one and, suspecting the worst, asked me outright who had died. My office is in my home; over the years, some patients had occasionally seen my young son in the elevator or going to his room, they had smelled dinner being cooked for him by the housekeeper, or they had heard the TV. They knew I had a child. They were devasted when I told them it was my son and cried for me, for him, admitting it was what they feared. As I write this now, it has been three and a half months, and there are still a number of patients who do not know. Where the work is perhaps less in-depth, their not knowing does not seem to feel critical. There are, however, several patients who do not yet know, but I would like them to because our work is more intense, and it feels as if I have a big, bad secret. I dread others' finding out; one wants to get pregnant, one is trying to adopt—how will this affect them?

FIRST DAY BACK AT WORK (SEPTEMBER 20, 1993)

The first patient I saw, precisely two weeks after my son was killed, was a 39-year-old married woman, with a five-year-old child, who has been trying to get pregnant for two years. Other than knowing someone had died, she had no idea what happened to me nor did she ask. She started talking about how desperately she wanted this second child and about the fertility problems she was having. Despite, or perhaps because of, my tragic loss and my own fantasies of another child, I felt extremely sympathetic to her longing for a second child. I was relieved she did not know about Shaun's death because I felt it would have inhibited her rightful need to grieve for what she had not been able to achieve. She told me that she found it very reassuring when a friend recently told her, "At least you have one child." I was, however, unable to help her with that perspective. I was glad someone else had; it would have felt like "sour grapes" coming from me. I fear if she finds out that I lost my child, she will be ashamed. She shouldn't be. I care about her, and her pain is so palpable.

By contrast, that day, another long-term patient asked me who had died. She had feared it was my son and was devastated when I confirmed it. She cried bitterly for me and for Shaun. I felt strangely grateful that she hurt, too, and to know that Shaun's death had so affected her. She is 39, just out of a divorce, and also desperately wants a child. She has had to struggle with the dual issues of finding a man and having a child. This patient, however, has accomplished what she set out to do. She recently fell in love with a man, older and handicapped, but willing and able to afford to have a child with her or to adopt. I marvel at the recoverability of the human soul. She was distraught and despairing after the breakup of her marriage, yet one year later she is embarking on a new life. Could this be possible for me? I cannot imagine it. This patient is most dear to me, and I enjoy every moment that she conquers fate. She asked what she could do to help, and I told her to let me keep doing my work. I worry that this truly sensitive person could fear that I might be jealous, but I am not. She must know how much I want her to be happy.

Grief is such a difficult emotion. A funeral director/social worker went so far as to say that

> Jacqueline Kennedy Onassis, with her magnificent public stoicism at the funeral of the assassinated president, set grieving back a hundred years. She created an example of dignity for the world that people emulated. . . . The only harm in emulating this brave woman arose when people did not stop to think that in private she cried and probably screamed just as we all do. Bereaved parents actually are ashamed of their own comparative "lack of control" as this attitude filtered down to the general population.

Harriette Sarnoff Schiff, author of *The Bereaved Parent* (1977, p. 16), questioned what kind of control should have to be maintained by the parent of a dead child at such a catastrophic time. I questioned what kind of control to maintain as an analyst with a dead child.

It was not until this first day, when I saw I could function, that I realized I would be continuing with work.

ABRUPT TERMINATION (SEPTEMBER 23, 1993—2 WEEKS)

That first week, a patient who had happened to read my son's obituary wrote to me:

Even though we have a professional relationship, we also have a very personal relationship, albeit one way. The news of your personal loss—tragedy— makes me want to reciprocate to you all the attention, caring, and advice you've given me. Of course, I feel close to you as you are the only one I have confided in about so many things.

The patient came for this one session and quit treatment that day. She cried bitterly for my loss and told me she could not bear talking about herself, that all she wanted to do was to comfort and hug me. We embraced; we did hug and cry—actually, I don't remember if I cried. She is a 35-year-old married woman who is having difficulty conceiving. I asked if she felt that she could not talk to me about wanting a child or having a child because of my loss. She denied it but quit nonetheless, with assurances that she would contact me should she need me. The assurances sounded strangely hollow, yet I understood her need to flee from my terrible situation, as if the death of my child could be "catching." (Interestingly, almost ten months later, this patient referred a relative of hers.)

The rest of my patients remained. Freud was right about the nature of productive work: at least for the time that I was in session, I could escape a little from the horror of what my life had become.

OTHER WAYS PATIENTS FOUND OUT
(DECEMBER 15, 1993—3 MONTHS)

This week, *New York Magazine* published my Letter to the Editor where I discussed Shaun's death. The letter was in response to an article they had published about a couple whose seven-year-old son had died of a brain tumor and who subsequently adopted two daughters. This same couple had heard about Shaun's death and contacted me, and, as the first family I knew who had also lost a child, helped me to feel less alone in my tragedy. The husband introduced and accompanied me to several meetings of Compassionate Friends (a bereavement group for parents who have lost children). I wrote too because part of me wanted the world to know about Shaun's death. I also suspected some patients who did not know might read the letter.

One did. She described how, when she originally received the call from the Rabbi, she had no idea it was my son who had died and had thought (wished) it was some distant relative. She herself had lost her father within the past year. She told me she read the letter three times to be sure it was really me. She then volunteered to contribute to a Memorial Fund I had set up in Shaun's name at his school. She talked about how guilty she felt having talked about her problems, which by comparison to my son's death, now seemed unimportant. I told her that my work with her and my other patients was, in fact, very important and was helping me to survive and that she should go right on doing what she was doing, namely letting our work continue. She seemed relieved by this reassurance.

Feeling guilty about being preoccupied with their own problems, which they felt were insignificant by comparison, was a dominant theme for patients once they found out it was my child who had died.

When Shaun was dead three and a half months, I received a written response to my published letter from a current patient:

Dear Dr. Chasen—

After reading your letter in this week's *New York Magazine,* I was *very* sad to hear of your son's tragic death. I actually had the gut feeling all along that this is what had happened to you, but was hoping it wasn't what I thought, and was also afraid to put you in a difficult position by your having to tell me.

But in this card I wanted to reach out and send to you a little emotional support for a change. You are a very strong woman to be able to go on with your sessions so quickly, but I suppose it is also therapeutic for you. You are a very special person—a great therapist. I truly feel that I respect your words and your way in guiding me, or at least pushing me into the right direction when necessary.

Thank you again. Take care (and see you soon!)

When I talked with her about this note, she said she had asked me who died at the end of our second session but then never brought it up again. I know I would not have told her at the end of a session, and somehow I too did not bring it up at the next session. She said, "It reminded me of my first therapist—some guy called to say the therapist was unavailable, and I never went to sessions again. When this happened to you, I thought maybe I wouldn't see you again. I was really anxious at the beginning. If it was bad as I thought, how could you go on as a therapist? I was scared you'd get upset—afraid I wouldn't know what to say or do. I know there are no real rules. I thought you'd say what happened when you were ready to." She cried, saying, "I can't believe it happened. I feel really bad. I keep thinking what a tragedy it is—the worst thing that happens to a parent. It's close to home. It makes me think about what the future holds."

She then started talking about the traumas in her own life: her parents' divorce, her father's remarriage, and the birth of a half-brother. "Part of me is thinking about the similarity of my half-brother's age (eleven), part of me is relieved to know about Shaun's death. I was always wondering, but scared to bring it up. I didn't want to be pushy. Maybe partly I didn't want to know. I cared so much I couldn't bring it up. I thought about it all the time. I get really nervous about bringing up things that are diffi- cult." I asked "Why?" "My father taught me to hold things in. If it's bad, he broods for months or years. We don't deal with things. I had that same bad gut feeling when my parents told me about their divorce. Then when my stepmother was pregnant, we saw her gaining weight, but my sister and I said, "No, she's not pregnant, she's older [38]." She had returned to her issues, through my loss, perhaps with a different perspec- tive. I said, "Maybe I wanted my patients who didn't know, to read the letter." She said, "I'm glad you wrote." I responded, "I'm glad you wrote."

MY SUICIDAL WISH (JANUARY, 1994—4 MONTHS)

> We thank with brief thanksgiving
> Whatever Gods may be
> that no life lives forever;
> that dead men rise up never;
> That even the weariest river
> winds somewhere safe to sea.
>
> A. C. Swinburne

Now I fully understand how the thought of suicide is so very comforting. Last year, a young patient came to see me after a suicide attempt. He told me that he had had suicidal ideation since he was a child and brought me a poem, written when he was eight, about how he would one day attempt suicide by taking aspirin. This is, in fact, what he attempted at nineteen. During the course of our brief treatment, he described how whenever anything would go wrong, he soothed himself with the fantasy that since he could always kill himself, "it really didn't matter." I was horrified that so young and so talented a child would have carried the burden of this fantasy for so long. Now I have the same fantasy myself. I worry, however, what impact my suicide would have on my patients, particularly him. I especially worry about a failed suicide attempt and bought *Final Exit* (Humphry, 1991) to learn how to do it successfully.

That first week, this same young patient decided to stop treatment. He did not know that my son had died. Our work was far from finished, and I tried to persuade him to continue treatment, but he was determined to "go it on his own." Previously, during the summer, he had told me that he might quit because he didn't want to become "dependent" (though he had only been in one-time-a-week treatment for less than a year). While I wanted to continue work with him for his sake, I was relieved he quit, for my sake. He was the patient I worried about most should I decide to commit suicide. Not a very good role model. I was now relieved of that particular constraint.

One of the century's most famous intellectual pronouncements comes at
the beginning of *The Myth of Sisyphus*. "There is but one truly serious
philosophical problem, and that is suicide. Judging whether life is or is
not worth living amounts to answering the fundamental question of philosophy" [Styron, 1990, p. 23].

My patients' relief that I am working and their need for me has given
me strength. I feel I would betray their trust if I killed myself. They
would have to truly understand that to lose a child is a blow from which
one might not *want* to recover. There is a constant longing to see Shaun
and hold him and touch him: as Anna Quindlen put it, "the constant
presence of an absence." Shaun's death leaves me feeling unneeded and
useless. The feeling of being needed, wanted, and useful by my patients
counteracts the uselessness for a time, but when I am alone, suicidal
thoughts soothe.

VARIOUS PATIENT REACTIONS
(JANUARY, 1994—4 MONTHS)

Another patient who knew Shaun casually through passing each other in
the hallway, and of his death, has been with me for many years and has
been talking of terminating this June. One session she talked of feeling
trapped in the treatment. We analyzed a dream where she saw me as
forcing her to remain in treatment. She then told me of a recent slip;
when she was asked how long she had been in treatment with me, she
told the person, "I'm treating her," instead of "She's treating me." In
part, she feels that she cannot leave me because my son died. She was
right, though I did not confirm her perceptions. So I challenged her and
asked her how she would feel about leaving even sooner, perhaps in
February or March instead of June. She immediately responded that she
would not want to and astutely told me, "You just got upset." Defensively
I said, "I merely wanted to ask you." I will miss her and did not want
her to leave at this point. She feels I will miss her and that she needs
to take care of me, though she admitted she "would be giving up a lot
too." I felt resentful of her wanting to leave at such a vulnerable time
for me, "after all I had done for her." Later, we talked about caretaking
being a complicated issue for her, and she admitted that, as the eldest
of eight siblings, she was angry about always having to help her mother.
It was grudging help. I myself was unable to admit that being taken care
of, being needy now, was a complicated issue for me. She reassured herself
by saying, "I know I don't have to take care of you." I wasn't so sure.

HOME OFFICE

By choice, I have an office in my home. I would often hear my son
moving about while I was working. Perhaps he would drop something or

leave the living room to enter his room. They were always wonderful sounds. My patients did not really hear them, except perhaps to know he was home. As he got older and felt he needed to reach me for something "critical," such as whether he could go down and play basketball, he would occasionally call on the second telephone while I was in session, which I always thought was rather ingenious and daring, since he knew he was not to disturb me while I was working. At 7:45 P.M., when I finished work, I would open the doors to the living room and there he would be. I always loved working at home and hearing those noises. The silence now is deafening. As I write this so soon after his death, I don't know how my story will end. Will I ever achieve that mysterious state that Elizabeth Kubler-Ross calls "resigned acceptance"? I really do not know. Twice, two different patients asked me how I was doing. And twice, I told each of them, "It's unbearable." I cannot say otherwise.

Fuzzy, a three-and-a-half-year-old Yorkshire Terrier, my present to Shaun on his ninth birthday, is our dog. Fuzzy has become a part of the therapy process for many of my patients; one in particular brings her a bone every week. Once, she asked me who was going to walk Fuzzy now that Shaun was gone, and I couldn't answer because I started to cry. Most of my patients are on the couch, so they cannot see when I cry, though I rarely cry during sessions. During Shiva, I had been given "permission" to cry, if I had to, by the numerous colleagues who gave me numerous pieces of advice in their desire to help. Though it was brief, I was not ashamed of crying. Yet I'm not used to my patients seeing me so vulnerable. My colleagues suggested, "Let your patients comfort you," but it's hard to accept, or maybe it is the reason for the comfort that is so terrible. The main way they comfort me is by continuing to come and letting me do my work.

NEW PATIENTS (JANUARY 1994—4 MONTHS)

Two weeks ago, a new patient called and my initial reaction was not to take him. I felt I could not take anybody new. I thought the reason I had been able to work was because I knew and cared about my current patients. However, counterphobically, I forced myself to see him and realized by now I could work with even a new patient or two. But I had no desire to tell him about Shaun, even though, or especially, because he had two boys, eight and eleven.

When I was a relatively new analyst and became pregnant, I worried about the transference and countertransference of my pregnancy. When my son was a baby, I worried what my patients would think if they heard him cry, though he was safe with a housekeeper. They rarely heard him. What joyous worries those were by comparison.

DREAM ANALYSIS (JANUARY, 1994—4½ MONTHS)

One patient, married with a young daughter, surprisingly still does not know. She's quite depressed, in a difficult marriage, with a bright, demanding child, a high-pressure, difficult job, and a large extended family with numerous problems. She has reason to be depressed. Perhaps those reasons stopped an otherwise extremely empathic person from sensing, or wanting to know, what happened. There is a part of me that wants her to know, as we have that deep a relationship. Yet I dread it because I fear that she will feel unentitled to her depression, or her happiness, in comparison to my grief.

I kept feeling it was disrespectful not to tell: that she had shared so much with me, how could she not know? She then brought in the following dream after four and a half months.

> I was in the backyard of a house where I mostly grew up. Where the house ended, it dropped off into a wooded area. Stairs went down to a stream. I saw my niece there, her name is Debby (the same age as Sally, blond and fair). Another child is with Debby. I realized my brother and sister-in-law were not around. It was dangerous for her to be there without a grownup. So I talked to her and told them to come with me. I started to look for my brother—she's his daughter. How could he leave her there? Then I realized that Sally and Debby are together and I can't find them. I don't know what happened to them. Essentially they're kidnapped and cannot be found. I think Sally will be found but not Debby. But what if Debby's found alive and not Sally. I think they're dead. I have the feeling Sally will never be found and she's dead and it's my fault. More than feeling responsible, I feel pain, loss that I don't have her anymore, that she's not alive.

This was the dream for which I was waiting. Her initial associations were that she felt the house was where she lived for a long time with her parents and that she was the child who gets lost and dies. She also talked of her worry about her own daughter. I asked if she felt there was any connection to therapy. "I'm not sure of a connection." I reminded her of the death in my family. She said, "I sent a card, but when you didn't say anything, I thought I shouldn't bring it up. I didn't think about it. I hope nothing happened to your child. It is too terrible to think about." At that point, I confirmed that it was my child who was killed and suggested she may have unconsciously noticed the silence in the apartment, the lack of smells of dinner cooking. She cried,

> I don't know how you manage. I'm sorry. I saw him one or two times. Blondish. I feel like saying "I wish it weren't true." That split second and you can't bring him back. At the time, I thought it just couldn't be, just couldn't be your child. I hope you can sleep and eat, and that people are being good to you, that nothing else terrible is happening. I never thought in a million years that that's what this dream would mean.

The following week she asked me, "What is most helpful to you? I keep thinking about how you're managing. It's obviously devastating. I know you're a very strong person. Did you think of being in a group with other parents? It's such a tragedy. How can you recover? Oh yes, you said work helped." I told her, "Other than work, it's unbearable." She responded, "That's honest." I then put into words what I sensed might be difficult for her to say. I asked, "Was it hard to come back today?" "Yes. I kept thinking about what I wanted to say. But I wanted to come because I wanted to talk to you."

EFFECTS OF AVOIDANCE
(MARCH 17, 1994—6½ MONTHS)

Can I be writing this? Is it my child who is dead? No, this is a nightmare, and I will wake up and he will be alive and well. But every day, I keep re-realizing "my baby is dead." The thought of my dead child does not leave me for one minute. But sometimes instead of the sharp pain, there is a dull agony. I continue to see my patients, which has saved me in some ways. But to go on without him forever is still unimaginable. Friends are a tremendous support, and watching movies on a VCR makes the time pass a little. I find I do not remember movies I have seen more than a year ago, so the entire movie world is open to me. I've now survived major holidays without Shaun: Rosh Hashanah, Yom Kippur, Halloween, Thanksgiving, Chanukah, New Year's, Valentine's Day. My birthday is in three days, and I'll be going to the cemetery. I dread Passover. I dread Mother's Day. I dread the day he would have been bar-mitzvahed. I dread his birthday. I dread his death day.

Two days ago, one of my patients who knows (I think I've divided my patients into those who know and those who don't, just as I've divided time into before the accident and after) came in and said, "I don't feel my therapy with you. I can't connect or take anything. I feel empty. Part of me feels paralyzed and scared and it has to do with Shaun. I fear that one day I'll come here and you won't be here anymore. Dead. Crazy. Moved away. Decide you can't be a therapist anymore." I said, "Are you also asking how come I'm not dead or crazy?" She replied, "I can't come in and ignore it, but there's nothing to say. It's too painful to confront together in the open. And also it's your life and what right do I have?" I assured her that she had rights. She continued, "I can't get over the pain you must be in. Figuratively, it means I can't fathom it and literally I can't get past it. I feel it here, and I can't stand the discrepancy. I come here and you seem okay." I responded, "I am in terrible pain all the time, but when I'm working, I'm okay." She said she felt relieved "that you're experiencing what's real." I interpreted, "You felt since I'm okay here, maybe I'm okay outside, and that would be crazy." She asked,

"Do you think it's therapy?" I answered, "Yes, but maybe productive work of any kind is healing. I've been dealt an impossible blow, but I am learning." She then asked, "Do you think I experienced a thin (shallow) connection because the connection is thinner?" I answered, "No. I think your not talking about it made you feel alienated."

For a period of time, I was relieved that no one asked me about Shaun, and I was content to escape into the work, knowing full well that we were all avoiding the issue. But I needed to avoid it for a time.

THE BURDEN OF DETAILS (APRIL 14, 1994—7 MONTHS)

Today is seven months, one week. A patient came in saying that somehow she felt sad, despite having had a gala birthday party that weekend. At her party, she discovered two guests who knew some details about Shaun's accident. My patient described how she had been praying that I had not actually seen the accident but learned through one guest that I had. She described how sad she was every time she came to our sessions, how she always thought about Shaun and what had happened to him. I was very touched, because other than her intense initial reaction, she had rarely talked about it. I thanked her for caring, and she knew I was crying, and she wept with me. She then described talking about me with another guest at her party whose father, a colleague of mine, had paid a Shiva call. The daughter had wondered to my patient how I could live and whether I was suicidal. My patient told her that she couldn't understand it, but somehow I felt "whole" for her, that she felt I was there for her during our sessions. She told her friend that I had said that work was healing, but that work would not be healing enough for her. I felt I had to admit that I truly did not know how I was surviving, that somehow I was. I added that it was not only work but the love and support of a wide circle of friends and family. I did not tell her about my own therapy and Compassionate Friends. I did not want her to feel that work was a panacea I had as a "solution" while she didn't, but I could not bring myself to tell all. I could not tell her that somehow you survive, that you don't die though you want to. If anyone would have told me my twelve-year-old would die and I would continue to live, I, too, would have thought it was impossible to go on. But you don't die.

We then talked about her plans for adopting a child and whether she feared she couldn't share her happiness because of my loss. Important issues to be worked on.

Another patient was telling me how cruelly her religious brother-in-law treated his two children, boys about eight and eleven. I was very involved in the intricacies of my patient's handling of these boys and the similar treatment she herself had had at the hands of her ultrareligious parents. She then said how hard this must be to listen to, because here was a father who clearly didn't deserve these children, and I, who she was sure was a loving mother because I was a good "mother" to her as my patient, had lost a child. I was startled, because, engrossed in the analysis, I had not made that particular connection, though once she said it, I realized how true it was. I also realized that she, too, is suffering for me and with me.

My infertile patient is now pregnant. My sympathy for her previous dilemma now faces a big challenge as I wonder if I will be jealous of her emerging big belly. At the same time, I cheer her perseverance, glad she overcame fate. At least some of us can. The other day, she started obsessing about the possibility of her early death, her mother having died of cancer at 52, and we talked about her desire to control fate. It was an opportunity to tell her about Shaun and to share with her how uncontrollable fate really is. I chose not to. And I will continue to choose not to tell her, because I feel it will truly unnecessarily interfere with her happiness over her pregnancy.

LAUGHING (APRIL 20, 1994—7 MONTHS, 2 WEEKS)

The other day, I had a big laugh with a patient. She had come to her session having eaten two Reese's Pieces Peanut Butter Cups and informed me she planned to eat the remaining eight pieces after her husband left their apartment. She is overweight but, more significantly, loathes her body and doesn't have sex with her husband, whose body she also doesn't think is good enough. After listening to her talk about her longing for a man with a perfect body, I ask her how it was that so many fat or ugly people were able to have sex with each other. She said she didn't know. I added, sort of impulsively, "All those people are out there screwing around, having fun, and you're eating Reese's Pieces." This struck her as terribly funny, as the truth can sometimes be, and she started laughing hysterically. It was contagious and I found myself joining her. When she left, she thanked me for a good laugh and said something about throwing the candy away, though nothing about having sex. Could I have laughed so hard? She knows my son is dead. What will she think of me?

LETTER FROM AN EX-PATIENT
(APRIL 26, 1994—7 MONTHS, 3 WEEKS)

I know that your son Shaun was killed in an accident in the fall. Since you didn't tell me, I've been afraid to intrude on the privacy of your grief— but I had to write. I *have* written—innumerable times—but I still don't know what to say to you. Simplest put, I wanted to send you my love and my grief for you, for your son, and to tell you that I have been, I am,

thinking of you. And, damn conventions of psychotherapy, I wish I could
truly comfort you in some way for this unbearable loss. You have meant a
tremendous amount to me—you know you've been sort of a mother to me—
and I know very well how deep your love for Shaun must have been, must
be.

You and I became mothers within a year of each other, and I have been
thinking a lot about the answer you gave me when, newly pregnant, I asked
you if children made you happy, and you said, simply, "Yes." We shared
that, and much else about becoming and being mothers—you helped me so
much with being a mother, not least by letting me glimpse the profound
attachment and care you had for your child. The life he did live was obviously a beautiful, tender and caring one. I hope that somehow the precious-
ness of his life, as he had time to live it, is consolation to you in some
degree for the time he was robbed of.

Her letter moved me to tears, and I was deeply grateful for her love. I
responded briefly:

Your eloquent and beautiful letter touched me deeply and gave me comfort.
I am glad you knew Shaun just a little and shared your memories with me.
I too remember our shared motherhood, and will treasure those remem-
brances. In some way I am glad that you know, but am sorry you had to
find out. Thank you for writing, it meant a great deal to me.

I wanted to write much more or to call her, but just could not "damn
conventions of psychotherapy." The web of this tragedy extends beyond
current patients, and the relationship with past patients remains as strong
as with current ones.

TO TELL OR NOT TO TELL
(SEPTEMBER 12, 1994—1 YEAR, 6 DAYS)

Today, one patient complained, "Why did you tell me the details about
Shaun's death? I was not saying I wanted to know. . . . I don't know if
you should have told me or not. In a way you were saying I really trust
you, and I am more a member of your family if I know what happens.
But it is not where I am at. I am still lying on this couch and you are
sitting on the chair." It was two sessions prior in which I had told her
the exact circumstances. Just before her session, my Rabbi[3] visited me,
and she overheard our talking about the memorial for Shaun (a playground is being built at Rodeph Sholom[4] with donations received in his

---

[3] Rabbi Robert Levine, Senior Rabbi, Temple Rodeph Sholom, New York. My deepest
thanks to you.
[4] The Shaun Beckwith-Chasen Memorial Playroof Fund, Rodeph Sholom, 10 West 84th
Street, New York, New York 10024.

memory; though Shaun was a scholar, his favorite subject was "recess," and I thought a playground would please him). She added, "And you have all these books on your shelf about grief, and it is the anniversary of the time I found out. I didn't have anyone I could talk to. I even wanted to ask your doorman about what happened. I felt there was no one I could talk to who is in my position." I was reminded of her pressure and clearly remembered why I had shared more details. I told her, "I thought you had a right to know." When she pressed, "Why?" I answered, "It was an extraordinary event, and you seemed to be asking. You even said you wanted to ask the doorman." She then became very distressed and said she was starting to "dissociate," having an "out of body experience." She added, "You are not paying attention to me, like my mother. I think you told me because you wanted to tell me." I said, "You wanted to know but you didn't want to know." She responded with, "You are putting it all on me, but part of it is you." I confirmed that I had decided that, with this tragedy, if my patients wanted to know, I would reveal more than I ordinarily would. She said, "I was angry that you told me. The content was so horrific; that you were there. It was not what I imagined. Not only that you could have gotten killed, but that you watched Shaun get killed. I never thought you would be there. It is too horrible to even think about. I just felt really stunned. I feel like I am acting like a baby, but it has affected me. I wish I could have been comforting to you. I am reacting very primitively, not very grown up. As my therapist, your sharing anything personal is different. And you are my mother, and Shaun was my sibling. It has that flavor. Now I have to deal with it and spend time, money, and emotional energy dealing with it. And knowing that you must get upset when I talk about it and not be able to listen. I have to think about your feelings and my feelings, and I don't have the appropriate feelings. It is such a scary, scary concept to think that happened. Now I can imagine the whole thing in my head and it makes it more horrific. Maybe it is better that we talk about it. But it is not the kind of thing you really can talk about, because it has to do with you. It makes me feel sad, angry, inappropriate, unless I am very adult-like, thinking about you. I can't talk about how I really feel about it because it is such a tragedy for you."

I ask, "Do you want me to say I am sorry I told you?" "No, but I feel as if I didn't ask you." I continue, "Do you feel I imposed it on you?" She said, "I felt I was expected to rise to the occasion. But I didn't, so I feel like I failed. I should have been more comforting. The whole thing is still so unbelievable, I don't feel I am on the outside, but it doesn't make me feel better to be on the inside. I always thought you had an enviable life. This makes me look at you in a different light." I asked what was enviable, and she answered, "You were a grownup, you had grownup things, a practice, an apartment, a son. You were pretty set. Now you are not set."

She then started crying. "It is very tragic. I feel my mother's life is ripped away. I feel closer to you than my family. This is more important to me than it is to other patients. Your life is unsettled, and that is what is most upsetting." I assured her, "It sounds as if you are feeling empathy for me." "Yes, I had to be angry first because it is scary to feel so sad." I interpreted, "So, you need a mother and I need a child. We'll see if we can work something out." We both smiled.

Another patient who knew the same details of the accident but through other sources, was getting married that week. She had just completed a rancorous prenuptial agreement, which almost resulted in the marriage's not taking place. A particularly generous person, she had been absolutely determined not to be taken advantage of this time, not her first marriage, and was courageously willing to cancel the wedding if she had to. We talked about her philosophy; she knew this was a risky marriage but was determined to proceed. Shaun's accident, with her knowledge of all the details, made her determination stronger because, she added, "There is a total impossibility of predicting the future, as witness the tragic death of Shaun. So I've decided to live life as it comes." I wished her well and told her I felt this time around she was going into the marriage a grownup.

TIME PASSING (OCTOBER 6, 1994—13 MONTHS)

Another patient, often oblivious to the passage of time, had been in a destructive relationship for over twelve years. He finally left a year ago and was slowly starting to date. He told me the following dream, apologetically saying "It'll be disturbing to you. I hope it won't upset you."

> I dreamt my sister Susie had the same sort of accident that happened to your son. I felt horrible that I didn't spend more time with her when she was younger. Then in the dream I thought it was a dream. It felt real and very upsetting. I thought it's a good thing it's only a dream and didn't really happen. I was very relieved.

His association to Susie was the name of a possible new girlfriend, as well as his sister's name. He felt that "anything can happen at any moment, like what you were saying. When you said it, I thought of what happened to you. I was concerned about telling you this, bringing up something upsetting. I felt guilty." I told him I think about Shaun all the time and started crying, adding, "Maybe we both need to cry. We haven't talked about it for a long time." He said, "I think about it every time I see you. And I feel like I'm whining, that my things are unimportant. My friends know a lot about their therapist's life—it seems unusual. Knowing puts me more in touch with your emotional life. It's something I can't

help but think about. I wonder how it affects therapy." I asked, "How?"
He answered, "That I have trivial problems by comparison, and I wonder
how you perceive that. Is it difficult to concentrate? I haven't felt it, I'm
just wondering. It's strange to tell you this dream and upset you." I asked,
"You're not supposed to upset your therapist?" He said, "Something like
that." I said, "If Shaun's death is to have any meaning to you in particular, it would be in having you experience the passage of time realistically." He agreed and proudly asserted, "I certainly didn't waste time
with Susie."

CONCLUSION (APRIL, 1994—WRITTEN AT 7 MONTHS)

This winter when it snowed continuously was the perfect weather to reflect
my mood, cold and dead. I rarely left the house because outside something could always remind me of Shaun, and I would not be able to control
it. At home, some of the pain was controllable if I avoided listening to
opera or any music or watching television because it might be a show
we watched together or eating foods we ate together. Now it is the beginning of spring. How can it be that flowers are starting to bloom, that life
goes on around me?

During Shiva, a colleague said to me about work, "Now you will know
what is really important and what is crap." It is not so. Nothing, nothing
seems important compared to his death. How can random chaos teach
you anything about what is important. So I just muddle along, with a
broken heart. Perhaps that is what I've learned so far. That you can.

Recently I asked Elie Wiesel how to overcome despair. We had been talking
about things touching on despair, and on God, hence my question. This
man who more than most has reason to despair, this man who lost his
family in the death camp and himself barely survived, looked at me with
those deep, dark eyes that have looked into the abyss and said, "You want
to know how to overcome despair, I will tell you. By helping others overcome despair" [Lord, 1995, p. 79].

ADDENDUM
(NOVEMBER 14, 1995—2 YEARS, 2 MONTHS)

In one of the bereavement magazines which have now become a regular
part of my reading, Robert Frost, who had lost five children, said, "If
I had one thing to say about life, it would be, It goes on." It had never
comforted me to know that life went on, to be reassured that "time heals
all wounds." It seemed, sometimes still seems, obscene that I could go
on, be healed, after my child was killed. Yet I never feel that way about
other parents whose children have died; it is all right for them to heal.

The stabbing pain has turned into a dull agony. I am aware of the "constant presence of an absence." I function. I more than function. I've changed. I was relieved to be told by "Alive Alone" (a Virginia-based self-help organization for parents who have lost their only child or all their children) that, at two years, one was still considered "newly bereaved." They consider three to five years a turning point.

I am deeply grateful to my patients, those who do not know and those who do. For those who do not know, they made me feel I carried on professionally, that somehow I had retained my style. For two who know and left, for having the courage to do it, so that I could discover limits. And for those who do know and stayed, for having the courage to continue with me, the courage to talk about their problems in the face of my pain, and the courage to get better.

I am in the process of adopting an eleven-year-old Russian girl.* That I have the desire to continue mothering is a tribute to my darling son who gave me so much joy.

REFERENCES

Lord, J. H. (1995), *No Time for Goodbyes.* California: Pathfinder.
Humphrey, D. (1991), *Final Exit.* New York: Dell.
Schiff, H. S. (1977), *The Bereaved Parent.* New York: Crown.
Styron, W. (1990), *Darkness Visible.* New York: Random House.
Swinburne, A. C. (n.d.), "Garden of Prosephene." *Pocket Book of Verse,* ed. M. E. Speare. New York: Cardinal, 1951.

BEREAVEMENT GROUPS AND PUBLICATIONS

Alive Alone, 11115 Dull Robinson Road, Van Wert, Ohio 45891.
Compassionate Friends, FDR Station, POB 324, New York, New York (212) 517-9820.

---

*The adoption was finalized on April 9, 1996.

2

More Human Than Otherwise

Working Through a Time of
Preoccupation and Mourning

ERIC M. MENDELSOHN

ANNA

My second child, Anna, was born on July 11, 1991, and died on June 4, 1992. She suffered from severe heart disease, microcephaly, and other conditions that would affect her prospects for life and health, but none of her illnesses was apparent at birth. When she was six weeks old, she became cyanotic and was hospitalized. Almost immediately, my wife and I learned that Anna was critically ill and had several heart lesions that made her long-term prospects guarded at best. While we were told how her immediate crisis might be managed, we became aware of the microcephaly and other conditions that drastically influenced our picture of her future. We learned that Anna would not qualify for a heart transplant, would have a limited life expectancy, would have severely compromised cognitive and social capacities, and, if she lived, would endure repeated medical crises and increasingly heroic surgical interventions.

The medical team temporarily stabilized Anna's condition and, through their willingness to identify with us and share their personal reflections, provided the support and empathy we needed to assimilate unbearable information. We also enlisted the help of a close-knit network of friends and family who came through magnificently. Especially when under duress, I seek companionship, and for me, opportunities for bearing witness and intimate conversation were crucial and sustaining. As will be seen, the needs for self-expression and affirmative connectedness to others carried over into my work with patients during the year of Anna's life and death.

After two weeks of consultations and agonizing soul-searching, we decided not to go ahead with a surgical procedure deemed necessary to keep Anna alive. It was thought that Anna was being temporarily sustained by an infusion of medicine and that, once this treatment was withdrawn, she would die, probably within hours, at the outside within days. The medicine was discontinued, but Anna lived. It was not the last time she would confound predictions.

We brought Anna home two days later. Originally, we were frightened; Sarah, our older child, was 17 months old, and we dreaded exposing

I am grateful for the comments and suggestions of Colin Paolo and Drs. Ken Barish, Irwin Hoffman, and Michael Wald, who read earlier versions of this chapter.

her firsthand to Anna's dying. We were helped through this by the medical team who said, basically, that we were projecting; the issue was ours, not Sarah's. Their willingness to speak plainly about difficult subjects not only helped us work through our fear, but also became a source of inspiration for my clinical work.

As the days passed after Anna's return home, life resumed the semblance of an everyday rhythm. While in some ways time was suspended, we also began to notice the progression of the calendar, and the needs for working, respite, and income were felt. I resumed seeing patients a week after Anna came home. My wife and I were still involved in an extended death vigil, but surprisingly, we gradually resumed normal activities.

In the months that followed, in recognition of Anna's unexpected resilience, the medical predictions became more ambiguous. Anna was, for the most part, free of pain and was curious, responsive, and affectionate. Even given the certainty of some degree of mental retardation, her social and cognitive development suggested she could become a person among people, and we began to think of her as an odds-beater. There was an ongoing series of consultations about her prospects, and the questions about cardiac shunt surgery were revisited. By most accounts, Anna was still expected to die, but we enrolled her in an early intervention program designed to increase her long-term adaptive capacities. Contradictions abounded.

Gradually, we reconsidered the decision not to pursue the shunt surgery. By early spring, the predictions had become even more open-ended. It was now thought Anna might live for "some years," and her overall development was far better than anticipated. With deep misgivings about the pain and terror she would suffer and with dread about what we would endure as a family, we decided to proceed with the surgery. Anna nearly died immediately after surgery, but then recovered rapidly and, six days later, returned home. The remaining five days of her life were a blessing. Now absorbing more oxygen into her bloodstream, Anna had more vigor and a healthy color. She made new cause-and-effect connections, anticipated leave-takings with a goodbye wave, and became preternaturally loving, stroking and kissing us with a purposefulness and directness we will always remember. She died suddenly on a Thursday morning, probably of a previously undetected arrhythmia. At the time of her death, she was expected to live.

Anna has continued to be part of our lives. After her death, we made a book about her life for Sarah and, in the next year, established a fund in her name. The success of the fund helps us feel a sense of ongoingness as her parents and inspires feelings of pride in her accomplishments. For all that was tragic, we are grateful for the good year of life that she had, and there have been unexpected and continually inspiring opportunities to affirm our bond with her.

This narrative reflects some of the experiential background for my work with patients during and following the year of Anna's life.

TECHNICAL CONSIDERATIONS

Analysts working in times of personal difficulty contend with circumstances that intrude, materially and affectively, into the analytic field. Issues related to practical management, maintenance of boundaries, self-disclosure, and the changing nature of the analyst's self-experience inevitably arise, and modifications of the usual working arrangements are considered (Singer, 1971; Silver, 1982; DeWald, 1990; Gerson, 1994). Some authors have called attention to regressive trends and heightened countertransferential pressures that must be recognized and dealt with (Abend, 1982; Arlow, 1990). Among other perspectives, it may be useful to consider psychoanalysis as a profession that must sometimes be practiced under difficult circumstances.

Anna was first hospitalized midway through my August vacation and remained in intensive care until just before my scheduled return to work following Labor Day. At first, resuming work was sufficiently far off that I did not need to think about how to manage it. A week later, while we were still assimilating medical information and weighing choices about treatment, I began to think about contacting patients. By this point, it was clear that, whatever happened, I would not be able to return as scheduled. The first decision was who would contact my patients and what message would be given. I began a routine, which carried through that year, of discussing technical and countertransferential problems with a number of trusted colleagues and close friends. While I did not pursue formal supervision, the practice of discussing feelings and reviewing decisions with colleagues was maintained consistently. These ad hoc consultations were enormously helpful and reassuring as they served to dispel fantasies that I had lost my clinical bearings, and in their encouraging and affirmative tone, they previewed the support and matter-of-factness shown by patients. Despite my fears that anxiety and self-interest were clouding my judgment, colleagues who know me well apparently experienced me as myself and repeatedly let me know it.

I decided to tell patients that my return would be delayed by at least a week due to an illness in the family, and since I could not say with certainty whether I could begin the following week, I said I would call them again to let them know. Those with whom I spoke directly expressed sympathy and concern; no one made reference to personal inconvenience. The experience was reminiscent of sharing difficult news with good friends, but the sense of professional boundaries was reflected in the relative lack of specific questions. I am sure my tone conveyed, "We'll talk in more detail, but in the office, not now." In the following days, many patients left messages of support on my office machine, and for the first of many times, I experienced my patients as comrades.

When I returned to work, Anna was still expected to die, now "possibly within days or perhaps a few weeks." I felt a need for the distractions and comforts of clinical work and could not see staying away in an open-ended way. Yet, how to resume work under these circumstances? I had read Singer's (1971) paper dealing with an analogous situation in his work and had a desire to tell every patient, as Singer had done. However, I had reservations about indiscriminately imposing this news. My inclination was to explore patients' reactions to my messages and to the delay in resuming and tell them that it was likely there would be more cancellations in the immediate future. I would then see what developed. I felt I would work better if I could acknowledge what was going on, but I expected there would be differences in what felt right with different patients.

Many patients asked, openly and with little delay, what had happened, and in these cases, I let them know. My reasons for telling patients were that the circumstances of my life had already significantly disrupted their therapies and were likely to do so again. In addition, I was obviously distressed and wanted to provide some explanation for that. In line with the view that the analytic situation is founded on respect for the patient's freedom of choice, I felt my patients should be offered information they could respond to as one informed participant to another. Finally, and most importantly, I was, at that time, sufficiently preoccupied that I felt that not revealing at least some information about what was happening would foster mutual alienation; I imagined I would feel I was keeping a secret and expected I would be more distracted if I did not acknowledge my circumstances than if I did. Extrapolating from experience in other situations, I expected that the acknowledgment would help me feel more present and enable me to move on and attend to other issues.

What I found was that, when it proved possible to tell patients, I did indeed feel closer and more involved. Moreover, it was those patients whom I told who were more able to express their feelings and fantasies about my situation. This experience runs counter to the usual assumption that divulging personal information inhibits, rather than fosters, the experience and expression of transference (Abend, 1982; Lasky, 1990). I suspect things developed in this way for me because I felt more fully present when I was able to talk about my experience, and this emotional presence encouraged my patients' expressiveness.

By contrast, in those therapies where the circumstances were left more ambiguous, there was a greater degree of mutual estrangement and caution, a circumstance not conducive to the open expression of feeling and fantasy. Of course, in some cases at least, these were therapies in which things were just getting under way or where there was already an entrenched pattern of avoidance. What I think is most important is to create conditions that facilitate the analyst's emotional participation. For me, this involved acknowledgment of personal circumstances. For other analysts, it may not.

A few patients directly said they did not want to know. A common expression of this position was, "I know something serious is happening, but I don't want to know specifically. I would feel burdened, and I don't want to have to think about you in that way." Other patients could not be this direct and communicated their desire not to know in derivative material. I respected the wishes of those patients who preferred not to be told, and in some instances, this response later became a fruitful issue for analysis. Some patients who initially chose not to be told changed their positions later, and subsequent work illuminated transference and countertransference issues that contributed both to the not telling and to the eventual shift.

Spoken or unspoken, the experience of Anna's life and death colored my work with patients throughout that year and after. There were many cancellations during the year for various medical consultations and, at the time of Anna's surgery, two weeks when I was away from the office as much as I was there. When Anna died, a colleague and I made the calls informing patients that I would be away for another week. The combination of fairly frequent interruptions of the regular schedule, my ongoing preoccupation, and patients' open and covert expressions of interest, concern, resentment, and obliviousness continually affected the analytic work.

Although my theoretical views and technical practice are identified most closely with interpersonal psychoanalysis and despite a belief in the therapeutic value of candor and directness, my ideological commitments involve an element of reaction formation. In ways that remain disconcerting to me, I can be quite formal and reserved. While my way of working had, for some years, included an intensive focus on both participants' experiences of the therapy relationship, I had never previously confided in patients about my personal concerns, and I sometimes felt I was in deep and treacherous waters.

I wrestled with the question and frequently discussed with colleagues whether my self-disclosures were exploitative. Was I seeking comfort, was I wanting patients to admire my strength, was I seeking absolution for my guilt? I knew I sometimes enjoyed the self-disclosures, and my patients told me so. Was this a problem? This self-questioning gradually assumed less urgency as I discovered that the self-disclosures began to seem ordinary; that is, they had a place in difficult circumstances, helped me work, may have helped some patients, and did not seem to impede what increasingly came to feel like everyday analytic practice. Of course, this is a generalization and, day by day, it was more complicated and variable than that. However, as I will describe, I do not believe that the self-disclosures had a disruptive effect, which I believe would have been the case had they been driven by defensive or exploitative aims. Like Singer, I found that my decisions expressed a largely unwitting vote of confidence in my patients and engendered a deepening of the mutual appreciation for what we share as people. Just as the experience of Anna's illness confronted me with the limits of my control, I developed a previously unanticipated, reassuring sense of flexibility about the management of patient–therapist boundaries. It became clearer that the maintenance of appropriate roles depends far more on a mutual commitment to the integrity and purposes of the work than it does upon any obsessionally maintained, unvarying asymmetry, and I felt a new sense of conviction regarding the resilience and plasticity of the analytic relationship.

In saying that patient–therapist boundaries were respected, I want to make clear what occurred. There were, to varying degrees, explicit exchanges of information. As in most cases of telling something important, there were many conversations that built on each other and times when concern with my circumstances faded into the background. Patients communicated concern and support in sessions, phone calls, letters, and cards, and after Anna's death, there were moving expressions of condolence and charitable donations in her name. At times when I was obviously pulled in many directions, patients sometimes brought me coffee or a sandwich. Moreover, especially after the first weeks, there were open expressions of a desire *not* to talk about my situation, a searching out of assurances that this was acceptable, and increasing freedom to turn our attention to other things. Patients conveyed resentment about the disruption of their therapies, and there were both genuine and strategic expressions of apology for ignoring my situation.

When I disclosed information, the extent of the detail varied considerably from patient to patient. In a few cases, the level of intimacy was such that I included information about the decision not to do the surgery. This was the hardest to disclose because it was the greatest source of guilt. I worried that patients would no longer regard me as a caring person but found, to my considerable relief, that patients could discern and empathize with my ambivalence. These experiences support Singer's (1971) view that the usual and necessary role relationships and asymmetry tilt analytic work in the direction of exploring patients' narcissism and infantile dependency. As a result, capacities for concern, altruism, keen observation, and accurate empathy are often neither recognized nor fostered.

THE EFFECTS ON CLINICAL WORK

Dyadic models of the analytic field expand the locus of inquiry to include not only the analysis of the patient's past-in-present, but also the vicissitudes of mutual influence in the patient–analyst relationship. In these models, while an asymmetrical tilt is preserved, experiences and influences initiated by the analyst are seen as inevitable, valid, and potentially beneficial foci for analytic work. In this section, in somewhat schematic form, I present examples of how the experience of Anna's illness and death was represented, avoided, and worked through within the dyad. The variety of effects ranged from apparently helpful to disruptive to ambiguous and ongoing.

There were some cases where the experiences stimulated by my life circumstances appeared to be facilitative, leading to an intensification of the work. Sometimes these effects were rapid and dramatic. For example, a woman who had initially described herself as shallow and indifferent began work with me some months after Anna's first hospitalization. She had a longstanding pattern of engaging others and then leaving relationships without so much as a backward glance. She considered herself manipulative and exploitative and had apparently left a trail of perplexed and wounded lovers and professional colleagues. She seemed quite unsettled when I canceled sessions for Anna's surgery and asked why I would be away. Her response when I told her was uncharacteristically intense. Later, when I informed her that Anna had died, she began weeping uncontrollably. What was most impressive was how surprised she was by her own reaction, and for some time after, she expressed bewilderment about the strength of her feelings. She said, half apologetically, that she knew she wasn't really crying about my daughter but said she had been moved by my willingness to include her and by the obvious grief and love I felt. In the next weeks, she allowed herself many poignant "backward glances," recalling, with guilt, the abrupt way she had left her husband and dreaming about long forgotten childhood losses. The developments in our relationship seemed to foster an experience of long-delayed grieving. The patient's recognition of the bleakness and emotional deadness that characterized her family atmosphere in childhood and her growing ability to recognize and nurture her own longing for attachment and dependence became central themes in the treatment.

In other cases, there were difficulties. One patient, who had planned to end treatment after years of intensive work, anticipated the birth of his first child. Always exquisitely sensitive to my moods, he sensed and frequently commented upon the difficulties he knew I was experiencing. He talked about feeling guilty and inhibited about exploring his sense of joyful anticipation and his anxieties about his wife's pregnancy and the upcoming termination. While these issues were dealt with to some degree, the work had a superficial quality as we moved toward termination. I was prepared to end as planned, soon after Anna's death, when the patient, for the first time in years, became panicked. He confronted me angrily; he needed more therapy but wondered whether I was in a position to help him. Jolted into awareness, I realized how difficult it had been for me

to experience, in any depth, his need to protect me as his wife went
through her pregnancy and delivered a healthy baby. Further, I gradually
realized that, already bereft, I had distanced myself from mourning the
loss of someone with whom I felt particularly close. In the months that
followed, we were able to take up these issues and, in a sense, experience the termination year that we missed.

There were several cases where, surprisingly, in otherwise intensive
work, although patients were informed about my circumstances, issues
related to Anna's living and dying did not appear to become woven into
the analytic experience in any central way. It is these cases and those
where, even after the fact, there was no disclosure that lead me to wonder
what I missed. Recently, in reviewing my notes of one case where I
recalled little focus on the patient's experience of what was happening
to me, I saw he had dreamed of taking me with him on a trip. I was
his "traveling analyst," accompanying him on a series of signal personal
and professional voyages. There were get-togethers involving family and
friends from childhood. At one gathering, he could not find me. Someone
said I was "off with the children" and he could hear the sound of crying.
He felt abandoned. What was both remarkable and dismaying was that
I had no recollection of this dream and cannot say what we did with it.
Interestingly, this is a patient who recently told me he experiences me
as an open person, willing to talk about most anything of concern to
him. However, he thinks there is one area where I draw the line; I won't
talk about my daughter's death. When he said this, I felt puzzled in a
self-righteous way; whatever does he mean: I *welcome* talking about Anna.
Then I came across the dream and felt he had identified a key area of
avoidance.

In several other cases, the impact of my life circumstances and our
reflections on what we had and had not made of this were explored after
considerable time passed. One patient, a young physician, always made
a point of saying he did not want to know anything about my personal
life. Sessions were *his* time, and there was a concrete distinction made
between his interests and mine. Every second of every session counted
in his effort to purge himself of the annoying, petty persecutions of daily
life. Even brief "digressions" to discuss scheduling or his lateness in
paying were treated as ways I robbed him of his time and freedom. With
this pattern firmly established, I fully expected him to say he did not
want to be informed when I returned to work after Anna's first hospitalization. Much to my surprise, he immediately asked what had happened.
I was taken aback and signalled my lack of acceptance of his interest by
referring to his oft-stated desire not to know anything about me. Seeing
his disappointment, I quickly said that I would tell him, adding that I
had been surprised by his directness. I told him my daughter was very
ill and was not expected to live. He was stunned, speechless. Then, perhaps

in response to my rebuff, he quickly resumed his usual mode of working. In the next months, there was little reference by either of us, either to my circumstances or to my rejecting response to his inquiry.

During that year, his wife became pregnant and, especially after his son was born, he began to imagine what I must have gone through. He had not been prepared for how deeply he felt about his son, whose loss seemed unimaginable to him. During this time, I reflected back on our work together and began to rethink the development of the distance between us. While it was true he had drawn a line in the sand from the start and presented himself in an unusually thin-skinned way, it was also the case that I often felt critical with him. I then focused on a persistent area of idealization; he insisted on a view of me as a consistently hardworking man of high energy and rich cultural interests. He saw me as continually reading, cultivating stimulating friendships, and pursuing challenging professional goals. By contrast, he was a couch potato with an addiction to MTV. What had gone by without comment was that, gradually, we had begun to spend a few minutes in many of our sessions discussing rock music. It was clear that we were both into it and that my knowledge was every bit as encyclopedic as his. At this point, I told him that I thought we both had been avoiding, for quite some time, the recognition of ways in which we were alike. This ushered in an increased sense of pleasure and collaboration in our work, an experience that was, at least indirectly, facilitated by a belated acknowledgment of our kinship as fathers and prima donnas.

In reviewing these experiences, I am impressed by the ordinariness of what transpired. The mixture of stimulating and facilitative interactions, disruptions, missed opportunities, and second chances is likely representative of most analytic work. This everyday quality reinforces the sense that the analytic relationship is both resilient and flexible enough to absorb disruptions and to thrive under trying circumstances.

CASE MATERIAL

This section includes two extended case vignettes. These cases illustrate in more detail how my experiences became part of ongoing analytic work and how circumstances ordinarily viewed as external to and potentially disruptive of the analytic process were dealt with in ways that reflected these patients' characteristic conflicts and relational patterns.

The first patient, Nathan, was a successful attorney who initially presented as deferential, compulsively attentive to others, and disconcertingly selfless. Despite his implacable solicitude, however, he actually felt resentful and intimidated by ordinary emotional claims and, for many years, avoided intimate, interdependent relationships. He spoke of himself in impersonal terms and once dreamed of "dematerializing" when he was in danger. After years of intensive work, he had gradually come to feel more resilient and substantial. He was considerably more connected to his thoughts and desires, more able to translate his wants into tangible achievements, and better able to set limits. He had extricated himself from a loveless marriage, remarried far more happily, and several months before Anna's birth, had become a father for the first time. He nonetheless remained somewhat inhibited, private, and subtly estranged, often unable to imagine alternatives to the anticipated dangers of submissiveness and isolation. There was a growing bond of affection and honesty between us, but he felt wary about the depth of our connection. There were recurrent feelings of being encroached upon and a sense that I would never let him go. When he spoke of his desire to end analysis, he typically said he could only imagine leaving abruptly or staying forever. There was no possibility of *really* working toward termination and experiencing the loss of the relationship.

Nathan's family background was characterized by boundary mix-ups and an endless succession of provocative, double-binding messages that were ostensibly innocent and well-intended. Nathan often found himself in the middle of uncannily unnerving parental arguments in which his role was emissary and lightning rod. He learned the subtleties of obfuscating language and lost track of whose ideas he was promoting. Separateness and self-interest were, to the degree they could be dimly imagined, regarded as unpardonable betrayals. Nathan's previous therapy had been wrecked when he responded to his therapist's importunings by providing several referrals of patients whose sexual interconnections left the therapist unable to maintain boundaries.

As was typical for Nathan, his hyperawareness of my experience with Anna threatened to crowd out his ability to focus on his own thoughts and feelings. By this point in our work, however, he was more able than he had been earlier to articulate and work on this dilemma. His initial responses to the news of my circumstances were cautious and subtly exploratory. When I first called to say I would be delayed returning to work because of an illness in the family, he sounded uncharacteristically distressed and left two follow-up messages saying he hoped things were going well. When we resumed in person, he immediately asked for information. When I told him, he was at a loss for words and quickly moved to other topics; however, he repeatedly returned to my situation by anxiously voicing reservations about talking about his daughter. I wondered if he were looking for a green light. He said he feared adding to my pain but quickly doubted his own genuineness. He was afraid he was feigning concern and worried that he really only wanted assurances that I could deal with his feelings. In so quickly moving into this characteristic muddle, I felt he was unconsciously reassuring me that he and I were very much back at work.

In the next weeks, Nathan said he continued to feel inhibited. He imagined that, if he asked me questions, he would cause me pain, and since I wasn't saying anything, he did not want to interfere with my freedom to have worry-free time. I asked what made him think his talking about his situation, or mine, would upset me and said he seemed to overlook the possibility that I might want to talk. He then brought in pictures of his daughter, still carefully studying my reactions. At the same time, he began to wonder if his reticence were more his issue than mine. He linked his reluctance to talk openly to his longstanding need to "keep things to [him]self" and to his family situation, in which the expression of personal need inevitably was experienced as burdensome or disorganizing by his parents. There had been many struggles over autonomy and compliance, and he was given enemas when he failed to "produce." Overtly compliant, but secretly angry, he evolved a dissociative solution: "You can have my body but not my soul." For the first time, the sexual aspect of this attitude, which had previously been ignored, was engaged as a live issue between us.

Nathan enjoyed feeling freer to talk openly and realized he had been fighting a low-grade depression, which he linked to his decision to cut down from three to two sessions a week following his daughter's birth. This move had been presented as a financial necessity. I noted that he had difficulty mourning this loss; in fact, he had acted as if the change made no difference. He then contrasted his unwillingness to respond to things that affected him with my ability to tolerate sadness and said that, despite what I was dealing with, I was able to work vigorously and effectively; perhaps it was good to talk about things after all! Soon after, he resumed three sessions a week.

Several weeks later, Nathan asked about Anna's condition. I said her prognosis was now more uncertain; she might live for some time, but her prospects were limited. He said, very simply, how hard this must be for me and then articulated some of the ambivalence he thought I might feel about her survival. I experienced what he said as tender and straightforward, much in contrast to his usual cautious hedging and practiced self-effacement. I told him how much I appreciated his freedom to speak directly. Soon after, he dreamed he found an injured bird; "It couldn't fly. Its muscles weren't developed enough, and I walked with it, flexing its wings to help it fly." His associations were to his daughter, who was starting to walk; to Anna, who was damaged; and to his own sense of himself as crippled and fearful. As he talked about the wounded bird, he cried openly for one of the first times.

That spring, a good friend of his died after a long illness. Nathan had been quite involved and now prepared to take on a mentor role with his friend's son. He said he wept when he heard the news but, in the next session, was remote and closed off. He said, "I'm reluctant to share the experience because I'm afraid I'll lose it somehow." Soon after, he reported a dream. "I dreamed my daughter was a little baby, and I turned to whomever I was with and said, 'You know, at that age my father had a feeding tube implanted in my throat, so they only fed me through the tube.' I wondered what happened to the feeding tube. I wonder if I just absorbed it." He associated the feeding tube to seeing his friend in the hospital and to the peculiar, antiseptic atmosphere that characterized his family. Absorbing the tube meant that he had taken in the detachment and dissociation of feeling and had grown up as a mechanical man. (There were no conscious associations to Anna.) Yet, despite this, Nathan felt he was changing. He said he had been awakened by his daughter's crying and realized he no longer had to watch himself to make sure he didn't get "overly frustrated" or "angry." He could experience his daughter's "demandingness" as "natural for her age."

There were several missed sessions when Anna had her surgery. When he asked, I told him the reasons for the cancellations. He expressed cautious hopefulness, reflecting his awareness that the best outcome remained mixed and complicated. When Anna died, I reached him directly but cannot recall what we said. When I returned to the office, there was a card from him saying, "I want to tell you how sorry I am. I had begun to think it wouldn't happen. If I can help in any way, please let me know. You've done so much for me." When we resumed, he told me he'd seen the death notice in the paper and reread it daily. He was very reluctant to tell me this and felt tempted to hold it privately. In the sessions that followed, he talked about feeling angry at me, wanting to "slam" me because I hadn't been as available to him. The wife of a work colleague died, and he dreamed of a child who failed to grow. He connected this to Anna but also saw the child as representing himself. He felt his daughter's growth and development were stimulating "the conscious and unconscious memories of [his] own childhood."

In the weeks that followed Anna's death, he focused on how I was managing. He observed that I did not avoid talking; I responded to his questions and pursued his interest, no matter how obliquely expressed. He contrasted this again with his tendency to be avoidant, a tendency, he realized, that was now significantly diminished. In the last session before my summer vacation, he said he thought it had been a difficult, but very helpful, year of work. He could now not only be aware of other people's sorrow, but realized he felt freer to love and to mourn. He then described an event from the Summer Olympics that he found particularly moving. A runner was nearing the end of a long-distance race when he tore his hamstring. Barely able to stay on his feet, he looked as if he would not make it to the finish line. Suddenly, the runner's father came out of the stands, and the two of them completed the race with their arms around each other.

I believe Nathan needed to test me repeatedly during this year to see whether I could maintain my interest and openness with him despite my grief and preoccupation. Because he tended to dichotomize self-interest and responsiveness to others and continued to feel that *really* difficult issues were best suppressed, he was reassured by the experience of observing and contributing to my efforts to manage. His ability to openly state his need to be self-involved, *and* to realize that he also cared for me, helped him develop alternatives to submissiveness and withdrawal. My sense is that the intrusion of my life circumstances into the analytic work did not prevent, and may have enhanced, a fuller experience of attachment and loss in a somewhat disconnected, emotionally inhibited man. His closing image of runner and father holding each other as they approached the finish line anticipated the termination process that followed over the next two years. The resistances and impasses that developed regarding termination were considered, more fully than might have been the case before, as experiences we both created and both had to work to resolve.

The second patient, Steve, an artist in his late twenties, was a friendly, placid man, gregarious, but lonely in a crowd. He maintained a wide circle of friendships but had underachieved professionally and was strikingly oblivious to opportunities for romantic or sexual involvement. Steve's underlying pessimism and resignation became apparent only if one stood back and considered how much he had failed to pursue. Occasionally, he was able to speak openly of his despair. At those times, he said he believed he would fail anyone who loved him. Steve could not fathom how people found the strength to persist.

Steve's sense of self was profoundly shaped by two tragedies. His father died of cancer when he was eight months old, and he was raised as an only child by a devoted but depressed mother. In trying to compensate for what she felt he had lost, and as an expression of avoidance, his mother became overly "understanding" and failed to define limits and expectations for achievement. Steve was cared for and worried over but felt subtly neglected. He recalled that no one ever insisted he clean his room, and he felt he was allowed to procrastinate or quit when faced with difficult challenges. When Steve was in college, he and a friend went backpacking in a remote area. While fording an icy river, his friend was swept downstream, became wedged in a cluster of rocks and logs, and succumbed to hypothermia while Steve watched helplessly from shore. His friend died, and Steve recalled "going on auto-pilot." At the time he began treatment, his profound survivor's guilt and relentless, subtly enacted self-punishments were masked by an earnest, amiable pseudo-relatedness. At heart, however, he did not consider himself to be among the living.

In the first two years of analysis, Steve primarily experienced me as a father whose support and insistent focus on areas of self-neglect, grandiosity, and subtle arrogance helped him become somewhat more self-accepting and self-aware. He described a shift in perspective, from feeling he had never had a father to a sense of having lost his father. He characterized this change as moving from a state of "absence" to one of "loss." He felt somewhat more alive and in touch with his anger.

When Anna was first hospitalized, it was still fairly early in our work. There was little direct focus on the events in my life, but in keeping with his personality style, Steve's responses were unfailingly kind and solicitous. I occasionally found him attentive in ways that were moving and quite attuned. Once, when we had scheduled a session at an alternate time because of Anna's surgery, he correctly guessed I was coming to the office directly from the hospital and brought me a sandwich, which I thankfully accepted. We were both struck by the contrast between this experience and earlier times when he brought me copies of his drawings and virtually insisted I take them. It was only later, however, that we became aware of how his caring for me during that year recreated an aspect of his experience with his mother, this time with Steve as the depressed, but solicitous parent, and me in his place, as the child contending with unbearable loss.

Anna's death ushered in a shift in the primary focus of the analysis. Whereas earlier the exploration had centered on the experience of the death of his father, now increasing attention was paid to his life with his mother. With growing intensity and conviction, Steve developed a sense of me as depressed and wondered if depression were a hallmark of my character. Certainly, I seemed particularly depressed since my daughter's death. He experienced this view of me both as unsettling and facilitative. He said he suspected that it was his unconscious diagnosis of my depression that had led him to select me as his analyst in the first place. Were I not depressed, the experience with me would lack familiarity, and he would not have been able to get in touch with his despair, guilt, and refusal of opportunity. At the same time, he began to wonder if I could help him. Perhaps I was *too* depressed.

During this time, aspects of Steve's symbiotic-like involvement with his mother were clarified. There had always been a tacit agreement between them to avoid challenging or confronting each other. They glossed over disappointments and criticisms and avoided talking about the sense of resignation that defined their shared experience. Steve's mother helped pay for the analysis, an issue of secondary gain that reinforced his connection to her. In his dreams, she was often depicted as a beatifically smiling, oblivious bystander to his life-threatening crises. At one point, he characterized them as "Siamese twins, joined at the grief."

Nearly two years after Anna's death, at a point when Steve's experience of me as depressed and as, perhaps, too passive and listless to help him was emerging more vividly in the transference and at a time when he was making determined efforts to develop clearer boundaries with his mother, he dreamed that he saw two figures, a man and a human-like horse, fused together at the shoulder. They shared a circulatory system. As long as they remained pressed together, both would live, but their lives would consist of nothing but a resigned, enervated wait for time to pass. If they moved, both would die. The figures were reclining, as on an analytic couch.

This dream brought the depressive fusion explicitly into the transference-countertransference field. In the months that followed, Steve wondered if he should continue working with me. He told me he had sometimes felt suicidal but had avoided saying so for fear of "worrying" me. He complained that, despite growth in self-knowledge, he was no closer to professional or romantic success than when we began. He focused increasingly, angrily, and more freely on his criticisms of me and the analysis. For my part, I felt encouraged by his freedom to be critical and sympathetic to many of his doubts and concerns. I had often pictured both of us as retreating from potentially vital confrontations and had wondered if the drift in the analysis reflected failures of courage; I too wrestled with feelings of guilt, in my case about having been released from the burdens of caring for my daughter. In my blacker moods, I blamed myself for "failing to jump in" by opting not to pursue immediate surgery for Anna. Was I, like Steve, avoiding mortal challenges because I was afraid? In certain ways, we both wrestled with the ambiguity of personal control and responsibility.

As these questions dominated my experience of the analysis, I noticed that, despite the difficulty of these issues, my primary feelings were hopefulness and relief. I did not know what would happen, but for the first time, the work felt truly alive. I took his doubts and criticisms seriously and agreed that, at various times, we both had felt like passive bystanders and helpless victims. I focused his attention on his immediate experience of me in the sessions, and interestingly, he began to say that, in fact, I did not seem "that depressed" to him. While he would never describe me as "ebullient," I had, in a persistent way, continued to work closely with him through a time of loss. What seemed to occur was that his criticisms and confrontations facilitated the development of a sense of separateness, and this freedom to imaginatively and expressively move left both of us very much alive. Steve realized that he had tried with me something he felt unable to manage with his mother; he had said what was wrong and had defined what was making him feel dead.

In the months that followed, Steve, for the first time, was able to recall, with vividness and immediacy, the experience of his friend's death. The moment by moment review of the events and of his state of mind at the time was almost unbearably painful. I had often said that his survivor's guilt was a central factor in his failure to thrive. Now, however, Steve, with a sense of conviction that was new to him, could see how persistently and implacably he had attenuated opportunities for vital living. In the year since his dream of the two merged figures, Steve has begun to attain professional success, has moved toward financial self-sufficiency, has taken on the responsibility of an ambitious business venture, and has pursued relationships with women with a newfound insistence on sexual and romantic fulfillment. As Steve emphatically points out, we have not achieved a "happy ending," but there are hopeful signs of liveliness and friction.

In the work with Steve, a man whose character defenses and unconscious guilt impeded full use of analytic opportunities, the experience of working with me during a time of personal preoccupation and loss appears to have facilitated the intensification of a symbiotic transference. The dovetailing of our depressive issues led to therapeutic complications but also created the potential for a vivid, immediate experience of reliving in the transference–countertransference interaction that has had a mutative effect.

THEORETICAL CONSIDERATIONS

The clinical situation in psychoanalysis has evolved as a setting in which the patient's unconscious experience and relational patterns can be brought to light and experienced with immediacy and pertinence. The analyst maintains the boundaries of the relationship and continually monitors the nature of the interpersonal exchanges, protecting herself and the patient from the dangers of seduction, loss of focus, and exploitative misuse of the relationship. Every school of psychoanalysis regards attentiveness to frame issues as essential for the conduct of meaningful clinical work (Levenson, 1984).

Personal experiences of the analyst that, through choice or necessity, are carried into the analytic setting require us to closely examine issues of boundaries and role definition. Particularly when these experiences are disturbing and preoccupying for the analyst, requiring immediate response or long-term working through, the analyst must contend with a series of problems that bear upon the integrity of the analytic process. In this section, I will briefly comment upon three areas of concern taken up in the literature dealing with special circumstances in the analyst's life: self-disclosure, countertransference, and the therapeutic alliance.

It is by now commonplace to question the "myth of analytic anonymity" (Singer, 1977). It is accepted that, efforts to maintain a neutral ambience notwithstanding, the analyst inevitably reveals a great deal about his attitudes, values, personal aesthetics, anxieties, and blind spots

(Levenson, 1984; Greenberg, 1986; Aron, 1991). Moreover, a growing number of analysts now include within their technique the selective use of deliberate self-disclosure as a means of facilitating the analytic process. Such self-disclosures may involve sharing associative processes (Bollas, 1983) or affective experience (Ehrenberg, 1992). Most authors, however, regard the deliberate disclosure of the analyst's extra-therapeutic experience as improper technique, a form of countertransferential acting out bolstered by rationalization. In many instances, this disapproval even extends to unusual and trying circumstances such as the analyst's serious illness. Abend (1982), DeWald (1990), and Lasky (1990), for example, believe that, when manageable, the best position for an analyst who must interrupt and resume analytic work during times of serious illness is to provide information only about scheduling and the analyst's ability to continue the work. Further self-disclosure is to be avoided if possible because it may derail the analysis by interfering with the patient's fantasy elaborations and subtly manipulating the patient.

From a perspective that discourages self-disclosure, my way of working during the time of my daughter's illness and death was in error. In this view, what would have been optimal under the circumstances would have been either to have delayed resuming work until I felt better able to maintain anonymity or to have begun work knowing that my patients would perceive a great deal about my affective state. I would then have proceeded without validating, disconfirming, or in any way interfering with the fantasy elaborations built upon their observations. For a variety of reasons, I found it impossible to delay, in an open-ended way, my return to work. In addition, I had already established a way of working that involved exploring the contributions of both patient and analyst to the creation and working through of the transference–countertransference interaction. I hoped that selective disclosure of information about my life circumstances, to those patients who indicated they wanted to know, might, by acknowledging traumatic events I could in no sense ignore and by confirming my common humanity with my patients, actually enhance the possibilities for analytic engagement. While it is, of course, possible that my views are colored by denial and self-fulfilling prophecy, my impression now, three to four years after the events described, is that my self-disclosures neither derailed nor blocked the analytic process. For me (but likely not for some others), the *failure* to have spoken might well have been disruptive.

In considering if, how, and under what circumstances deliberate self-disclosures of extra-analytic experience should be made, it seems important to take into account both the emotional situation fostering the desire to communicate and the analyst's core beliefs about the analytic setting. Self-disclosures that are responsive to the analyst's desire to continue honest analytic work under adverse circumstances will likely be experienced by patients very differently from those offered for narcissistic or exploitative reasons. The analyst's willingness to searchingly and rigorously assess her own needs and to consult with colleagues enables her to think through decisions regarding self-disclosure under trying circumstances.

Analysts experiencing serious illness have described regressions in functioning, including reliance upon reality-distorting defenses and lapses in judgment (Abend, 1982; Arlow, 1990). It seems unarguable that the challenges to adaptation posed by trauma and loss render the analyst more than usually vulnerable to selective inattention and to the self-soothing rationalizations of misbehavior that result in misuse of the therapy relationship. For these reasons, some writers counsel holding fast to one's customary way of working during times of acute stress (Lasky, 1990). The familiar, well-established rationales for clinical decision making are seen as bulwarks against the dangers of anxiety-driven innovation.

In reflecting on my experience of working during the time of Anna's illness and death, it does not seem that I was impaired in my functioning as an analyst. This is not to say that I was unaffected; indeed, the experiences of that year influenced me profoundly and significantly shaped my work. At the same time, I felt healthy and personally uncompromised, even if preoccupied and grieving. I was aware of deriving comfort from my work with patients and of feeling helped, both by my patients' kindness and solicitude and by their willingness to persist in the work when I was feeling distressed. Once, soon after Anna's death, a patient described a panic attack she'd had the night before. She couldn't breathe and was about to go to the emergency room when she thought she must be identifying with my daughter, experiencing the heart palpitations and shortness of breath she imagined Anna felt before dying. She said she realized that, as much as she felt I cared for her, I would never love her as deeply as I loved my daughter. She concluded by saying she envied Anna. As I listened to this striking recitation I experienced what seemed to be an incongruous feeling; I was grateful to her for speaking so unselfconsciously.

In receiving and enjoying comfort and affirmative regard from my patients, was I exploiting the therapy relationship? In departing from my usual stance of not sharing personal difficulties with patients, was I acting out my need for attention and solace? To some degree I was. And yet, working from a position that values active inquiry into the particulars of here and now experience, I believe I fostered circumstances in which the effects of my participation could be examined and freely discussed. I have no question that many patients were more restrained than they otherwise would have been, but, under the circumstances, that might have been the case during that year, even had I not altered my technical approach.

Moreover, given my inclination to inquire about patients' observations and interpretations of my subjective experience, my patients' reactions, both to my personal circumstances and to my evolving relation to the analytic situation, readily became grist for the mill. The question to be considered at times of personal trauma might not be whether counter-transferential influences will appear in the analytic work. The answer to this question will invariably be yes. The more meaningful issue may be the accessibility of this countertransference experience to both patient and analyst.

The question of the acceptability, to both participants, of the analyst's emotional situation bears on our conceptualization of the therapeutic alliance. Traditionally, this term refers to the processes through which the patient and analyst accomplish their collaborative work. It can be defined narrowly as the juncture of the observing, reflective capacities of both participants or, more broadly, as involving the joint creation of a space in which vivid experience, as well as reflective analysis, can be fostered and sustained. Erwin Singer (1971), in his groundbreaking description of working analytically during his wife's serious illness, pointed out that the analytic situation, as it is usually defined, tilts in the direction of infantilizing patients and disregarding their strengths. The relative neglect of the analyst's human kinship with the patient and the emphasis on the analyst's competence and the patient's immaturity and narcissism create a skewed, confining situation. My experience suggests that the concept of the therapeutic alliance might be broadened to include the recognition that the analytic relationship is, at heart, a collaboration between two people who are "more human than otherwise" (Sullivan, 1938). The opportunities for the patient to experience the analyst in ordinary, de-idealized terms; for the analyst to receive from, as well as give to, his patients; and for patients to recognize their capacities for generosity, concern, and forbearance would seem to hold considerable therapeutic and analytic potential.

The imposition of tragic circumstances may afford a chance to deepen analytic collaboration if patient and analyst are able to enlist their capacities for flexibility, resilience, and generosity of spirit.

REFERENCES

Abend, S. (1982), Serious illness in the analyst: Countertransference considerations. *J. Amer. Psychoanal. Assn.*, 30:365–375.

Arlow, J. (1990), The analytic attitude in the service of denial. In: *Illness in the Analyst,* ed. H. J. Schwartz & A. L. Silver. Madison, CT: International Universities Press, pp. 9–25.

Aron, L. (1991), The patient's experience of the analyst's subjectivity. *Psychoanal. Dial.,* 1:29–51.

Bollas, C. (1983), Expressive uses of the countertransference: Notes to the patient from oneself. *Contemp. Psychoanal.,* 19:1–34.

DeWald, P. (1990), Serious illness in the analyst: Transference, countertransference, and reality responses—and further reflection. In: *Illness in the Analyst,* ed. H. J. Schwartz & A. L. Silver. Madison, CT: International Universities Press, pp. 75–98.

Ehrenberg, D. B. (1992), *The Intimate Edge.* New York: Norton.

Gerson, B. (1994), An analyst's pregnancy loss and its effects on treatment: Disruption and growth. *Psychoanal. Dial.,* 4:1–18.

Greenberg, J. R. (1986), Theoretical models and the analyst's neutrality. *Contemp. Psychoanal.,* 22:87–106.

Lasky, R. (1990), Keeping the analysis intact when the analyst has suffered a catastrophic illness: Clinical considerations. In: *Illness in the Analyst,* ed. H. J. Schwartz & A. L. Silver. Madison, CT: International Universities Press, pp. 177–197.

Levenson, E. (1984), The interpersonal (Sullivanian) model. In: *Models of the Mind,* ed. A. Rothstein. Madison, CT: International Universities Press, pp. 49–67.

Silver, A.-L. (1982), Resuming the work with a life threatening illness. *Contemp. Psychoanal.,* 18:314–326.

Singer, E. (1971), The patient aids the analyst: Some clinical and theoretical observations. In: *In the Name of Life,* ed. B. Landis & E. S. Tauber. New York: Holt Rinehart & Winston, pp. 56–68.

—— (1977), The fiction of analytic anonymity. In: *The Human Dimension in Psychoanalytic Practice,* ed. K. Frank. New York: Grune & Stratton, pp. 181–192.

Sullivan, H. S. (1938), The data of psychiatry. In: *The Fusion of Psychiatry and Social Science.* New York: Norton, 1964, pp. 32–55.

3

Trauma and Disruption in the Life of the Analyst

Enforced Disclosure and Disequilibrium in "The Analytic Instrument"

ANDREW P. MORRISON

My wife died in January 1994 following an 11-year struggle against cancer. She was an analytically committed psychotherapist, and, among other things, we were mutually respecting colleagues. We shared adjoining offices on the third floor of our home and, of course, greeted each other frequently during the work day. When our doors were open, I would hear her talking on the telephone, or I would stop to talk or smile on my way down the stairs. All of this familiar ritual ceased in the fall when my wife terminated her practice. After her final incapacitating illness and death, her office door was closed, as her part of the suite remained eerily silent. My own patients were keenly aware of the change in our/my circumstances, and in this chapter I want to reflect both on the response of *my* patients to my wife's illness and death and on my own responses to the reactions of my patients. While writing this chapter itself may well be part of my own process of mourning, I want to focus on my feelings about my patients' feelings and gestures in the hope of broadening the conceptualizations of "countertransference," "intersubjectivity," "analyst enactments," and "selfobject needs and self states of the analyst" in the face of trauma and loss in the analyst's personal life. I will present some personal historical and theoretical background and then clinical examples of the intersubjective experience of patient and analyst in the face of this change in the analyst's life.

My wife's cancer was first diagnosed almost eleven years prior to her death, when our only child, a daughter, was five. My wife received the full complement of what was then considered optimal treatment in an excellent medical system, which included surgery, radiation, and various combinations of chemotherapy. During the first ten years of her illness, she felt essentially well and strong throughout periods of treatment, remission, and spread of the cancer. She chose to face her disease directly and openly, sharing facts and feelings freely with friends and family. She paid particular attention to the matter of self-disclosure with regard to her patients and wrote about the process of deciding what and when to tell patients about her illness, how to handle matters of accepting new patients, termination and referral, and so on (Morrison, 1990, in press). She presented her thoughts about these matters widely in the local therapeutic community, and thus, many of her patients, as well as many of

41

my own, knew directly of her illness. Others of my patients observed my wife struggling to get up the stairs in the last weeks of her practice and learned of her illness in this way. She and I discussed our approaches to sharing this information about the reality of our personal situations, and I took my lead from her forthright decision to share as indicated the facts of her illness with her patients. For those of my patients who had no knowledge of our situation, I eventually spoke of my wife's illness and the fact that I would be taking some indeterminate time away from practice.

Our mutual decisions about disclosure were influenced by horror stories that we each had heard about analysts/therapists who had not revealed their terminal illnesses to patients, thus providing no chance for them to anticipate, terminate, and grieve; by our own personal styles and values regarding authenticity in work with patients; and by the fact that so many of our patients could see for themselves that something dire was going on. I chose to tell those of my patients who had not observed my wife's struggle (or, perhaps, my own) in adequate time for us to discuss their reactions and together to anticipate my absence. Technically, this approach to disclosing the actual situation seemed useful to my patients as a means of handling a difficult reality. I didn't fully anticipate, however, my *own* vulnerabilities or the extent of my responses to the range of my patients' reactions to my painful life situation. It is this intersubjective, shared experience that I want to examine in this chapter.

I came to think of the particular nature of this aspect of my work with patients as *enforced disclosure,* since for so many of them there would have been no way of concealing the reality of or protecting them from its impact on them and me. I reflected on how different this might have been had my wife and I *not* shared adjoining office space in our own home or had she not been in the same field and been so public about her approach to dealing professionally with her illness. While providing therapy would be a means of *escape* or *distraction* from painful or traumatic circumstances for some colleagues in situations analogous to mine, in this instance there was no potential evasion through work available to me. It felt, at times, as though my very privacy was taken away—there could be no solace, no forgetting, no pretense of normalcy that might have obtained had my office been elsewhere, in an anonymous building in town. On the other hand, I felt, at times, guilty or responsible for the impact of this enforced disclosure on the direction or nature of my patients' concerns. They didn't have the freedom, it often felt, to pursue the range or direction of their own associations and inner processes but had to deal with and respond to the concerns presented to them by my external reality and their assumptions about my responses. While this fact, of course, offered ample opportunity to pursue transference feelings, these often seemed forced and imposed, not reflecting the free and meandering direction dictated by the patient's own personal need or experience. On the other hand, because of the reality circumstance, there seemed no alternative to this conundrum. (I sometimes speculated that I might have done more to protect my patients, like moving my office out of the house.)

These were some of the concerns with which I approached my practice during my wife's final illness and death. I felt raw, vulnerable, and quite preoccupied much of the time and tried to assess whether or not I was able to offer my patients that magnitude of analytic attentiveness toward which I routinely aspired. I consulted with a respected colleague who had previously gone through a similar experience, and he speculated about the wisdom of taking a break or, at least, making alternative arrangements for those patients who presented the greatest stress. I thought seriously about this suggestion but decided that, for now, at least, so long as I was able to reflect upon and try to sort out my own feelings relating to my patients, I would probably be able to continue to be helpful in my work. This chapter will attempt to describe that monitoring process.

THE ANALYST'S VULNERABILITY

Not much has been written about the analyst or therapist's response to environmental trauma or stress in their own lives (e.g., illness in family members, catastrophic personal events, divorces, etc.), although some material is beginning to appear about the therapist's efforts to deal with his/her own illness (Morrison, 1990, in press). An important paper by Bacal and Thompson (1994) points to the inevitable selfobject needs of the analyst with regard to his patients, emphasizing such factors as the expectation of respect, payment, some sense of therapeutic impact and patient improvement, and a means of dealing with the shame that often accompanies therapeutic impasse and patient complaints of not being helped. These relevant concerns often are not considered in examining the contributions of the analyst to the intersubjective field with his patient.

From my own experience with my wife's illness and death, I would add another dimension that differs somewhat from the contribution of Bacal and Thompson. I will call this dimension the quality of the *self-state* of the analyst at a particular time. By this, I refer to the stability, tranquility, and equilibrium of the individual analyst's sense of him/herself as he or she engages with the patient. This sense of self relates to those qualities of self-representation defined by Stolorow (1975) as cohesion, stability over time, and affective coloration. Traditional analysis has tended to consider the analyst in terms of "the analyzing instrument"— a mechanistic structure beaming perceptual energy towards the patient's unconscious, a tabula rosa receiving messages from the patient's unconscious, which then can be decoded by an ever-alert analytic observing ego. I think this model tends to leave out the inevitable fluctuations in attentiveness, interest, or empathic and perceptual clarity that each of us evinces at different moments in our work, as our "analytic instrument" is subject to the vagaries of human experience and the inevitable mutual discourse between the internal worlds of both participants.

Environmental trauma—in this case, illness and loss of a loved one—inevitably exerts a destabilizing impact on the self-state (or sense of self) of the analyst and shakes up the calibrations on that delicate appliance, "the analytic instrument." From my own experience, this destabilization does not automatically mandate a break by the analyst from his work. Rather, I suggest that deliberate and focused attention to this dimension of the analyst's person—the cohesion, stability, energy, and equilibration of his sense of self (that is, the *self-state* of the analyst)—enables the analyst to place himself into the analytic matrix as he interacts with, responds to, and has feelings about the expressions of his patients. This awareness by the analyst of his own contribution to the intersubjective moment with his patient can often be turned to major benefit for the therapeutic process.

In the following examples, I will try to recall and express the feelings I experienced as my patients became aware of and spoke about their perceptions and fantasies regarding my wife's illness and death, its impact on me, and, hence, its impact on them and their therapy. This account will be about both patients and therapist and about the relationship between them.

CLINICAL MATERIAL

In general, as I reviewed these matters, there were no major surprises in my responses to patients (although there were several unexpected reactions of particular patients that will be described later). I continued to have complex countertransference feelings with the same patients as previously; those with whom the clinical relationship had flowed fairly easily continued to proceed in a relatively uncomplicated way. I believe, however, that there tended to be an *intensification* and *amplification* of the particular countertransference experience with certain patients. Given the reality of my own more vulnerable and fluid self-state, as well as the potential for that intensification of selfobject needs noted by Bacal and Thompson (1994) because of my own loss and mourning, examples of amplified countertransference feelings and subtle countertransference enactments (Jacobs, 1991) may have accrued in certain specific clinical interactions.

Ms. A

A married mother of three in her thirties, Ms. A had been in treatment for a good number of years, during which time her extensive fear of death had been one focus of our work. Ms. A had frequently seen my wife as she passed her office or noted her walking up or down the stairs. Fantasies about her as the "good mother" or the "safe, caring therapist" had been frequent, as my wife appeared in dreams as a benevolent, caring, female figure often in contrast with a remote or harsh male. Ms. A had learned of my wife's illness rather early from acquaintances and, for some years, had been scanning the environment for signs about how she was doing. Her antennae about this (as about other issues in her life) were exquisitely sensitive, and yet, at the same time, she strove to protect herself from her observations or memories by denying their importance to her or their relevance to our work together. I, on the other hand, had been working towards helping her to tolerate the intensity of her feelings and the pain of her memories and observations, and one major source of my countertransference frustration in work with her had to do with her tendency towards denial and disavowal of her most important and relevant feelings.

As my wife's illness progressed, Ms. A kept track of events and would report these in treatment (e.g., the presence of medical items in the car; the pace of my wife's gait in coming up stairs or the quality of her voice while talking on the phone; whether or not she was wearing makeup, with inferences about the significance of these factors) but then would proclaim their irrelevance. Her concern manifestly was for my loss, but also for what would happen to me as my wife became terminally ill and if, ultimately, she died. Would I still be available to Ms. A after my loss and in my grief? Also, this eventuality would leave us together in the suite of offices, alone, and without the salving, safe presence of my wife. I tried to explore the meaning of this potential absence to her, both in terms of her fears for my own capacity to be present for her and of her fantasies of potentially having me for herself.

Her characteristic response to my inquiry was that it was irrelevant or "bad" for her to have such thoughts or intrusive on the privacy of my own space or feelings. For example, she might comment on "the deafening silence next door"—she had long experienced relief to hear the sound of footsteps in my wife's office or closet—but then would quickly state that this wasn't important or shouldn't be part of our work. "What's the purpose of talking about this? Is this good to do?" She "shouldn't" notice these things, shouldn't know about my wife's illness, certainly shouldn't be "curious" about the details of my personal life. Also, she would state that she didn't want to know about me, didn't want to know anything about my wife's condition. "I don't want it to be a factor."

In the best of times, I could become impatient with Ms. A's perceptual style and her commitment to denial and disavowal as defensive methods. I took therapeutic solace from her remarkable capacities to observe and to remember and also from realization that this defensive style had evolved in the context of a family that emphasized, at all times, a cheerful countenance and a social network that valued deception and suppression of feelings. However, during the last stages of my wife's illness, I had particular difficulty with Ms. A's defensive responses. I grew irritated with her need to deny or to negate her feelings. In retrospect, I think this was particularly so because I personally had no such recourse. Since I was constantly and inescapably confronted with a painful reality and because of my own personal commitment to facing and sorting out feelings, I was particularly impatient with Ms. A's defensiveness. It felt to me as though her wish to evade feelings about my wife's illness deprived me of *her* selfobject responsiveness to my needs. Also, it had been my wife's unswerving decision to face her realities and feelings directly, and I think that I therefore had less than usual patience for Ms. A's maneuvers and needs. It had always been my message to Ms. A that the psychoanalytic method had as its ultimate goal the uncovering and understanding of feelings, painful and otherwise. Because of my own vulnerabilility at this time and because of my intensified selfobject need for a shared ("twinning") value on truth and veracity regarding feelings, I was quick to grow impatient with Ms. A's response.

While I think, in general, that I was able to monitor my exasperation so that it did not encroach much on my therapeutic work with her, there were two instances in which I became aware of enactments reflecting my own vulnerability and personal state. In the first of these, at a moment when Ms. A was emphasizing that she didn't want my wife's condition to be a factor in her life or our therapy I blurted, "But it is!" In this response, I think I was attempting to block her access to disavowal as a means of avoiding the range of her feelings about my wife's impending death, including confrontations with her own mortality, feelings about sickness in her family, her fears and wishes about my future aloneness and availability, and so on. Rather than exploring the ramifications of her wishes to avoid, I was saying, "No, you can't!" I think that behind this fierce refusal was a feeling akin to, "Listen, *I* can't get away from this reality that my wife is dying. I'm going to try to stop you from escaping it." In retrospect, it seemed that Ms. A's denial felt to me like a negation of my inescapable situation. My maneuver to confront her with reality, rather than to explore her wish to avoid thinking about it, represented an invocation of the well-utilized "truth" morality of psychoanalytic theory by which avoidance and self-deception are eschewed. Under less pressing circumstances, I believe that I would probably have asked her to talk more about why she didn't want my wife's condition to be a factor in her life. In the past, such inquiry had yielded feelings of humiliation that illness and death were so terrifying to her—"I should be able to handle this better, like everyone else does."

In another session, when she was talking about how badly she felt about what she observed regarding my wife's condition, I wondered aloud whether she might feel angry at me for forcing her to know about such matters, for not protecting her against being confronted with details about my wife's illness. She denied this, but several times more during the session, I alluded to the obligatory or enforced nature of disclosure about the illness and about my personal life. I believe that one such inquiry would have been therapeutically useful, but my repeated questioning reflected more my own complex feelings about my patient's involvement in the circumstances. I have spoken about my guilt over exposing my patients to my wife's dying (i.e., the question of "enforced disclosure"). I think also, on some level, that I was resentful of her repressed curiosity about all that was going on and was angry at *her* for her denied, but palpable, interest. Through my repeated inquiry into her anger at me, I think I was turning the tables away from my own feelings of anger at her persistent, unacknowledged involvement in my situation and projecting them onto her instead. Under less loaded circumstances, I might have attempted tactfully to look into her curiosity and her wish to know the details of my family's plight. As it was, I think that my attempt to monitor my feelings about Ms. A's veiled intrusiveness helped at least to keep the analysis on track and workable.

My annoyance and anger at Ms. A was indeed elicited, in part, by the manner in which she inserted and denied her feelings, but I suspect that more was involved. Hers was the presence of a healthy, vigorous younger woman *not* plagued by the tormenting illness and pain that afflicted my wife. There was probably a level in which I was angry at my women patients in general, both because their circumstance differed from that of my wife and because, through gender identity, they were similar to her as well, tending to confront me with the pain of my forthcoming loss. I will consider these factors further in the final section of this chapter.

Ms. B

In the four years of her treatment, we had worked extensively on Ms. B's squelched grief over the death of her father when she was a teenager. The trauma of that loss had been followed by her developing a chronic illness shortly thereafter and then by the decision to move far away from her mother and home. The relation of all these events to one another, as well as her reticence to accept the ambiguities of life and her wish to replace these with decisive certainty, had been a focus of our attention. Ms. B also had learned early of my wife's illness and had been appropriately concerned and distressed about the situation. Like Ms. A, she expressed difficulty in thinking about the outcome of my wife's progressive deterioration. Also as with the first patient, I found myself, at times, impatient with her, in this case with her wish to avoid amibiguities (including the ambiguity of timing regarding the course of my wife's illness). While I am not aware of any particular enactments that emerged from these feelings towards Ms. B, one particular interaction was stressful to me because of issues it raised, but which provided as well an avenue for deepening of the analytic work between us.

Always tactful and concerned about intruding on me and "your personal pain," Ms. B started one meeting apologetically by stating, "I'm terribly afraid that when your wife dies I'm going to have to stop treatment." As I recall my reaction, I felt upset, hurt, and angry at this prospect of "yet another" loss—first my wife and then this patient. I was able to contain and reflect upon this reaction and continued to explore it with her. "Well, if she's not there any more," Ms. B opined, "someone else will have to take care of you, and, of course, that would have to be me." At first I was startled but then was able to "decenter" from my personal focus on my reaction to my wife's potential death to Ms. B's concerns, as I wondered at her assumptions that I would need such "taking care of," that she would have to be the responsible party, as well as about the meaning to her of having to "take care of" someone important to her.

I inquired about these matters, and she associated to her adolescence and to the death of her father. "After my father died, my mother was a total basket case; she couldn't take care of anything—me, herself, the house. I had to rally, take over—to do everything and to take care of her." Thus, concern about the potential loss of this patient, because of assumptions about my vulnerability after my wife died, turned into a productive therapeutic exploration. It required my reviewing my own feelings and stepping aside—decentering—from my own vulnerabilities and concerns to allow Ms. B's issues to expand into the space between us and so to maintain the exploratory focus. I am suggesting, however, that my initial (internal) response to Ms. B's remark reverberated with my own sense of myself as being uniquely exposed and sensitive to loss. "Indeed, who *would* there be to take care of me after my wife dies? Will I need taking care of? What function will my work, my patients (such as Ms. B) serve in this task?" By reflecting directly on these feelings and then being able to utilize them as part of the work at hand—exploration of meaning and history with Ms. B—I was able to maintain the therapeutic process.

Further elaboration by Ms. B led to her understanding that the decision to go far away from home to get away from her mother's dependency on her after her father's death and the onset of her disease paralleled her expectation that she would have to leave treatment at the point of my wife's death. A further element to be unraveled was her assumption that our (my wife and my) daughter (with whom she identified) was the same age currently that she had been when her father had died. All of these parallels raised strong feelings and the doubt that she would be able to contain them. While I too was aware of my own anger, fear, and sadness raised by her initial statement, I was able to explore her concerns and, ultimately, to question with her whether my needs and response to my spouse's death would necessarily be identical to those of her mother. With this question, we were *both* addressing as well the matter of ambiguity that had been such a thorn in Ms. B's side—neither she nor I actually knew for sure how I would manage with this momentous loss. My posing the question, however, raised the *possibility* that I might continue to be able to provide what she needed from her treatment and that she mightn't have to make the same decision (to leave) that she had made as a teenager. The therapeutic process proceeded usefully after that interchange.

Ms. C

A young woman who had been hospitalized a decade before for depression and an eating disorder, Ms. C had moved away from her family and was in the process of trying to put her life together in a different environment. She had been initially hopeful in this psychotherapy, feeling that I was responsive to her needs and to her inquiries (in contrast with previous therapists and her parents). She was, however, discouraged and gloomy about the prospects of her life, particularly about any hope of having a normal social and dating experience. The major focus of treatment was on the nature and origins of her massive self-loathing, with a therapeutic goal of altering these feelings about herself.

Ms. C learned of my wife's illness through observation. Her fantasies previously had been that my wife was a competent and caring person. When she noted on one occasion her difficulty in walking, Ms. C asked if she were sick, and I told her that she was. "Is it serious?" she continued. "Yes," I said. When I explored her response and clarified my wife's condition, she seemed shocked and then explained that she was very frightened of this illness and didn't want to think about it. She was uncomfortable with her dependency needs but then proceeded to enumerate them and to get angry at me. "You'll be so preoccupied that you won't be able to continue to respond to me, to give me what I need. Things will change—I'm sure of it! Just my luck to finally find a therapist who I like and who I can trust, and then *this* happens. You'll disappear on me." She continued to say that she wasn't going to get caught needing someone who wasn't going to remain available to her. It never works to depend on someone—maybe she should just cut back on therapy. Then her expression changed as she berated herself, "But what right do I have to have those feelings, when you're going through all this sadness. In fact, I don't have any serious problems compared to you and your wife. I shouldn't even be wasting your time."

Predictably, my "buttons" were pushed, and I felt annoyed with Ms. C. As with Ms. A, she was saying that she wanted to avoid thinking about my wife's illness—an option totally unthinkable and unavailable for me. Certainly, there were many times when I would have grasped at that option, and the fantasy of escaping to work might have been one of them. However, because of the proximity of my office to that of my wife and because her circumstance was widely known in the professional community, work tended to be an inescapable continuation of encounters regarding the facts of her illness and physical decline.

Secondly, I wasn't in the fittest condition to contain and process Ms. C's anger at my potential unavailability. A part of me wanted to shout back, "Shit, I've got other things on my mind at this time than your fears that *I'll* disappear." Also, "I'm trying as best I can to keep focused on you, to be here for you, and you're mad that I might not be there. You want to cut back? Go!" And, "You don't have serious problems compared to my wife and me? Shouldn't waste my time? RIGHT YOU ARE!" However, I was able to contain and reflect on these feelings without enacting them (through angry response or an emphasis on external reality) as I had with Ms. A. Instead, we continued to explore her fears, her anger, and her disappointment as she anticipated my unavailability. I did confirm that I would probably be away from the office for some length of time in the foreseeable future, but we discussed the option of a particular therapist who would be available to help her during that time. This shared negotiation offered her some sense of control over her fate in therapy in a way that differed from her earlier parental interactions.

Ms. D

A woman who was perpetually angry at me because I *wasn't* the same therapist who had "abandoned" her several years before by moving away and refering her to me and because I seemed too remote and "superior" (like her father), Ms. D was one of my patients who had no idea about my wife's illness. On one occasion when my wife was hospitalized, I had to cancel some sessions with Ms. D. During that phone conversation she asked whether I was sick, and I took that occasion to explain that my wife was ill and had been hospitalized.

During our next session, Ms. D asked for details about my wife, and after inquiring about her concerns, I explained the situation to her. I recall feeling rather relieved that now, at last, she too knew about my wife's condition. I now felt ready to tell the few remaining patients who were unaware of her illness, and then Ms. D and I could proceed with full "authenticity" (based, as it was, on full disclosure). After first expressing her perfunctory condolences, Ms. D began to launch into her anger at me for not having told her sooner. "What kind of relationship is this, when something as serious as that is going on in your life, and

I don't even know it? You should have told me earlier. It just confirms what I've always said—that this isn't real between us. It's just a sham to call this a relationship. It confirms my view of you—cold and distant."

"'Cold and distant?'" thought I. "For heaven's sake, lady, I've just told you about my current personal life, and you tell me that I conceal from you." We had wrestled for some time about my "aloofness," her experience of my style in relation to that of her father and of her previous therapist and, significantly, about the nature of the therapeutic relationship. "Conceal?" my interior musings continued. "What the hell more do you want?" Aware as I became of my own anger, in contrast, we continued therapy as we discussed her thoughts and wishes about what she would have liked for me to have told her and *when* and what such attentiveness would have signaled to her. What she wanted, of course, was to have had me turn to her in my grief for support and understanding, instead of the "charade" of normalcy that had surrounded therapy. In fact, Ms. D's own mother had died some short while before, and she had expected her father to look to her (his only daughter) for solace. While she experienced no profound conscious grief at the loss of her (remote) mother, she was furious as her father turned for sympathy and tenderness, not to her, but to a new girlfriend.

DISCUSSION

I have tried to present glimpses of the interaction between some of my patients and me and of my internal musings, during a particularly stressful time in my own life—the terminal illness and death of my wife. Knowledge of this situation or delayed apprisal of it affected both my patients and myself, influencing, in some instances, the nature of our interactions and, in all instances, the feelings experienced by both of us. My own personal reality—both internal and external—influenced my patients' experience of our therapeutic encounters, just as patients' response to my circumstance had a profound impact on my own feelings and sense of myself at given moments. This mutual interaction and mutual construction of the relationship between patient and therapist is what Stolorow and Atwood (1992, pp. 3–4) refer to as the "intersubjective field," created by "mutual reciprocal influence" (Beebe and Lachmann, 1988), in this instance, between patient and therapist. With respect to my personal participation, I am suggesting that my own traumatizing circumstance and vulnerability created a subjective sensitivity to strong and, at moments, destabilizing affects that were atypical of my routine participation as analyst and therapist. The self-state (or particular self experience) of the analyst at a specific moment in time, particularly under circumstances of severe stress, must be added to the mix in the formulation of a given intersubjective field.

It is, indeed, relevant to this account that the patients I have selected to illustrate my enactments or countertransference feelings during my wife's last days are all women. It seems to me that several factors, besides those of chance and clinical process, influenced these choices. Principal among them is the likelihood that mutual identifications—both of women patients with my wife and her circumstance and of me associating my women patients with my wife—led to a relative blurring of the therapeutic frame during this period of my own self-state disequilibrium. Women patients may, in general, more freely express their reactions, concerns, and needs than their more contained and/or constricted male counterparts. As noted earlier, women patients also may more readily have elicited my anger (in part because of my own identification of them with my ailing wife). This anger may, in fact, have vitalized and illuminated recollections of the treatments at this difficult time in my personal life. Perhaps, too, something transmitted from *me,* the therapist, made it less problematic for me to interact with my male patients at that stressful time. Might it have been a more flowing and easy empathic bond from my male patients towards me that caused them to "buck up" and "restrain" their own needs during my time of distress? Ironically, of course, such restraint might ultimately have compromised the depth of work attained with some men because of their identification with and response to my pain at that time or because of my own preoccupations.

I'm not sure about all the factors regarding the gender composition of my sample; suffice it to say that my thoughts about the complexities of transference–countertransference feelings during that time two years ago have brought to mind interactions with these four women patients. In thinking about my male patients, I have an image of Mr. X, a quite remote, intellectual, bipolar young man who, for years, had seemed fundamentally consumed by his own self-doubts and impairments. He appeared to take relatively little note of me or my presence, except to comment occasionally on my various lapses or insufficiencies. He was one of the last of my patients to know of my wife's illness, and I decided to tell him about it because of some imminent inevitable absences (as with Ms. D). To my great surprise, Mr. X expressed great concern and sadness. Tears came to his eyes as he rose from his chair, came over to me, and embraced me tenderly. I was very moved and found myself learning about a whole new side of Mr. X that we continued to explore from that point onward in his treatment. His was, then, a reaction that posed no conflict or difficulty to me but offered surprising empathic resonance, as well as an opportunity for mutual authenticity, thus opening new and productive channels for further therapeutic exploration.

I will close with an example from Ms. A that illustrates, I believe, the reestablishment of a more equilibrated, expectable self-state in me, the therapist. In a session some months after my wife's death, which included a three-week absence from practice, during which Ms. A met with a colleague of mine, she complained that talking about my wife's death just made things worse. She spoke of a part of her that wished I had closed my practice. I inquired about that wish, and she declared that she would then be sure that no one would be treating things "as though nothing has happened." She again reiterated her desire that my wife hadn't died, and, as I probed, Ms. A expressed a concern that she might "just come in here and forget about her." I then commented that, were I to stop my practice, she wouldn't have to come, could put it out of her mind without feeling guilty about it. "That probably would feel like a great relief," I suggested, while at the same time noting that she would also greatly miss her connection to me. I also commented on her concern that my continuing practice seemed to suggest that I treated my wife's death as though nothing special had happened.

There were other directions that I might have taken that therapeutic moment, but I include it as an example to indicate that I felt less raw, less likely to respond confrontatively to her provocation, and better able to explore the range and intricacies of her feelings regarding my wife, my responses, and her relationship with me. In other words, I believe that the nature of my countertransference reactions—what I am calling the analytic self- state—had returned towards a level of equilibrium, stability, and neutrality approximating the usual, expectable quality of the analyst/therapist in performing her/his therapeutic tasks. Of course, a perspective informed exclusively by a social–constructivist or intersubjective view might not emphasize those same factors to define the expectable analytic context!

CONCLUSION

During this period of evolution in our field towards greater awareness of the therapist's responsiveness in *relation with* the patient, it is important for us to be aware of the nature of what our patients learn about us and about what impact trauma and tragedy have on us—the "analytic instrument" of traditional analytic formulation. In this chapter, I am suggesting both that certain circumstances of the treatment situation may impose on *our patients* inevitable information and knowledge about our own life circumstances and, further, that these circumstances frequently impose an equally likely, though unsought, destabilization and disequilibration of *our own* personal capacity for analytic neutrality and "evenly hovering attention." I am calling the patient's experience one of *enforced disclosure* and the analyst's experience as the quality of his or her *self-state*.

Certainly, many current writers are focusing on the inevitability of self-disclosure by the therapist in treatment (e.g., Hoffmann, 1983, 1992; Renik, 1993), but in this chapter I attempt to illustrate the occasional occurrence of inescapably traumatic or unusual elements influencing self-disclosure and revelation. These elements will likely impact harshly as well on the optimal calm and self-reflection of the analytic process for both participants, imposing an expectable *fluidity* in the self-state of the analyst. Through reflection on my own personal experience, I am suggesting that attention to these elements in the therapeutic encounter is vital. I have tried to show that awareness of our fluid self-state can be useful to the analyst in helping to monitor the analytic process and in deciding when it is best to interrupt practice (in general or with specific patients). Awareness of these issues is important in order to grant therapists *permission* for and *self-acceptance* of those inevitable deviations from the optimal states of attentiveness and calm that may accompany personal stresses in their own subjective realities. Such awareness optimally enhances and helps to make authentic the therapeutic process and may, in fact, increase its depth through immersion in the issues of loss, death, and sorrow that such disruption necessitates.

REFERENCES

Bacal, H. & Thomson, P. (1994), The psychoanalyst's selfobject needs and the effect of their frustration on the treatment: A new view of countertransference. Presented at the 16th Annual Conference on the Psychology of the Self, Toronto, Canada.

Beebe, B. & Lachmann, F. M. (1988), Mother–infant mutual influence and the precursors of psychic structure: In: *Frontiers in Self Psychology: Progress in Self Psychology, Vol. 3,* ed. A. Goldberg. Hillsdale, NJ: The Analytic Press, pp. 3–25.

Hoffman, I. Z. (1983), The patient as interpreter of the analyst's experience. *Contemp. Psychoanal.,* 19:389–422.

——— (1992), Some practical implications of a social–constructivist view of the psychoanalytic situation. *Psychoanal. Dial.,* 2:287–304.

Jacobs, T. J. (1991), *The Use of the Self.* Madison, CT: International Universities Press.

Morrison, A. L. (1990), Doing psychotherapy while living with a life-threatening illness. In: *Illness in the Analyst: Implications for the Treatment,* ed. H. Schwartz & A. Silver. New York: International Universities Press.

——— (in press), Ten years of doing psychotherapy while living with a life threatening illness: Self-disclosure and other ramifications. *Psychoanal. Dial.*

Renik, O. (1993), Analytic interaction: Conceptualizing technique in light of the analyst's irreducible subjectivity. *Psychoanal. Quart.,* 62:553–571.

Stolorow, R. D. (1975), Toward a functional definition of narcissism. *Internat. J. Psycho-Anal.,* 56:179–85.

——— & Atwood, G. (1992), *Contexts of Being.* Hillsdale, NJ: The Analytic Press.

4

An Analyst's Pregnancy Loss and Its Effects on Treatment
Disruption and Growth

BARBARA GERSON

Several years ago, when I was 17 weeks pregnant, I suddenly developed problems in my pregnancy as a direct consequence of having an amniocentesis. After 4 weeks of complete bed rest, I had to have the pregnancy ended. These stark facts, together with their immediate and long-term emotional effects, have altered and shaped the paths and textures of the treatments of many patients with whom I was working then. The meaning and effects have varied, of course, for each patient in relation to his or her unique dynamics and with the kind of relationship we had developed. For many, however, the impact has been a major one, and the levels of meaning have emerged gradually. As I have become more comfortable with the sudden and random turn my life took and with the intense and initially unknown feelings I had, I have become better able to talk about the events with my patients and better able to give them permission, often unstated, to unwrap their thoughts, fantasies, and questions with me. In this paper I discuss this path, often bumpy, awkward, and uncertain.

When I first developed a medical problem after the amniocentesis, I was put on bed rest for an undetermined length of time. During those first few days, I regained some sense of balance and felt relieved that my pregnancy seemed viable. Given my hope and medical indications that the pregnancy would continue for the remaining months, I decided to return to my work with adult patients—by phone or at home. In preparation, I busied myself with practical details for at-home work. The challenges I found, however — my patients' and my own reactions, feelings, and problems—far dwarfed the pragmatic arrangements.

THEORETICAL PERSPECTIVES

What I present fits into the larger context of the effects on treatment of crises in the life of an analyst. There is a very small literature on the effects of analysts' miscarriages on treatment (Hannett, 1949; Barbanel, 1980; Lazar, 1990), and there is a larger literature about analysts' pregnancies (Lax, 1969; Fenster, Phillips, and Rapoport, 1986; Penn, 1986;

This article appeared originally in 1994 in *Psychoanalytic Dialogues,* 4:1–18.

Imber, 1990). There is also a growing body of work about the effects of serious or life-threatening illnesses and the deaths of loved ones on analytic work (Singer, 1971; Givelber and Simon, 1981; Friedman, 1991; Schoolman, 1988; Weinberg, 1988; Schwartz and Silver, 1990). There is consensus that such life crises profoundly affect and alter the analytic space.

Lazar (1990) wrote most vividly about the effects of her seven pregnancies, two of which ended at five months and three in early miscarriages. She noted that her patients felt deeply involved and reacted strongly when her pregnancies were lost at late points, especially, she added, "in the face of their own covert and explicit hostility" (p. 200) and were alert to her deeply felt feelings. She discussed some of the difficult reactions analysts may experience at the ensuing loss of anonymity—self-protective anger, guilt, and partial withdrawal—as well as her increased respect and awe for patients' perceptiveness. Her patients' reactions included relief at the miscarriage, guilt about envious and destructive feelings, unconscious enactment of self-destructive punishments for their wishes, concern about the analyst, and intensified experiences of their own prior grief or losses. Her own reactions included outrage at some patient responses, deeper connections with the grief of others, and horrified helplessness as still others played out self-destructive dramas responsive to her loss. She also noted her positive reaction of "heightened countertransference, concern, and dedication to the ongoing work" (p. 225).

A duality of disruptive effects, which for some patients are ultimately useful and for others insurmountable, and of growth-evoking consequences from the analyst's life crisis has been noted throughout the literature. Lazar spoke of "the analyst's survival of repeated loss and yet continued functioning" (p. 225) as offering the patient a powerful reassurance. Singer (1971) discussed the positive aspects of his sharing the fact of his wife's serious illness with his patients. Their reactions, he said, showed the "positive manifestations of potentials and attitudes usually and unfortunately expressed by them in non-productive and pathological terms" (p. 62). Friedman (1991) also noted that her own serious illness evoked previously unknown positive feelings in some of her patients. For example, one man experienced, through his concern for her, "long repressed feelings of caring and empathy toward his mother whom he viewed either with indifference or disgust for most of his adult life" (p. 417). She also noted, though, that some patients chose not to begin work with her when she revealed her illness. Dewald (1990) elaborated the potentially disruptive effects in his discussion of his serious illness, which required a ten-week absence from his work. Increased transferential reactions of anxiety about aggression and dependency were particularly prevalent.

Two questions or issues repeatedly occur. The first concerns how much factual information needs to be provided to patients. Abend (1990) refers to this question as "the crux of the matter" (p. 104). Increased self-disclosure seems to be the norm, with specificity in disclosure most commonly encouraged. Thus, some urge self-disclosure according to the level of patient's developmental stage (Barbanel, 1980) or stage of treatment (Dewald, 1990). Orientation to self-disclosure seems to vary with overall theoretical orientation to analysis. For example, Abend (1990) acknowledged with great regret that he could not maintain a classical nonrevelatory stance with his patients after a several-week absence due to a serious illness. He had planned to provide no factual information, but: "To my surprise, that proved all but impossible. . . . Within three days after I began to see patients, I had found . . . compelling reasons to tell all but two of my analytic patients something factual about my illness" (pp. 107–108). Nevertheless, he recommended little alteration in analytic stance about disclosure. On the other hand is the view of Peddicord (1990), a more interpersonal analyst, who wrote that he told some patients without conflict the fact of the death of his infant son, who was born prematurely. He explained: "For me, it would have felt unauthentic not to disclose it . . . [it was] a bridge to genuine relatedness" (p. 271). Leibowitz (1992) discussed her decision to tell a pregnant patient about her own choice to remain childfree following infertility problems. Greater freedom and more genuine intimacy in the analysis and in the patient's life, as well as increased exploration of issues around jealousy, envy, and competitiveness, followed. The decision about what information to impart becomes more complex as analysts' crises become more complex, in terms of chronicity, ambiguity, or ongoing effects.

A second question—more important, I think, than how much information to impart—is how to deal with the consequences of the crises on treatment. Dewald (1990) asks, "How extensively can/should the patient be encouraged or helped to describe and deal with the multiple conscious and unconscious reactions to the analyst's illness?" (p. 83). He concludes with what has become a widely quoted admonition that the "full gamut of patients' responses, affects and associations to the illness" needs to be explored "in the face of countertransference temptations . . . to promote premature closure . . . or to use the experience for exhibitionistic, masochistic, narcissistic or other neurotic satisfactions" (p. 89). He adds, "To the extent that such reactions in both participants remain unacknowledged or unanalyzed, important resistances and counterresistances to deeper analytic work will persist" (p. 89).

My experiences indicated that patient and analyst reactions need to be analyzed not only because deeper analytic work would be impossible without it but because such analysis itself is, or can be, the "deeper" analytic work. In other words, the interpersonal/relational and intrapsychic experiences and reactions generated by the analyst's life crisis can provide the field in which the "knottiest" analytic issues are confronted.

This was the case for patients with a variety of reactions and dynamics. Those with sharply negative reactions to my loss called most obviously for analysis of what appeared to be a disruption of the treatment; however, the lasting impact and generalizing effects of my crisis continued for other patients as well, with my loss providing a turning point in their treatment.

CLINICAL MATERIAL

In order to show how I came to view the exploration of reactions to my loss as being "the deeper analytic work," I present clinical material and my thinking as they unfolded chronologically, at three different times over a three-year period—during my initial pregnancy difficulty, in the immediate six months to a year after my loss, and in the ensuing two years since then. I talk in some detail about two patients whose negative reactions presented difficult challenges for me. The first is Sara, whose mother had given birth prematurely to a baby who then died. Later I present Peter, who did not want me to have a baby. I also talk more briefly about the early impact of my pregnancy difficulty on two other patients, for whom the crisis ultimately provided a new focal point in their treatment: Louisa, who was herself pregnant at the time, and Marie, who did not want to know anything about babies or about me.

Before turning specifically to the clinical material, I want to clarify the criteria I used to decide whether to work on the phone or at home. I anticipated that there would be more involuntary self-disclosure resulting from working at home. I also thought patients who saw me at home would be more closely exposed to my high-risk pregnancy and whatever vicissitudes that might involve. Therefore, I evaluated the degree of personal revelations and ambiguity the patient seemed able to tolerate without feeling overstimulated or excessively anxious. I also considered whether a patient might later feel abandoned when we returned to the more normal office setting. A criterion that was unconscious at the time was the degree of negative transference my patients presented. An unconscious fear of others' aggression has been noted by others (Imber, 1990; Schwartz, 1990) to accompany illness and pregnancy, and they note that this may evoke distancing from the analyst.

The Immediate Crisis: Working at Home

Sara is a single woman in her 20s, highly successful in her profession despite a history of substance abuse and depression. Sara had noticed my pregnancy early on. She said she was thrilled at my pregnancy and that it made her feel like a baby sitting on my lap; later she amended this to feeling like the one inside my belly. She thus far had experienced only positive feelings about my having a child, identifying with the one who would be within me, not the patient who was outside me. The content of her sessions at my apartment was clearly influenced by my pregnancy problem. She focused on the pregnancy problem and premature delivery her mother had when she, Sara, was a young child. That baby died soon after birth. Although she had brought up this death earlier in her treatment—she was now in the third year of twice-weekly therapy—her memories now contained vividness and urgency as she saw me reclining as her mother had. Years later, she said being with me at home plunged her back into a terrible time. She had a disturbing memory of her father yelling at her not to jump on the bed, but she did not stop. Although she "knew" that her jumping did not cause the baby's death, she still felt guilty.

As Sara discussed her memories, she began to have numerous criticisms of my apartment. She objected to the absence of a comfortable waiting area. She disliked various art objects, which seemed unlike anything she would have. She noticed that a piece of furniture was in disrepair and expressed anger that I would not have repaired it. Her most serious objection was to the dirty dishes in the sink, which she discovered one day as she wandered into the kitchen when leaving. Initially I did not take her criticisms seriously. I myself wished that my concerns were about dirty dishes or a broken chair. The seriousness of the complaints soon became evident, however, and her negative feelings about my home continued. As I understood their importance, I acknowledged her anger. The meaning of the anger, personal and symbolic, emerged later; I return later in the paper to Sara at the time of my pregnancy loss.

Two other patients had significant initial reactions to my difficulties. Louisa, an artist in her 30s, was herself pregnant. She was also in the termination phase of a long analysis. Louisa had been excited about my pregnancy, which she also had noted quite early. The issue of how similar or different we were as women had been a long-standing concern, and she was happy that we were finally alike in a tangible way. In acknowledgment of both our similarity and differences, she had brought me a pregnancy gift. It was something she was using in her pregnancy, and she accurately sensed that I would be unlikely to come across it in my more traditional circles.

Her first sentence when she came to my apartment, however, was: "I don't know if I'll be able to come here—it's bad for my baby. Too much stress." I was surprised by her reaction, by her perception of me as dangerous, which I understood as largely transferential. I was also disappointed and realized I was more vulnerable than usual. As she spoke about her fear that my misfortune would be destructive to her, she said her fear passed. It was to return later, during her next pregnancy, in a different form, as fear of my envy. She returned briefly to analysis then, when we were both better able to understand and work through its meaning.

On the other hand, Louisa was the only patient who expressed worry about my physical health, apart from the viability of my pregnancy. I understood her worry then as related to her anxiety about abandonment associated with her termination. I interpreted this to her. She responded by correcting my interpretation, saying that she had a human concern about me, just as she would with a friend. Much later, I was able to understand my quick interpretation as, at least in part, reflecting my own denial of my physical vulnerability. She, also pregnant, had easily recognized the permeable boundary between unborn baby and mother. She, like Erwin Singer's (1971) patients, was able to respond to my crisis with increased empathy and "constructive relatedness." I learned to accept her nontangible pregnancy-problem gifts, her concern, and her empathy.

Marie presented a different problem for me. Marie had been in psychotherapy for many years. She was married and intensely ambivalent about whether she wanted to have a child or could be a loving mother. Unlike many others, she had not yet recognized my pregnancy. When she came to my apartment, she immediately told me her belief that I had pneumonia. I was shocked by the idea, since it seemed so clear, as I lay on the couch with my legs on pillows, that I was pregnant. As I explored her idea that I had pneumonia, she said that my voice had sounded very different over the phone. She explained that pneumonia can change the sound of one's voice and be serious enough to require remaining at home, but not so serious that I could not work. I was struck by a sense of unreality, created by the enormous gap between us at that moment. Although we had known for years about her denial, I experienced firsthand, more fully than ever, the degree of distance, alienation, and disorganization her denial could create. She had constructed a fantasy identity for me that I did not want and that I could not bear at the time. In retrospect, I realized that I also had been working hard to organize my sudden changes into an identity that would help me feel continuous at such a time of discontinuity. Her organization of me was too jarring a construction. I also believed that I would soon inevitably have to discuss my pregnancy with her.

I decided to tell her then what was going on, a deliberate self-disclosure driven mostly by my sense of urgency. She was shocked and embarrassed and was then able to tell me that she had noticed I was gaining weight. She had never considered pregnancy as an explanation. This interchange pointed us to look at central questions between us. What did she know about me? How much did she want to know? How well did she want me to know her? We both became aware of how much she wanted us both to live in a make-believe world devoid of birth, death, and tragedy.

In trying to understand the impact of the initial phase of my crisis, I am struck by the intensity of many of the sessions, for myself and for patients. I had consciously instructed myself to temper interpretations and interventions, to become less active at a time of increased personal stress. But I did react more intensely to patients. I was more susceptible to transferences, distortions, and patients' reactions. My therapeutic armor was weaker, and my stance altered with patients. My reactions were truly more self-revealing. This shift seemed to crystallize central themes between my patients and me. These themes were often ones that had been difficult for us to confront, as illustrated by the clinical material. With Sara, the themes of danger between us and of differences between us began to emerge. With Louisa, themes around intimacy were highlighted, with issues of envy poking through. With Marie, the themes were about secrecy and ways of hiding the dark side of intimacy. The patients' "real" experiences with me during this time brought to the foreground core transference-countertransference issues. In struggling with unavoidable realities, the nature of our relationships emerged with clarity.

Pregnancy Loss: Time of Grief

When I suddenly found that I would have to have my pregnancy ended, I canceled sessions for a time. A week later, I called my patients to say I would be returning to work at my office. This ushered in a time of work amidst acute grief, a state that was visible to most. The content of many sessions seemed reactive to my loss. For example, Marie, the patient who had denied my pregnancy, reviewed an abortion she had as a teenager. She expressed the fear, sadness, and loss that she had hidden with bravado and denial since then. Louisa, the pregnant patient, continued to show heightened concern and empathy as the time of her termination and delivery of her baby approached. She brought me names of noted high-risk obstetricians, "for the next time." Most typically, patients attempted to go easy with me, not to bother me with their most serious problems when mine were so obvious.

With some patients, however, my loss elicited or intensified negative reactions. They felt rage, fear, or disdain for me. Sympathy was replaced by pity, and I became a sign of danger to them, a reminder of chaos or a carrier of badness. I found this reaction most difficult to work with at this time. In addition to the customary difficulties of negative transference, remaining grounded required an enormous amount of psychological energy at a time when I felt depleted. Some of the attacks meshed with my own self-criticism. I felt less freedom, as did my patients, to work with material that so obviously came from events from which I had no distance yet. My feelings were raw, and there was no way to hide them.

When I called Sara, the patient who had objected to my home, to tell her of my return, she responded that she was not going to return right away. She did not want her Christmas holidays marred by my grief. I

heard her need for distance as another expression of her negative transference that I had become a bad mother, someone who would ruin her
good times. I winced internally and struggled with a temptation to over-
compensate for my anger with leniency. We were set on the rocky course
that had begun when we met in my apartment and that continued for the
next several months. She returned to analysis a week later with only the
briefest acknowledgment of my loss. She began spending large amounts
of money outside sessions and was rapidly in debt. I felt continually put
into the role of limiting superego or restrictive mother, with my efforts
to perform as her analyst regarded as spoiling her good times.

Sara acknowledged that she was probably reacting to the disruptions
in treatment and related this disruption to seeing my home. The dirty
dishes and broken chair were proof to her of my depression. Now that
she was feeling less depressed, she did not want a depressed therapist.
She bristled when I inquired into her wandering into my kitchen and
accused me of judging her. Finally, we reached a point that seemed
inevitable. She announced that she had run out of money and needed to
stop treatment. I felt frustrated and defeated. My attempts at exploration
around obvious meanings—her guilt over my loss as reminiscent of guilt
over her mother's earlier loss, her anger at my vulnerability, competition around fertility, her fear of her destructiveness or her desire to
protect me from these feelings—all missed. More to the point, she said,
she felt used by me. I should not have seen her at home or returned to
work so quickly. She accused me of doing both to help myself. There
was, of course, some truth in this. I did need my work, particularly at
a time of personal loss. I thought that when any of the two-way aspects
of the relationship became apparent to Sara, she believed that I would
gobble up everything. Despite all my efforts, she left treatment for the
time.

Another patient, Peter, confronted me more directly with his rage at
my loss. Peter was a married man who had several children. His relationships with them were characterized by distance and judgment. He
had been angry at my pregnancy and related his anger to a fear of my
abandoning him. "You say you'll come back to work, but I know you
won't." In the last session before my medical problem began, Peter
revealed his wish that I would have a miscarriage. Then, he said, I
could become pregnant again, but this time by him. I heard this as a
"fantasy," feeling safely pregnant. (Lazar, 1990, also mentions feeling
initially protected from a male patient's sadistic fantasies toward her
baby, pointing to some commonality in analyst self-protective mini-
mization of attacks.)

I chose to start working with Peter over the telephone at the time of
my pregnancy difficulty, with the two of us planning together for him to
start sessions at my home. He verbalized reluctance about seeing my

home and life more closely, anticipating jealousy and envy. I was aware of wanting distance from his intrusiveness. Fear of his anger or anger at his destructive wishes remained unconscious at the time.

When Peter returned to the office, he spoke about my loss in a way I found particularly painful. Referring to the amniocentesis, he said, "You thought you were doing something helpful, scientific, and look what happened." A few sessions later, he began to raise questions about my choice of doctor, challenging my judgment. He often seemed afraid to enter the office, and I could feel his looking me over in minute detail. He commented that I was not looking well, my hair was getting gray, I seemed older. Eventually he was able to tell me that coming into sessions scared him. He had never seen grief so close up and had certainly never felt it. He wanted to be far away from me.

Not surprisingly, I began to dread his sessions, feeling that I had to gird myself for what I experienced as berating and invasive attacks. I felt immobilized with him, uncertain of how to proceed. I wondered about whether to raise what I believed was affecting our work his stated wish for me to have a miscarriage, so close to when I had one. This wish had remained underground since then, and no easy access to it came up in sessions. Finally I brought it up. Initially, Peter did not remember, but soon memory reemerged. He was terrified that I would want to destroy him in retaliation. He felt that I had become a mother of death, rather than a mother of life to my baby and then, he thought, inevitably to him. I wondered how I could harness and use my increasing anger with him. I came to realize that however understandable or important his reactions might be in his historical context, their hostile interpersonal quality was primary at the time. I began to respond directly to his attacks as they occurred. For example, I said that I had not destroyed my baby when he again used that image. Instead, I told him that I had suffered bad luck. Thus reassured, he began to talk more openly about how serious and sincere his wish had been for me to lose the baby and said that it had not just been in the realm of make-believe for him. It was indicative of his mean spiritedness, he said. Later we were able to talk about it as a manifestation of his hatred. l came to see how I had not recognized his hate during my pregnancy.

As Imber (1990) discusses in her paper on countertransference during pregnancy, it does seem particularly difficult for the pregnant analyst to tolerate intensely negative transference in her patients, since this requires tolerating similar feelings within herself as "concordant countertransference." In addition, the "apparently blurred reality-fantasy distinction" (Schwartz, 1990, p. 121) so common in illness or loss seems to have affected both Peter and me. As I recovered by grieving and regained the distinction, we were able to continue the work with heightened attention to his hatred.

Long-Term Consequences

As the first six months to a year passed after my loss, and the period of my most intense grief eased, the routines of treatment became reestablished. However, since patients had shared in such an intimate part of my life, the question of what they wanted to share or know about in the future became a more open one. I faced a recurring question of what I wanted to share. Was treatment going to return to what I thought of as its preloss state? Early on, I went through a period of not wanting to self-disclose, when it was painful to be reminded in sessions of my loss. Later, when I was more comfortable with the loss and the ambiguity of my situation, I was more open to discussing my loss and to the possibility of self-disclosure. Arriving at this point was a process of gradual evolution.

My decision about what and when to reveal rested on many factors. I thought about the degree to which the unusual analytic situation itself had stirred a patient's anxiety and might be inhibiting his or her ability to proceed with the work. At times, a direct answer to a question seemed to allow a patient to proceed with the work. At other times, a direct answer inevitably flowed from the work, as illustrated later with Sara. I also considered the patient's explicit communications. Most often, when the patient did not side with wanting a self-disclosure, I did not provide one. I am not, however, suggesting that I withheld essential information explaining the disruption in treatment. As I presented earlier with Marie, my patients had already known about my pregnancy difficulty and loss, even in the face of their denial. We were now working through residual questions and anxieties. Finally, I considered transference communications as well as my personal needs and countertransference reactions. I did not self-disclose if a question had a hostile intent, violated my standards of privacy, or appeared to be functioning as resistance.

In retrospect, whether or not I self-disclosed seemed secondary in its impact on treatment. Although I considered the issue a great deal, it seemed that the internal freedom I felt was more important in helping me be receptive to patients' explorations. When I felt unconstrained internally, I could let subjects wander wherever they might and could consider with less anxiety whatever questions arose.

Sara, the patient who had left analysis accusing me of acting in self-interest with her, returned to analysis six months later, saying that the sudden change in my boundaries had been terrifying. She said the change replicated her family, where we knew there had been no boundaries. Her mother treated her like a chum, and her father like a desired girlfriend. Although I had certainly understood her family enmeshment, I had not appreciated how much she needed to see me as rigidly nonrevealing. This assured her that our boundaries would be maintained and that I would be different from her family. When that image was no longer possible, her rage and fear were suddenly released at me.

We had mostly explored the impact of the change in boundaries, rather than the pregnancy loss itself. Sara was saying that she needed me to resume a stance that had firm boundaries between us, while she continuously tested me in her offhand manner. Had I been to a certain restaurant? Why did I have such strange artwork? What did my husband do? She tossed the questions out casually, not waiting for answers. She denied any reaction to my loss, although some of her concerns raised the question of transferential linkage. Specifically, she wavered back and forth between urgent desire to become pregnant and disavowal of any interest in pregnancy. She said she did not want to wait until she was "too old" and then later that she never wanted a child.

About two years later, while associating to a dream, Sara revealed that she has continued to perceive me as in "chronic mourning for my unborn child." I felt a sense of relief that we might finally pick up the strand of meaning my loss had for her. She had, after all, been identified with the baby, felt as if she were the baby. I noted to myself that I had become a static image for her and wondered what that might mean. She continued to muse about her dream and about me. She said she always thought of my unborn baby as a girl. It occurred to her now that this was her fantasy, not necessarily the reality. She asked, almost casually, "What was the sex of your baby?" I waited a moment for her next association, taking this as another of her questions that required no answer. I was suddenly jolted to realize that she was waiting for me to respond. We sat in a silence that seemed interminable, until I answered her directly: "That's something I don't talk about."

I realized later that I had not explored the meaning of her question. I responded instead to the boundary disturbance, to the intrusion I experienced into my most intimate parts. I also realized that my answer was the most self-disclosing response I could have given. She nodded in reaction and tried to gloss over her feelings of shame, hurt, and anger. The next session she talked about her shock that I had so bluntly said no, that something was off-limits. Although she was still hurt, she felt freed by my answer. In direct identification, she began to exert more control over what she told people about herself. We have returned many times to my answer to her and its meaning to her. The issues that have emerged later in treatment have continued the themes implied in that exchange and its elaboration. What is her access to me? What about her desire for me, sexual and nonsexual? Can she feel as needy as a baby with me? Is she safe with me? Am I safe with her, able to contain her feelings of assaultiveness? Her focus on whether or not to have a baby herself receded as these other issues became elaborated.

Sara's anxiety about safety with me was similar to Peter's worry, which he connected to his wish to destroy my baby. Peter's interest in my childbearing status diminished for a year. Then he began frequently to refer to adoption in a negative way. For example, he described someone as overbearing and insecure and added, "He was adopted, you know." Peter was now able to acknowledge that he was being mean to me, observing that perhaps I had adopted or planned to. He began to talk about his wish now that I would have a baby. He preferred that I would become pregnant again, but, if not, that I would adopt. Why this was so important to him and his continuing hostility toward me became recurring issues for the next months. He thought his stake in the outcome was obvious— to mitigate his guilt over his destructive wishes. I was a constant reminder of his hatred. He wanted and needed to think of me as someone who faced disappointment, a model to counteract his own withdrawal from pain.

I believed that his recognition of his hostility was a sign of growth. It eased the edge of his continuing anger, but I still had many moments of feeling provoked. I also noted how hard it was for Peter to think of my outcome, or resolution, in terms of me, rather than in terms of what he needed. He was terrified of thinking of me as separate from himself or of knowing me as real. At one point, he angrily demanded facts about my childbearing status. I thought that I might tell him if I did not feel that I were capitulating to a demand. He backed away quickly when the possibility of self-disclosure became evident. This became another important event between us symbolizing his desire to keep the tides of movement and growth away.

CONCLUSIONS

I believe that my pregnancy loss became a focal issue around which patients and I confronted central themes. For Peter, it was hatred, lack of empathy, and difficulty seeing others as separate from himself. For Sara, it was boundary concerns—overlaps and differences. I wonder how the analyses would have proceeded in the absence of such a focal event. Although it seems likely that we would have dealt with the same problems, I do not think that the treatment would have had the same impact on us. My vulnerability made me particularly receptive to some of the ill effects of Peter's dynamics and gave a heartfelt urgency to confronting his reactions. Sara questioned whether she would have had the same anxiety about feeling safe with me if there had been no actual shifts in boundaries. She thinks she would have found another inadequacy to keep from trusting, and I agree.

Few situations, however, could have created the same intense environment. I think the impact on me and the interpersonal impact on my patients and me have been instrumental in driving the analysis forward.

It seemed clearer to my patients that we were a dyad or team, both authentically involved in a task deeply important to both of us. These relationships became more special because we had gone through my crisis together, as well as my patients' crises with my crisis. The heightened uniqueness of the relationship is reminiscent of what Otto Will (1971) describes in his work with schizophrenic patients, in which heightened intensity also exists. It is also consistent with Levenson's (1991) emphasis on the "interactional and real" events between patient and analyst as mutative. As stated by Fiscalini (1988), in order for change to take place, there must be a "coincident living through of the interpretive issues in the immediate analytic relationship in a new and more mature manner" (p. 134).

From my own experience and the small literature on miscarriage, I have thought about one gender difference in reaction to analyst pregnancy loss. Some female patients, such as Sara and some of those presented by Barbanel (1980) and Lazar (1990), do harbor fears of their own frightening destructiveness and fantasize that their envy or hateful wishes have led to the miscarriage. Female patients, however, do not seem to directly express a wish for the analyst to miscarry. Such direct expression of a wish to destroy, when it occurs, seems to be limited to male patients. Lazar presented a male patient with sadistic fantasies toward her baby. When she miscarried a later pregnancy, his initial reaction was relief that he would not have to tell his wife about her pregnancy. She reported feeling outrage at his reaction. Since the discussion of analyst miscarriage is quite limited, and there is only a small number of male patients presented, it is difficult, of course, fully to understand how generalizable these cases are. It may be, though, that the observed gender difference in expressing a wish to destroy or hurt the analyst's baby is more a difference in the expression of aggression, rather than in the underlying fantasy or wish. Given the reports (Barbanel, 1980; Lazar, 1990) of female patients who prematurely terminate therapy or arrange for some break in their treatment, as did Sara, it may be that we need to work more directly to elicit nonverbalized or repressed destructiveness in women.

In considering the many aspects of the effects of my loss on treatment, I have thought about how jarring it was to many of my patients to discover how closely we inhabit the same worlds—of dirty dishes, unrealized dreams, grief, and struggle. Although patients are often well-attuned to our complexities and experiences (Hoffman, 1983), it seems harder to move beyond the vestigial wish that the analyst and, by association, they are protected from the grittier parts of life and mortality. It has become clear to me and, I think, to many of my patients that none of us live far removed from the fates of nature, that our lives are shaped by luck and chance far more often than we like to think. I have found this comforting and freeing in some unexpected ways. It has helped me feel closer to the rhythms of life, gentle and harsh, and to the gifts of the connections I have, including those with my patients. I hope that some of them may have been helped by our experiences together to face their own fates.

REFERENCES

Abend, S. (1990), Serious illness in the analyst: Countertransference considerations. In: *Illness in the Analyst*, ed. H. J. Schwartz & A. L. Silver. Madison, CT: International Universities Press, pp. 99–113.

Barbanel, L. (1980), The therapist's pregnancy In: *Psychological Aspects of Pregnancy, Birthing and Bonding*, ed. B. L. Blum. New York: Human Sciences Press, pp. 232–246.

Dewald, P. (1990), Serious illness in the analyst: Transference, countertransference, and reality responses—and further reflections. In: *Illness in the Analyst*, ed. H. J. Schwartz & A. L. Silver. Madison, CT: International Universities Press, pp. 75–98.

Fenster, S., Phillips, S. & Rapoport, E. (1986), *The Therapist's Pregnancy*. Hillsdale, NJ: The Analytic Press.

Fiscalini, J. (1988), Curative experience in the analytic relationship. *Contemp. Psychoanal.*, 24:125–141.

Friedman, G. (1991), The impact of the therapist's life-threatening illness on the therapeutic situation. *Contemp. Psychoanal.*, 27:405–421.

Givelber, F. & Simon, B. (1981), A death in the life of a therapist and its impact on therapy. *Psychiatry*, 44:141–149.

Hannett, F. (1949), Transference reactions to an event in the life of the analyst. *Psychoanal. Rev.*, 36:69–81.

Hoffman, I. Z. (1983), The patient as interpreter of the analyst's experience. *Contemp. Psychoanal.*, 19:389–422.

Imber, R. (1990), The avoidance of countertransference awareness in a pregnant analyst. *Contemp. Psychoanal.*, 26:223–236.

Lax, R. (1969), Some considerations about transference and countertransference manifestations evoked by the analyst's pregnancy. *Internat. J. Psycho-Anal.*, 50:363–372.

Lazar, S. (1990), Patients' responses to pregnancy and miscarriage in the analyst. In: *Illness in the Analyst*, ed. H. J. Schwartz & A. L. Silver. Madison, CT: International Universities Press, pp. 199–226.

Leibowitz, L. (1992), Considerations concerning the decision to reveal personal life experiences: The impact of the analyst's voluntary self-disclosure about not having children. Presented at Postdoctoral Program in Psychotherapy and Psychoanalysis, New York University, January 31, New York City.

Levenson, E. (1991), *The Purloined Self*. New York: Contemporary Psychoanalysis Books.

Peddicord, D. (1990), Issues in the disclosure of perinatal death. In: *Self Disclosure in the Therapeutic Relationship*, ed. G. Stricker & M. Fisher. New York: Plenum Press, pp. 261–273.

Penn, L. (1986), The pregnant therapist: Transference and countertransference issues. In: *Psychoanalysis and Women*, ed.]. L. Alpert. Hillsdale, NJ: The Analytic Press, pp. 287–315.

Schoolman, J. (1988), Remission: An experiential account. *Prof. Psychol.: Res. Pract.*, 19:426–432.

Schwartz, H. J. (1990), Illness in the doctor: Implications for the psychoanalytic process. In: *Illness in the Analyst*, ed. H. J. Schwartz & A. L. Silver. Madison, CT: International Universities Press, pp. 115–149.

———— & Silver, A. L., eds. (1990), *Illness in the Analyst*. Madison, CT: International Universities Press.

Singer, E. (1971), The patient aids the analyst: Some clinical and theoretical observations. In: *In the Name of Life,* ed. B. Landis & E. S. Tauber. New York: Holt Rinehart & Winston, pp. 56–68.

Weinberg, H. (1988), Illness and the working analyst. *Contemp. Psychoanal.,* 24:452–461.

Will, O. (1971), The patient and the psychotherapist: Comments on the "uniqueness" of their relationship. In: *In the Name of Life,* ed. B. Landis & E. S. Tauber. New York: Holt Rinehart & Winston, pp. 15–43.

5

Reflections of a Childless Analyst

LYNN LEIBOWITZ

As an analyst who, at one point, very much wanted to have a child, tried unsuccessfully for several years to do so, and then arrived at the decision not to have children, I have had to work through the impact of my choice on how I see myself, both as an analyst and as a woman. I also have had to grapple with feelings about how my patients view me, particularly when we talk about choices involving childbearing.

In this chapter, I will be exploring the challenge created by patients' questions, comments, and assumptions about my parental status, as well as the issue of personal boundaries around self-disclosure. I will also discuss some of the transference/countertransference issues underlying questions about parenthood (e.g., envy, competition, idealization, devaluation, and separation). I will reflect on clinical material from my present perspective, discussing both the past realities and contexts from which it emerged, along with my current thinking about the material.

This discussion is embedded within the context of my evolving and changing ideas about the work itself. The issue of childlessness has been a highly charged focus of contact between me and some of my patients. This issue has acted as a catalyst for me to change my ideas about the nature of therapeutic relationships and about my participation in the analytic process. I will be describing an evolution in my thinking, which was influenced by the interplay of my reactions to patients' communications about parenting and nurturance, their reactions to my reactions, and by my own personal development. While the issue of childlessness is central to my discussion, it is largely illustrative of a broader issue, which is the process of change in how I view psychoanalysis and psychotherapy: as more engaging, involving, and interactive processes, fueled, in part, by the more open use of countertransference.

Many of the case examples begin with patients asking, "Do you have children?"—a question with which, at the very least, the inquiring patient is pushing at the conventional boundary of the therapist's "neutrality" and "anonymity." The question can represent an attempt to enter territory laden with profound feelings for both therapist and patient about gender identity, self-image, or wishes for nurturance. The question about children contains varying meanings, depending on the patient, the therapist, and the nature of the therapeutic relationship. The feelings stimulated within the therapist vary tremendously, depending on how that particular clinician feels about his or her own identity as a parent, would-be parent, or nonparent. When my patients ask me this question, I feel they are attempting to dig further into themselves and into my identity.

To put this discussion into a meaningful context, I will briefly describe my own experience of trying to have a child and the gradual shift from a life crisis to a slightly ambivalent, but mostly positive, resolved choice.

My husband and I decided to have a child about 12 years ago, when I was 33. After not conceiving for six months, we went for a diagnostic work-up. The work-up revealed a fertility problem. We spent five years undergoing painstaking medical tests, various invasive procedures, surgery, and the careful timing of the expulsion of various bodily fluids to be repeatedly examined and measured for reproductive potential. This was a draining and emotionally consuming process. My quest for a child became a preoccupation, which sometimes felt desperate and isolating. At times, it was painful to see a pregnant woman or to be around children or other couples with children. After exhausting all the medical technology, my husband and I realized we could not have a child biologically. At that point in our lives (I was 38; my husband was 40), after having gone through intense and prolonged emotional pain and inner exploration, we decided not to have a child. Both individually and together, we needed to work through feelings about ourselves as people unable to create a child and as nonparents. This process of becoming clear and positive about the decision was a long and arduous one. It involved a lengthy process of inner exploration, acceptance of fate, life phase considerations, existential issues, and feelings in our relationship as a couple. These were all factors in coming to terms with the choice not to become parents. Although I believe people always have some ambivalence in the choice to have or not to have children, I am comfortable with our decision.

Because I feel mostly resolved about this aspect of my life, I can explore childbearing problems and decisions with patients more readily than if I were still trying to conceive. It is not always easy, however, to experience myself as a clinician who does not have children and who enjoys many aspects of nonparenthood. While I can feel good about the decision to be childless, it has had complex and challenging psychological consequences, which I will discuss further on.

The role of analyst is both analytic and "nurturing" (in the sense that patients come to us for help, and we as analysts are engaged in facilitating the psychological growth of our patients). The interplay of a kind of parenting (hopefully, without the same degree of control, investment, and judgments that usually accompany parenthood) with the sort of boundaries required by the analyst's role makes for a complexity of intertwined wishes and enactments between analyst and patient. Patients often wish that I would be their "good parent." Some of the subtle conflicts I feel about my choice not to be a mother come into play in my relationships with my patients.

THE WORK WHILE TRYING TO CONCEIVE

During the time that I was trying to have a child, I recall some painful moments with several patients. In reflecting on these experiences, I have seen how I have changed as an analyst and how the painful feelings related to the struggle to conceive affected the ways in which I related to my patients' questions and perceptions of me.

A 29-year-old woman, whom I had been treating for about two years, asked me if I had children. At that time, early in my career, I did not believe a therapist should answer such questions, particularly without first exploring the meanings behind the question. When I asked her what her fantasy was, she said that I probably was not a mother because I did not seem as warm and concerned as I would be if I were a parent. At the time, I was hurt by this, believing myself to have been warm, caring, and concerned about her and a warm and caring person overall. Moreover, even though I was not a mother, I very much wanted to be. This analytic moment stirred up doubts within myself about my ability to be caring and warm. In that moment, I also thought to myself, "Think about all those mothers who are not particularly warm or nurturing people and some who are even abusive toward their children." I thought I needed to defend myself against a not uncommon myth about nonmothers being "nurturance defectives." I believed my analytic role required me to keep many of my feelings in check, to the extent that warmth and concern, particularly when pulled for by this particular patient, were aspects of myself that I withheld. In addition, her tendency to complain and never feel fully satisfied contributed to my occasional lack of warm feelings for her; nevertheless, had I not felt on the defensive about her remarks, I could have explored more fully her feelings *and* mine about how we affected each other. The issue was not really about my parental status.

Another patient, a 26-year-old male, who had been in weekly psychotherapy for about eight months, asked if I had children. Again, I asked what he thought. He said that he assumed I did not because I did not look tired and out of shape, which is what he would have expected a mother to look like. Shortly thereafter, I told him I did not have children. We considered the issue of my not being the kind of older, nurturing mother figure he wanted his therapist to be. In fact, he did not see me as really caring at all about him and experienced me as somewhat cold and distant. As with the previously mentioned patient, I had usually felt warmly toward him, was very interested in him, and had felt like I had been connected to the painful journey we had embarked upon together. The injustice I felt at being seen so differently than I believed myself to be, coupled with my painful struggle to have a child, left me less able to encourage my patient and myself to explore the ways in which we were depriving each other. In both this and the previous case, I was not as free to explore my reactions openly with patients as I have since become, not only because of the inhibiting effect of my struggles to have a child, but also because of my personal and professional development as an analyst. I have recently become more aware of how I had been unconsciously remote with patients at times. In addition, working through identity issues tied in with not being a mother or "nurturer" has helped me to feel less defensive about not being who my patients might want me to be in the transference.

A particularly painful experience occurred during a final attempt to conceive with the help of medical technology. My husband and I had gone to Philadelphia to be evaluated for *in vitro* fertilization. We had been anxiously optimistic about the *in vitro* program. While there, after a particular test, we were told that the procedure would not work for us. Our last hope of conceiving a child together had been destroyed. Shortly after returning to New York, I met with a patient. I felt depressed and tearful. I was beginning to mourn never being able to have a biological child. I imagined I looked as though I had been crying recently, and I wondered how I would get through the session without crying and pouring out my sadness. I decided that if the patient asked why I seemed upset, I would say that I was experiencing great sorrow over a personal matter. I thought I might even reveal the nature of my sorrow if she asked further questions.

The patient was a 34-year-old doctoral student and mother of two children. I had been seeing her for about one year for weekly psychotherapy. She did not seem to notice my mood or state of mind. She said nothing, either manifestly or in latent form, that seemed to relate to my depression or unavailability, nor did her manner toward me indicate any reaction to my mood. She did not relate in a particularly friendly or protective way. It was "business as usual." I felt hurt and angry at her lack of sensitivity to me. I decided not to bring her lack of awareness to her attention, because I thought doing so would be self-serving. I also preferred to focus away from my pain and on what she was discussing.

I have learned from this and other experiences that, if I am considering revealing personally sensitive information, I am generally more likely to do so if I trust a patient deeply and if I feel that our relationship is developed sufficiently enough that we can use such a disclosure fruitfully in our work. With this patient, who seemed unaware of my pain, I could have addressed this insensitivity in a later session without necessarily revealing the content of the experience that led to my sorrow. This patient was usually narcissistically angry and somewhat distant with me. She was often aware of her coldness and rejecting feelings toward others, but not necessarily toward me. There were many opportunities apart from this particular experience that I could have used to engage my patient in exploring her insensitivity and other feelings toward me. Had we earlier created more of a foundation by openly exploring our relationship in this way, I might have felt more inclined to bring up her ignoring my mood or my sad feelings that were taking me away from her. Perhaps I was experiencing an insensitivity from her that was similar to that which she had experienced from her parents.

In reflecting on why I did not introduce my feelings directly into the session at that time, I believe there were two separate but related factors: one had to do with my approach to treatment at that time, which did not utilize my countertransference in as direct and open a way as I do now, and the other had to do with not wanting to open up a personally painful area with this patient. In part, I did not see how I could move past my private pain to explore the interpersonal issue in a way that would have led to a new experience of each other and to new insight into my patient's (and my own) dynamics. When immersed in a personally painful struggle as I was, I did not see beyond the self indulgent aspect of self-disclosure. I was not seeing the potential analytic usefulness of a two-person engagement, triggered by my pain and her insensitivity to it. I suppose that one reason not to disclose the analyst's personal pain to a patient would be the fear that revealing this pain would be manipulative and self-indulgent rather than serving to further the analytic exploration.

I now consider any feeling or motive, no matter how ignoble, to be worthy of analytic attention with patients. That does not mean, however, that I plunge into anything with anyone. As I stated earlier, I believe that my sense of how open a patient and I have been with each other, how much trust and connection have been established, are key to how inclined I would feel to reveal personally painful feelings or information about myself to a patient.

During the struggle to conceive, I had difficulty with some of my patients' perceptions of me as nonmaternal. Whatever doubts I had about myself as a nurturing or caring person were exacerbated by the frustration of not being able to fulfill my longing to be a mother. Morever, my patients' anger at me for not fulfilling their longings for me to be more "motherly" added to my sense of inadequacy. The wish to be loved by my patients rather than to find sufficient satisfaction in my role as analyst added fuel to my countertransference. There are assumptions that are often made about people who choose not to have children or who accept not having children—they are selfish, inflexible, or have unresolved feelings about mother. These assumptions can be painful to both those who have struggled to have a child and those who have decided not to. People do not generally apply these assumptions equally to people who choose to have children. On the other hand, the above assumptions could all

apply to my character at times. My defensiveness about these characterological issues was magnified when they were superimposed on my
difficulty conceiving and, later, on the choice not to have children.

THE WORK SHORTLY AFTER THE DECISION
NOT TO HAVE CHILDREN

After deciding not to have a child through alternative means such as
adoption, my husband and I began to come to terms with not having children. Two female patients had asked me if I had children. In contrast to
my previous reactions, I chose to respond directly to both. I had been
working with each one for more than a year, both on a once weekly basis.
The first patient was in her forties and had two grown children with
whom she had tremendous conflicts. I told her that I did not have children. When she asked why not, I told her that my husband and I had
been unable to have a child biologically and had eventually decided not
to adopt. The patient immediately expressed empathy with how difficult
that must have been; however, she did not seem to want to discuss me
any further. My answer had satisfied her. However, earlier in treatment,
I had not answered some of her personal questions because I thought she
was testing me to see if I would develop a therapeutic style more to her
liking: she wanted therapy to be conducted like an AA meeting, promoting
trust through self-disclosure and eliminating any sense of hierarchy. Because
we had worked through much of her transferential resistance to me as a
judgmental authority figure, I now felt free to answer her question. I
wished at the time that she would have been more open to exploring the
meaning of her question and her feelings about my response, but she
wanted to control how close we could get. The fact that I felt satisfied
with answering her question meant to me that our connection had matured
and grown. She was asking out of interest in knowing more about who
I was, and I felt freer to let her know who I was. She never again brought
up questions about my parental status, either overtly or covertly.

The other patient who asked me about not having children was a woman
in her sixties. When she spoke about me to others, she referred to me
as her "lady," as if I were a precious possession she valued and loved.
She was overly involved with both her elderly sister and her adult son,
constantly worrying about both of them. In terms of the therapy relationship, this patient maintained a positive transference in which she could
express her hostility and guilt about those she was dependent upon while
preserving me as "good." Usually preoccupied with anxieties and phobias,
she vacillated between relating to me as if I were a nurturing mother or
a beloved child. When she asked me if I had children, I told her I did
not, then told her why. This patient seemed empathic. I was aware that
she accepted me, but also that she saw me as more of a child because I
did not have the experience of motherhood.

I believe I told this woman more than necessary because I wanted her to know I had wanted to have a child. I was responding to what I sensed was behind her question, and I still felt defensive about being perceived as less understanding or caring because I was not a mother. Unfortunately, we never engaged in a more direct discussion of our feelings about my parental status at that time. This patient was overly protective of, and continually worried about, her son. I think she accurately perceived my thoughts about her maternal overprotectiveness—that she was struggling with her ambivalence about letting go of him but was desperately anxious about autonomy and separation. She had undermined her son's ability to grow up and become a responsible, self-sufficient adult. I believe her question about my parental status implied that I would better understand and support her anxious overprotectiveness if I were a mother. If that were indeed her feeling, I believe she was wrong—I think I would still recognize anxious attempts to impede separation as detrimental to both parent and adult child.

Yet to some extent, she may have been right. This recognition comes from other experiences around motherhood in my life. My own mother often anxiously attempted to overprotect and forestall separation, and at times I was identifying with this patient's son. Moreover, I could see the detrimental impact of this patient's difficulties with separation on her own functioning and growth, because I could see this in my mother. Because I am not a parent, I probably identify more with the child's struggle to be free and autonomous than with the parent's desire to hold on and protect. This patient continued to cling guiltily to her elderly sister but made some progress toward becoming less submissive in relation to her. The therapy was cut short by this patient's sudden death, which followed her sister's by several months. I could not help but think of her dying as a reflection of her difficulty in ever fully separating from her sister, who had been like a controlling and overly protective mother to her.

During the time just after my husband and I decided not to have children, questions about my parental status rarely came up. When they did, as with these two patients, I was inclined to answer directly, partly because I consciously felt comfortable with my decision and thought that offering factual information about the underlying difficulties might lead to further engagement and exploration. In hindsight, however, I realize that I was not fully conscious of the anxieties that got stirred up by being perceived as a nonparent and a woman who chose not to have children, even though the two patients I mentioned seemed to be sensitive to the sad side of my ambivalence. These patients also might have been wondering if I could identify with them in their struggles with their children. Today, I would be more inclined to engage directly in clarifying where my patients and I stand in relation to the questions behind the questions about my parental status.

THE CASE OF DONNA

At this point, I am going to present some case material that illustrates some of the transference and countertransference issues that can arise when childbearing choices become part of the patient–therapist dialogue. I am also going to explore the impact of my self-disclosure on my relationship with this particular patient.

My patient, whom I will call Donna, was a 35-year-old European woman who worked full time in an administrative position. She had been in a weekly treatment, refusing to increase frequency, largely because of her wish to keep her feelings under control: she felt some shame and fear in being vulnerable with others. I believe she wanted to maintain a safe distance from me because her relationship with her mother had been so painfully enmeshed. Donna moved to the United States 13 years ago after marrying an American whom she had met in her home country. She moved here to put some distance between herself and her parents, particularly because she was finding it difficult to create her own life with her husband. Donna's mother had disapproved of her marriage and had urged her to get an abortion once she became pregnant. Donna agreed to have an abortion and, since then, had blamed her mother for this decision. She felt that her mother did not want her ever to marry anyone or have children. According to Donna, her mother—like all the women in her family—had only married because she had accidentally gotten pregnant. It was Donna's conception that triggered her mother's marriage, and Donna carried the burden of her mother's unhappiness.

Donna's father was a dogmatic man who let himself be pushed into the background by his wife, a volatile and unpredictable woman who used physical ailments and suicidal gestures to manipulate her family into trying not to upset her. Donna recalled many times when her mother yelled, hit, and threw objects during family fights.

Donna entered treatment six months after her abortion. She admitted to being ambivalent about the pregnancy. Just before the abortion, while she was pregnant, Donna and her husband had agreed to become foster parents to a 14-year-old boy, whom I will call Paul. Donna complained of depression following the abortion and of difficulty in making decisions. In the same way that she felt manipulated into the abortion by her mother, she also felt manipulated by her husband into taking in their foster child. She experienced her life as a series of events controlled by others and for which she had little, if any, responsibility. She did not see her marriage as a choice either, since she thought she had married out of pity for her husband, who would have been deported otherwise. Donna's stated goals for therapy were to become a more assertive and independent person and to "cut the umbilical cord from my family."

The sessions I am presenting took place two and a half years into treatment. During the treatment and after the abortion, Donna and her husband had been trying to conceive. She had had a miscarriage, which had been a great disappointment and had fueled her fears that she might have infertility problems. At the time of these sessions, my husband and I were well past trying to have a child, and I was content with our decision not to become parents. (I have since learned, however, that my acceptance of and mostly positive feelings about being childless do not mean that interaction with others about this issue does not stir up internal conflict.)

Donna had a dream in which she and I were talking to each other through a closed door. She related this to seeing me as unapproachable and as keeping a distance from her. She also acknowledged that maybe she did not try to know me because I might disappoint her if she learned certain things about me, such as that I were divorced or that I lose control of my emotions. In the next session, Donna told me that she was pregnant. In this session and the next, she spoke about her ambivalence about having children. She expressed concern about losing herself to her child. We explored her experiencing herself as not having choices, particularly when she becomes a mother, much as her own mother experienced motherhood.

What follows are some process recordings from the next five sessions:

D: You have small children, don't you? You take vacations when the schools do.

L: Could there be any other reason I would take vacations at those times?

D: Yes, could be. Well, do you have kids?

Keeping in mind Donna's dream about the distance between us and her reluctance to grapple with the reality of who I was, I decided to answer her. I knew this might be an entree into an exploration of choices about childbearing and gender identity issues.

L: No.

D: Why not?

Here is another point where I had to make a decision. How much did I want to reveal? This was relatively new territory for me, and I decided to venture into it. I was glad Donna was trying to deal with me as I really was.

L: My husband and I had tried for years to have a child and couldn't. We then decided not to.

D: Why?

L: It was a long process, trying to have a child. We eventually reached a phase of our lives where we felt good about not having a child.

D: (cries) It must be hard for you with me.

L: Because of my pain? My jealousy?

I was aware that Donna feared that I was envious of her.

D: I know I hate to see pregnant women. I want to be away from
      them.

Although pregnant, Donna feared she would have a miscarriage, so she
still felt like an infertile woman. I believe she was also indicating, at this
point, that she was anxious that I would reject her for being pregnant.

L: There was a time when I felt like that. I came to understand it as
      a competitive issue: they have what I don't. I don't find it difficult
      with you. I empathize with the pain of trying to get pregnant, but
      I feel good about my decision. I sometimes have some pangs when
      I'm with children. I think there will always be some ambivalence.

D: I don't feel like a real woman. I don't know why I'm having a
      child. Do I really want to, or am I doing it to feel like a real
      woman?

In the next session, Donna talked lightly about a few topics and eventually acknowledged that she was avoiding talking about her pregnancy
with me. She said that she was protecting herself from the anger and
envy she thought I would be feeling. Donna's associations focused on
the lengths to which her mother would go to try to keep Donna from
feeling envy or jealousy. We also acknowledged the hostility her mother
must have felt in relation to feelings of envy and jealousy. Donna ended
the session saying, "When I like someone who's pregnant, I can be happy
for them, but I don't want it rubbed in my face." Donna continued to
project both her own feelings and her mother's feelings of anger and
envy onto me, despite my telling her as honestly as I could how I felt.
At the time, I was not conscious of feeling envious of Donna; however,
now I'm more respectful of the possibility that I may have had other
unconscious feelings that I was unaware of.

Donna was late for the next session. She said she had been crying for
days because she was afraid she might have a miscarriage. She also said
that her mother did not tell her about her cousin's pregnancy because she
thought Donna would be upset, since Donna had undergone an abortion.
We talked about her mother's message that a person cannot enjoy another's
experience if it is associated with one's own deprivation, along with the
notion that what you do not know will not hurt you. I then asked Donna
if she was talking about what she perceived as my anger and envy of her.

D: You'd rather not see me. I can imagine how I'd feel. I'd be upset.
      My friends didn't tell me about their pregnancies because it's not
      nice. If I miscarry, I'd be happy for my pregnant friend, but I
      wouldn't want to hear about her pregnancy if she called me.

L: And I wouldn't want to be reminded of my deprivation?

D: Yes. You said it was a conscious choice not to have kids. This is
      new for me. It's hard to believe. I have a friend who's cold—not
      like you. It makes sense to me that she doesn't want to have kids.
      My best friends in Europe also don't have kids and that's okay.
      One has problems with men and wants to be in control. Maybe
      I'm stereotyping. Another friend is scared to be like her mother,
      so she doesn't have kids. You don't fit. You're very balanced. My
      friend is selfish.

L: Are you concerned I might be like your friends?

D: You're like Maria, my best friend. She's different than me. She's
      a good person. She has set ways of lifestyle.

L: You mean inflexibility

D: It's not negative. Things are set up to be comfortable in.

These are some of the assumptions about nonparents that I referred to
earlier. They give rise to a defensive stir in me when my parental status
is linked with characterological issues.

L: I want to get back to what we were saying about my being
      reminded of my deprivation by your pregnancy.

D: In the beginning it was involuntary not to have a child. How does
      it become voluntary?

L: I feel you're projecting your mother's difficulties with envy onto
      me. What does it do to you if I'm envious?

Looking back, I realize that I did not want to go further into my own
process of moving from desperately wanting a child to eventually choosing
to be childless, given my options. At that time, I was not aware of feeling
envious of my patient and, perhaps unfortunately, was not so open to the
possibility that I could be unconsciously envious or uncomfortable with
what her pregnancy evoked in me. I, therefore, focused on the projective aspect of her perception, while offering an opening to discuss the
impact on her of my possible envy. I also could have pursued the meaning
of voluntary versus manipulated decisions about children in her life.

D: I feel obligated. I should be walking on eggshells.

L: So I won't be angry and envious of you?

D: Yes. I feel like crying every time I leave. I'm selfish and rude if
      I'm insensitive to you.

In the next session, Donna brought up the issue of being protective
of others' feelings. I asked about that happening with me.

D: I don't want to hurt your feelings.

L: You insist you know how I feel. You don't believe me. Are you
      protecting me or yourself?

D: I don't want to hurt your feelings. I'm worried about the
      consequences—making my life miserable.

Donna talked about her fear that I would not remain "neutral," that she
did not want to know much about me. While she differentiated me from

her mother in that I would not retaliate in the extreme ways her mother would when she was hurt, Donna was clearly uncomfortable with the shift in our relationship due to my self-disclosure. For my part, I was not distinguishing my conscious feelings from unconscious feelings to which my patient might well have been reacting. At the end of the session, she said she was feeling angry at our discussion.

At the beginning of the next session, I asked about Donna's anger from last time.

D: I felt backed into a corner. *I want to pretend not to be pregnant with you.* Why did you tell me about yourself?

L: Your dream about the wall between us suggested you felt a distance from me, and I felt you were ready to want to know more of me. Also, you asked me if I have children.

D: This was not really a choice for you since you couldn't have a biological child.

Donna's distinction about my not fully choosing because I could not have a biological child with my husband is an important one. At that time, however, I did not appreciate her point since I felt I had eventually accepted the loss of that option without significant underlying repercussions. Several years later, at the time of this writing, I have begun to get glimmers of underlying feelings and issues that my defenses had managed to ward off and transform. In essence, my patient was questioning my facade of seeming complacency with childlessness. Another interesting statement of hers that I missed at the time, "I want to pretend not to be pregnant with you," I now hear as her unconsciously letting me know that she felt *pregnant with me*, as if I were the child within her. I imagine this was a burden she did not want "to bear." She was perceiving a vulnerability on my part. Because I was not acknowledging my vulnerability, she was left carrying the load.

Donna then moved from her focus on me to what was happening with her foster son Paul, who did not want to talk about being a foster child. Had I been listening to Donna then as I am now while writing about this session, I would have related Paul's denial to my own. I was not acknowledging the pain of the loss of the wished-for child, as Paul was not acknowledging the loss of the wished-for parent. Instead, I drew the parallel of Donna being like Paul, who gets angry and tries to deny and avoid the situation in order to avoid pain. Donna then told me a dream:

D: We were in European beds. They're divided in the middle. I'm in bed with my mother. We were grown-up. I thought, "I can't take this!" I went into bed with my father. There was more safety: I was more to myself. My mother eats me up. I felt stifled in the dream. I felt upset like I've been feeling with you. You remind me that I need to walk on eggs (an interesting slip). I pretend with my mother.

L: Did I burden you by telling you about me?

D: Yes. I think you told me because you want to get to my issues.
        The subject throws me off. I'm forced to deal with how I project
        onto others, then manipulate.

I did not see at that time the connection Donna was making between her
mother's vulnerability and mine. Instead, we were both focusing on my
strength and the weaknesses of Donna and her mother.

In the next session, Donna talked about her pregnancy excitedly. She
had seen her baby in a sonogram. She also talked about seeing herself
as a person who had a choice about the past, particularly in terms of
decisions she had made. She and her son Paul had been able to talk
openly about adoption over the past week. I asked how she had felt,
talking with me about her pregnancy. She said it was okay, that it did
not feel like an issue. She asked how I had felt. I said that I felt happy
for her and touched that she had shared her excitement with me.

Subsequent to these sessions, Donna was able to explore in depth some
key issues around becoming a mother, especially in connection with her
relationship with *her* mother. She became less ambivalent about becoming
a parent and seemed to be more open and free in how she related to me.
She made further gains in treatment, including increased openness with
and separation from her family of origin. She also gained a sense of
herself as making choices, taking less responsibility for trying to control
how others feel. Eventually, Donna ended treatment close to the birth of
her child and brought the baby to my office when she returned for a later
session. Despite whatever unconscious feelings I may have had about her
pregnancy and child's birth, I was consciously gratified by our work together
and felt that I shared part of both the pain and the joy she experienced
in the transition to motherhood. In hindsight, I realized how much deeper
the work might have gone had I been less defended against my unconscious motivations and vulnerability.

My inclination to answer Donna's questions about my decision not to
have children and to reveal very personal information about myself has
caused me to ponder not only why I answered her as I did, but also why
I would or would not share such personal information with other patients.
As I said to Donna, I believed she wanted to know more of me and was
ready to deal with me as a real person, rather than maintaining some
denial and idealization in order to preserve a positive and safe image of
me. I felt that she was starting to take a risk by becoming more personal
with me. I welcomed this shift in her and also wanted to be known by
her, rather than distanced through idealization. Because I knew that secrecy,
careful overprotectiveness, and denial were so much a part of Donna's
self-protective maneuvers in relating to her mother, I think I decided
quickly, when asked about myself, not to collude with this pattern. I
wanted us to face each other squarely and allow our emotions free rein—
as "free" as we could be at that time.

I have just mentioned the more conscious motivations for my personal revelations to Donna. I have since become aware of some other, less noble motivations and have had to look at some of the problematic aspects of my approach to Donna's questions and subsequent feelings. In part, I believe I wanted to show my patient that I was not like her mother and that I was emotionally strong and self-sufficient. I also was unconsciously hiding my ambivalent feelings about being childless from myself and my patient. These motivations might have led me away from a deeper exploration of why Donna was asking me about myself at that time and what it is she might really have been asking about *herself*.

CONCLUSIONS

Some aspects of countertransference are unknowable to the analyst, myself included. As I. Z. Hoffman (1991) wrote in his comprehensive discussion of the shift toward a social–constructivist view of the analytic situation:

> Because the participation of the analyst implicates all levels of the analyst's personality, it must include unconscious as well as conscious factors. Therefore, what the analyst seems to understand about his or her own experience and behavior as well as the patient's is always suspect, always susceptible to the vicissitudes of the analyst's own resistance, and always prone to being superseded by another point of view that may emerge [p. 77].

Furthermore, some aspects of the analyst's personality might make self-disclosure more appealing or readily forthcoming. My investment in helping females, myself included, sever the learned tie between reproductive potential and self-valuation was probably an important factor behind my wish to more openly engage in this issue with Donna. Perhaps I wanted to suggest myself as an example of someone who had successfully grappled with this issue.

While struggling to have a child and then trying to reconcile the decision not to, my responses to patients who asked about my parental status were charged with multiple meanings in terms of my own psychology and how I perceived the relationship with each patient. The clinical examples I discussed reflect different meanings and differing relationships, depending on the particular patients, my evolution in my process, and where we were together in our relationships. Revealing personal information is a form of self-disclosure, but for me the factual disclosure is not as significant as the meaning behind the questions and behind my choice to disclose. In thinking about the broader issue of self-disclosure of the analyst, several ideas come to mind. In my wanting to be seen in a more "real" way by Donna, I think of Greenberg's (1986) re-definition of neutrality as aimed at creating an optimal tension between the patient's internalized old and new objects. Part of my wish to disclose had to do with wanting Donna, for example, to relate to me as a "new object," as distinct from her mother. Although my disclosing was not part of a conscious, technical decision based on a relational model, Greenberg's concept is a useful one in reflecting back. Ehrenberg (1974) makes the point that the analyst need not understand the underlying meanings behind the analyst–patient interaction before disclosing, but rather the disclosure itself might be a means to gaining understanding; clarity might come later. This was certainly true for me in the case of Donna.

Within the past year, my philosophy of treatment and my style as an analyst have shifted. I am far more interested in plunging into my own unconscious material as I have become more aware of and accepting of underlying characterological issues within myself. Because I make more active use of my countertransference, my patients are more openly analyzing themselves as well as me. With this increased involvement and intensity in my relationships with my patients, I am discovering more about myself as a childless woman, and I am thinking about how I might be different with patients if I were a mother. I might be less dependent on my patients for fueling my narcissism because more of my narcissistic (and not so narcissistic) gratification might come from the engagement with my child. As a nonparent, I think I identify more with the child in parent-child struggles, as in one of the cases I discussed earlier. I think I also retain more childlike identifications and, therefore, sometimes rely on patients to fulfill my childlike longings, for example, to be thought of as attractive, brilliant, and likable. On the positive side of being childlike, is my enjoyment of play with my patients. I enjoy the direct engagement that comes with humor, teasing, and the dropping of formality. I believe that in parenting, we are pushed to give up our role as children. I do not know how I would be different as an analyst were I a parent, but I imagine that if I were a mother and having to take the role of caregiver/protector/guide, I would probably feel the effects of being the elder more often in relation to my patients. It is hard to predict how my style and focus might change: would I become more "parent-like," allying more with wisdom, reason, containment than I do at present? Then again, I might identify with my child and learn even more about being playful, creative, and "uncivilized" in my style.

At this stage of mid-life, I am seeing that not having a child creates a challenge for finding personal meaning through my work and through relationships. Some of the longings that remain unsatisfied from my relationship with my mother might have been worked through in the process of parenting. Instead, I get strong maternal feelings at times with patients. I have had the fantasy, for example, of wanting to adopt one 45-year-old patient. I also experience the reverse: wanting to be appreciated, loved by patients in a way that I might not want so much from them were I a parent.

Childbearing is heavily laden with a multitude of meanings for all of us. Usually, our sexual and gender identities are closely connected with creating and raising children. The experience of infertility can easily lead to feelings of shame and inadequacy. Because so many self-esteem and self-image issues tie into childbearing, we might have difficulty talking freely about this area with our patients, particularly when we have deviated from the traditional path of easily deciding to have children, followed by relatively problem-free conception and birth. Because I am fairly free of conflict about my eventual decision not to have children and feel that most of the pain of the struggle to have a child is probably behind me, I feel open to revealing something of my experience and choice to patients, should childbearing issues emerge in the treatment. Over time, I have come to realize that although I feel satisfied with and sometimes very positive about the choice not to have children, it does not mean that there are not psychologically complex and challenging sequelae to that decision. When patients raise issues and questions about childbearing, it is bound to evoke a wide range of feelings in me, both consciously and unconsciously. I seem to vacillate between strength and vulnerability, a sense of both triumph and loss as I contemplate the meaning that nonparenthood has had in my growth and development as a person and as an analyst.

Through my work with patients, I am learning more about the significance of my nonchoice about childbearing and eventual choice not to have a child. In retrospect, Donna taught me about my defensiveness against my underlying vulnerability and about my wish to appear strong and self-sufficient. She also sensitized me to questions I had stopped asking myself, such as what does one lose or miss in the transition from wanting a child to choosing not to have one.

On the other hand, facing myself as a nonparent through my work with patients has helped me to see the value and intensity that analytic relationships have in my life. The love and hate I can now feel in my work as an analyst might well rival that which I would feel as a parent or I have felt as a child. Although my patients are not my parents or my children, they call forth basic and personal feelings that force me to grapple, grow, and develop in ways I might have been pushed to were I a mother. In my development as an analyst, I have moved from a somewhat detached, intellectualized stance to a much more involved and open way of relating. When asked if I have children, I now usually answer directly and explore my patients' thoughts, fantasies, and feelings about me as a nonparent in relation to themselves. I openly engage in exploring transferential and countertransferential feelings of wanting to be the parent or the child with particular patients. It can be both playful and poignant to get in touch with the wishes to parent or to be parented by each other, to feel and express both the longings and the regrets. I see the analytic process as an intensely intimate one, and I thrive when my patients are willing to struggle for intimacy with me. The rewards and gratification of this work, like those of parenting, involve reaching new places within oneself. Mutual dependence and intimacy lead to eventual separation and change within both parent and child, analyst and patient.

REFERENCES

Ehrenberg, D. B. (1974), The intimate edge in therapeutic relatedness. *Contemp. Psychoanal.*, 10:423–437.

Greenberg, J. R. (1986), Theoretical models and the analyst's neutrality. *Contemp. Psychoanal.*, 22:87–106.

Hoffman, I. Z. (1991), Toward a social-constructivist view of the psychoanalytic situation. *Psychoanal. Dial.*, 1:74–105.

Chloë by the Afternoon

Relational Configurations, Identificatory Processes, and the Organization of Clinical Experiences in Unusual Circumstances

MICHAEL A. CIVIN
KAREN L. LOMBARDI

Late on a Friday afternoon, December 14, 1990, we received a telephone call from our adoption agency. In her rather typically unempathic way, our case worker advised us that if we *really* wanted the baby girl we were waiting to adopt, we needed to be in Asuncion, Paraguay, by the following Tuesday morning.

The call was so jarring that the next few hours will remain forever blurred. We had been expecting to go to Paraguay to pick up the baby, who had been born on November 3, but we had been told that the end of February was the earliest we might hope for. Despite the countless hours we had spent staring at her blotchy newborn pictures, despite the obsessive search for every ounce of meaning we might squeeze out of the few scraps of information we had, and despite the fervor of our debate about a name for her, Chloë and our almost inexpressible hopes for the future had remained even more distant and abstract than the end of February. Our paranoid anxieties had been so fueled by years of frustration and recent bureaucratic incompetence that neither of us dared suspend our disbelief. But with the call, we were no longer faced with the vagueness of "perhaps the end of February." We could now picture ourselves holding our daughter on Tuesday morning. We booked the airplane flight and launched our own flight into mania. We had two days to buy everything we ever might need as parents, pack, and deal with our professional obligations, both to our students and our patients.

In this chapter we wish to address a few of the issues that emerged in our dealing with our professional obligations, beginning with an examination of what we said to our patients, why we chose to say the things we said, and the impact on treatment of both the event and our way of handling the event. One salutary consequence of remarkable and unusual events, such as the one we are describing, is to provide us with an opportunity to bring into sharper focus the ways in which we have been organizing our clinical experience. These are events and circumstances that we cannot integrate seamlessly into our ongoing clinical experience without pausing to reflect. In fact, these unusual events often force us, or at least offer us the opportunity, to think about some of the rarely inspected aspects of our work (see e.g., Civin, 1991; Lombardi and Rucker, 1991; Wilner, 1991).

We are arguing that, even under the close and careful scrutiny of well-trained, serious analysts, the very repetitiveness of much of our work may conspire with our tendencies to dissociate salient aspects of our experience, particularly those aspects that neatly complement our patients' disavowed internal worlds. However, when we experience a notable rupture in the ongoing continuity of our work, these otherwise dissociated complements may become more visible against an unfamiliar backdrop. This sudden, emotionally overcharged separation from our patients will serve as an illustration.

Like most conscientious analysts, separations from our patients are generally cushioned by a period of preparation before the event and a period of exploration after the event. The ritual had become so automatic that its affective momentum was diminished and it rarely occurred to us to question, for example, our levels or choices of self-disclosure. Unlike August vacations, this separation would have no period of preparation, nor did we even know exactly when we might be coming back.

Before disappearing into our respective offices, we spent a few anxious minutes together in the kitchen discussing what exactly it was that we wanted to say to our patients. At the time, naturally enough, we were so suffused with conflicting emotions and the compelling urgency of turning those emotions into action that thinking felt like forced confinement. We seemed to be in agreement that, in general, the less we said, the better. This was not because we felt there was any special analytic frame or analytic neutrality to be maintained. At least on the surface, ours was a much more pragmatic decision. We had so much to do and so little time in which to do it, that we simply didn't have the time it might take to "process" the information about the adoption with our patients. On the other hand, we felt it was important to let them know that, despite the hastened departure, there was no cause for alarm. Since we actually had no idea when we would be returning, we decided to pick a "safe" date of January 7 and to set up our schedules for that week. We were satisfied that this was an adequate, if somewhat innocuous, solution.

We believe that our experience in this instance demonstrates that, to a large extent, relational configurations are sufficiently entrenched within each analytic dyad that it really matters very little whether or not a patient is or is not "adequately prepared" for a separation or how much self-revelation accompanies the briefing and debriefing. On the other hand, scrutiny of the choices made, as well as the whole gamut of the analyst's affective experience (Searles, 1965) in making the choices, may reveal to the analyst otherwise concealed, but important, aspects of the identificatory process that is occurring in each of the dyads. Under ordinary analytic circumstances, we may fail to scrutinize these choices, because, under the sway of our own dissociative complement to the patients' internal object world, we may not perceive ourselves as having made choices.

However, in unusual circumstances, such as our excited and hasty leave-taking, what we are choosing to do may become more apparent. We will illustrate these ideas using clinical vignettes and Heinrich Racker's (1968) ideas on concordant and complementary identifications.

MICHAEL'S LIST

As soon as I got into my office, I got out my appointment book and made a list of all the patients I was scheduled to see over the next three weeks. There are many ways I might have made such a list: for example, in the order I was going to see them, alphabetical order, or random order. In my immediate state of mania, I found myself unable to embrace an obsessional organization. No matter how I started making the list, I found myself jumping around in a way that seemed random. After completing the list, I paused to review it and realized that there was one patient that I had omitted entirely, even though I saw her four times a week. This omission prompted me to examine my list again. I began to suspect that at the top of my list were the patients I was eager to call, then came a group I found it easy to conceive of calling, farther down came the patients I felt some discomfort about calling, and at the bottom came the patients I didn't want to call. At the time, I didn't know what sense to make of the patient I had forgotten about completely.

As I made the first few calls, I became aware of an alternative way of understanding my strategy. I reviewed the list again. The first group, those I was eager to call, were, by and large, patients with whom I had been working for a while, whom I considered healthier and more related and with whom I felt I could communicate most, if not all, of the array of emotions I was experiencing—concern and anxiety, excitement and joy, fear and dread. This would represent the group of patients with whom my work featured the most therapeutic symbiosis (Searles, 1965, 1979) or concordance (Racker, 1968). In retrospect, I might speculate that the second group of patients, those I found it easy to conceive of calling, but was not eager to call, represented patients with whom I was more likely to engage in what Racker has called complementary identifications, and in this instance, Searles might term pathological symbioses. At the other end of the spectrum, those patients whom I had no wish to call would fall into the realm of Searles's autistic countertransference, which is an alternate form of complementarity. I should make it clear that, even with the first group of patients with whom I was eager to speak, I had no conscious intention of sharing my array of emotions. I had a preprogrammed message to deliver, but, in fact, most of these patients asked me questions, perhaps in response to an unconscious, but equally preprogrammed, message. I found myself responding in similar but subtly different ways.

In the following clinical examples, we will illustrate some of the ways in which the extraordinary clinical circumstances occasioned by our hasty, but personally joyous and anxiety-ridden departure provided a backdrop against which some previously concealed analytic experience became projected into the foreground. The first three of these examples come from the father's practice and the final example from the mother's.

Clinical Example 1: The South American Patient

Among the group of patients with whom I found myself eager to speak was a patient who was born in South America, but who had lived since her teenage years in this country. In response to this woman's politely concerned question, I revealed that my wife and I were adopting but omitted a detail that I included in response to others' queries, namely that I was going to South America. This was a woman who had entered therapy because she found herself inextricably mired in a marriage in which she tolerated but suffered with her husband's frequent absences and probable affairs. In the process, she had stifled any other outlets for herself, despite ample talent and education. Now after considerable therapy, she had returned to her career and was thriving in it and socially, but remained deadlocked in her marriage. Her early years, before her parents had separated and she had left for this country with her mother, had been especially painful ones, repressed to the point that she produced almost no memories of them beyond a feeling of having failed to be an attractive enough child to prevent her father from having his constant affairs. In retrospect, I believe that my failure to reveal that I was to become a father in South America reflected the many ways in which, in the therapy, I dissociated my experience of being a bad father for her, as her husband denied his part of their difficulties. My inability to extract myself from the complementary partial identification with her internal paternal introject combined with her dissociated sense of herself as a failure as a woman.

In fact, it was this complementarity that had limited our ability to extend the progress we had made in the therapy to her marriage. Amplified many times by my own anxieties about becoming a father and brought into focus by the uniqueness to this dyad of my omission of the detail of South America, I was able to note an important aspect of the treatment. In fact, I quickly forgot my observation under the pressure of the moment. With this patient I was not aware of any perturbation in treatment caused by the failure to prepare her, nor did I ever become aware of any changes in the treatment brought about by the self-disclosure.

After my return, the therapy progressed much as it had before, with one notable exception. In my first session back, she noted my suntan and joked about my going to Florida and just saying I was adopting a baby. Again, I found myself censoring the South America detail, but this time as I did so, my previous thoughts returned. Over the next several months,

I frequently became aware of my previously dissociated sense of having failed her in her dealings with her husband and was able to place this sense in the context of her inability to deal with the sequelae of seeing her father, husband, and therapist as having failed her. I think it is no coincidence that she soon found herself able to confront her husband about his betrayals and abandonments. As far as I know, they resolved their difficulties in a reasonably successful manner and were able to continue their marriage.

Clinical Example 2: The Adopted Friends

Among my patients were two profoundly borderline women in their late twenties who had entered therapy independently at much the same time; they were referred by different people but were, it soon emerged, virtually best friends. These two women had grown up together in the same small community, gone to the same schools, played on the same teams, shared sleepovers, and, most importantly for the purpose of this chapter, had shared one aspect of self-definition, which kept them close to each other, even as in other ways their lives drifted apart. Each of them was an adopted child, and growing up they were, as far as they knew, the only adopted children in their class and among their circle of friends.

As patients, they presented many similar concerns—frequent and severe depressive episodes with terrifying suicidal ideation; tremendous difficulties sustaining relationships of any kind, let alone intimate relationships; and many forms of impulsivity, intense neediness, and dependency. Although the one had a more flamboyant and histrionic manner and the other a more constricted and secretive manner, they were, in so many ways, two peas in a pod, and I often tended to group them in that way.

As I reviewed my list, it crossed my mind that it was strange that the more histrionic of the two was nearer the top of the list, though certainly not in the group I was eager to call, while the more constricted of the two was at the bottom. This awareness gnawed at me, especially as I found myself refusing to call the latter, even after my conversation with her friend, a conversation that was unremarkable in any way. I knew that they were likely to speak to each other within the day, and thus I felt under more pressure to maintain an egalitarian posture, and yet I found any excuse to avoid making the call. Eventually, I forced myself to dial her number, and much to my relief I heard her answering machine pick up and, in turn, I left my standard message.

In fact, there was almost no notable difference between the actual phone call I had with the one patient and the answering machine message I left with the other. The former patient had asked no questions, nor had she expressed any surprise about the hastiness of my departure.

I imagine that, to a large extent, I continued to ruminate about these two young women because adoption had consumed my mind and they talked so often about their adoptions. Even so, what emerged increasingly was my differing reactions to the two of them. Against the stark backdrop of my markedly different countertransference experience, I began to differentiate between them in new ways.

The more constricted woman was a patient whom I had fancied myself glad to have in treatment. In fact, I had made several fee concessions to her in order to facilitate her being able to come in more than once per week. Despite her periods of depressive constriction, I had seen her as bright and verbal, capable of moments of insight, and equipped with a deep fantasy life, which she often revealed in rich dreams and waking fantasies. Suddenly, as I found myself burdened by dealing with her, I came to see much of my former way of relating to her as complementary to her greed. To the extent that I saw myself as kind and good, she and I were both preserved from the experience of her devouring need for me, as well as her utter dissatisfaction with anything that I had to offer. At the same time, in a complementary manner, we were spared the awareness of my inadequacies as a compensatory object and the fact that I, greedily, had a world and life of my own, with my own needs and wishes that took precedence over my devotion to her.

Later on, as I thought about my relief at getting her machine and not having to deal with her, I felt better able to integrate a fundamental, previously dissociated, aspect of the transference–countertransference. This young woman had often talked about her younger sister and her experience of her parents' favoring of that sister. She, and I, had made a good deal of the fact that her sister was not adopted and that their mother referred to the younger sibling as her "real" daughter. Prior to this event, however, I had been unaware of the many ways in which she experienced *me* rejecting and humiliating her, as well as the ways in which I attempted to conceal the fact that I had more important priorities in my life than her. In this case, the patient's dynamic was one with which I did have some familiarity, but the power and pervasiveness of that dynamic had evaded my awareness because of the strength of my own complementarily dissociated sense of guilt and inadequacy.

But my thoughts did not stop there. Even equipped with this understanding, I found myself seething with anger at this young woman, who possibly still had not received the message, that she could hate me for finally getting the daughter that I had longed for. While the prior thoughts had been relatively easy to integrate, the force of my hatred for her caught me short and left me without an explanation. In the few months after my return, now knowing that this hatred existed, I endeavored to nurture it within me during our sessions instead of suppressing it into complementarily dissociated enactments. Gradually, I came to understand the hatred of her, which she experienced emanating and attacking her from within, in the form of a maternal introject for whom her very existence represented a profound narcissistic injury. As my understanding and my own cherished baby grew, it occurred to me that I had been unable to attend to this aspect of our interactions, as fundamental as it was, because in part I too had feared addressing directly the question of narcissistic injury surrounding an adoption, thus facilitating my identification with her internal object world.

Clinical Example 3: The Forgotten About Patient

The patient whose name I had forgotten to include on the list was a woman in her mid-twenties with whom I had first worked while she was an inpatient, hospitalized for suicidality and profound depersonalization and depression. At the time of this episode, after some three years of four times per week analysis, she had been doing well enough to return to college with excellent results and, for the first time in her life, maintain both steady employment and a stable relationship with a man. Both patient and therapist seemed to experience a great deal of gratification about these results outside the consulting room. However, our work within the room had maintained a boringly repetitive, virtually stagnant, quality for some time. The feature of our work that had been most striking to me in the prior year was her simultaneous devotion to me as the most important person in her life, the one safe and stabilizing influence about whom she could have erotic and loving thoughts as well as hateful and deprecating thoughts, while at the same time steadfastly refusing to know or acknowledge anything about me as a person. This refusal took considerable effort since some rudimentary aspects of my personal life are available for my patients' inspection because of where I practice. For some time, my office was in an upstairs wing of our house, and after having offices built adjoining the house, my wife and I share a waiting room. Still, large parts of many sessions were devoted to this patient's ruminative speculations about whether the house was mine, whether I was married and had children, how old I was, what sorts of things I liked, and so on. At times, these speculations felt highly erotized, but at other times they felt like pro forma ruminations, filling up time and space that otherwise might remain empty. My primary tack with these speculations had been to explore with her why she would not ask me to clarify her uncertainties, if these were matters that were of such importance to her that they deserved to occupy so much of her therapy time.

From my point of view, I had been aware of a number of differing countertransference responses to her. At times, I felt a corresponding overvaluing of her as my best patient, my most interesting patient, or my favorite patient. At other times, I found her erotically stimulating. But a good deal of the time, I found myself either bored with or somewhat disgusted by her ruminations, which I experienced as increasingly pathetic.

Although each one of these countertransference feelings was powerful, none of them seemed adequate to explain to me why I had omitted her from the list. My immediate justification was that she was too fragile to tolerate the suddenness of the separation and, even more so, the reason behind my leaving since it would shatter her fantasies and consequently destroy her stability. But this justification did not sit well with me. It had been quite some time since she had been so unstable, and talk of suicide or even depression had been absent from the sessions for some time. Nor did I have any reason to suspect that she needed her fantasies about me to continue living. Her relationship with her boyfriend had grown more serious. In the several sessions immediately prior to the episode under discussion, she had even broken free of the ruminations to the extent that she preoccupied herself with thoughts of him as much as with speculations about me. In addition, I had other patients whose current depressions and suicidal potential were greater than hers. I had not forgotten to include these patients on my list, nor had I any special hesitation about calling them.

In fact, I began to realize that I had no particular fantasy at all of how she might react to the call, nor was I terribly concerned. I did not dread calling her. Quite to the contrary, I felt no hesitation about picking up the phone and making the call because I had no sense of her at the receiving end. Even in my speculation about having forgotten her, I had forgotten her. In fact, I felt no link whatever with the patient with whom I would have expected to feel most connected. The call, once made, was entirely perfunctory. After it, I experienced a momentary sense that something was amiss, but, grateful to be done with the call, I quickly put the thought behind me.

When I returned, she noticed my tan and began as she always did, even when I had gotten a haircut, by telling me that she was letting me know that she noticed because she didn't want me "to get away with it" or to think she hadn't noticed. She then proceeded to spend virtually the entire session wondering aloud whether I had gone somewhere with my wife and children, whether I had gone on a Club Med vacation with the patient who followed her, and what it might be like to go away with me and whether she ever would. Often, in the past, I had listened to similar fantasies and ruminations and organized them as one or another version of an abandonment fantasy, fueled by her internal experience of a mother who had been alternatively overvaluing and rejecting and a father who expressed his love by leaving the house on drinking binges in order to avoid his incestuous urges.

Now as I listened, enlightened by the experience I had of forgetting her several weeks previously (and during the entire time we were in Paraguay), it occurred to me for the first time that so much of our complementary overvaluations, erotizations, and apparent investments in each other, in fact, concealed an entirely different and much more primary issue. In truth, we had little connection with each other at all.

I came to suspect that the reactions I was having now of emptiness and disconnectedness were reactions that I had all along but had dissociated in my complementary identifications with a maternal introject whose relationship with her daughter had been similar to what Spitz (1965) calls primary passive rejection. The first words I had ever heard from this young woman had, in fact, reflected this relationship with her internal object world and predicted the relationship that we would enact not having for several years. She had said, "I feel like I'm not me." Her internal object world was comprised of objects who feigned extraordinary concern, but demonstrated little or none. Her maternal introject did not alternate between concern and rejection; she was primarily rejecting. The internal father expressed boundless love and protection but alternated between treating her as a sexual object and leaving the house to drink. In my complementary identifications with these aspects of her internal world, I too had feigned concern and, as made clear by my forgetting of her, experienced none.

Clinical Example 4: Girls Who Need Their Mothers

At the time, I was seeing two girls in once a week treatment, one a five-year-old and one seven. In each of these cases, for what I thought at the time were different reasons, I spoke to them individually on the telephone and told them the reason for my abrupt departure. The seven-year-old, who had profound depressive anxieties, I consciously intended to tell from the beginning, so as not to contribute to what I was sure would be intense and unwarranted worry about me and an accompanying anxiety about her own sense of herself as animate and related. When she was two, she was present in a hotel room when her mother was beaten and made briefly unconscious by her father. This became a focal incident in their mutual identification with each other. As I spoke first to her mother on the telephone, I heard her in the background saying, "I'm afraid to speak to her. It's something terrible, isn't it? I know it's something terrible." When I explained to her that I was leaving for Paraguay to bring back my baby, underscoring that I was really fine and that I would be back soon, I heard relief in her voice. She said, "I was afraid you were going to tell me something terrible. As long as you're all right." When we first met on my return, she had a present for Chloë, a wooly pink lamb with a bell around its neck, which she had picked out herself on a shopping trip with her mother. She asked if she might give it to the baby herself. Not quite knowing what to make of it at the time, but assuming that she somehow needed to check out the existence of the baby, I brought her into the house, where she met Chloë (and my own mother) and handed her the present herself.

The second child, the five-year-old, was herself born in Colombia, the second of two adopted girls in her family. My decision to tell her the reason for my absence was less volitional, although equally conscious, because it felt more like an enactment with her mother, who seemed to take over and place herself in the middle of the interaction between the child and me, saying, "Oh, you must tell her this; she'll be so excited," calling her over to the phone at the same time that she was communicating both the content and the affective excitement herself. She was not adopted until she was nine months old, and issues of loss of her previous mother and a sense that she was not truly her mother's child were elaborated as a mutual identification between her and her mother. By the time the child came to the phone, I had nothing left to tell her but to repeat what her mother had said; the child accepted the news with little of the excitement that the mother predicted and left me feeling a bit deflated, as if I had attempted to give the child a gift—the gift of sharing an identity around adoption—which she had not wanted. On my return, she also had a present for the baby—a picture frame that she had *not* picked out, but was clearly a present from her mother. She, unlike the first child, was completely uninterested in the present itself but was also very curious about seeing Chloë, which again I arranged. (I should note that there were other children in my practice at the time and that seeing Chloë was not an issue for them or for me.)

In reflecting on my enactments with these girls, who were very different from each other, I began to focus on certain similarities, some of which I had previously been aware and others of which had remained unconscious in me. For example, on a manifest level, the presenting problem of each of these girls was separation anxiety. They were each second daughters, very close in age to their older sisters, who were seen as sociable, secure, and well-integrated. They were each very close to their mothers and not especially close to their fathers. At the same time, there was something profoundly askew in their relationship with their mothers, which related to their own sense of impending internal disorganization. Both mothers, because of their own issues, became intensely anxious around what they experienced as their daughters' unabating need for them. I, up until this point, consciously felt myself to be quite comfortable with the intense need these girls felt for their mothers, as well as what I saw as their worry for their mothers' welfare. What I had not consciously experienced was the extent to which their damaged mother introjects complemented my own damaged mother introjects, which I lived, in a very concrete way, through two ectopic pregnancies and previously failed in vitro attempts and adoption attempts. The reparative aspects of having my own child helped me integrate my own previously dissociated damaged mother identifications and freed me to work more vigorously on those issues in these children. Their need to verify my daughter's existence and to experience my own maternity in a concrete way related to their need to verify their own existences both in communion with and separate from their own dead mother introjects.

DISCUSSION

In our lives as clinicians, we have experienced no event as disorienting as the whirlwind of disruption and excitement that accompanied our sudden discovery that we were on our way to pick up our daughter. In this chapter we have presented a few clinical vignettes that reflect some of that experience. We believe that these vignettes lend some credence to the position that, by and large, our dyadic relational configurations are so deeply established that sudden disruptions or the presence or absence of self-revelation matter little in the progress of the analysis. Within wide limits, the patient will experience us in a variety of ways, just as we will experience the patient in a variety of ways, both consciously and unconsciously, regardless of what we say about ourselves or find ourselves forced by circumstance to do.

Nonetheless, against the backdrop of dramatic personal events, analytic experience that had been invisible previously may be projected into the foreground. The clinical examples presented here demonstrate some of the ways in which such invisible organizations of experience, previously hidden in complementary identifications with aspects of the patient's internal object world, were brought to light during just such a personal event. The overarching suggestion here is that some experiences that have been viewed customarily as treatment destructive or, at the very least, detrimental may, in fact, prove to be unparalleled opportunities for analytic insight.

REFERENCES

Civin, M. A. (1991), Unusual occurrences in the consulting room and the structuring of clinical experience. Spring Meeting, Division 39 (Psychoanalysis), American Psychological Association, Chicago.

Lombardi, K. L. & Rucker, N. G. (1991), Parallel dreams as a form of transitional relatedness with the silent patient. Spring Meeting, Division 39 (Psychoanalysis), American Psychological Association, Chicago.

Racker, H. (1968), *Transference and Countertransference*. New York: International Universities Press.

Searles, H. (1965), *Collected Papers on Schizophrenia and Related Subjects*. New York: International Universities Press.
—— (1979), *Countertransference and Related Subjects*. New York: International Universities Press.
Spitz, R. A. (1965), *The First Year of Life*. New York: International Universities Press.
Wilner, W. (1991), Unusual unconscious communications and enactments: Illustration and exploration. Spring Meeting, Division 39 (Psychoanalysis), American Psychological Association, Chicago.

The Ongoing, Mostly Happy "Crisis" of Parenthood and Its Effect on the Therapist's Clinical Work

CLAIRE BASESCU

We all necessarily live in two different economies, one an economy of finite resources, the other an economy of flexible and expanding resources. In the economy of finite resources, an arithmetic of addition and subtraction applies, and all games are 'zero-sum' games: if you spend time in the office, you are not spending that time at home. . . . In the economy of expanding resources, the games are "win-win" games: the arithmetic is multiplicative, credit can expand indefinitely; a day of rewarding effort can send you home frisky and exhilarated; . . . It is almost impossible to keep these two ways of thinking in focus. Each reflects important truth and dangerous error. Most people have temperamental preferences for one style or the other, but either, by itself, produces nonsense.

Mary Catherine Bateson
Composing a Life

I leave home to go to work at a moment when my older child, a five-year-old (at the time) son, is feeling particularly sad and vulnerable. I am able to reassure him before I leave, but ten minutes later, the phone rings in my office as a patient sits in my waiting room. I answer and hear my son sobbing on the other end. "I need you," he says. "I never see you. You're never home. Please come home early. I'm so lonely." We talk for a while, as the clock ticks forward and then into my patient's session time. My son calms down somewhat. I agree to come home as soon as possible. I get off the phone, shaken, and begin the session with my patient. A friend, not a therapist, hearing the story says, "Well, therapy begins at home." His point touches on the irony, which cannot possibly escape any therapist/parent, of at times depriving one's children for the sake of one's patients. Or, at least, it can seem that way at such a moment. I know there is a difference between causing temporary discomfort in my children and inflicting lasting psychological damage, and, as a parent, I am always trying to differentiate between the two. And clearly, it was not only for the sake of my patient that I wanted to get off the phone and get to work, but for my own sake, to satisfy my need to maintain my professional life. Whose "need" is it anyway?

I am in a session with a young woman physician, who is on the couch. Just before the session began, I called home to check on my baby daughter, who is four months old and sick with a fever and cold. I heard her crying in the background as I spoke with the babysitter. Suddenly, during the session, I remember that it has been more than four hours since the baby's last dose of Tylenol, and I am the only person who would know this. I become extremely anxious in the session as I think of my daughter in pain at home, crying. Finally, I interrupt my patient, tell her what is happening with my baby and me, and tell her that rather than continue unable to concentrate, I am going to call home. I do so, and the session continues. My patient is not at this point interested in exploring her reactions to most things having to do with me. She proceeds with her agenda. I am aware of feeling embarrassed and vulnerable to some disdain on my patient's part for my worrying about such a small malady. After all, she is a physician and faces life and death every day. This is an ongoing transference/countertransference theme in the work with her. She had an extremely neglectful narcissistic mother; while she longs for the kind of attention and nurturance I am giving to my daughter, she is also very contemptuous of herself for wanting it and of me for giving it. She, therefore, cannot be directly responsive to *my* vulnerability and pain that I have revealed in the session. While I have been attentive to my daughter, I also have acted on my commitment to my patient, in refusing to pretend to concentrate when I found it impossible, in deciding I wanted to be "all there" in listening to her in the session. None of this is explored directly between us at the time. However, my patient, from time to time, comments that she appreciates that I am "a real person," in contrast to a previous therapist, who scrupulously avoided revealing personal information about herself.

Such moments of role conflict, confusion and clash, are par for the course, everyday occurrences for the therapist who is also a parent. To be sure, they occur for every working parent, in any line of work, and require large stores of humor and resilience to manage. For the parent who is a psychotherapist, the definitions of work and family roles overlap in complex ways.

Because we consider ourselves to be "experts" on, or at least students of, the psychology of human beings, their development, relationships, and emotional lives, there is a continual, ongoing interplay of ideas and feelings between office and home. We are doing the same thing at home and at work: we are involving ourselves, immersing ourselves in the processes of growth and development of other human beings. We are trying to respond appropriately and creatively to the needs of other human beings, while also taking care of ourselves. We are doing this primarily in dyadic or small-group interactions and in intimate situations. In addition, in psychodynamic psychotherapy, parent–child relations and the experience of childhood are viewed as ever-present layers of current experience and are a large part of what patient and therapist are trying to understand: how the patient has become who he or she is in the interpersonal world of a particular family. Thus, the immersion in family life and parent–child relations at home can inform one's understanding of transferences and countertransferences at the office.

While, certainly, the dual roles of therapist and parent are integrated in fundamental ways and inform each other, they are also very different in many ways and may conflict or seem to conflict with each other. For one thing, at home, our hope is to respond optimally to our children's emotional needs so as to prevent ongoing psychological problems from developing. At work, our task is to help undo or redo problematic development that has already taken place without our involvement. As in my opening example, at times, our dual commitments to our patients and our children in this regard may conflict with each other. For another, we interact at work primarily through talking, though the playful qualities of creative therapeutic work have been noted in recent years (e.g., Ehrenberg, 1990). At home, we have a much wider array of interactive modalities, including play; touch; concrete caretaking, like feeding; as well as talk.

A third crucial difference is that the boundaries of our responsibility for the other person's life are vastly different in the two situations. Legally, morally, and practically, our adult patients are ultimately responsible for their own lives, for their own decisions, and their own fates. This issue of personal responsibility is one that many a therapeutic pair struggle with and explore extensively. It is often an area of psychological development—development out of childhood and childish modes of relating—which many adults have not successfully completed. As parents, we are legally, morally, and practically responsible for our children. However, our job as parents is to teach self-responsibility and to gradually relinquish our caretaking role. Since many adults have not successfully negotiated this transition throughout childhood, it may feel to the parent/therapist like the same task at home and in the office. However, the distinction between the fact of physical adulthood and the fact of physical childhood cannot be obscured by psychological similarities between some adults and children. The tension between one's physical status as an adult and one's mental self-perception or self-experience of being a child is one that adult patients must struggle with and therapists should not overlook. Therapists' experience of the kind of responsibility we have for our children, as distinguished from the kind of responsibility we have for ourselves in our relationships with our adult patients, is a useful source of creative tension in the therapist.

This chapter grows out of my interest in the interpersonal view of therapy as an encounter between two whole, complex, unique human beings who bring all aspects of their personal selves to the encounter. I have been inspired by several examples in recent literature of therapists attempting to write in more thorough, honest, and revealing ways about aspects of their own personal situations impacting on their clinical work (e.g., Friedman, 1991; Hirsch, 1993; Gerson, 1994). These recent articles, while building on previous work, have attempted to forge new territory in their inclusiveness of both countertransference exploration and exploration of nontransference aspects of the patient's participation. Such efforts are encouraged by theoretical articles that attempt to articulate and delineate principles of the interpersonal approach to psychoanalysis.

For instance, in a recent article Fiscalini, (1994) writes:

> Interpersonal analysts repudiate the traditional concept of the blank-screen analyst, or so-called opaque mirror, and consider analytic anonymity a myth . . . Interpersonalists are not concerned with "purifying" the analytic field; from their perspective this is not only unnecessary, but indeed impossible. Since, in the interpersonal approach, the analyst's personality is seen as forming an integral part of the transference and as inevitably revealed in it, the clinical focus is more on its open examination, by both patient and analyst, and less on trying to constrain or legislate its inevitable appearance [p. 123].

My interest in this chapter is to explore parenthood as *both* a particular example of a personal aspect of the therapist's life, which can become a useful stimulus in the clinical work for patient and therapist *and* as a unique set of life experiences that shed particular light on clinical issues and the clinical situation.

In my title, I call parenthood an "ongoing crisis" because it is an ever-present and ever-changing, very salient, powerfully absorbing, and at least potentially anxiety-producing part of the therapist's life, even when things are going smoothly. In addition, it carries with it, inevitably, innumerable small and large crises when things are not going smoothly. Responsibility for a human life, in addition to one's own, is a position of both tremendous power and tremendous vulnerability, and it involves a total transformation of one's life. I call parenting a "mostly happy" event because, although there is certainly often a great deal of pain associated with the experience, there is usually a greater abundance of joy. The fact of the happiness associated with parenthood may make its impact on therapy unique among crises. For instance, in considering the impact of events in the therapist's personal life on therapy, the literature often contains an emphasis on negative, painful events such as illness in oneself or a family member. Exceptions are marriage, pregnancy, and parenthood. These events in the therapist's life may be more likely to evoke envy in patients and guilt in therapists; on the other hand, they may also stimulate thoughts and feelings in both parties about joy, contentment, love, the meaning of life, and so on.

I write as a 40-year-old mother of two children, a son, now age six, and a daughter, now age three and a half. My son was born when I was beginning my third of five years of analytic training; my daughter was born one week after I completed all the formal requirements for graduation. Thus, from birth to the present, they were both intimately involved in my development as an analyst, though I had worked as a therapist for several years before beginning analytic training. I see adults, couples, and occasionally older adolescents in my private practice. Therapists who are parents and work with children may confront some different issues from those I explore in this chapter

While I was pregnant for the first time, I read much of the fairly extensive analytic literature on the therapist's pregnancy. However, I found only a few articles or book chapters dealing with the experience of parenthood and its effect on therapists (Fenster, Phillips, and Rapoport 1986; Marlin, 1988; Guy, 1987). In terms of what was in the literature, once the children were born (i.e., no longer physically in the room), it was as if they were no longer an issue. This was far from my experience. They were a powerful issue for me and for many of my patients. I became interested in formulating and writing about my experiences. (I also developed and began to run a workshop called "Integrating the Roles of Parent and Analyst.") Perhaps there is so much more literature on pregnancy because pregnancy is a literal physical "intrusion," which even analysts committed to a model of analytic anonymity cannot ignore or deny.[1] When the children are just in the therapist's head and heart, it may become more possible for patients or even for therapists to imagine that they are no longer there in a relevant way. As clinical theory expands to include what is in the therapist's head and heart, it becomes necessary to consider how more aspects of the therapist's identity are relevant to the clinical encounter.

I am also the child of a psychologist-psychoanalyst father. As the child of an analyst, with an office in our suburban home, I became accustomed to the experience of my father's secret life of intimacy with others. I watched from the window as patients entered and exited the office, and I wondered what was going on in there. Perhaps because I found my father somewhat contained and difficult to read, I was even more curious and intrigued by the relationships he had with his patients. I imagine that I was quite envious, at times, of the attention they were getting from

---

[1] It may be that some of the turmoil, which many writers have noted in patients around their therapists' pregnancies, is the result of patients' sensitivity to their therapists' anxiety about being exposed, or revealed, as real persons in the therapy. In other words, rather than reacting only to the pregnancy per se (without underestimating the emotionally evocative nature of pregnancy, the beginning of life itself), patients may also be reacting to the discomfort of their therapists about having to reveal themselves, something that many therapists, whether by characterological and/or "technical" constraints, often prefer not to do.

him. I asked him what psychologists do, and he said, "They study what makes people tick," and "They help people with problems; everyone has problems." I was fascinated. I sometimes "joke" that I went into the field so I could finally find out "what was going on in there [the office]." Of course, when I finally did have an office of my own, I found myself, not him.

The impact on children of the "secret life" of the analyst/parent is one I know from the child side, but not yet from the parent side, as my children are not yet old enough to be really curious about my work life. They are somewhat curious, particularly since I recently moved my office into a part of our home. They ask to meet my patients. They can go to work with their dad, a lawyer. They can meet his clients and can watch him in court. But they can't come to work with me. It is difficult to know how I will explain to them what I do. I would like to demystify it as much as possible.

My father came from an era in which the mystique of both psychoanalysts and fathers was a more acceptable, even favorable, valued/prized thing. While the remoteness and mystifying aspects of conventional technique in psychoanalysis have had their rewarding aspects for those who practiced that way, there has clearly been a price to pay. I see in my father's writing (Basescu, 1977, 1987) an attempt to "come out from hiding," a hiding that perhaps both his character and his profession had encouraged. In papers like "Anxieties in the Analyst: An Autobiographical Account" and "Behind the 'Seens': The Inner Experience of at Least One Psychoanalyst" (1987), he attempts to reveal his personal experiences. This was his contribution toward moving the field towards a more open, two-person model of therapeutic interaction. It was not until well into the writing of this chapter that I could consciously see the influence of that conflict in my father and first "mentor" on my own attempts to integrate my personal and professional selves.

In a paper called "The Impact of Being an Analyst: Harmony and Dissonance in Personal Life," Barbara Messer (1991) discusses the results of interviews she conducted with experienced analysts about the relationship between their work and personal lives. Strikingly, she begins her paper by noting her reluctance to write about her own experiences: "I might be exposing myself to people for whom some degree of anonymity might be important" (p. 64). Instead, she decided to interview other analysts. Messer explores many aspects of both the integrating and disintegrating aspects of being an analyst on a person's well-being. The principle of confidentiality dictates that the therapist's ability to share his/her work life with others is extremely limited (even in professional forums including paper writing, where clinical data has to be transformed to protect patients' privacy). The principles of neutrality and anonymity mean that the therapist cannot share his/her personal life in work settings. She writes:

> Analysts perceive their work and personal lives to be substantially inte-
> grated by way of fundamental values and principles of the field. At the
> same time there are other basic tenets of the field that ironically work
> counter to these principles and could actually undermine the analyst's expe-
> rience of integration. The possibility that analysts may unknowingly make
> accommodations that compromise their internal integrity and interpersonal
> relationships requires serious attention. Future inquiry needs to address the
> effect on analysts' psyches and relationships of, for example, naturally and
> routinely withholding information, splitting off central elements of their
> lives one from the other, and fairly constant and habitual self-conscious-
> ness [p. 73].

Messer wonders whether analysts holding differing theoretical positions
on the issues of neutrality, anonymity, self-disclosure, the "real" relationship, and the analyst's genuineness and humanness might experience
differing degrees of self-consciousness or dis-ease with themselves at work
and at home. She asks, "if . . . differing positions on these issues have
the power to affect the analyst's own experience of integration, might
different positions on these issues not also influence the patient's integration?" (p. 74).

While my father's choices strongly influenced my feelings about integration of the personal and professional, my mother's choices did also.
As was common for women of her generation, she had given up her
career (in the performing arts) to raise a family. There was a great deal
of frustration and unhappiness associated with this, for her and for all
of us because of her unhappiness.

While in graduate school, I began therapy with a woman therapist.
Her manner of professional self-confidence and authority led me to a
conviction that she was unmarried and childless. I arrived at one session
to find a child's sled outside her door. I was in shock and reeling inside
as my thoughts propelled me to the possibility that my assumptions were
untrue. I asked my therapist if the sled belonged to a child of hers, and
she told me that she was married and had three children. There may have
been no single event in all my years of analysis with more than one analyst
that had a greater impact on me. The (erroneous) certainty I had had
before the revelation made it so powerful. The power of my feelings made
me realize how *deeply* entrenched in my view of myself was a split in
identity, that I could be either a powerful, competent careerwoman or
connected through bonds of nurturance and love to a husband and children, but not both.

The discovery of my therapist's dual identity and the discovery of my
own, at least partly unconscious, assumption that it was impossible to
be or do both reverberated through my life. Primarily, I felt excited and
hopeful and very curious about how my therapist did it. However, I had
many other feelings about the fact of her children. I felt competitive with

her, for having it all, and with them for having her in a way I knew I couldn't. I felt envious of them for the ideal mothering I imagined they received. My memories of this experience have helped me in understanding some of the feelings my patients have struggled with. One reaction I did not have, given my background of a mother who was home, but which I have experienced from some of my patients whose mothers did work, is a reaction of anger, condemnation, and worry about my neglecting my children.

CLINICAL MATERIAL

In this section, I will discuss a variety of clinical situations where the issue of my parenthood has been salient for my patients and for me. Far from an exhaustive survey of the territory, my hope is to explore further some of the variety of ways the issue arises.

First is an example of an encounter that raised issues about role conflicts, female identity, envy, and choices.

A woman patient in her mid-thirties, with whom I have been working for several years, is talking about a daughter whom she gave up for adoption at birth when the patient was a teenager. The patient is now married with no other children. During the time we have worked together, I have given birth to two children. Her daughter is on her mind now because it is the child's eighteenth birthday, and she has had thoughts about sending a letter for her to the adoption agency in case the child looks for her. Today, she is also talking about her feelings of loneliness, her longings for a feeling of family, which have led her to be overly attached to people and situations that are not good for her. She feels that *her* mother will always be "the center of the family." I feel concerned about the ways in which she seems to continue to feel intimidated by her mother (me?) into playing a child role and to feel there is room for only one woman in the family (in the therapy?). I ask, "What about your own family?" She talks about her relationship with her husband, which is sometimes satisfying and at other times difficult and unsatisfying. She relates two dreams, one in which she is on a raft and a huge whale is nearby, terrifying her, and a second, in which her mother is chosen for a job and she (the patient) is let go from the company. I find myself thinking, "Have the baby or be the baby," linking in my mind my patient's lost child and her struggles to grow up. This is a line I know my mother's therapist had said to her when she was a young woman patient contemplating motherhood. I have always considered this line to hold some truth and yet to be misguided and sexist, in that it seemed to view parenthood (possibly only mother-hood) as the only path to maturity. My patient is an artist who is committed to her work, but not yet commercially successful. She has said before that she and her husband have decided not to have children. Some of her reasons have seemed rational, especially her desire for the freedom to pursue her artwork wholeheartedly; others seem to be an outgrowth of some very troubled aspects of her relationship with her mother and troubled aspects of her sense of self. In working with her, I have had to consider my attitudes about whether childlessness can be a healthy choice.

As she relates her dreams, I find myself thinking about my children, particularly my daughter, who is slightly older than the patient's niece to whom she is very attached, but who lives in another city. I am thinking about how much I love my daughter, how comforting and satisfying our relationship is to me. I am feeling sorry for my patient because she does not have this solace in life, as well as this source of self-esteem, which serves as a buffer against some of the slings and arrows of work and other relationships. However, I am also thinking about how difficult the job of parenting is, and my patient does not have the material means I have at the moment. I think of all the horrible moments of depression, of feeling trapped, overwhelmed and overworked, exhausted and deprived of so many aspects of life, especially in the beginning of a child's life.

I ask my patient about the whale in her dream, and she says she thinks it is her feeling of loneliness.

I decide to ask her about children, worrying that this is my issue, not hers. I say, "Is your decision about having children resolved?"

She says, "What makes you ask?"

I say, "Your thoughts about your daughter, your feelings of loneliness, the longings for a family of your own."

She begins to cry heavily and says, "I don't see having a child as a solution to my problems of loneliness. I look at my mother's life and it's not what I want. I guess I could do it differently, but she just gave up so much. . . . I would be afraid, I would be so needy, I would eat my child up. . . ."

At some point, I say, "Well, you are very aware of the neurotic, narcissistic aspects of the decision to become a parent."

She says, "I guess I can see some good sides to it for me."

She is a relentlessly honest and self-critical person. She is right, I think, about what she sees as the possible narcissism involved in the choice to have children. But that's not all that's involved. Is she depriving herself of something that could be a rewarding experience for her? If I avoid bringing up the issue, am I enacting with her the role her mother has, the woman who has the family (who "gets the job") while she herself is on the outside? On the other hand, is it my "parentcentric" bias, because that is the choice I have made, which is influencing my concern about this issue for her?

She leaves the session crying hard, saying, "I'm surprised this stirs up so much emotion in me. I guess there's more to talk about."

In the following session, she continues on the theme of children. She reports a dream.

> My mother and I are on bicycles, riding along, talking, having fun. This is the thing we had in common . . . it was okay, it didn't have to be everything. We are heading for a hill. Just before the bottom of the hill, my mother grabs my handlebars and plunks a big sack onto the handlebars. It's really heavy, the sack is moving, there's something alive in the sack. I can't make it up the hill. The bike is weaving. My mother is ahead. I'm glad she's ahead. There's a little road to the side. I throw the sack off. I head down the road, on a little path, to a pretty beach. There are many people, family and friends, working on a big art project. Some big natural project, with shells, an environmental sculpture, the kind of thing I'd do if I had a lot of money. I woke up.

She had associations to her mother's controlling qualities. "If it's not done my mother's way, it's not done at all," and said, "I would defy any daughter of my mother to want to have children. It's like dragging a bag of concrete up a hill and we all owe her for it all the time."

She reported another dream about a forbidden lover and associated this to her passionate relationship with her artwork, which feels forbidden to her; through art, she said, "I feel so alive, so connected to life. I'm really afraid to do everything I can to embrace it." She talked about being in church the day before, thinking about a traditional lifestyle for women, worrying about what other people will think of her for making a different choice. I said, "Worried about what I think?"

She said, "When you asked me that question last week, I really thought of you as someone who loves being a mother; it works for you, otherwise you wouldn't have had a second child. So yeah, you're part of the congregation too. I feel really lonely. What you said last week gave me a lot to chew on."

This set of interactions precipitated by both her feelings about her daughter and mine about my daughter has brought her to a greater focus on her own choices. I feel I may have failed to challenge sufficiently her holding back as an artist and wonder if this may be out of smugness about my own lifestyle, or envy of her artistic gifts and her freedom to devote herself to her art, or even unconscious guilt about my complicity in my own mother's sacrifice (of her career as an artist).

Does the sack in my patient's dream represent the burden of a baby, the burden of her mother's neediness, or the burden of my neediness? In the beginning of the dream, she seems to have made some peace with being different from her mother (or me): "This is the thing we had in common . . . it was okay, it didn't have to be everything." Her mother puts the sack on her bike; is her mother saying, "Be like me, you can't escape the burden. You can't be free." Is that how my patient experienced my questioning her about parenthood? She seems in the dream and in her waking life to more firmly and clearly define herself in response to this whole episode. I am still concerned about the extent to which she defines motherhood in terms of her own mother, reflecting a lack of separation: "I defy any daughter of my mother to want to have a child." I take into account that my patient has a dramatic style of expressing herself, but her statement may also reflect that to simply define her choices as coming from herself, not as reactive to someone else, remains somewhat frightening.

In this case, my patient's decision not to have children was the central point, around which many other issues revolved, including our mutual envy, a defensive position, alternating with more mature attempts at self-definition and self-responsibility.

Envy has arisen for me in another context, where I had a strong negative reaction to a woman patient who was choosing to stay home with a young child and not work. I found myself questioning her motivation for doing so, with a decidedly negative bias. Later, I realized I was partly motivated by envy. If I had to be out in the work world struggling, so should she. That she may have had the inner freedom to make a choice that I did not have was difficult for me. My choice to work may not have been an entirely free choice, but one partly motivated by pressure to live up to family (paternal) standards of achievement. Knowing this, I was freer to explore the meaning and ramifications of my patient's choice for her, as well as of my choice for me.

The issues for me as a parent/analyst have changed over the six-and-a-half year period since my first child was born and, undoubtedly, will continue to change. In the early months of returning to work after the births, guilt, anxiety, and preoccupation with the child were intense. (Marlin, 1988 and Fenster et al., 1986 address these feelings.)

Therapists who have private practices usually choose or feel compelled to return to work when their children are still infants. I was back at work when my children were two to three months old. It was very difficult to leave the babies in the care of others. I felt intense separation anxiety and wondered if my children did also. I tried to observe them to evaluate the impact of my leaving.

The intense feelings required a lot of work to tolerate and think through. At times, they were overwhelming; at other times, productive inner work occurred. The children grew, and survived, and thrived for the most part.

I also felt guilt towards my patients at this time. My children were more important. Their needs were all-encompassing. I worried about short-changing my patients. I wondered whether I should work at all. Over time, during various children's health crises, I wondered whether I should cancel sessions because I was simply too tired or too preoccupied. Some of my patients felt resentful of what they rightly perceived to be my divided attention. Some were sympathetic, others felt guilty (for "taking you away"), while others seemed oblivious. While struggling with my own intense emotions, I tried hard to focus on my patients' reactions and explore them openly in the sessions, but this was often difficult. My vulnerability at this time in my life was double-edged for my patients and myself—both useful and disruptive, growth-promoting and growth-inhibiting. Following are some clinical examples of the impact of my vulnerability on the therapy process.

A patient with a history of extreme neglect and "parentification" (having to take care of her alcoholic mother) had a dream during my first month back at work after giving birth to my second child, a daughter, about a woman who was at work and unable to concentrate. Her associations were to her own mother who neglected her and to how she had to pretend she didn't notice and that everything was fine. I wondered aloud if the dream referred also to her and me. She said yes, relieved that she could "tell it like it is." Her perceptiveness made me uncomfortable, and I was aware that she could be "taking care" of me in not objecting to my divided attention, but merely being elated to be able to talk about it. This same patient, about nine months later, came to a session when I was in the middle of a babysitting crisis (my regular babysitter was sick). My husband had agreed to come home early to take care of the children but was late. My patient arrived at the office (which was down the hall from my home); I let her into the waiting room with my children hovering in the background and told her I'd be a few minutes late. My husband finally arrived. I was furious. I went to my office about 10–15 minutes past the session time. My patient said, "Are you sure you're in shape to work?" I said, "Yes." She, an artist, very adept at "reading" people, but formerly not very trusting of the accuracy of her perceptions or her right to have them, said, "I don't think so. I'm leaving," and left. I was relieved but ashamed, ashamed of being so out of control of my life, ashamed of the possibility that I could not accurately judge my own state of mind. My sense of relief signaled that she was right to leave. My desire to have the session expressed my need to regain a sense of control: "All is well; things are proceeding normally," after the tumult of feelings (anger, helplessness). I probably would have regained my composure and sense of control quickly and been able to work. However, at what price? Perhaps my patient was partly fleeing from her own fear of what my lack of control would stir up in her, her own fears of being out of control.

She returned at her next session, very pleased with herself, feeling strong and courageous in having unilaterally made the decision and taking care of herself. I respected her decision and did not charge her for the session. Nevertheless, my discomfort about myself, my lack of control and "nonperfection," prevented me from fully exploring this incident with my patient at the time. I believe now, having worked through somewhat more my own issues about perfectionism and control (parenthood, in part, having facilitated such work), I would be more able to inquire fully about her reactions to this incident, including not only her feelings about herself, but her perceptions of me. She too had many issues about her image and presentation to others and had fears about her perfectionism and criticisms of herself and others.

The incident reverberates with another issue that had been powerful in the therapy with this patient. During the time I was pregnant with and gave birth to two children, she was trying to become pregnant herself and was encountering serious infertility problems, which ultimately did prevent her from bearing children. Throughout her ordeal, I was impressed with my patient's courage in dealing with her grief as openly and fully as she did and in fully exploring her reactions to me and my pregnancies. I was sometimes concerned that she might have been better off not working with me, but she never talked about leaving for that reason. I wondered whether this issue played a part in the incident where she walked out, in that she was allowing herself to enact what must have been an aspect of her feelings towards me, wanting to get away, relief that I was the one who was suffering and not she, a feeling of freedom and power, maybe even aggression and destructiveness, in relation to me.

When my second child was 20 months old, she required surgery for removal of her chronically infected adenoids and tonsils. After initial meticulous planning of the timing of the surgery, the surgery had to be rescheduled at the last minute, so that I had to call patients and cancel sessions abruptly. I found myself explaining the situation somewhat differently to different patients, with fewer or more details, depending on the person and the nature of our relationship. Patients' reactions varied also. Some asked questions, others didn't. I believe patients' motivations for asking or not asking questions in such a situation vary widely and are very useful to explore. Simple curiosity seems natural, but patients have often had their natural curiosity rebuffed or exploited in some way. In reacting to the news of the surgery, one patient spoke of her perceptions of me as "unlucky" and "vulnerable" where before I'd seemed "lucky" and "invincible." She found this useful, but "scary." She was concerned she would have to take care of me and not focus on herself. She wanted to help but not give up her own needs. Another patient recalled the impact of his own childhood surgery. A third reacted to the last minute cancellations, finding them upsetting and disruptive; however, he "pulled [himself] together and dealt with things," and felt stronger for it. I found myself responding with intense feelings to a patient whose mother was undergoing surgery during the time of her session, which was two days before my daughter's surgery. While I was concerned that my identification with her might obscure the reality of her experience, I also felt I was able to be acutely attuned to her feelings of anxiety and pain as she thought of her mother.

As the children get older, I find myself less consumed with issues of dependency and separation and more concerned with issues of character development. For instance, when patients talk about their childhoods and the impact of their parents, I sometimes find myself thinking, oh, I have to remember never to do that or that's something to try to do. I find myself thinking about my children at a case conference or in a session when an event is being discussed that occurred at an age that is close to that of one of my children. This can be helpful because it gives me a developmental context with which to evaluate the event being described. It can also be distracting, excruciating, and anxiety-provoking as I think about my own child's vulnerability.

At the moment, I have many more patients who do not have children than who do. However, I have some who do. There can be feelings of comraderie and shared pleasure and pain, feelings of competitiveness; I often admire my patients' parenting and learn from them. I have at times been troubled by a know-it-all attitude in myself towards patients who are having difficulties with children who are younger than my children (i.e., "I've been through that; I know all about that"). This can be a defensive reaction to my own vulnerability, that is, "Thank God there's something I've negotiated successfully," and not wanting to empathically connect with my patient's vulnerability. On the other hand, patients sometimes are grateful for advice or suggestions. There are usually transferences and countertransferences that come up around such interchanges that require exploration. I feel better when I am also aware of appreciation for a strength in the other person that I don't have. The most troubling countertransference arises when I feel something in a patient's parenting is wrong or damaging or abusive. I have not had this experience often; I more often feel my patients are too hard on themselves, or they are honestly struggling with a difficult issue, and whereas I might make a different choice, theirs seems reasonable too. When I do have a very clear negative response, I say it. I feel it's better to have that on the table, rather than hidden or withheld.

Perhaps, most profoundly, the experience of parenthood has taught me about the power of psychic resources inherent in the human organism, beyond the control of parent or therapist, and at the same time, about our vulnerabilities to the actions and reactions of others. In children, we see both these aspects writ large. I have been aware both of the need to "get out of the way," as my children and patients grow autonomously and discover themselves, and of the need to receive and respond to my children's and my patients' needs to express love and to feel loved, connected, and affirmed.

My last clinical example illustrates a patient's struggle to feel connected and separate and my response to his struggle.

The patient is a young man in his twenties, who has intense transferential experiences involving my children and his fantasies about me as a mother. He had a depressed mother with poor self-esteem, with whom he identified and towards whom he felt responsible as a caretaker. He was expected to be self-sufficient, while also tending to her emotional needs. His own dependency needs went underground, surfaced in the form of acute symptoms like school phobia, and remained as an unevolved morass until early adulthood, when problems in romantic relationships with women became so intense as to severely disrupt his equilibrium, and he began therapy. He says, "I worry about your children. I worry about my selfish needs. I want you to have more evening hours, but I don't want to take you away from your children. I pray that you're a good mother, that you give them love, attention, help them develop self-esteem, be self-centered, don't make them feel they're a burden. I want so much to believe you're a good mother and that you have a good marriage." In one evening session, he said, "I have mixed feelings about having this time, I feel like you should be home with your kids. But I need you; I feel guilty. I really worry about your kids, about whether you're a good mother. ('You're not sure I am.') No, I'm not. How could I be? (At one point, I say, 'How do you know I'd go home, I might take myself out to dinner.') Oh God, I can't imagine that. I only think of you going from home to work, to home. I don't think of you by yourself. If I do, I have to picture you *thinking*. I can't picture that, it's like D (former girlfriend) going off to work, having a job, her own life, not constantly focused on the relationship. How can she do that? ('If I'm with my kids, it's okay.') Yes, yes, it's good, it's very important. (I ask, 'How do you think my kids feel about having a working mother?') My first thought is, they feel fine, we can fend for ourselves. That was always the way it was talked about in my family. You kids can fend for yourselves. ('So, they would act like it's okay, but you know it's not.') That's right, it's not. Like I hear stories about women going back to work three months after their kids are born and it kills me. . . ."

Another time, he hears pigeons hooting outside my office, but thinks it's my daughter crying. "I'm imagining how she's feeling . . . alone, abandoned, and you're not there; you're up here with me, not me, any patient, I can't think about it as me, if I thought about it, I'd feel too guilty. . . . I'm angry with you. Why are you up here with me and not with her. . . . I imagine she's feeling, why doesn't mommy come, she doesn't love me, I'm worthless. . . ." At another point, he says, "I think of you watching your baby with that incredible amount of love [as Garp watches his children sleep in *The World According to Garp*] and I think of me as that baby, feeling so loved and lovable . . . it makes me happy and sad . . . happy cause it's so amazing, sad because I can't feel it, I can't imagine feeling it . . . it's so amazing it's taken me this long to talk with you like this. . . ."

This patient uses his fantasies about me as a mother in a concrete way to work out profound issues about self-esteem, love, lovability, and separation. "I want to think of you as a perfect mother. What if you're not? What does that mean about you and me?" He is trying to understand how he can internalize a sense of lovability so that he will not remain as dependent as he feels on others moment-by-moment for good feelings about himself.

In the countertransference, it is interesting to me that I do not feel guilty towards my children for leaving them at the times when he is most concerned about that. My lack of guilt leaves me freer to explore his reactions as a projection of his own feelings. However, in response to this patient, I do find myself thinking more about the impact of the separations on my children and about how I evaluate my children's needs and make decisions regarding them. I realize what a subjective process this is, how varied parental perceptions can be in this regard, and how easy it is to fool oneself self-servingly in the process.

My patient is looking for a solid feeling inside himself that would make it possible to tolerate separations and absences without undue unease. He is also talking about the separation that comes from having a separate self, from *being* separate, not just separated.

More than with any other patient, I often imagine myself in a maternal role with this patient. He is my son, in varying ages, up to adolescence. I often think about my own son when I am with him and about the complex nature of mother–son relationships. I think about what feels healthy in my relationship with my son and what this patient has not internalized from his relationship with his mother. It is something about sturdiness, about people who love each other with space between. Occasionally, I tell him a story about an incident with my son that reflects this quality. He says, "I *love* hearing that stuff," and seems elated to imagine the possibility of relating in such a manner. Later, he may also feel sad: "I didn't have that," or hopeless: "I didn't have that, so how will I ever be okay?" His ability to imagine relating in such a way, I say, reveals his ability to do so. "Just walk away? Just let my mother off the hook? I can't do that yet," he says (bringing the issue of anger and will into it). As time goes on and we return over and over to these themes (which are not only being imagined and talked about, but lived out in the relationship between us), he begins to glimpse a freedom and a future for himself that is new.

In this chapter I have tried to explore some aspects of the continual, ongoing interplay between experiences of parenting and therapy-work that I have had and thought about. I have hoped to address parenthood as a set of unique life experiences that shed light on both the content and process of therapy, and I have hoped to contribute to the growing body of literature that examines the therapy relationship as a two-person encounter between two unique human beings.

REFERENCES

Basescu, S. (1977), Anxieties in the analyst: An autobiographical account. In: *The Human Dimension in Psychoanalytic Practice,* ed. K. Frank. New York: Grune & Stratten.
—— (1987), Behind the "seens": The inner experience of at least one psychoanalyst. *Psychoanal. Psychol.,* 4:255–265.
Bateson, M. C. (1989), *Composing a Life.* New York: Penguin Books.
Ehrenberg, D. (1990), Playfulness in the psychoanalytic relationship. *Contemp. Psychoanal.,* 26:74–95.
Fenster, S., Phillips, S. & Rapoport, E. (1986), *The Therapist's Pregnancy: Intrusion in the Analytic Space.* Hillsdale, NJ: The Analytic Press.
Fiscalini, J. (1994), The uniquely interpersonal and the interpersonally unique. *Contemp. Psychoanal.,* 30:114–134.
Friedman, G. (1991), The impact of the therapist's life-threatening illness on the therapeutic situation. *Contemp. Psychoanal.,* 27:405–421.
Gerson, B. (1994), An analyst's pregnancy loss and its effects on treatment: Disruption and growth. *Psychoanal. Dial.,* 4:1–17.
Guy, J. D. (1987), *The Personal Life of the Psychotherapist.* New York: Wiley.
Hirsch, I. (1993), Countertransference enactments and some issues related to external factors in the analyst's life. *Psychoanal. Dial.,* 3:343–370.
Marlin, O. (1988), Parenthood in the life of the analyst. *Contemp. Psychoanal.,* 24:470–478.
Messer, B. (1991), The impact of being an analyst: Harmony and dissonance in personal life. In: *The Psychoanalyst: The Interplay of Work and Identity.* A monograph of the Westchester Center for the Study of Psychoanalysis, 1:63–75.

Thank You for Jenny

JESSE D. GELLER

My wife Ruth and I have two daughters, Elizabeth (31) and Jennifer (25). Jennifer was born profoundly deaf. The discovery of this cruel fact in 1973 confronted me with a series of crises unlike anything I had ever encountered before. Two decades later, in the spring of 1993, Dr. Gerson invited me to write an essay about the ways in which our efforts to cope with the crises triggered by Jennifer's deafness have influenced the way in which I do psychotherapy and think about my work. Even after obtaining Jennifer's permission to do so, I said yes only ambivalently. The balance of my feelings were initially tipped in a negative direction.

The conflicts I was experiencing at the outset derived from several sources. Objectifying my relationship to Jenny is repugnant to me. I feared that writing about her for a professional audience would alienate me from the most private and precious meanings of my relationship to Jenny. I also tend to be suspicious of parents who portray their children's disabilities as "gifts," "messages," or even as "opportunities for learning." I usually find their tone to be too sentimental, too heroic, or too self-congratulatory. In fact, I am wary of all retrospective attempts to specify direct and inevitable lines of influence between early and subsequent events.

Very different narratives could have been fashioned out of the facts, events, and anecdotes that are included in this chapter. Nevertheless, as I discovered while writing this, I believe that the continuing process of learning to be a father to Jenny has influenced my views of just about everything of importance that happens in psychotherapy. (In distinctive ways, each of my daughters has had a decisive impact on what I hear, see, feel, think, and say during therapy session.) For the present purposes, however, I will restrict myself to discussing the influence of Jenny's deafness on my attitudes toward the nature and functions of communication and miscommunication in the therapeutic situation.

WHO IS JENNY?

My representation of Jenny and the meanings that I ascribe to her deafness have changed many times over the course of our lives together. Where once I construed Jenny's deafness as her most defining feature, I now conceive of her deafness as only one aspect of her highly distinctive and inspiring personhood. I made the following "slip of the tongue" the week

---

The title is borrowed from an article my mother (Geller, 1984) wrote about Jenny.

Jenny was diagnosed. I mistakenly told a friend she was "profoundly retarded," rather than profoundly deaf. Today, I regard her as a highly intelligent, creative young woman. She is a college junior at the Rochester Institute of Technology. She is trying to decide whether to become a teacher, a social worker, or a graphic designer/artist. Jenny embodies an affirmative answer to my brother Norman's question, "Is it possible to be both real and cool at the same time?" Her vitality is contagious. She is the Picasso of lip readers. She signs with eloquence and style. Her voice is aesthetically pleasing. She is making a life for herself in the "Deaf" community[1] and, if she chooses, can "pass" in the hearing world. Like her older sister, Liz, Jenny is a loving and lovable person. She is generous, empathic, and sensible. Her sense of irony is well developed. Her courage and successes deserve to be celebrated. This chapter is, in part, a thank you for all that Jenny has taught me.

To understand why and how Jenny exerted a positive and pervasive influence on my work requires some knowledge about the barriers to contact and communication resulting from profound deafness. Because profound deafness is a rare occurrence, I assume that most therapists are unfamiliar with the emotional, interpersonal, and cognitive consequences of being born without the ability to hear the human voice. Deafness is far more than simply a loss of hearing. So before proceeding, I will provide some basic information about the diagnosis of deafness, hearing aids, the misleading notion of lip reading, residual hearing, and the developmental difficulties Jenny has endured as she has proceeded from infancy, through childhood, and into her adolescence.

DEAFNESS: SOME FACTS AND THEIR IMPLICATIONS

The diagnosis of deafness is usually determined by the degree of hearing loss in the speech range. Auditory loss is measured in decibels, or units of sound. A slight hearing loss is 20 decibels or less. With this limitation, one may experience strain in hearing when tired or inattentive, in distant theater seats, or when articulation is soft or poor. Persons whose hearing loss averages 40–60 decibels in the speech range struggle to decipher even shouted conversations. Without the help of hearing aids, they cannot learn speech or language normally.

---

[1] Following a convention proposed by Woodward (1972), an increasing number of deaf people distinguish, conceptually, between the audiological condition of not being able to hear (spelled with a lower case "d") and the "culture" of Deafness (spelled with a capital "D"). The latter concept is especially important to those Deaf people who do not consider themselves disabled or handicapped, but who identify themselves as members of an "ethnic" community that has a distinctive language, sensibility, and culture of its own. Jenny is currently struggling, heroically, to define her relationship to Deafness.

Jenny suffers from a profound degree of hearing loss. A child whose hearing loss averages 80 decibels (about the volume of a garbage disposal) in the speech range is considered to be profoundly deaf. Jenny's first audiological examination indicated that she had a "sensori-neural" hearing loss of 95 decibels in her right ear and 100 in her left ear. This means that without a hearing aid, she can detect only sounds that are louder than a lawn mower, food blender, or jet plane. Jenny's deafness was not diagnosed until she was 19 months old.

My wife Ruth "knew" something was "wrong" with our baby's development by the time Jenny was five months old. Pediatric ignorance, incompetence, and arrogance, as well as the power of a family system in denial, postponed the diagnosis of Jenny's "invisible" handicap. Ruth and I watched the first audiologist test Jenny through a one-way mirror in a cold room in the basement of Yale–New Haven Hospital. We could not tell what the results were indicating. We were traumatized when he told us that Jenny was profoundly deaf because of physical damage to either her inner ear or to the nerves leading to the auditory cortex. The audiologist then predicted that Jenny would not benefit from hearing aids and that she would never acquire usable speech. He also claimed that not providing Jenny with "sign language"[2] immediately would retard her intellectual development and inevitably lead to serious mental illness. He presented these conclusions coldly, as if they were incontrovertible facts, rather than the biased opinion of a "manualist."

Centuries-old questions about how best to educate prelingually deaf children are still being debated acrimoniously by deaf educators. The polarized positions taken by the so-called "oralists" and "manualists" resemble religious wars. I quickly lost faith in their "expertise." There is an appalling lack of objective data to help parents decide whether a child who is deaf from birth or who lost his/her hearing before learning to talk should be taught speech or sign language. There is, for example, still no reliable method to determine the nature and extent of a prelingually deaf child's "residual hearing," as well as how much it could be amplified. Residual hearing is the term audiologists use to refer to the hearing that remains after a hearing loss. This hearing may be limited

---

[2] Sign language is a broad term that encompasses a variety of sign languages used with and among the deaf, for example, Seeing Essential English, Manual English, finger spelling, and American Sign Language (ASL). In contrast to the other systems, ASL is not a mere transliteration or visual representation of spoken English. Until recently, it was viewed by the hearing merely as a way of pantomiming using gestures. Thanks to the research of William Stokoe (1960), it is now recognized that ASL satisfies every linguistic criterion of a genuine language. It has a distinct lexicon and syntax as well as the capacity to generate an infinite number of propositions. Oliver Sacks (1989) discusses ASL in *"Seeing Voices"* in a way that can provide psychotherapists with a highly illuminating perspective on the emotional and cognitive development of the deaf, as well as the hearing.

to the ability to detect the presence of sound, or it may also include the ability to discriminate between sounds. People with similar audiograms may have very different speech discrimination abilities.

Three months after she began wearing a hearing aid, Jenny uttered her first word. It was "baby." Our joy was immense. This developmental landmark indicated, contrary to the first audiologist's predictions, that the new computerized hearing aids could provide Jenny with some usable sound. It also signaled that she was rapidly learning how to connect lip shapes to concepts. It appeared as though she might even be abundantly endowed with the talents required to transform noise into the sounds of speech. And so, in full knowledge that we were playing "Russian roulette" with Jenny's future, we decided to educate her orally. We dared to hope that someday Jenny might achieve linguistic competence and intelligible speech.

Owing to many factors, ambitious goals such as these can be realized only after many years of arduous effort, if at all. Binaural hearing aids amplify sound but do not, themselves, discriminate between messages, competing messages, or background noise. Even with maximum amplification, Jenny can hear only low frequency sounds, mostly vowels. Thus, for example, the word "impossible" might sound to her like "i-a-i-al." Imagine trying to learn a foreign language by listening to it spoken over a static-filled radio station. Under optimal circumstances, this is somewhat akin to the challenges Jenny experiences when trying to listen. A further complication is the fact that the linguistic information that can be extracted from the movements of a speaker's lips, even by experts, is often incomplete or misleading.

Sacks (1989) has likened lip reading to "a complex art of observation, inference and inspired guesswork" (p. 15). These mental abilities are a major component of lip reading because many speech elements and words look identical on the lips, although they sound quite different. To cite just a few examples, the letters "m," "p," and "b" look alike on the lips, as do "s" and "z." Unstressed syllables, articles, some prepositions, and many other entire words (for instance, "a," "the," "in," "at") are not usually visually detectable in speech presented at a normal conversational rate. To a lip reader, the words "baby" and "paper" are indistinguishable, as are "mama" and "papa." Even when a sentence provides contextual cues, it is maddeningly difficult to distinguish by lip reading the words "but," "bad," "ban," "mat," "mad," "man," and "pad." It has been estimated that, at best, deaf persons recognize three or four words for every ten that are spoken. Dolnick (1993) has, therefore, likened lip reading to filling in the blanks in a fast and ongoing crossword puzzle.[3]

---

[3] More extensive discussions of the information summarized above can be found in the works of Meadow (1980), Padden and Humphries (1988), Sacks (1989), and Peterson (1994).

Looking backward, Ruth and I now agree that it was "irrational" faith in Jenny that sustained our optimism during the many and recurrent periods when there seemed to be no visible progress toward linguistic competence and intelligible speech. I am convinced that, if it had not been for Ruth's untiring perseverance and unselfish devotion, Jenny would never have acquired the listening and speaking abilities that enable her to participate in *our* world, the hearing world. In the next section, I will begin to examine how the difficult tasks we imposed on Jenny, ourselves, Liz, our friends, and our relatives contributed to my continuing education as a therapist. To paraphrase an African proverb—the raising of a deaf child is so difficult that it requires the contributions of the entire village.

PERSONAL TRANSFORMATIONS

In 1973, the year Jennifer's deafness was confirmed, I was 34 years old. I was still very much in the process of personalizing and integrating the theoretical viewpoints of my teachers. My first psychotherapy supervisors were influenced primarily by Helmuth Kaiser (1965) and David Shapiro (1965), who in turn acknowledge their indebtedness to Wilhelm Reich (1949). My supervisors encouraged me to develop a refined sensitivity to the ways in which patients and therapists withdraw from intimate and collaborative dialogues. Kaiser placed authenticity of communication, rather than the creation and working through of insights, at the center of his theory of therapy. My own view, after many years of practice is that the search for the "truth" and the subjective experience of "truth-telling" each make a positive contribution to the success of psychotherapy and that they jointly set in motion various forms of experiential and interpersonal learning. Thus, I assume that, while promoting insight and/or authenticity, therapists provide their patients with repeated experiences of feeling understood, which in turn, activate the processes of internalization (Geller, 1987, 1994). Most broadly stated, a single, efficacious, communicative exchange can be conceived of as serving multiple therapeutic functions simultaneously.

When Jenny was born, a durable sense of myself as a "good-enough" therapist was in the process of becoming a more stable aspect of my professional identity, thanks in part to my experiences raising our daughter, Liz. With Liz, I was already learning that I was capable of loving unambivalently and unselfishly. The love I gave and the love I received from her supported my striving for maturity and virtue. I took to fathering Liz rather intuitively. Our first infant thrived on what came naturally and spontaneously to Ruth and me. Liz permitted us to nurture, comfort, and protect her. From birth onwards, she provided me with palpable evidence that I was capable of providing her with experiences that promoted her growth and development.

These affirmations were especially important to me during the earliest stages of my career, for they made it easier for me to tolerate the feelings of incompetence and fraudulence that inevitably accompany training to become a psychotherapist. They counteracted my inclination to interpret my difficulties in mastering the roles and functions of a psychotherapist as a negative reflection upon my character development. As my confidence regarding my capacity to be benignly influential grew, it became increasingly possible for me to use diminished, as well as amplified, feelings of therapeutic competence as information about the particular patient with whom I was working.

By contrast, raising Jenny from the very outset was often grueling, painful, and difficult. Early on, before Jenny's deafness was diagnosed, Ruth feared that there was something inaccessible, perhaps even "autistic," about her. Jenny seemed to disregard our efforts to soothe her. Liz loved eating. Jenny was lactose intolerant and suffered from severe colic. Liz was joyously active. Jenny was hyperactive. When frustrated, Liz got angry while Jenny, on the other hand, became rageful. Liz cried. Jenny screamed. Liz enjoyed going to sleep at night. Jenny had serious problems falling and staying asleep. Often, Jenny stayed up past midnight until she virtually collapsed. From ages three to ten, she regularly was awakened by nightmares and insisted on spending the rest of the night in our bed.

In short, our home felt like a residential treatment center under siege. The stress and fatigue Ruth and I had to deal with inevitably took their toll upon our marriage. So, too, did our frequent quarrels about the meaning and management of Jenny's sleep disorder. Ruth advocated the comfort provided by structure and routines, as well as by the setting of limits. I insisted that going to sleep fueled Jenny's intense separation and annihilation anxieties. Both perspectives were valid. Both were also incomplete, and as I came to realize, my own interpretation reflected to some degree the projection onto Jenny of the unfinished business of my own childhood. For example, my reactions to Jenny's deafness were anticipated by my reactions to her colic. I am told that, like Jenny, I suffered from severe colic during the first six months of my life. While little is known about the long-term developmental consequences of colic, my own speculations have led me to believe that whatever its origins, colic diminishes an infant's trust in his/her caretakers and leaves behind a legacy of sensory-dominated, presymbolic memories of being both alone and afraid. When activated, these memories enter awareness in the form of diffuse, intense, and "unnamed" somatic sensations. Like the inability to hear our loving voices, I believe Jenny's colic further diminished her capacity to call forth self-soothing representations when separated from us.

What remained constant throughout these chaotic years was Ruth and my shared love for Jenny, our commitment to Jenny, and our faith in Jenny. Moreover, Ruth and I were in agreement that Jenny's deafness was retarding her acquisition of the representational capacities required to differentiate, describe, and regulate emotional experiences. Jenny had not, after all, heard the human voice until she was almost 20 months old. She did not know that words existed or that everything—objects, actions, and abstractions—has a name. She did not begin speaking in syntactically organized sentences until she was three and a half. (Some analysts take this developmental achievement as signaling the beginnings of secondary process thought.) Furthermore, it took many years before Jenny could participate comfortably in the interactions that take place when we tell each other stories. For these and other reasons, misunderstandings and miscommunications were daily occurrences in our home.

MISUNDERSTANDING EVENTS IN PSYCHOTHERAPY

Misunderstandings are an ever-present danger when trying to communicate verbally with a profoundly deaf person. I shudder to think about the number of times that Jenny interpreted what we were asking of her "inaccurately" or "incorrectly." In turn, Jenny frequently experienced us as not understanding her needs and/or being unresponsive to them. From infancy until she was about eight and a half, Jenny had severe and prolonged temper tantrums in response to our perceived lapses of understanding. Efforts to console Jenny after these misunderstanding events often inadvertently intensified her frustration at not being understood. Jenny raging inconsolably until she collapsed in exhaustion was a recurrent feature of our average expectable environment. Like the girl in the nursery rhyme, when Jenny was good she was very, very good, and when she was bad, she was horrid. Lacking a shared vocabulary, I believe, exacerbated the expression of the more selfish and aggressive aspects of her nature and delayed her emergence from the "egocentrism" (Piaget, 1965) of early childhood.

Difficult as they were, these experiences impressed upon me how important it is for therapists and patients to attend with exquisite care to patients' reactions to feeling misunderstood (Geller, 1992; Geller and Rhodes, 1993). The analysand in Judith Rossner's (1983) novel *August* put it this way, "With a shrink a little mistake goes a long way" (p. 23).

Much remains to be learned about how to turn to advantage the interactional phenomena and intrapsychic processes set in motion by lapses of understanding on the part of therapists who are usually perceived as understanding. My evolving approach draws upon Greeson's (1967) discussion of mistakes or technical errors and on Kohut's (1971) formulations regarding empathic failures. It includes the following working clinical hypotheses.

I assume that therapists, for varying reasons, underestimate the frequency with which their patients feel misunderstood. Early in my career, I was sensitized to this possibility by Reich's (1949) assertion that every patient, without exception, begins therapy with a more or less explicit attitude of distrust or cynicism, which, as a rule, remains hidden. More recently, Rennie (1985) has documented that many patients do not signal, either verbally or affectively, that they are preoccupied with negative reactions to the therapists' characteristics or with their therapists' way of working because of timidity, deference to authority, and stereotyped politeness.

There is ample clinical evidence to indicate that there are consistent and psychologically important differences in the recognizability, intelligibility, and communicability of the feelings and memories triggered by empathic failures, narcissistic injuries, and the stresses of separation and loss (Geller, 1984, 1987). These reactions can span the range from the "objectless" and impotent rage of the frustrated infant to the subtle, refined, thoughtlike blend of anger and forgiveness experienced by adults who have achieved that attitude Levinson et al. (1978) refer to as "deillusionment." The present-day consensus among psychoanalytically informed clinicians is that patients who are suffering from narcissistic and borderline, as compared to normal-neurotic, levels of character pathology are vulnerable to experiencing disorganizing, grossly unmodulated, and conceptually obscure states of emotional upheaval when "disappointed" by valued others. In a like manner, I have found that much of what enters the awareness of such patients when they perceive that they have been misunderstood by their therapists is inchoate or undifferentiated with respect to its ideational and affective content, rather than merely disguised or denied.

Thus, a crucial diagnostic distinction that a therapist must make, at any given moment, is between reactions to feeling misunderstood, which are being kept "private" for fear of jeopardizing the relationship, and those for which patients' genuinely have no words. Incorrect assessment of these independent sources of silence and secrecy can further intensify a patient's suffering and reinforce the conviction that one's feelings are incomprehensible. As these diagnostic formulations are meant to further suggest, the precise framing of a therapist's verbal responses requires an ongoing assessment of the levels of symbolic functioning at which patient's reactions to lapses of understanding are being experienced and expressed.

HELPING PATIENTS TO COMMUNICATE

Especially during her early years, Jenny often felt as if she couldn't make herself comprehensible or understood. Until she could produce words intelligible to strangers, we served as Jenny's interpreters. As in the movie *Johnny Belinda*, people in our community often treated our little girl as if she were "a dummy." Even now, despite her remarkable academic successes, Jenny often refers to herself as "stupid." I feel actual sensations of pain whenever I think of how often Jenny had to reckon with feeling ignorant and learning disabled on route to acquiring linguistic competence.

These experiences impressed upon me the importance of inquiring as to whether a patient feels that he/she is participating in therapy competently and intelligently. What I am discovering is that many patients feel like "failures" at therapy itself. Feeling like a failure as a patient is, as I now realize, a normative aspect of the experience of individuals whom investigators refer to as "alexithymic" (Krystal, 1979; Geller, 1984). Alexithymic individuals suffer from extreme difficulties distinguishing feelings from body sensations and putting them into words. Consequently, like Jenny during her childhood, much of their experience remains "unformulated" (Sullivan, 1940). I am especially likely to observe Jenny's presence in my conscious and preconscious processes when I listen to such patients. It is she who has made it possible for me to identify directly and immediately with patients who are unable to describe their wishes and feelings vividly and "interestingly" (Geller, 1994). These identifications then find expression in the ways in which I help patients talk about the what, when, how and why of the more troublesome aspects of their lives.

Whenever possible, I try to help my patients achieve greater clarity and specificity regarding what they are experiencing. Not surprisingly, Ruth and I made prominent use of "clarifications" when conversing with Jenny. Clarifications essentially paraphrase, reflect, or summarize what has been communicated. At first, we found ourselves using clarifications when we were trying to make what was incomprehensible comprehensible. We used them to reassure her that what she had intended had actually been communicated. We used clarifications to validate her perception of "reality." Our clarifications would, we hoped, provide her with the reassurance that *we* took upon ourselves the primary responsibility for the failure of a communicative exchange.

Providing patients with clarifying descriptions of inner states strengthens their feeling that they are competently or successfully engaging in psychotherapy. For example, I rely on a clinical strategy Loewald (1978) refers to as "active mirroring," when patients' reactions to real and alleged lapses of understanding are inaccessible to self-reflection and verbalization. Active mirroring essentially refers to verbal responses that restate or translate the felt meanings inherent in a patient's communications into statements that are more explicit, concrete, "hot," and intimate or more well organized than are those used by the patient. By going beyond what a patient has said, active mirroring thus blends the qualities of clarifications with those of interpretations. I give center stage to this clinical

strategy when I am trying to help a patient transform vaguely apprehended negative reactions (e.g., "I felt upset . . . bad . . . weird . . . when
you misunderstood me") into more precise emotion-words (e.g., angry,
afraid, embarrassed, hurt). Nurturing the formation of affects that are
recognizable as being of one kind, and not another, helps the patient to
feel capable of expressing his/her pain articulately. Increased eloquence
reduces the intensity of painful emotions and makes them more available
for self-exploration. As Fenichel (1954) put it, words "tame" affects.

Active mirroring can, furthermore, be used to lend vitality to patients
who express their negative reactions to feeling misunderstood in a "disem-
bodied" fashion. When clinically indicated, I will translate words like
"anger" or "fear" into body-centered metaphors that stand closer to
the physicality of immediate experience. As an example, I will speak
of "a broken heart," "a lump in the throat," or "a pain in the neck"
when an intellectualizing patient speaks about failed love, sadness, or
anger.

In order to foster the creative and responsible use of language—two
of the cornerstones of effective psychotherapy—I try to voice all of my
interventions so that they affirm and highlight what a patient is trying to
accomplish, rather than what he/she is trying to avoid. For example, when
commenting on what a patient is resisting, I do not use terms such as
"running away" or "hiding," but rather talk about retreating to a safe
place.

The following vignette can be used to illustrate how these technical
principles inform my work as a psychotherapy supervisor. The dialogue
is an excerpt of the final minutes of the fourth hour of a course of
psychotherapy being conducted within the Yale Psychological Services
Clinic. The therapist is a fifth-year clinical psychology graduate student,
whom I am supervising. The patient is a 27-year-old single man who
recently returned home after spending 10 years in another city, to take a
managerial position in his father's very successful real estate business.
His father, whom he idealizes, is about to retire, and he and his brothers
are competing for power and the father's approval. What do you hear in
the following exchange?

P: I was thinking on the ride home last week that it feels like I just
    scratch the surface and then it's time to go. What are your
    thoughts or your policy here about meeting more often?

T: Do you feel like the issues you're bringing to therapy don't have
    the chance to get addressed adequately?

P: No. It's that there's a lot of background stuff that I feel like it's
    going to take a while to get through. Later on, I'd probably want
    to go back to meeting once a week.

T: So you feel in a hurry to get to some later phase of therapy?

P: I don't know. Maybe not. You're the boss—you tell me.

T: I don't think of myself as a boss. I view our work here as a
      collaborative endeavor. But that said, I'd like to suggest that we
      wait another two weeks, and then let's re-evaluate this issue again.
      I can understand how you might be impatient with this process.
      But it's often a slow one—and we really are in the beginning
      stages.

P: I am the kind of person who doesn't like to wait too long for
      things.

T: Uh-huh. At the same time, the therapy doesn't end at 8:30. Look
      at all of the thoughts and memories that were generated in here
      last week that you've been working over since then.

P: Sounds good. See you next week.

Because of the ambiguities inherent in language and the sheer number
of possible meanings of any complex statement, the patient's metaphor-
ical reference to "scratching the surface" and subsequent request for clarification regarding the therapist's thoughts or policy about increasing the
frequency of visits can be variously interpreted. Does his question represent a retreat from the direct expression of the wish to meet more
frequently? Is he deferring to the therapist's legitimate authority or
presumed greater knowledge about the benefits of various dosages of
therapy? Is he expressing impatience and disappointment in the process
of therapy? Is he criticizing the therapist for being superficial?

The therapist chose to ask the patient whether the issues he is bringing
to therapy are not getting adequately addressed. Alternative affirmative
wordings of this intervention might have been, "You are really eager to
get to the heart of things," or "Perhaps you both wish and fear that our
sessions will cut to the bone." Even interventions that challenge or call
into question a patient's expectations about how therapy works can be
stated affirmatively (Schafer, 1983). For example, in response to the
patient's saying that there is a lot of "background stuff" that he must get
through and that, once this is accomplished, he would want to go back
to meeting once weekly, the therapist decided to ask another question:
"So you feel in a hurry to get to some later phase of therapy?" Once
again, a less "accusatory" formulation of this idea is possible, for example,
"Perhaps you feel that my knowing a lot about your background (early
childhood?) is crucial to the success of your therapy? Maybe there are
other ways of thinking about this."

A follower of Kohut (1971) probably would argue for an intervention
that affirmed the patient's feeling that it is important to him that the therapist understand what led up to his current predicaments. What I wish
to emphasize here is that changes in stylistic choice might have strengthened the patient's confidence in his ability to use psychotherapy and his
sense of self-determination. I wonder what the fate of the session might
have been if the therapist had inquired whether the patient felt somehow

misunderstood, rather than asking him if his issues were not getting adequately addressed. The question, as posed, is an invitation to criticize the therapist's competence or expertise.

Let me weave in here a related issue raised by this clinical vignette. The patient reacted to the therapist's second question by retreating from his implied proposal and by emphasizing the inherently hierarchical nature of the patient–therapist relationship with respect to issues of authority and power: "You're the boss." My supervisee and I agreed that his reactions to the patient's deferring to his authority included a host of his own uncertainties about how to coordinate the exploratory, supportive, and managerial responsibilities inherent in the role of psychotherapist. In my experience, therapists-in-training tend to be more comfortable interpreting their patient's reactions to them as "authority figures" than with managing the fact that they are persons in positions of authority who are empowered to define when, where, and for how long they will meet with their patients.

DEAFNESS AND ALIENATION

The stance of "alienation" has always appealed to me. My exemplary sufferers include Holden Caulfield, James Dean, Jack Kerouac and the anti-heroes of Paul Simon's songs. I have romanticized the role of "outsider." With Jenny, the gravitational pull exerted upon me by these positive images of alienation began to lessen.

In her autobiography, Helen Keller (1990) wrote that "Blindness cuts one off from things. Deafness cuts one off from people" (p. 48). Jenny has experienced alienation in all of its painful incarnations. To me, Jenny's inability to hear the human voice is at the heart of the alienation she suffered during infancy. During adulthood, voice qualities are usually thought of as serving primarily to enhance or modify the meanings of words.[4] During infancy, vocal qualities are one of the primary vehicles through which parents communicate with their hearing offspring. Jenny was deprived of the pleasure-giving, protective, and adaptation-enhancing sounds of lovingness and the soothing tones of lullabies. I still feel the sadness of these facts in my throat and chest.

At the heart of Jenny's alienation during childhood was her severely curtailed ability to learn by listening to and telling stories. It wasn't until age seven that she discovered the difference between TV programs and commercials. Before she came to understand that plots organize stories, she created her own kinetic montages by rapidly changing TV channels.

---

[4] Research indicates that in many instances the acoustic properties of the voice are far more important than the actual words chosen in conveying attitudes an emotions. Voice qualities tell us, more or less precisely and directly, the extent to which an interactant is energized by, invested in, and moved emotionally by what he/she has said or heard (e.g., Rice and Kerr, 1986).

Narration involves far more than the exchange of information. Stories make it possible to express the idea of "necessity" or, in contrast, of "possibility." Negotiating endings or making transitions with Jenny was very difficult because we were unable to convey to her the temporal order of things. Trilling (1965) has observed, "It is in the nature of narration to explain. It cannot help tell how things are and even why they are that way" (p. 126). We could not enlist the aid of stories to serve these didactic purposes. For example, we could not read Jenny fairy tales or cautionary tales that illustrated our values.

When Liz was four, she began to ask her grandmother (my mother) to tell her "stories from her mouth" (not from a book). Their narrative content usually concerned my family's history. Liz loved most to hear anecdotes about my childhood or about the time my mother told my brother, Norman, that his great grandfather was a black slave to counteract a racist comment he had just made. Jenny was ignorant of this family tradition. This limited her sense of "kinship" and deprived her of the myths that organize my family's saga. Jenny's delayed language acquisition also deprived her of the opportunity to laugh with us at my father's jokes. Many of his jokes contained Yiddish expressions that signaled our family's religious heritage and cultural identity. This, too, was unknown to Jenny. At age 10, she asked me what the "Holly Bibble" was. I was stunned. She did not know about the existence and importance of the *Holy Bible*. This forced me to recognize, once again, the magnitude of Jenny's estrangement from the hearing world.

My efforts to combat Jenny's isolation, her underdeveloped sense of personal continuity and her limited storytelling capacities took many forms. For instance, in order to help Jenny develop a more integrated perspective on the evolution persons and relationships over time, we created family photograph albums. Like interconnected narratives, photographs that are arranged chronologically can reveal the relations that exist between what was, what is, and what will be. Most importantly, I became much more attentive to the informative and rhetorical, as compared to the merely expressive, functions of the nonverbal channels of communication. I do not think that I am overstating the case when I say that these experiences and experiments had a substantial impact on the evolution of my therapeutic style and on my abiding interest in harnessing those agents of therapeutic change that are less dependent on the more purely linguistic aspects of language.

THE EVOLUTION OF MY THERAPEUTIC STYLE

In therapy, as elsewhere, there are identifiable and broadly categorizable "styles" of communicating the fruits of one's listening. A therapist's communicative style and its variations can be discerned in the way in which he/she formulates answers to the following types of questions: How often should I speak? When and how should I exchange the positions of listener and speaker? How expressive can I permit my face to be? In what proportions should my presence express warmth or coolness, informality or formality, activity or passivity, spontaneity or restraint? To what extent should my communications expand on what patients have already said, as opposed to offering a new and different perspective on their experiences?

I struggle with these questions differently today than I did in 1971, the year my daughter Jenny was born. At the time, I called into the question the value of all "techniques." Like most existential analysts, I believed that a preoccupation with technique led to the "stylization" of the therapeutic dialogue and to a resultant dilution of its authenticity. On the other hand, I often felt uncertain about what stylistic choices to make for my patients, especially if they were "fragile" or "difficult." I frequently knew what I wanted to say to them before I found the appropriate voice for the occasion. Today, in order to maximize the possibilities of interacting authentically with my patients, I think consciously and systematically about the proper timing, sequencing, and use of clarifications, confrontations, and interpretations. This shift was parallel to and congruent with my very different experiences raising Liz and Jenny. Liz seemed to thrive on what came naturally and spontaneously to Ruth and me as parents, while extraordinary effort and a great deal of conscious strategizing were required to accommodate to Jenny's communicative requirements.

During communicative exchanges that are proceeding optimally, the activities of listening and talking are themselves taken for granted. They recede from awareness. This makes it possible to focus one's attention exclusively on the content of the conversation. Communicating with Jenny always did, and still does, bring into sharp focus the problematic aspects of the activities of listening and speaking themselves. Jenny's ongoing struggle, moreover, is a constant reminder that our capacity to understand one another is always incomplete and imperfect.

Jenny titled one of her recent paintings "I hear with my eyes." Vision is her principal source of knowledge about speech. Once I fully understood this, I became increasingly attentive to the positioning of my face vis-à-vis Jenny during communicative exchanges. Looking down or turning away severely curtails the clarity and intelligibility of the information received through lip reading. Concurrently, I became much more attentive to the ways in which I used gestures, postures, and facial expressions to communicate to her my thoughts and my feelings.

I can trace my greater facial expressiveness as a therapist to my efforts to find visual equivalents for the vocal qualities Jenny could not hear. I tried to communicate with my face the grunts, sighs, tones, murmurs, and other vocal qualities through which we give form to our feelings. I brought to awareness the didactic possibilities inherent in the games I had played, unselfconsciously, with Liz. For example, having a game of catch with Jenny became an opportunity to practice reciprocity. Like jazz singers, we sang scat and babbled together in rhythmic synchrony. I taught Jenny how to box and dance.[5] As previously noted, I also took primary responsibility for the success or failure of a communicative exchange with her.

At this point in my career as a psychotherapist, I possess a distinctive, consistent, and personally satisfying style of communicating with my patients. It can be characterized as "responsive," "expressive," "demonstrative," and "conversational." I do not think that I am deceiving myself in suggesting that the experiences described above moved me in this direction. I also do not think it is too fanciful to claim that Jenny stimulated my interest in the formidable technical challenges posed by patients who are unable to receive the sensuous fullness of the therapeutic dialogue. Jenny alerted me to the possibility that patients' problems processing sensory information are an often overlooked impediment to therapeutic progress. Her inability to hear the human voice sensitized me to the importance of assessing my patients' capabilities for receiving, storing, and recalling the verbal and nonverbal aspects of the therapeutic dialogue. I began posing to myself such questions as: How many sensory systems are effectively called into play when X is in the presence of his/her therapist? What range of sensory experiences are aroused in X when listening to his/her therapist? What do patients look at while they are listening? How does X coordinate looking and listening? What sensory modalities does X rely on when constructing mental models of the therapeutic relationship?

I now accord patients' difficulties processing sensory information a prominent place in my evolving theory of therapy. One of its conceptual starting points is that the cognitive styles patients bring to therapy can exert a restrictive influence on the distinctiveness and variety of their sensory experiences.[6]

---

[5] I find it almost karmic that I brought to my experiences with Jenny a working knowledge of the ways in which dance therapists use sensorimotor dialogues to establish a sense of relatedness with otherwise noncommunicative schizophrenic patients (Geller, 1978).

[6] My experience as a psychotherapy supervisor suggest that the sensory processing of therapists-in-training tends to favor incoming auditory stimulation. A concern with understanding what patients are saying or are hesitant or unable to verbalize may inherently bias therapists' sensory awareness in the direction of audition. Moreover, in the psychotherapy literature, information that is available to therapists' "eyes" tends to be regarded merely as an ancillary source of data about patients. I believe the well-educated therapists' observational skills are as well developed as are his/her listening skills.

In the therapeutic situation, psychopathology often reveals itself in the form of difficulty "listening." Difficulties with listening are, for example, commonplace among patients whom Bowlby (1973) would designate "insecurely attached." Compulsively self-reliant patients experience themselves, for example, as turning to their therapists more fully for help when they are listening, as compared to when they are talking. In order to deal with their anxieties about becoming dependent on their therapist, compulsively self-reliant patients tend to impose, prematurely, their own meanings on what their therapists are saying. I do not take it for granted that they are open to receiving the "supportive" aspects of my communications. On the other hand, I now often take it as a signal of a growing readiness to ask for and to take in help when a compulsively self-reliant patient tells me, "I'm not getting any better."

A compulsively care-seeking attachment style also interferes with effective listening. Compulsive care-seekers feel under a constant pressure to pay close attention to everything their therapists have to say. This makes it particularly difficult for them to think about what has already been heard or to attend to the felt internality of their own experience. To paraphrase Lacan (1966), whereas compulsively self-reliant patients begin therapy by listening to themselves without listening to their therapists, compulsive care-seekers begin therapy listening to their therapists without listening to themselves.

Variations can also be discerned in the ways in which patients process information available to their "eyes." Some are "blind" to the meanings, attitudes, and feelings conveyed by their therapists' facial expressions, gestures, and postures. Those who are fearful of affect-laden face-to-face contact cannot see whether or not their therapists' facial expressions say, "Yes, I am listening," "Yes, I am present," "Yes, we are together," and "Yes, I am interested in you." Deprived of this information, they remain uncertain as to whether their therapist is conveying "serious interest" and "sympathetic understanding." This uncertainty can significantly undermine the therapy. Indeed, Freud (1912) proposed that offering patients serious interest and sympathetic understanding laid the groundwork for what we now call the "therapeutic alliance."

Jenny has told me that, when she turns off her hearing aids, the way things look to her is also transformed. Her return to silence is often accompanied by a reduction in the speed with which objects and persons appear to be moving. At the extremes, this slowing down process feels to Jenny as if the world is "dying." What these anecdotes are meant to suggest is that the interdependence of looking and listening must be taken in consideration when trying to understand a patient's experience of the therapeutic dialogue. To illustrate: A female patient recently told me a dream in which a former teacher is reading her a poem. In the dream, she is seated behind him, and they are facing away from each other. Her first association to the back-to-back seating arrangement was that it felt both "highly personal and impersonal." She stated further that the positioning of their bodies made it easier for her to attend to the "message" and "not the messenger." What we are coming to understand is that the anxieties associated with seeing and being seen interfere with her ability to listen.[7] Furthermore, it was only when she was relieved of the anxieties of looking at me that she could begin to look *within*. As she is further realizing, when wishing to look *in* on her own thoughts and feelings, she sometimes merely looks *at* her behavior evaluatively. The difference between these two modes of self-observation is as great as the distance traveled between saying, "I'm not dead" and "I am alive."

TRAGEDY, PITY, AND ACTIVE MIRRORING

Psychotherapists are frequently called upon to help patients face and deal with the tragic aspects of living. My current caseload includes a mother who is grieving the death of a beloved infant daughter, a social worker who was sexually abused by her father, an impaired physician who sexually abused one of his patients, and a young musician who is dying from a rare and incurable heart disease. I take it as an a priori assumption that who I *am*, or what I am capable of experiencing is as important as what I *do* in determining whether I will be able to help these patients move through the process of mourning. To illustrate this conviction, I offer the hypothesis that, to the extent that a therapist is threatened by experiencing "pity," his/her capacity to clarify or give meaning to suffering and misfortune will be curtailed. I doubt whether I would have come to this particular belief if Jenny hadn't put me in touch with my most vulnerable "selves." Unless I am deceiving myself, Jenny taught me something about how not to shrink away from problems that can neither be altered by doing nor avoided by not doing. Like inoperable deafness, some forms of psychopathology cannot be "cured." Their devastating consequences can, however, be mitigated if we can learn to manage and contain the painful feelings that they awaken.

Until I had to reckon with Jenny's deafness, I had little appreciation of what I didn't know about the emotional consequences of being caught up in a tragic situation. Prior to Jenny's diagnosis, I had experienced, during my adulthood, only superficial levels of despair, disappointment, and terror. I paid lip service to the notion that "bad things happen to

---

[7] Another female patient taught me that, when speaking, a patient may paradoxically feel invisible. According to my patient, she compulsively engaged in lengthy monologues when feeling anxious or ashamed in order to create the illusion that she was hidden behind a wall of sound.

good people, for no good reason, all the time." But since that time, I have learned to live with the awful burden of unanswerable questions. The origins and causes of Jenny's deafness are not known. On occasion, I fill the vacuum with self-punitive/blaming fantasies about the unforeseen consequences of my actions. In my youth, I inhaled.

Seneca (quoted in Moffat, 1992) was right, "Great grief is dumb" (p. 21). In the weeks following Jenny's diagnosis, I was rendered mute by the intensity of my sorrow. I felt wordless in the face of my raw emotions. I felt like a helpless "victim." I felt condemned and abandoned by God. I fell prey to intense self-pity, and for the first time in my adulthood, I felt that people were making me, not only Jenny, the object of their pity.

As defined by dictionaries, the word *pity* literally means "to suffer with," as do its synonyms, sympathy and compassion. Nevertheless, antipathy toward pity and self-pity are recurrent themes in our culture. The positive meanings once ascribed to pity are nowadays attributed only to sympathy and compassion. For example, the deaf poet David Wright (1969) has written that pity "is a sentiment that deceives its bestower and disparages its recipient. . . . Its acceptance not only humiliates, but actually blunts the tools needed to best the disability. To accept pity means taking the first step towards the self pity, thence to the finding, and finally the manufacture, of excuses. The end-product of self-exculpation is the failed human being, the 'victim'" (p. 8).

Jenny helped me to reclaim the original, positive meaning of pity. My bias is that all human beings need both to pity and to be pitied throughout their lives. Wisdom, according to Jewish thought, is associated with an all-forgiving pity toward humanity and a wry sense of humor regarding human weaknesses. Jenny's disability forced me to recognize that we are all bound together by shared vulnerability. I feel a certain kind of solidarity with those whose suffering is caused by vice, depravity, and deficiencies of will. To die alone is, in a sense, everybody's fate. As Coleridge (1977) put it, "Pity is best taught by fellowship in woe." In becoming the object of pity, I began to realize that one can feel pity towards someone who is not otherwise pitiful or pathetic. That others "felt sorry" for me did not undermine my sense of self-as-agent. Because I evoked pity in others, I took my own suffering more seriously. Sometimes my self-pity represented the first step toward empathizing with the enormity of my predicament. Nothing softens a man's sense of ironic detachment more than the felt inability to protect his handicapped child.

Although it is not the full explanation, I recognize a connection between these transformative experiences and my current interest in the technical problems and countertransference issues encountered in the psychotherapy of patients who are unable to receive, without conflict, their therapist's help or caring concern. I have begun to explore whether patients and therapists are capable of distinguishing between pity, sympathy, and compassion. My own emotional reactions to a patient's suffering or misfortunes usually include a complex blend of pity, sympathy, and compassion. Although conceptually and introspectively distinguishable, pity, sympathy, and compassion all seem to emerge from the same matrix of biophysiological states. I cannot detect a highly distinctive pattern of autonomic activity for each of these emotional states. On any particular occasion, they may be of equal strength or aggregate in various configurations. Pity tends to be salient when patients are in the grip of powers and forces they cannot control, and I am resonating with the magnitude of their misfortune, rather than with their strengths, sensitivities, and resilience. Whether experienced singularly or in combination with sympathy and compassion, I have found that pity can facilitate my efforts to understand, empathically, a patient's suffering.

Responses to my inquiries about such experiences seem to indicate that most of my colleagues share the modern disdain for pity, and consequently, they are threatened when they recognize that they are experiencing pity towards a patient. My experiences as a psychotherapy supervisor have led me to conclude that therapists-in-training who hold a predominantly negative view of pity have particular difficulty empathizing with their patients' suffering, especially if they believe that the suffering was "caused" by the patients' own actions or is being used strategically to "manipulate" others.

I have also been trying to determine whether or not there are subtle "meta-messages" that enable recipients to determine whether the other is expressing pity, sympathy, or compassion. At present, I am moving towards the conclusion that all expressions of caring and concern, regardless of how they are intended, are potentially ambiguous with respect to the respective strength of these feeling states. Some patient's difficulties in receiving their therapist's empathy, I now believe, cannot be fully understood without taking into account that there are no unequivocal cues that distinguish the expression of pity, sympathy, and compassion. To the extent that a patient fails to make these distinctions, he/she may experience any expression of caring concern as disempowering, patronizing, stigmatizing, foreboding, limiting, demeaning, or belittling. In my experience, devoting attention to uncovering the meanings, functions, and consequences of this potent source of misunderstandings—for both patients and their therapists—may be the first step toward the establishment of a therapeutic alliance. Conversely, neglecting this task can give rise to therapeutic impasses or to the breaking off of treatment.

EPILOGUE

In this chapter, I have attempted to establish linkages between my experiences raising my daughter Jenny and my views about the barriers to contact and communication encountered in psychotherapy. While struggling to bring it to a natural conclusion, I recalled that psychoanalyses are rarely, if ever, "complete" (Freud, 1937) and that the termination of a particular therapy should not imply the cessation of the therapeutic process. I also paused, remembering the day I delivered an earlier version of the chapter.

On that occasion, Jenny and five of her deaf college friends were in the audience, as were Ruth and Liz. I had hired an interpreter who translated my lecture into American Sign Language. Love and work came together on that triumphant day. Since then, we have been humbled again by the emergence of the new and ever changing tasks that are being dealt with by each of the members of our family. It is for this reason that I aspire to practice psychotherapy in a way that honors Kafka's (1961) overarching conclusion that "the decisive moment in human development is continuous" (p. 55).

REFERENCES

Bowlby, J. (1973), *Attachment and Loss, Vol. 2: Separation.* New York: Basic Books.

Coleridge, S. T. (1977), *Portable Coleridge.* New York: Viking.

Dolnick, E. (1993), Deafness as culture. *Atlantic Monthly,* 272:37–53.

Fenichel, O. (1954), *Collected Papers* (first series). New York: Norton.

Freud, S. (1912), Recommendations to physicians practising psychoanalysis. *Standard Edition,* 12:109–120. London: Hogarth Press, 1958.

—— (1937), Analysis terminable and interminable. *Standard Edition,* 23:216–253. London: Hogarth Press, 1964.

Geller, J. D. (1978), The body, expressive movement, and physical contact in psychotherapy. In: *The Power of the Human Imagination,* ed. J. Singer & K. Pope. New York: Plenum Press, pp. 347–377.

—— (1984), Moods, feelings, and the process of affect formation. In: *Emotions in Health and Illness,* ed. L. Temoshok, L. S. Zegens & C. Van Dyne. Orlando, FL: Grune and Stratton, pp. 171–186.

—— (1987), The process of psychotherapy: Separation and the complex interplay among empathy, insight and internalization. In: *The Psychotherapy of Separation and Loss,* ed. J. B. Feshbach & S. Feshbach. San Fransisco: Jossey-Bass, pp. 459–579.

—— (1992), *The Meanings and Uses of Misunderstandings in Psychotherapy.* Society for Psychotherapy Research 24th Annual Meeting, Berkeley, CA.

—— & Rhodes, R. (1993), A task analytic approach to studying the resolution of misunderstanding events in psychotherapy. Grant application: Fund for Psychoanalytic Research.

—— (1994), The psychotherapist's experience of interest and boredom. *Psychotherapy,* 31:3–17.

Geller, T. (1984), Thank you for Jenny. *Parents Magazine,* 59:66–67.

Greenson, R. R. (1967), *The Technique and Practice of Psychoanalysis, Vol. 1.* New York: International Universities Press.

Kafka, F. (1961), *Parables and Paradoxes.* New York: Random House.

Kaiser, H. (1965), *Effective Psychotherapy: The Contributions of Helmuth Kaiser.* New York: Free Press.

Keller, H. (1990), *The Story of My Life.* New York: Bantam.

Kohut, H. (1971), *The Analysis of the Self.* New York: International Universities Press.

Krystal, H. (1979), Alexithymia and psychotherapy. *Amer. J. Psychother.*, 33:17–31.

Lacan, J. (1966), *Écrits*. London: Tavistock.

Levinson, D. J., Darrow, C., Klein, E., Levenson, M. & McKee, B. (1978), *The Seasons of a Man's Life*. New York: Knopf.

Loewald, H. (1978), *Psychoanalysis and the History of the Individual*. New Haven, CT: Yale University Press.

Meadow, K. P. (1980), *Deafness and Child Development*. Berkeley: University of California Press.

Moffat, M. J. (1992), *In the Midst of Winter*. New York: Vintage Books.

Padden, C. & Humphries, T. (1988), *Deaf in America: Voices from a Culture*. Cambridge, MA: Harvard University Press.

Peterson, P. (1994), *Mother Father Deaf: Living Between Sound and Silence*. Cambridge, MA: Harvard University Press.

Piaget, J. (1965), *Moral Judgments of the Child*. New York: Free Press.

Reich, W. (1949), *Character Analysis*. New York: Orgone Institute Press.

Rennie, D. L. (1985), *Client Deference in the Psychotherapy Relationship*. Society for Psychotherapy Research 16th Annual Meeting, Evanston, IL.

Rice, L. & Kerr, J. (1986), Measures of client and therapist vocal quality. In: *The Psychotherapeutic Process: A Research Handbook*, ed. L. Greenberg & W. Pinsoff. New York: Guilford, pp. 73–105.

Rossner, J. (1983), *August*. New York: Houghton-Mifflin.

Sacks, O. (1989), *Seeing Voices: A Journey into the World of the Deaf*. Berkeley: University of California Press.

Schafer, R. (1983), *The Analytic Attitude*. New York: Basic Books.

Shapiro, D. (1965), *Neurotic Styles*. New York: Basic Books.

Stern, D. B. (1983), Unformulated experience, *Contemp. Psychoanal.*, 10:71–99.

Stokoe, W. C. (1960), *Sign Language Structure: An Outline of the Visual Communication System of the American Deaf*. Studies in linguistics, occasional papers, 8. Department of Anthropology and Linguistics, University of Buffalo, New York.

Sullivan, H. S. (1940), *Conceptions of Modern Psychiatry*. New York: Norton.

Trilling, L. (1965), *Sincerity and Authenticity*. Cambridge: Harvard University Press.

Woodward, J. (1972), Implications for sociolinguistic research among the deaf. *Sign Lang. Studies*, 1:1–7.

Wright, D. (1969), *Deafness*. New York: Stein & Day.

9

When the Therapist Divorces

PETER J. SCHLACHET

My wife and I had shared an office suite before our separation; our respective patients had regularly encountered the other's and observed that the other office in the suite was occupied. Since we had previously practiced out of our home apartment, all patients were aware that we were a couple, and various of my patients, at least, would comment from time to time, in one fashion or another, on my wife's ongoing presence and their reactions to our being together. The office arrangement was a constant stimulus for transference reactions, both positive and negative.

When we separated, it was agreed that I would temporarily move into the office suite, while she moved her office to another location. The rooms of the suite were arranged so that the one I would use as the sleeping area could be a closed-off, unobtrusive space. Nevertheless, my patients were, from one day to the next, faced with a change in what they encountered with each visit: the configuration was different; something was altered; there was no longer traffic around that other office. Even though I made no overt remark about these changes, questions quite naturally followed, and I was confronted, without being properly prepared for it, with difficult choices: with steering between the Scylla of undermining my patients' perceptions of reality and the Charybdis of burdening them with the incipient tragedy brewing in my personal life, a burden with which I already felt myself to be severely encumbered.

Never mind the pain of my separation and impending divorce: beyond the misery with my changed circumstances was the nagging feeling that I was perhaps in some way culpable, that these events represented some profound shortcoming of my own which my patients would surely discern, or about which they would at least query me. Not only was the searing shame which such thoughts evoked a source of intense distress, but how could I now help my patients with their relationships when beset by doubts that I could sustain my own? And would they not confront me with these same questions? The temptation to hide was acute, even though I was cognizant of the fact that, as Grunebaum (1993) correctly observes, "not telling the patient is not a neutral action." I did not know at the time that even more severe trials were in store for me.

I was confronted with the question of how I construed the analytic situation and what was properly and appropriately to be encompassed within its frame. Yet how could I continue to care for my patients and their needs in light of these feelings and considerations?

Nevertheless, I opted to reveal as little as possible to them, to say nothing, and to respond with content only when patients' reality testing hung in the balance. On contemplation, my conviction emerged clearly in focus that the analytic ambiance requires certain constant properties in order for its mutative impact to materialize. Greenson (1967) emphasizes its predictable nature: both patient and analyst need to know how events in the consultation are to transpire. The adventure of exploration into the unknown realms of the unconscious, like Verne's famous expedition into the bowels of the earth, already entails more than enough thrills and perils. As a minimum, the dimensions and specifications of the vessel and the nature of its crew must be familiar, consistent, reliable. That companions in this hazardous enterprise can be trusted and relied upon to provide aid, comfort, and assistance as needed is essential. A sense of safety engendered by the collaborator and the external surroundings is requisite to encourage risking the hazardous inward journey.

In addition, that collaborator must convey a certain stance, the "analytic attitude" (Schafer, 1983), for the patient to feel safely held during the rigorous exertions of the work. The analyst's empathic stance (Schafer, 1983; Greenson, 1967; Kohut, 1971) is an essential facet of this posture, as is the "evenly hovering attention" (Freud, 1912), by which he/she remains attuned to the variety of conscious and unconscious currents and interchanges constantly transpiring in the situation.

Crucial for this to occur, however, is the suspension of the analyst's narcissistic needs. There are very few circumstances in life in which we completely suspend our own self-interested concerns: the analyst in the analytic situation is one of them. Patients' concerns and preoccupations, their experience, feelings, thoughts, fantasies, attachments, aversions— in fact, everything about them which illuminates their human condition— are the sole concern of the analyst. Even the analyst's own inner experience becomes, in this situation, part of the finely tuned receiving instrument whose sole purpose is to further illuminate every facet of the patient's inner and outward life and style. Abend (1986) puts it this way:

> We are obliged to sharply curtail the instinctual gratifications permissible in our interactions with patients, to maintain a uniquely difficult kind of attention, delicately poised between the patient's productions and our own internal psychic activities, and to sustain a genuine neutrality toward whatever each analysand brings forth, regardless of our personal preferences, ethics, and values [p. 564].

Such is the ideal. But Abend (1986) also adds this proviso: "On the face of it, it is inconceivable that any one of us can sustain an optimum level of functioning in anything remotely like an absolutely unvarying state" (p. 564).

What happens, then, when the analyst is so preoccupied, so distracted by the impingement of unbearable life circumstances on these concentrated mental processes that this intense focus becomes too difficult to maintain consistently? It seems almost inevitable that patients will notice. Mine did. I was faced with comments such as, "You aren't with me today," or "You seem distracted." Of course, they were quite accurate.

In past decades, thinking about influences on the analytic situation had keen concentrated primarily on one or another facet of the patient's behavior or circumstance: patient-generated factors. The effect of direct situational alterations interpolated by the analyst may perhaps have been acknowledged, at least insofar as their impact on transference responses were concerned: changed circumstances such as a new receptionist, a new office-mate, a renovation, or a changed office location. But the fact that therapists, in addition to their potent impact within the therapeutic transaction, also have private lives and that those lives can similarly have an impact, both directly and indirectly, on events transpiring in the consultation room has not, to my mind, been sufficiently recognized or appreciated. The "blank screen," considered to be blank not merely with respect to what was to be etched upon it, but also with respect to what would emanate from it, is being shown more and more to be an illusion. Norcross and Prochaska (1986) remark that "the penchant for viewing psychotherapists as not having lives outside the consultation room afflicts our patients as well as ourselves" (p. 111). As the act of observing affects the quantum theoretical observation in physics, so the life and nature of the analyst impacts the events in the analytic consultation room.

More recently, literature has begun to burgeon—of which this book is one example—mirroring an increasing concern with the impact on the therapeutic or analytic situation of variables generated by the analyst and the analyst's life circumstances. As far as I have been able to discern, however, this literature deals largely with *forces majeurs, colpe del destino, Schicksalschlaege,* blows struck by fate, events that underscore our humanness, our frailties and our temporality, those slings and arrows to which we are all prey, caretakers no less than patients. We all become ill at one time or another; we all age; we all lose loved ones; and many of us have children—happily or otherwise.

While one could arguably claim that we have a direct influence on our own health and well-being—to a greater or lesser degree—and that we may affect those of our loved ones, with the exception of the last listed situation, these are not conditions for which any of us can take too much responsibility. And the last is, under most conditions, ordinarily considered a "joyful event." Not too much here to tweak the superego or to engender much finger pointing.

Furthermore, when the analyst is ill, the effect is often patent and apparent. Depending on the severity and type of illness, it may be potentially discernible to the patient or even recognizable for what the problem is.

Recently, I broke a leg—for the second time in a two-year span—and both my cast and my crutches were abundantly obvious to my patients. Their varying responses, highly indicative both of their transference feelings and their psychodynamics, were equally obvious, ranging from intense concern and preoccupation regarding my condition, both immediate and chronic, to total obliviousness.

When the analyst is pregnant, it may be similarly apparent to patients, although the nature of their reactions—or lack of them—can clearly mirror their transference responses to this new form of input to the analytic interchange. Analogously, they may become aware of the more subtly altered situation in which the therapist's capacity to function may fluctuate or become diminished by one or another kind of psychological or emotional transformation.

The patient's cognizance, conscious or otherwise, is thus: "Something has happened to the doctor. He/she is different in some way." The attributions with regard to the reason for or the nature of the change can, of course, vary enormously, from astonishingly sensitive discernments of the true state of affairs, all the way to total fantasy fabrications having no bearing whatsoever on the real nature of the situation. Blame can also quite naturally be very much a part of the reaction, since patients can easily experience lapses of whatever kind in the physical or mental presence of the analyst, as intentional negligence, indifference, or even abuse on the doctor's part. However, the analyst is mostly spared the onus of self-blame for such circumstances and can quite confidently maintain that "I was not party to what was inflicted on me by an unkind fate, even though I have to endure it and try, despite it, to tend to my patients' needs to the best of my ability and even though I know that it has some kind of impact on our joint endeavor."

But how is one to construe a situation where this cannot be said, where such analytic self-exoneration is not possible? How then is the therapist to respond to patients' reactions to these iatrogenic changes introduced into the sanctity of the consultation room or to their accurate observations of alterations in the attitude, concentration, empathy, capacity, or circumstances of the doctor? The problem of disclosure emerges as particularly difficult around patients' observations, questions, or reactions to changes such as these when the therapist also has decidedly mixed feelings about them: a fine line must be navigated between validating a patient's sense of reality, on the one hand, and the temptation either to confess and to seek absolution, or to deny responsibility or deviation, on the other. Such a quandary is potentially presented when the analyst divorces.

That many similarities exist between the types of situations I have posited will nevertheless be immediately apparent. Dewald (1994) astutely observes that

> reactions to any significant life event are only partly related to the nature of the event itself. The therapist's prior personality organization, the residual internal psychic conflicts that the therapist experiences and the nature of the adaptive and/or defensive style used to cope with them, the prior personal and professional experiences he or she has had . . . and elements in the therapist's current life situation will all influence [his/her] responses [p. 222].

This could as easily have been written about divorce as about illness, even though it addresses the latter. In fact, many of the observations that authors have made about the impact of illness in the analyst and the powerful concerns which it raises comprise equally accurate appraisals of the repercussions of the analyst's dissolving marriage. They have cited the momentous consequences of the intense stress, worries about the ability to function adequately; about the analyst's continuing positive self-perception, both as a person and as an effective professional; about one's stamina and capacity to endure; and about the need to continue working during the impacting experience, despite doubts about one's ability to do so. The importance of sustaining environmental structures is cited by Schwartz (1987), who states that, in the context of illness, "Underlying supporting structures ideally include a gratifying intimate life, a retrospective and prospective sense of personal history, and a view . . . only slightly clouded by denial" (p. 659). The perceived need on the therapist's part to continue working in the context of illness is recognized by Grunebaum (1993), who writes that

> motives therapists have for [continuing] working [despite illness] include self-esteem, the need to prove oneself competent and intact, fears and anxieties, and (as with other self-employed individuals) the fact that income depends directly on the number of hours worked [pp. 30–31].

These observations hold equally true in both kinds of life-disrupting situations, as much for illness as for divorce.

This chapter is intended to explore the impact and ramifications of the latter of these traumatic life events on the therapist and on the continuing therapeutic process in both individual and group therapy. I have endeavored to portray some of my experiences in the context of a bitter, long drawn out and traumatic divorce proceeding, throughout which I continued to work with my patients, and to examine how these experiences impacted both on my capacity to work with them in ongoing therapy and on the therapeutic process itself.

As my protracted divorce action dragged on, I would return to my office on numerous days directly from meetings with lawyers or from numberless interminable court hearings during which, in addition to having to endure humiliating and denigrating comments from opposing lawyers (such is, after all, their stock in trade) and from an inordinately sadistic and abusive judge, I was faced with potentially devastating financial jeopardy. I was indeed distracted, preoccupied, worried, often enraged at the callous and destructive character of court officials and of the incessant legal proceedings I had been forced to endure.

The very self-same concerns articulated by authors around illness became mine: How could I continue to feel competent and maintain a certain amount of self-esteem in the face of this onslaught? Could I sustain the financial burdens with which I was threatened, and would my practice be sufficient to meet them? Would I have the stamina to endure endless legal wranglings and still have enough vitality left to give my patients the undivided and unswerving attention they deserved and required?

Intrusions into that empathic and attentional bond took many forms. It was difficult not to relive the antagonisms I had left only minutes before; it was a challenge to calm the affronts and the rages they engendered, a problem to put aside the intricacies of legal maneuvers that promised pitfalls on every side. Memories of bitter scenes and confrontations would interpose themselves, especially when patients spoke about related matters. A patient described a fight with her husband: I recalled a particularly bitter one with my wife. Then the immense challenge of seeing the scene through her eyes, of not identifying with the husband, would erupt! It required of me the most resolute concentration, the most intense energy, even a certain amount of affective isolation, in order to continue the work at all in a reasonably balanced manner.

Parenthetically, that particular patient was able, in the context of our work, to achieve enough strength and perspective on her marriage to a sadistic and neglectful husband to ultimately divorce him. Although I had never consciously given any indication of my situation, she had heard about my divorce from another patient, one who had a special talent for ferreting out scuttlebutt about virtually anyone. Even though she was not able to articulate an identification with me—and she needed to precipitate her breakup indirectly, rather than to forthrightly sever the alliance— I believe that an unconscious emulation was one important element (of many) in her mustering enough strength to finally actualize what she had long wished for.

Even though I felt I had no choice but to carry on, I did decide that I could not burden my patients with my own colossally distressing situation. That would detract far too much from the purpose of our meetings: to heal their problems in living, not mine. But while I volunteered no information and provided what seemed to me virtually none, even in the face of direct questions, I could at least affirm their reality: I could—and did—validate their perceptions of change and of my state of mind when they commented on them, and, at times, apologized in that context for having let them down when I felt that was warranted. Some were able to express gratitude at the affirmation and relief in knowing that my inattention, when it happened, was not attributable to them: it was not that they were boring, uninteresting, disgusting, hopeless, or any of the numerous other things they might have thought, feared, or imagined. Often, this validation led us directly to secretly harbored, yet nameless, images of themselves, ways of experiencing themselves, learned in the painful and damaging contexts of dysfunctional parental families, which guided and determined their perceptions of every personal interaction, and which embodied the certainty of their sense that something about them was indescribably despicable. They could realize in our exchanges what they could not discern before: that so often it was not they who determined the responses they observed, but rather the idiosyncrasies of the other, that their perceptions occurred through faulty lenses and that these could be corrected.

In the group therapy setting, there is somewhat more flexibility inherent than in individual therapy: the group is often supportive, effective, and immensely helpful to the therapist—as is often said, the leader's best co-therapist. In that venue, my distractions and ruminations were less apparent and less intrusive for the members as they worked with one another, although I suspected that the somber atmosphere that pervaded my groups, on occasion, could well have been the result of my moody contribution. In that arena, with all the participants in clear view of one another, the subtle communication of feelings and attitudes by anyone present can often have a profoundly determining impact on the character of the group ambiance and the direction of the group's associations.

Possibly, it was because my groups meet later in the evening so that some lapse of time between the onslaught of courts and lawyers could provide a grateful insulation, not the headlong breathless dash from the degrading judicial setting to instantly compose myself as the authoritative, respected therapist in individual consultation—some hiatus interposed to regain my equilibrium and concentration, to reconsolidate my identity as a skilled professional. Perhaps not surprisingly, therefore, I found the articulation of this moody effect emanating from myself to arise notably more readily in the individual sessions than in the group sessions—until one fateful evening. The Intrusions on the sanctity of the consultation room were destined not to be limited to those introduced by either me or my patients.

My office is not usually locked when I am working. This policy facilitates patients letting themselves into the waiting area of the office suite without having to disturb me in session and saves my having to interrupt my work to admit them, a standing practice which was well known to my wife and had been shared by her when we had used the office together.

The bitterness of our lengthy divorce proceedings had escalated; the legal maneuvers burgeoned, with meetings, conferences, motions, and court orders multiplying geometrically and papers perpetually being served on one or the other side. One evening, as I was leading one of my groups at its customary day and time, the outside door of the office suite suddenly slammed—an exceedingly unusual event and one that startled both the group and myself. Immediately thereafter, a sharp knock sounded on the group room door. The group fell silent in tense alarm. Springing out of my chair, I flung open the door to confront my wife's best friend framed in the doorway, brandishing a legal document. This she thrust into my hand while uttering a few choice expletives and whirled to leave.

Momentarily tetanized with shock, outrage, and fury, and finding myself torn between wanting to annihilate her, but not wanting to have either that feeling or this intensely personal occurrence be exposed to or intrude on the group, wanting at the same time to protect the group from this mortifying horror, I exited the room and closed the door behind me as calmly as I could while I fumed at her, whispering through clenched teeth in rage and humiliation. How could she, herself a therapist, so violate the seclusion of the therapeutic sanctum, to trespass so brazenly on its privacy! In truth, I wanted to throttle her on the spot, but I also had to return to my group. We were, after all, in the middle of a session.

Opting to let her live, fighting to compose myself and to control my volcanic emotions, I reentered the group room. The group was still sitting in stunned silence, waiting for a cue from me. As I entered, however, they erupted into questions and irate expostulations: What was that about? Who was that person? How dare they intrude in this manner? What an outrage! Is anything wrong? Am I all right? I must have been white as a sheet. All I could think to do was to reassure them and to attempt to calm their quite realistic fears. And then the aftermath: Is the group safe? Can the sanctity of the group room be trusted? Has their confidentiality been irrevocably violated?

My first responsibility, I thought, was to alleviate their anxiety, to assure them that I had neither abrogated nor relinquished my role and function as group leader. To attempt to continue the group as if nothing had happened, however, I knew was impossible. Besides, there I was, sitting in my therapist's chair, still holding a legal summons in my hand. That was undeniable. I decided that the most appropriate thing I could do was inform them about the reality they had witnessed without confessing, confiding in them, or belaboring them with what would, for them, comprise burdensome or worrisome details. These patients were not aware of my ongoing divorce proceedings; I told them the event related to an ongoing legal action I was party to, that there was nothing really to worry about, that things were not out of hand, but that there was apparently more bitterness involved than I had been aware of. Hence, this untoward intrusion. I declined to provide further details.

Nevertheless, momentarily mollified, the group was able to move its focus to its own reactions and fantasies regarding the event. These centered primarily around their indignation, fear, and rage at the violation and penetration of the group's safe cocoon and at the affront to me. The extent to which group members invariably rely on the intactness of the group's boundaries, both to help them master their anxieties, and for containment and control, became at that moment abundantly apparent. With these boundaries no longer intact, their functions suddenly missing, the result was momentary panic. In addition, they had seen their leader suddenly accosted, possibly hurt in some incomprehensible fashion. The fantasy of the omnipotent therapist, the idealized father, the one who could protect them, both from their own eerie inner worlds and from the terrifying outside world, was suddenly dissipated. I was no longer all-powerful, magical, merely human and vulnerable, just as they themselves were—so how could I be trusted?

Indeed, the effort at "evenly hovering attention" so important in individual sessions and altogether crucial in the group setting was totally and utterly dissipated, impossible to maintain in this distressing moment. At the same time, they made the attempt to revive and repair my image, to tend to me, to protect me, railing at the intruder, inundating me with legal advice, voicing their protests at this injustice, and expressing their ministering their concerns.

A member with a paranoid underlay and a history of having been systematically brutalized as a child was genuinely afraid. He wondered aloud if the members of the group could be identified, if the intruder might return, and if this spelled the demise of the group. He was reassured by the other group members that they had no intention of permitting the group to be destroyed so summarily. Another, whose childhood was spent ministering to a psychotic mother and whose adulthood has been devoted to one of the helping professions, determined to write a letter "to whom it may concern" from the patient's perspective for me to include in my legal response, detailing and protesting the incident as an invasion of her own and her fellow group members' patient rights. That letter in fact arrived on my fax machine the very next day.

Still a third group member commenced a lengthy narrative of hostile fantasies: those he had as the incident was taking place and those he was having subsequently, regaling the group with a lurid and phantasmagorical catalogue of what he would have liked to do to the perpetrator. Finally, the fourth member, a massively other-oriented individual, reassuring both himself and the other members in an effort to ameliorate the general dread, observed that I seemed to be reasonably under control, that surely I would handle things quite effectively. The group ended with the members somewhat appeased and calmed, their respective dynamics having been played out around this horrific incident. Although still in considerable consternation, each could see a personal dynamic at work, both as a reliving of old echoes and as a coping modus operandi. We had shared and struggled together to surmount a very real trauma to us all.

Much work remained to be done, however; the reverberations of this incident continued for many months. At first, the group's energy seemed totally sapped by this shared trauma, and the momentum of the work ground to what seemed to be a total halt. Whenever the sense of safety came into question, the episode emerged as the containing metaphor; whenever anxiety took center stage, it became the embodiment of concretized danger.

Slowly, laboriously, however, the group began to use the experience more constructively. Periodically, the group members would inquire about my well-being, but transferential themes were more importantly in evidence. A member who had lost his father at a very tender age and who had struggled his whole life long to find another strong male with whom he could convincingly identify could assure himself that his loss was not to be repeated. Another who had been systematically brutalized by an exaggeratedly macho father was reassured that strength and sadism did not have to go together, and another with similar experiences could see that strength could be protective, not merely savage. I would reassure them minimally about the worrisome reality, but another element, one which I attempted to foster, also began to germinate: the group members shared the experience of having together encountered and surmounted a real danger. An esprit emerged more than it ever had in this group, a cohesion based on their firm conviction that they stood together and that they could cope together, both against inner ghosts and outward onslaught. The experience of strength which they shared was both joint and individual: each could feel enhanced, could savor a sense of augmented self-esteem, as well as a more intense relatedness.

No such dramatic encounters took place in the arena of individual treatment. While the impact of the events in my life was considerably more indirect there, it appeared to be no less real and perhaps not even more subtle. The groups I work with occasionally contain patients employed in the mental health professions, and some of those had heard rumors of my marital dissolution, so it was not long before various others were either informed about or strongly suspected my change in circumstance. Occasionally, patients would directly describe fantasies in which they imagined me now free to marry them or available for them to take care of me in my "hour of need." Astoundingly, one patient who could not possibly have had access to that information, a borderline individual, reported a dream very shortly after I had left my marital apartment, in which she saw me getting divorced. Although this was almost certainly a wish-fulfilling effort at a resolution to her eroticized transference feelings, she may well have discerned, in a fashion so often characteristic of borderline individuals, almost imperceptible nuances in my demeanor. We addressed the dream in terms of the fantasy wish for my availability, but for me, it was nevertheless a considerable shock to hear it related at just that particular juncture.

Many patients who were unable to approach feelings about my new situation by means of internal operations of one or another kind conveyed them in action terms, the meanings of which were often very difficult to bring into awareness. A woman lawyer, married for many years, began an extramarital relationship with a therapist who, she imagined, was a colleague of mine, although she had great difficulty recognizing that, perhaps, her illicit liaison represented a displacement of feelings she was having toward me. Later, she was able to use her feelings in more constructive ways. After tolerating what had been years of abuse from and infidelity by her husband, she finally permitted herself to recognize this painful reality, to screw up her courage and mobilize herself to respond appropriately, ultimately deciding to seek a divorce. Another patient, a bisexual young man, began a flirtation with an attractive female psychologist. Still another, who was unable to make the assertion more directly, permitted her husband to discover her longstanding liaison and thus precipitated the dissolution of her marriage.

Contemplating whether this spate of divorces and other forms of sexual acting out had something to do with the way in which I was conducting my work, I wondered if there was something that perhaps I was inadvertently, unintentionally imparting to my patients which could be helping to induce these forms of behavior. I had to question my own feelings and beliefs. I still had some clear opinions about the sanctity and importance of marriage, even though I had not myself been able to live up to my own ideals. Certainly, I had not yet settled within myself the volcanic feelings of bitterness and rage stimulated repeatedly—and during each bout of legal wrangling, almost daily—in the wake of my divorce. But I had scrupulously avoided permitting these feelings to intrude in my work with patients—or so I thought. Was I nevertheless communicating something to my patients, and, if so, how was I doing it and what was it?

In retrospect, it appears to me inevitable that I must have been doing so. Patients on the couch could discern the inflections in my voice, my choice of what to address or not to address, the almost imperceptible hesitations or too hastily offered interpretations, or my choice of words and expressions. Those patients whom I see in a face-to-face format could observe, in addition to my gestures and body language, the tenor and rhythm of my movements and my facial expressions or lack of them. All this must surely have provided some discernible information each time an issue related to divorce or the potential breakup of relationships emerged in the work. Despite my conscious effort to minimize these indicators, they are so automatic, virtually reflex, that, in these expressive modes, I could not have done other than, unavoidably, albeit inadvertently, to convey some measure of information about myself and my circumstance.

The patient often senses what the analyst is going through, even without more specific or articulated information; this is frequently reflected in the particular exigency of the transference being expressed by the patient. Possibly, this was the case with various of my patients. Viederman (1991) argues that anonymity is, in any case, virtually nonexistent and points out that "deviation from anonymity begins with the physical appearance and surround of the analyst, highly reflective of his world and his tastes" (p. 464). He also cites Gill (1982), who contends that "to properly interpret transference, one is forced to take note of the nidus of reality, inevitably present" (p. 464).

These questions of exposure are often difficult and painful ones to contemplate; they penetrate straight to the heart of the therapist's self-image as an effective, competent professional. Whereas when the therapist is ill, issues of stamina and capacity tend to be paramount, in circumstances such as those considered here, competence and insight are more centrally called into question. Denial is a potent problem and a powerful temptation, and even though consultation with a colleague becomes a priority and an important source of help, comfort, and encouragement, shame can be a serious obstacle to seeking such support. The resulting isolated struggle to cope with onslaughts as well as self-doubts can lead to lonely, debilitating, and inordinately stressful inner turmoil. Givelber and Simon (1981) recognize this denial and acknowledge the tendency among therapists to lean in the direction of grandiosity and the conviction of personal immunity. They observe that, in the face of loss, "a surprisingly large proportion of therapists take off almost no time. Certain feelings may be disavowed by the therapist who finds intolerable the awareness of states of neediness, fragility, and self-involvement" (p. 142). It is thus often difficult for the professional helper to concede the enormous extent of the debilitation that can result from such personal traumas.

From a broader perspective, it is apparent that there are numerous compelling and disorganizing sources of distress and distraction for the analyst, an array of potential occurrences which can be viewed as a continuum consisting of any number of intensely impacting life events. Divorce is a particularly extreme one, an event of life-disorganizing intensity, requiring what is often a complete transformation of the analyst's entire life; however, divorce is not unique in having such drastic consequences. Other catastrophic events—the death of a child, a spouse, or other close family member; financial setbacks; fires; floods; and a host of other such events—have similarly powerful repercussions on the analyst's ability to devote himself totally to the performance of his work. All represent interfering distractions which, to a greater or lesser degree, dilute the extent to which the analyst is able to apply his entire concentration to the issues that the patient presents: to the patient's life struggles. In the extreme, one can envision an entire such continuum of distractions and dilutions, ranging from cataclysmic ones, such as those just cited, to far lesser ones which (since, after all, we are all "more human than otherwise") can vie for the analyst's attention at any given time. While we typically view such peripheral and intrusive inner activity as dynamically related to the ongoing analytic interaction, echoing the transferential and countertransferential enmeshment of the two participants, it can also reflect the reality of the concomitant and ordinary human stresses impinging on the analyst's life, the daily tribulations that even the sanctity of the consultation room cannot always filter out.

On the other side of the ledger, the patient's recognition of the reality of the analyst does not necessarily always have to be detrimental. There are times when the patient can realize and appreciate the reality of the analyst's plight. That realization, not only of shared human ills and foibles, but also of the occasional genuine help which the patient is able to extend to the analyst, can be a beneficial experience for the patient, both in the recognition of that inner capacity, and in the awareness of being authentically responded to. Singer (1970) describes quite poignantly how sharing with patients the illness of his wife and his own grief became both for him and for them a positive, learning, and enhancing experience, as they struggled both to express their heartfelt concern and compassion and to empathize with his suffering and his impending loss. His recognition of their response to him represented a real and respectful acknowledgment, not only of their capacity to help, but also of their genuine feelings.

Divorce, however, entails other, particular characteristics and considerations heavily loaded with societal mores and evaluative considerations. Despite the reality of a divorce rate which sees the dissolution of more than one of every two marriages, sanguine acceptance of marital disintegration is not yet a societal norm. This is the source in no small part of the soul-searching and searing conflict which attaches to every decision to consummate this fateful move. And analysts, no less than their patients, are prey to these societal appraisals. In describing a favorable treatment outcome, for example, Viederman (1991) notes that "the patient married, had a family, and achieved a successful termination of analysis" (p. 457). The values which this statement mirrors are clear: marriage and family are positively valenced, their absence is not. This is only one such implicitly held standard; there are many, often held in common by both patient and analyst and rarely, if ever, verbalized or openly acknowledged. Given this ambiance, the potential repercussions in the transference of the analyst's divorcing, and particularly of the analyst's informing the patient of this fact, are potentially powerful and numerous. The analytic situation, although judgment neutral, is not value-free.

Nevertheless, it can be helpful for patients to recognize that, on occasion, partners in a relationship may discover that their values, aspirations, and *modi vivendi* are simply so vastly disparate as to render them in fact incompatible, that this is not a reflection on their worth, their lovability, or their characters, but a simple reality which must be confronted as such. When all is said and done, people differ. One rather obsessional young man found himself naggingly dissatisfied with a relationship of some years standing. His hopes tended in the direction of marriage and family, whereas the young woman with whom he was involved was quite content to drift along in a rather casual affair, her attachment to her parental family being, for her, paramount. This attribute had, in fact, constituted part of their initial attraction, since he too had been very closely tied to the parental fold; however, as he changed in the context of his treatment, he began to aspire to a family and children of his own. Nevertheless, he berated himself cruelly for his inability, despite repeated efforts, to move this relationship to a deeper level, to bring it to a point of a more lasting commitment, persisting in the harsh evaluation that he was incapable successfully to consummate a relationship to his satisfaction. His mother's nagging questions regarding the progress of the relationship only served to underscore his own harsh judgments, internalized from a father by whom he felt continually castigated as a ne'er-do-well. He was ultimately able to recognize that his girlfriend was unable to keep pace with the changes he had made in treatment and that, despite his best efforts, this was not reconcilable, that they were genuinely no longer compatible. He could see, without blame, that, despite their genuine fondness for one another, they were not suited, and he was thus able, ultimately, to relinquish the attachment, albeit with a great deal of anger, sadness, and a lengthy subsequent period of mourning.

There are, in fact, social norms, standards of behavior both inside and outside the analytic hour, to which we expect out patients as well as ourselves to adhere. These may encompass dress codes, forms of address, manners of presentation and exchange, gesture and physical expression or restraint, and various others implicit in any social encounter. We evaluate pathology, in part, by the degree to which patients are able to adhere to commonly held social expectations of behavior and self-expression. In fact, when encountering individuals from other cultures, for whom our own ordinary social mores may not be relevant or requisite, our assessing benchmarks may be quite confounded.

Similarly, when the values of the analyst conflict too intensely with those of the patient, the analytic enterprise may well be scuttled. The difficulty of so many analysts of finding a common ground for working with nazis, "skinheads," or psychopaths is based on profoundly held beliefs, attitudes, and feelings that run counter to the destructive or malicious behaviors which such individuals casually indulge in. The almost reflex reaction of abhorrence which persons of this ilk often engender is a graphic reflection of the influence that values and norms wield.

In a sense, the analyst becomes a model for expected behaviors. It is not unusual for patients in the throes of an intense positive transference to emulate the manner and dress of the analyst, and, we expect, in the context of termination, that the patient will, at least to some extent, internalize the analyst and the analyst's presumably less neurosis-engendering psychic operations. But these will also include those standards of behavior and those social values which have been, implicitly or explicitly, expressed in the context of the therapeutic endeavor. Despite what we may believe, the world, society, its mores, its values, or its impact do not stop at the consultation room door. Their infiltration is myriad, their impact no less real or intense than the incursion which my group and I experienced on that fateful evening.

How often have patients brought events or personalities, currently in vogue or touted in the media, into a session, either by associations or in dreams. The analyst's response to such importations, no matter how artfully disguised, the manner, tone, or wording of interpretations around them, no matter how astutely insightful, will inevitably convey something of the nature of his or her involvement, or lack of it in these contemporary issues.

However, this conduit for the incursion of the life of contemporary society into the consultation room serves not only implicitly to infuse value-laden material into the analytic space, but also to convey to the patient considerable amounts of information about the analyst.

Greenberg (1995) observes that

> Most relational analysts today . . . point out that a wide range of behaviors are self-revealing: answering a patient's question about one's personal life; sharing a countertransference feeling; asking a particular question (instead of another that could have been asked); making a particular interpretation; decorating one's office in a particular way; greeting (or not greeting) the patient; wearing a certain kind of tie; cutting one's hair. The list is endless, because everything that the analyst does reveals something to the perceptive patient [p. 195].

He notes further that "analytic anonymity is a myth. . . . Patients, especially those who are the most disturbed, know their analysts very well;

we reveal ourselves in everything that we say and do. Self-disclosure is inevitable; our only choice is how we accommodate to this fact of our professional lives" (Greenberg, 1995, p. 194).

Addressing the question of self-disclosure, one must, to be more accurate, distinguish between that which is conscious, planned, and intentional and that which is not. Jacobs (1995) underscores this distinction in addressing what he calls "the question of unintentional disclosure" (p. 240). In his opinion, "Patients clearly come to know us in ways that go beyond words, beyond our conscious intentions; through our office decor, manner of dress and bearing, tastes, habits, moods, predilections, and sensitivities, as well as through our values, attitudes, and ways of experiencing the world that are unconsciously transmitted" (p. 240). In addressing the particular question of disclosing divorce, when we decide that it is appropriate to do so, allusions are presumably intended to be within the realm of the former, conscious and purposeful, yet they may often be inadvertently in the context of the latter without awareness or intent. I believe this is true of many of our values, standards, mores, and expectations no less than of divorce. In Ehrenberg's (1995) opinion, however, any self-disclosing utterance is countertransferentially based. She asserts that "if we recognize our vulnerability to unconscious responsiveness in the analytic interaction, then we must consider that anything we say or do, including remaining silent, can be a form of countertransference enactment" (p. 214).

How is this apparent enigma then to be surmounted or resolved? Abend (1995) suggests that "astute and sensitive responsivity is the essence of good technique, and not whether one has fixed and proper rules for micromanagement" (p. 209), whereas Ehrenberg (1995) more pessimistically thinks that "the idea that we can transcend countertransference and restore 'objectivity' by rigorously dealing with our own internal issues as they threaten to 'get in the way,' is untenable" (p. 216). My own belief is that the answer lies in the analyst's therapeutic intent in the context of a genuine concern for the patient and the patient's welfare. This is equally true of the analyst's utterances as of his or her deportment, attitude, and presentation and can serve as a kind of righting mechanism, even when therapeutic matters may, on occasion, go astray. As the actor must be aware of the most minute gesture, manner, and expression in the development of his character, so, similarly, must the analyst let his understanding of the patient and his conception of the therapeutic direction and goal guide his most fleeting and subtle expression. Ehrenberg's (1995) comment is well taken: "The question . . . therefore, is not what response is 'right' or 'wrong' but how to use whatever occurs to greatest analytic advantage" (p. 216). The clear therapeutic purpose is the beacon that can steer even the most elusive expression in the analytic interchange. It can render the distinction between intentional and unintentional disclosure, I believe, effectively moot.

Finally, it must also be said that those inputs which we contribute to the analytic encounter—our values, our behaviors, our standards, our expectations, our likes and dislikes, our tastes and distastes, indeed the very selves which we bring to bear, whether intentionally or otherwise—we must strive to acknowledge and recognize for what they are and the effect they create, difficult as that endeavor may appear. Our subtle influences, as well as our purposeful interventions, must be equally seen and understood, the actuality of their weight appreciated and observed. Only by being open to these realities can we hope to understand the infinitely complex currents which transpire in this apparently simple situation in which two people converse together.

REFERENCES

Abend, S. M. (1986), Countertransference, empathy, and the analytic ideal: The impact of life stresses on analytic capability. *Psychoanal. Quart.,* 50:563–575.
—— (1995), Discussion of Jay Greenberg's paper on self-disclosure. *Contemp. Psychoanal.,* 31:207–211.
Dewald, P. A. (1994), Countertransference issues when the therapist is ill or disabled. *Amer. J. Psychother.,* 48:221–230.
Ehrenberg, D. B. (1995), Self-disclosure: Therpeutic tool or indulgence? *Contemp. Psychoanal.,* 31:213–228.
Freud, S. (1912), Recommendations to physicians practicing psycho-analysis. *Standard Edition,* 12:109–120. London: Hogarth Press, 1958.
Gill, M. M. (1982), *Analysis of Transference, Vol. 1: Theory and Technique. Psychological Issues,* Monogr. 53. New York: International Universities Press.
Givelber, F. & Simon, B. (1981), A death in the life of a therapist and its impact on the therapy. *Psychiatry,* 44:141–149.
Greenberg, J. (1995), Self-disclosure: Is it psychoanalytic? *Contemp. Psychoanal.,* 31:193–205.
Greenson, R. R. (1967), *The Technique and Practice of Psychoanalysis.* New York: International Universities Press.
Grunebaum, H. (1993), The vulnerable therapist: On being ill or injured. In: *Beyond Transference,* ed. J. H. Gold & J. C. Nemiah. Washington, DC: American Psychiatric Press, pp. 21–49.
Jacobs, T. (1995), Discussion of Jay Greenberg's paper. *Contemp. Psychoanal.,* 31:237–245.
Kohut, H. (1971), *The Analysis of the Self.* New York: International Universities Press.
Norcross, J. C. & Prochaska, J. O. (1986), Psychotherapist heal thyself, I: The psychological distress and self-change of psychologists, counselors and laypersons. *Psychotherapy,* 23:102–114.
Schafer, R. (1983), *The Analytic Attitude.* New York: Basic Books.
Schwartz, H. J. (1987), Illness in the doctor: Implications for the psychoanalytic process. *J. Amer. Psychoanal. Assn.,* 35:657–692.
Singer, E. (1970), The patient aids the analyst: Some clinical and theoretical observations. In: *In the Name of Life: Essays in Honor of Erich Fromm,* ed. B. Landis & E. Tauber. New York: Holt, Rinehart & Winston.
Viederman, M. (1991), The real person of the analyst and his role in the process of psychoanalytic cure. *J. Amer. Psychoanal. Assn.,* 39:451–490.

10

The Impact of Negative Experiences as a Patient on My Work as a Therapist

SUE N. ELKIND

For ten years, ever since I was a patient in two therapeutic relationships that ended in conflict with extraordinary disillusionment and anger, I have been striving to understand negative experiences in therapy. As part of working through the personal meaning of these experiences, I have been evolving ways of thinking conceptually about impasses and ruptures in therapy and consulting to patients and therapists grappling with them (Elkind, 1992, 1994, 1995). Negative experiences in therapy are difficult for all patients, but those who are also therapists have the additional challenge of assimilating and integrating their failed therapy into their professional work.

Describing negative experiences in therapy to others is not easy. I find it difficult to face once again in stark relief, unmuted by defenses, my primary wounds and vulnerabilities, the limitations of my analysts, and my inability to recognize and respond differently to their limitations and my own. Even though ten years have passed, I do not like to relive the experience of the destruction of the hope for myself that I invested in the long and intensive therapeutic relationships.

As a profession, we encourage patients to talk about traumatic experiences, and we admire those who have the courage to do so. But a therapist who talks openly about failed therapy experiences risks breaking a taboo and incurring diagnostic assessments and judgments from the professional community. I have pushed through the resistance about revisiting my negative experiences as a patient because I believe that an experience that has to be kept hidden cannot be organized in language and therefore reflected on and transformed. The experience remains encapsulated and frozen, unassimilated into the whole of one's being.

Even with a staunch commitment to writing about my negative experiences as a patient in order to consider their impact on my work as a therapist, conveying what happened remains a daunting task. Historical truth and subjective reality intertwine in shifting patterns. Not only do the interactions I select to convey change, but each becomes merely one scene in an infinite and changing kaleidoscope of personal meaning. I find myself faced with the fluidity of memory, not knowing how the current context of writing this chapter is influencing what I recall or how I weave a narrative, not knowing what factors influenced the memories that were encoded and preserved at the time. Determining the influence of the negative experiences as a patient on my work as a therapist both concurrently and over time augments these uncertainties and catapults me further onto the shifting sands of subjectivity.

MY EXPERIENCES AS A PATIENT

Before describing my experiences as a patient, I want to provide enough information about my early history to give a meaningful context for the transference issues that were activated. A firstborn and only child, I arrived seven weeks early in 1943, in the midst of World War II, and was quickly isolated in intensive care for a week. After my birth, my father returned to the army and was stationed in Europe during the first two years of my life. While I have no conscious memories from this time, I have been told stories about several early separations from my mother, who left to visit my father whenever possible.

My mother had two stillborn baby boys in the next four years. The first occurred when I was two and a half years old and resulted in a one month separation from her. The second stillbirth occurred when I was four years old and undergoing a tonsillectomy. We were again separated for several weeks. Both times, my mother was grieving and depressed.

I have no conscious memories of the emotional states I experienced or of the ideas I might have attached to the events that were occurring during these separations. But I do know that, throughout my childhood, I was inordinately anxious about leaving home. Separations and disconnections from significant others can still elicit a groundswell of grief and anxiety. A sense of myself as precious to my parents and of their life-preserving importance to me led to a precocious sense of responsibility for their well-being, as well as to a sense of the destructive potential of my needs. Separation and abandonment, within the context of a significant attachment bond, and the urgent need to preserve connection are issues that would inevitably arise in any depth psychotherapy. They were recreated in the transference–countertransference matrix of both my analyses but were not identified, so they led to ruptured terminations without understanding.

In my first therapy, I met with a psychoanalytically oriented male psychologist, whom I will call Dr. Hall, for two periods of therapy from the time I was twenty-six to thirty-three years old. I had completed my doctoral degree in psychology, been married for two years, and had a postdoctoral fellowship. I felt ready to take on the experience of being a patient.

After one year of twice a week therapy, which I used primarily to focus on the new experience of being pregnant, I terminated when our first child was born. I wanted to immerse myself in mothering without the distraction of focusing on anything else, which I did for the next three years. By then, I had a private practice, and I did not want to be apart from my daughter any more than I already was.

When our second child was one year old, my husband and I were struggling with our relationship, and I searched for a couples' therapist. I called Dr. Hall to ask if he would meet with my husband and me. He readily agreed and proceeded to meet with us. Later I realized that I would have liked him to meet alone with me first, to make sure that he was not abandoning my connection to him as an individual patient, but at the time, I was grateful to him for his immediate willingness to help both of us.

We began meeting weekly with Dr. Hall and soon added separate individual sessions twice a week. My husband and I quickly regrouped as a couple. Within the separate space for ourselves, without the impingement of small children or our work, and with the support of Dr. Hall, we restored our positive connection to each other. After one year, we ended the conjoint sessions and continued with our separate individual therapy sessions twice a week. We knew this arrangement was unusual, but the three of us believed that we could successfully manage whatever issues surfaced. We worked in this way for the next three years.

When I look back on this unconventional arrangement, I sometimes feel it worked well, but at other times, I feel that we failed to understand the influence of sharing a therapist on what occurred within each therapeutic relationship. A triangle was created, within which an oedipal competition between my husband and me for the attention and approval of the therapist-father operated but was not explicitly considered.

Eventually, I became pregnant with our third child, a happy and hoped-for pregnancy that also entailed anxiety because I was to be put on bedrest for the last six weeks. I also felt ready to terminate the therapy. My plan was to return to meet with Dr. Hall for several sessions after the birth of my baby to terminate the therapy. I wanted to reconnect with him after the long separation (my bedrest and his month-long vacation) and the enormous change that the baby's birth would bring about, rather than to terminate before the long break.

With six sessions remaining before his vacation, Dr. Hall announced that he was increasing his fee beginning with his return. I was extraordinarily distressed at the intrusion of Dr. Hall's needs and at the change in the frame on the brink of a long separation—a birth about which I carried anxiety, a leave from my practice, and a drop in income—and at the beginning of a termination phase.

I asked Dr. Hall to set aside the fee raise until we could discuss it after the long break. I wanted to use the remaining five sessions to talk about the impending separation from him and my feelings about the birth of my child. I did not want the stress of feeling angry when I was fearful of increasing the risk of an early labor. At that stage of the pregnancy,

I could bring on contractions by being upset or stressed. On another level that I did not yet have language for, I did not want to lose the idealized, omnipotent object/mother that I had created to keep me and my unborn child safe. I did not want him to metamorphose suddenly into a dangerous, threatening, potentially destructive separate being. Several years would pass before I came upon D. W. Winnicott's (1960) description of *primary maternal preoccupation,* which explained the intensity of my yearning to be protected from impingement during the last stages of my pregnancy.

In a manner that seemed to me to be unusually cold and unfeeling, Dr. Hall refused to set aside the fee raise. He regarded the fee raise as an impersonal act, a change he was implementing with all his patients. I told him the fee raise felt very personal to me, and I pleaded with him to look at it in the context of our relationship and my circumstances. He again refused. I felt humiliated and ashamed for begging, angry not only at being denied, but at his unyielding, harsh tone. I declared that I no longer wanted to be his patient if he was going to insist that I agree to pay the higher fee immediately. He responded that I was depriving myself of a "happy ending," like leaving high school without a graduation. He did not encourage me to remain a patient or help me focus on the opportunities that might be embedded in the power struggle. He allowed me to terminate in this way, and I was stubbornly unable to remain his patient.

I spent the next two weeks in anguish over the sudden and unexpected ending of the therapeutic relationship, ruminating over my motives, under pressure if I wanted to resolve the rupture with him before his vacation. Hoping for some resolution, I called for an appointment and returned for a final session during Dr. Hall's last week at work. In the session, I shared with him the insights I had arrived at about the meaning of my refusal to accept his increased fee. I saw myself as refusing to be blackmailed into paying a higher fee out of dependency needs and fear of abandonment if I refused to comply with what I perceived to be an unfair request. Dr. Hall did not encourage me to continue working with him. The opportunity to explore the psychological significance of my refusal to focus on his needs over mine, to experience a hard edge and conflict in a relationship, and to make links to the transference meaning of the power struggle was lost.

The emotional cost of the abrupt severing of the relationship seemed enormous, both at the time and now as I reconsider it. I grieved over the loss as if it were a death. Looking back, a death in the transference did occur of the daughter who wanted a loving, supportive father/mother to take care of her, especially when she was about to become the mother of a baby. But a working through and resolution of this transference (and countertransference) loss did not occur. Instead, although I did not understand it at the time, a reenactment of early trauma occurred, in which an unconscious belief or organizing principle, that the assertion (or mere existence) of my needs would precipitate unmanageable conflict and destroy connection, was confirmed. This *reenactment without understanding* constitutes for me the most traumatic aspect of the therapy. Without a conceptual understanding, I had no language with which to organize and make sense of the experience of hopelessness and despair that followed the ruptured termination. The consultations I provide represent my endeavor to spare other patients this trauma.

After my third child was four years old and my outer life was relatively stable, I contemplated reentering therapy. I wanted to understand why the therapy with Dr. Hall had ended in a rupture. Was my leaving healthy assertiveness in the face of his poor timing or a self-destructive stubbornness? What were other levels of meaning of this ending? I had thought long and hard about the transference issues that were involved and had many discussions with friends and colleagues. Like many patients, I assumed that I was responsible for the failure, and, not yet operating from a relational model, I had not yet risked reopening what happened with Dr. Hall in another therapy. I eventually chose Dr. Ross, an experienced and respected psychoanalyst. I hoped that the frequency and intensity of sessions with an analyst informed by psychoanalytic theory would allow affect states beyond language to emerge in the relationship and be organized in words.

After the first year, I increased the frequency of sessions from one, to two, and then to four sessions a week. Looking back, I can see that I tested Dr. Ross to see if he would repeat problems that occurred in the therapy with Dr. Hall. He successfully passed the tests, giving me room to have my thoughts and feelings without the impingement of his needs. Later, I realized how much I held back from engaging directly with him and expressing needs, fearful of precipitating unmanageable conflict. For example, I often hoped he would express an opinion about the ruptured termination with Dr. Hall, but he never did. Yet I never directly asked him what he thought was going on. I simply assumed that he had a rationale for his silence and that he wanted me to arrive at an understanding on my own. My avoidance of direct engagement and possible conflict or disappointment was outside of my awareness. Transference longings for a harmonious loving bond with a good father/mother and fears that I could disrupt the bond were operating, but I did not recognize them and Dr. Ross did not perceive or label them. When I try to imagine how I appeared to him, I picture him regarding me as an easy, undemanding, and satisfied patient.

On the positive side, Dr. Ross was helpful to me in understanding significant aspects of my relationships in my family of origin and in helping me take risks in these relationships. I was also meeting with him during a time when Dr. Hall initiated social contact, having no apparent memory of how the therapy ended. With Dr. Ross's support, I was able to face

Dr. Hall's anger and hurt when I reminded him that I had been a patient
with transference feelings and did not want to be his friend. I remain
appreciative of his support and availability as I worked through these
issues. In retrospect, I can see that both of us were more comfortable
when the focus was on a relationship outside of the room.

When these preoccupations diminished, I was left with little to talk
about other than pleasurable experiences with my family. I wanted to
deepen the therapy, but I did not know how. I talked about feeling stuck,
having a sense of not getting to the issues I wanted help with. I tried
implementing changes to bring about a shift, for example, instituting double
sessions once a week. I brought in dreams, but they did not lead us into
unconscious territory or into relationship and transference issues. Dr.
Ross acknowledged honestly that he was not good with dreams and understood that I felt stuck, but he also did not know how to effect a shift. I
know that staying within the familiar borders of my competent, functioning, ego-self was a powerful need that functioned as a resistance to
letting anything else occur. I was aware that he was enjoying the discussions
we had, but I did not formulate this awareness as countertransference.

I gradually fell into, with his cooperation and encouragement, a mode
of relationship in which I became an intellectual companion, living out
a yearned-for special connection to a good father. For example, he shared
his interest in Buddhist philosophy with me and gave me books to read.
I brought him tapes of a class that I was teaching, and he would listen
and comment. He revealed details about a class he taught, sharing his
dissatisfactions with himself. On one occasion, I brought back a catalog
from Karnac Books in London, and he asked me to order a particular
book for him that was not available in the United States. I forgot to place
the order, an unusual lapse for me, and he reminded me that he wanted
it. Neither of us analyzed the meaning of my "forgetting" or the meaning
of his asking me to help him. Each of these interactions were lived out,
not analyzed. I was unable to give up the gratification of feeling that we
had a special bond and the living out of a transference connection to the
father/mother.

In retrospect, I can perceive ways I tried to call attention to the problem
in the analysis, both consciously and unconsciously. For example, I asked
Dr. Ross if he had gotten consultation. I talked about psychoanalytic articles I was reading and about patients I was working with, commentary
that had embedded within it information about our therapeutic relationship, but he did not listen to my associations as commentary on our relationship, nor did he focus on the transference enactment dimension. Equally
unconscious, we were caught in a stalemate that was frustrating but safe
and gratifying for both of us.

Eventually, fate intervened, bringing with it an end to the stalemated
therapy. A crisis occurred in my life, which catapulted me into a state

of intense grief and despair (Nathanson, 1989). Already the mother of three children, I became pregnant due to a failure of birth control with what would have been my fourth child. I made the difficult decisions to have an abortion and a tubal ligation, expecting that I would cope effectively with both choices. Instead, I was completely overwhelmed by intense feelings of grief beyond any anguish I had ever encountered. For the first time, I desperately needed Dr. Ross and my analytic sessions. Uncontrollable and overpowering feelings of loss, rage, guilt, and self-loathing propelled me out of my comfortable mode of gratifying intellectual companion to him and into a state of fragmentation and frightened dependency. In this dreadful situation resided the fragile new step for me of letting go of precociously established defenses that preserved my self-reliance.

In the previous therapy, Dr. Hall had dropped me psychologically (or allowed me to drop myself) in a time of vulnerability and need, recreating in the therapeutic relationship an experience of abandonment that was a significant part of my early history. Now, Dr. Ross clearly seemed to be alarmed by the intensity of my feelings and the emotional demands they exerted upon him. He appeared shaken when I cried or talked about my unbearable emotional pain. He wrote out prescriptions for tranquilizers and sleeping pills, even though I clearly told him I did not want medication and that I needed a place to experience, not to mute, my feelings. I think it helped him to be able to offer me something concrete that might alleviate suffering.

Dr. Ross remained silent at times when I needed an empathic reflection of my feelings and longed for him to help me find a context of meaning for my experiences. I perceived his silence to mean that he was backing away from me psychologically and emotionally, communicating that he was unable to bear being with me in my distressed state. I was not able, on my own, to make genetic interpretations of what I was experiencing. In retrospect, I was living through the collapse of my analyst in the face of my needs, analogous to the perceived collapse of my mother when I was small and dependent on her for care.

At the beginning of each session, I would feel hopeful that something would shift, but each time I left feeling far worse. I began canceling my sessions, telling Dr. Ross I was too upset to come and did not want to risk leaving in a worse state of despair. He accepted these cancellations readily over the phone, telling me to come back when I felt better. I believed he did not want to face me, that I made him feel helpless and inadequate. Dr. Ross seemed unable to recognize that I needed him to urge me to come to my sessions anyway, to accept and therefore to contain me in my most upset and despairing state. He could not alter his responses, even with direct feedback from me about my need. Consequently, my sense of being "too much" was confirmed.

The sessions with Dr. Ross catapulted me into an intensified state of despair. I did not know where to turn for help. Finally, my husband arranged an appointment with a young, inexperienced counselor at Planned Parenthood who helped me through the acute crisis by moving toward every agonizing feeling: murderous rage at myself for taking the life of my unborn child, unspeakable grief at the loss of this child, breathtaking fury at my husband for urging me to have an abortion, and cold shock at the sudden loss of my fertility, until I ultimately could feel compassion for my husband and myself.

Once I was through the acute crisis, I began to meet once a week with an analyst from another institute, a woman I will call Dr. Marin. I explained to myself and to Dr. Ross that I needed help from a woman to work with issues related to the abortion and ending of fertility. Throughout this time, Dr. Ross expressed only relief about and support for my work with the counselor and with Dr. Marin. He never asked about the transference meaning of my turning to a woman for help or about any feelings of anger or disappointment in him. Fearing another failure in therapy, I was not able to face these feelings.

When Dr. Ross confided in me, only a few months after my abortion, that my painful experience had been helpful to him in allowing his young and unmarried daughter carry a pregnancy to term instead of insisting that she have an abortion she did not want, I felt only compassion for his daughter. I was not aware of anger at Dr. Ross for burdening me with personal information, or for telling me that I helped him help his daughter while he failed to help me. Looking back, I am astonished by my inability to access and express my feelings and by what this inability reflected about my fears of my destructive potential and the loss of connection. I am awed by the sacrifice I felt impelled to make to preserve the therapeutic relationship and by the sacrifices I must have unconsciously felt impelled to make to preserve my connection to my parents. I wish I could have been helped to recognize this dynamic within the therapeutic relationship, but at the time I feared that my rage at Dr. Ross would end the relationship, just as it ended the therapy with Dr. Hall. I regarded this outcome solely as a reflection of pathology in myself, not as a dynamic in the relationship or as related to Dr. Ross's countertransference. My shift to a relational perspective came later, the result of efforts to understand these experiences as a patient.

After a year of working concurrently with Dr. Marin, I finally tripped back into the anger toward Dr. Ross that had gone underground. Ironically, I had finally made the decision to terminate therapy. I went into a session and told Dr. Ross that I wanted to begin cutting back on the frequency of sessions in preparation for terminating. I shared my plan of stopping the double sessions right away and then gradually reducing the frequency to twice a week over the next several months. Dr. Ross responded that he did not think I should give up the double session. The fact that he was holding firm now to the importance of my attending a session when I was ready to stop, after having accepted cancellations at a time of desperate need, catapulted me into rage at the earlier abandonment.

I began for the first time to express anger at Dr. Ross's failures. At this point, we recreated and relived, without new conscious awareness, the crisis of one year ago. I left a Friday session in a state of rage that I was unable to tolerate on my own. I felt that I could not stand feeling this angry until the next session and, uncharacteristically, I called his exchange. When Dr. Ross returned my call, I told him that I was so angry that I did not know if I could stand waiting until the Monday session. I am certain that, if he had simply reflected back to me how frightened I must be about bringing so much anger into the relationship and how important this new step was, I would have calmed down and been able to wait. Instead, Dr. Ross immediately prescribed Xanax to help me sleep. I was stunned that he would repeat an attempt to prescribe medicine after we had been through endless sessions on the meaning to me of his prescribing medication and the importance to me of having my feelings. When I told him in this telephone call that medicine wouldn't help, he suggested increasing the dose.

This interaction, representing Dr. Ross's failure of the last chance I could offer him, brought home to me with utter finality the necessity of extricating myself from the therapy. I terminated in anger and despair one month later, with transference and countertransference issues remaining unaddressed, after more than four years of analysis. Fortunately, I was able to increase the frequency of sessions with Dr. Marin and continue in a productive analysis with her for the next four years.

WHAT CONSTITUTES A NEGATIVE EXPERIENCE?

Ultimately, I was able to use the negative experiences with both Dr. Hall and Dr. Ross to understand my areas of *primary vulnerability,* a concept I use to refer to areas of sensitivity that are shaped early in development that, when activated, threaten the sense of cohesiveness and continuity of self (Elkind, 1992). Painfully highlighted in both negative therapy experiences were my primary vulnerabilities related to attachment, separation, and abandonment, experiencing myself and my needs omnipotently as destructive to others, and automatically shaping myself around the needs of others in order to establish and maintain connection. I could now link the chaotic emotional states I endured to crises surrounding the traumatic separations early in my life. These were the primary vulnerabilities that led to my contribution to the countertransference–transference impasses I became caught in with Dr. Hall and Dr. Ross.

Eventually, I came to understand these primary vulnerabilities in the context of my family of origin issues. They emerged directly in the therapeutic relationship with Dr. Marin through dreams, associations, and interactions. In contrast to the therapeutic relationships with Dr. Hall and Dr. Ross, they were addressed within the analytic relationship. I was better able to bring up my feelings directly and to avoid falling into meeting her needs. Dr. Marin was more successful in keeping transference and countertransference dimensions in focus.

I regard the experiences in therapy with Dr. Hall and Dr. Ross as negative for several reasons. First, I feel that they failed to form an adequate conceptual, empathically based understanding of my core issues that might have provided a template or map for the therapy. I think of Loewald's (1980) view that an analyst has the responsibility to hold for the patient "an image of that which needs to be brought into its own" (p. 226), much as a parent optimally has "an empathic relationship of understanding the child's particular stage in development, yet ahead in his vision of the child's future and mediating this vision to the child in his dealing with him" (p. 229).

Dr. Hall lost this focus when he introduced the fee raise just before leaving on vacation and so close to my termination. In an unplanned social encounter several months after the abrupt termination, he disclosed that he was under considerable personal pressure at the time. Dr. Ross seemingly fell into a serious countertransference complex early in the analysis and could not extricate himself. In one of our last contacts he acknowledged that he had an internal block that prevented him from empathizing with me, and that he would live with feelings of failure. I know that my finely honed capacities to relate through empathy with others and my inability to connect with my feelings, needs, and desires when those of others seem more pressing contributed to his empathic block and made it impossible for me to extricate myself without the pressure of a crisis. However I also believe therapists are responsible for arriving at a working conceptualization of their patients and the transference and countertransference issues as they emerge in the therapeutic relationship. I believe that patients do find ways to convey enough of themselves, even patients as well-defended as I was, to help their therapists in this endeavor. I feel that both therapists failed in this regard.

Both Dr. Hall and Dr. Ross were unable to come to grips with their countertransference responses that allowed me to become a gratifying object for them. This countertransference resulted in the abandonment of an analytic stance and inability to preserve a sustaining therapeutic connection. The result was a *reenactment without understanding* of the trauma of abandonment that I had sought therapy to understand. The destruction of hope that this reenactment brought about was catastrophic to live through initially and then difficult to live with for some time. My investment in the profession and my interest in understanding the human psyche has enabled me to persist both as a patient and as a therapist, but I sometimes wonder what might have happened without them. What sense of myself would I have been left with, unmodified by other experiences?

THE INFLUENCE OF THE NEGATIVE EXPERIENCES
ON MY WORK

The negative experiences in therapy with Dr. Hall and Dr. Ross are embedded in my consciousness as a therapist. I know, not as an abstract possibility or academic fact or only through hearing someone else's experience, that therapeutic relationships are uniquely powerful and have the potential to leave patients feeling harmed. I invested incalculable hope in both analysts, risking the surrender of defenses that, albeit with cost, functioned as protection. In a psychologically unprotected state, I was at risk of retraumatization. I understand viscerally what happens when core vulnerabilities are activated and not contained, when analysts fall into countertransference reactions and do not work with them, when analysts lack the capacities that patients need, and when the disillusionment that patients sometimes endure feels unmanageable. This awareness is always with me and underlies my commitment to providing a resource for patients who have had or are at risk of these experiences.

I am going to focus first on the impact of my negative experiences as a patient on my work at the time I was living through them. A specific aspect of my work with certain patients was directly affected by the failures in my therapy. I would not necessarily say that I became a better therapist but, rather, that I strengthened a particular capacity. Whether this capacity was useful to my patients depended on their unique needs. In descriptive terms, I provided my patients with the attunement to their vulnerabilities that I urgently needed and wished for from my analyst. I then envied them for having what I lacked, a complex experience that I am only beginning to conceptualize after the fact.

Not long after I was struggling with Dr. Ross's inability to help me through my reaction to the abortion, I was working with two women who were each going through a descent, or dark night of the soul, precipitated by different fateful events in their lives. I noticed similar elements in my work with each of them, as well as less dramatic echoes of the same dynamics with other patients, but I will focus here on my therapeutic relationship with Celia.

Celia, a competent attorney ten years younger than I, entered therapy to work on problems in her marriage. In the two years we had worked together twice a week, we focused on the prolonged illness and ultimate death of her mother when Celia was seven years old. The loss had been traumatic for the family, but Celia was a quiet, self-reliant child whose needs went unnoticed. For example, she developed an allergic skin reaction and lost weight. Her ailments were treated solely as physical problems, unrelated to emotional needs. Her need to grieve and to be comforted was not apparent to her father or other relatives who were immersed in their own difficulties. Her older brother became a wild adolescent, acting out with drugs and skipping school. His flamboyant behavior drew attention away from Celia, who retreated further into herself.

I found myself experiencing powerful maternal feelings in relation to Celia, which I thought of as a response to yearnings that she could not express directly. Celia's persona was one of extraordinary competence and self-reliance. She was in charge of a large department in her law firm, highly regarded for her brilliance and intellect, yet my strongest connection to her was in relation to her vulnerability and need. Concurrently, in my therapy, Dr. Ross was primarily connected to my competent way of functioning in the world, not to the vulnerabilities that went unrecognized. I was also clearly more identified with myself as competent, rather than vulnerable, and was gratified by his countertransference. Staying related to my patient's vulnerability and need was also a way of paying attention to a neglected aspect of myself as a patient through the countertransference.

As an example of the strong countertransference undertow that operated with Celia, I found myself not wanting to leave her behind when I went on vacation, as if she were too young to be left, and I had a powerful impulse to give her a concrete object to hold. In the middle of our last session before the vacation, Celia told me that she had thought about whether to ask me for something special in relation to my vacation, like something from my office she could keep with her, but she had held herself back. I shared with her the powerful impulse that I had experienced to give her something to hold. This exchange, with some exploration of the meaning of her holding back and the meaning of my impulse, shifted the nature of our connection. We reached a shared understanding of the effect of her mother's illness and death on Celia's fear of showing her vulnerability and the resulting limitations to her capacity for intimacy and attachment. These capacities were directly related to the relationship issues with her husband that prompted her to seek therapy. I thought about, but did not share explicitly, my needs for an unbroken connection to my mother and my fear of inflicting on Celia the kind of abandonments I had lived through early in my life and in therapy. I know now that I yearned for, but never experienced or exacted from Dr. Ross, a similar attunement to my fears of abandonment and my defensive armor of competence.

In the midst of our work on these issues, at a time when the therapy was going well and Celia's marriage was improving, fate intervened for her as it had for me. Celia was seriously injured in a boating accident that left her suffering for months from acute and chronic back pain. She was housebound and unable to sit, not knowing if she would recover fully from her injury or suffer permanent disability. I was luckily able to make regular home visits so the therapy could continue, but the focus of our sessions changed drastically. I was now the recipient of her terror and despair for herself and her future.

In the middle of one of our sessions, she ordered me to leave: "Just go. Get out! You're not doing any good. You can't help." I distinctly recall how calm I felt in the face of her raw desperation. Knowing exactly what I had urgently needed from Dr. Ross, I understood that my task was simply to maintain a connection to her in this state. I was not deflected from this purpose by the intensity of her affect or by feelings of help-lessness in the face of her difficult fate. I told her that I wanted to stay for the full time even if I wasn't helping. But her despair only escalated, and she started crying and yelling at me, "Leave! I want you to leave!"

At another phase of my life, I might have left the session, perhaps feeling that I had failed, perhaps relieved to remove myself from her rage and despair, or perhaps believing that she chose to have me leave and I was correct to comply. I am convinced that my acute awareness of how utterly abandoned I felt by Dr. Ross and how desperately I wanted him to stay related to me in spite of my unbearable feelings gave me power and kept me focused. I was able to insist, with a vehemence equal to hers, from a position that I can only describe as one of centered clarity, "That's a *feeling* you're having, and it will *pass!*" I had no ambivalence: I wanted to remain with her and I did. The remaining ten minutes of the session were not easy. Celia was silent and appeared angry, but I perceived her to be calmer. We sat together in silence, punctuated by my occa-sional comments about what I was experiencing. Within the transference (and countertransference as daughter and patient) matrix, I was the mother who refused to abandon her despairing young child.

Had I left, I might have reinforced the destructive potency of her affect state by fleeing from it, repeating my own experience as a patient in analysis. Remaining related to each other was an invaluable experience for each of us, facilitated because my patient mirrored a vulnerable part of myself that Dr. Ross was abandoning. In responding to my patient, figuratively speaking, I, as therapist, vicariously provided both my patient and my acutely vulnerable self with yearned-for empathy.

After this encounter, Celia and I went on to accomplish the next step of therapeutic work, one that I felt Dr. Ross was unable to provide me. When her acute despair subsided and her situation became more manage-able, literally and psychologically, we were able to make links from her present experience to the underlying transference matrix. We explored, for example, the meaning of her reaction to being physically helpless, to being dependent, and to receiving nurturing and caring from another person,

in the context of her response to the loss of her mother and her determined efforts to take care of herself. Celia, through her physical suffering,
experienced a profound connection to her ill mother and a differentia-
tion from her at the same time. She came to understand her mother's
suffering, but she also managed her own travail in a different way, finding
a way to live with her pain and disability and to maintain a relationship
with her husband.

Providing Celia with an experience within the therapeutic relationship
that I could not have with Dr. Ross highlights another dimension of the
effect of my negative experience in therapy on my work as a therapist:
envy of my patients. One of the striking effects of my heightened intu-
itive awareness of my patients' needs and sharpened capacity to respond
empathically to them was the odd experience of envying my patients for
having me as their therapist. I know that, before my negative experience
in therapy, I might occasionally feel that another therapist could be more
helpful, effective, or insightful than me. I rarely had the sense that I was
a better therapist than someone else would be. The experience of actually envying my patients for having me as a therapist came as a surprise.

There was a striking absence of destructiveness in my envy of my
patients, which has led me to reconsider the concept of envy (see Feldman
and de Paola, 1994, for a recent discussion of the psychoanalytic concept
of envy). As I think about my envy now, I can perceive the following
sequence of events. As a patient, I experienced the loss of the omnipotent good object through the collapse of the analyst. I restored the omnipotent good object through becoming this object in relation to some of my
patients (therapists who are patients are also identified with their analysts)
and having it vicariously. Hate and aggression were directed not at patients,
with whom I was identified, but at the analyst. The aggression was chan-
neled into a competitive triumph (the analyst was not regarded as having
anything good but I, as a therapist, had what he lacked) and into a
consciously experienced murderous rage.

In both my analyses, an opportunity arose to make a shift from omnipotent self-reliance to reliance on an imperfect other, corresponding to
Winnicott's (1971) conception that patients become able to use objects
as part of a maturational process that depends on a facilitating environment. The change from object relating (when the object is under the
baby/patient's omnipotent control) to object usage (a capacity that develops
within a facilitating environment) occurs when the patient places the analyst
outside the area of the patient's omnipotent control. This occurs through
the patient's attempted destruction of the analyst and the analyst's survival
of the destruction. Unless this shift occurs, the patient can only relate
to the analyst as a projection of a part of the self and can never receive
something "other than me" from the analyst. For the shift to occur within
my analyses, the analysts would have had to recognize my dilemma as

the patient: personal capacities were inadequate to handle the tremendous need and deprivation that opened up, leading to profound anxiety about survival at the same time that a powerful refusal to rely on anything external to the self was operating.

The fact that both crises in my analyses occurred around reproductive issues is not surprising, not only in view of the connection with the early abandonments when my mother was pregnant. In becoming a mother, I could identify with an omnipotent, idealized mother and establish a mother–infant unit that was secure, an experience I did not have. I made of the male analysts idealized omnipotent good mothers and never-abandoning fathers and then could not tolerate their human inability to measure up to this expectation. I also believe that I became for each analyst an object they relied on and that I could not sustain this role. My seduction of each analyst into making use of me in this way was also a transference enactment in the sense of representing my effort to secure an unbreakable attachment. I wish that my analysts and I could have recognized this dynamic, but there was a collapse of the symbolic realm that rendered an analytic attitude beyond our reach.

MY CURRENT WORK AS A THERAPIST

This chapter would be incomplete without an example of the unusual consultations I have been providing for patients and therapists in serious, unresolvable impasses. As I was able to help patients like Celia and, at the same time, help myself, I developed an understanding of the power of intersecting primary vulnerabilities in therapeutic relationships (Elkind, 1992). Paradoxically, my negative experiences as a patient have had a powerful and positive impact on my clinical work. As a result of writing and presenting my conception of the intersection of primary vulnerabilities and defenses in therapist–patient dyads, I have been receiving unsolicited requests from both patients and therapists for the direct intervention of consultation. They want help resolving the impasse so that the therapy can either continue productively or come to a close with some understanding of what happened. I have been attempting to provide a new resource for patients and therapists and to understand its role and function. For the past five years, I have averaged at least five new referrals a month, which is indicative of how common the experience of a serious impasse or rupture is. In this discussion, I will focus specifically on the transference–countertransference responses that can arise and be worked with productively in consultations. I will describe part of a recent consultation through this lens, using the present tense to convey the sense of an uncertain outcome that characterizes each consultation.

I receive a telephone call from a young woman, Jeanne, who tells me that she has not been able to return to her therapist since they had an angry interchange in a session two weeks ago. She heard about me from a friend and wants an appointment for consultation. I explain how I structure the consultations and suggest that she leave a message for her therapist, asking him to save her ongoing appointment time and letting him know that she is seeking consultation. We find a time to meet.

When I open the door to my waiting room, Jeanne is in the midst of pacing back and forth, hugging her arms to her chest. She appears to be in her early thirties and is dressed in a suit, which is at odds with her high level of physical energy and emotional intensity. Exercise clothes or jeans would be more fitting.

She walks briskly ahead of me into my office and barely sits on the edge of the couch, leaning forward to talk to me as if her words will reach me faster. With a brief pause for encouragement from me, she plunges into a description of her therapy and her therapist, Dr. Kramer. She explains the events leading up to their fight, struggling to contain her anger and distress. The central importance of her relationship to her therapist, Dr. Kramer, is viscerally apparent.

Listening, I am aware of how hard it is to describe to someone else an agonizing breach in therapy, hoping for understanding, but fearful the response will make things worse. If the other person doesn't understand why the breach matters, the trauma intensifies and the sense of being beyond reach increases. I think a thought that arises often: how much easier it is to have empathy for someone other than myself. Psychotherapy, designed to help patients, sometimes provides a form of self-empathy for the therapist too.

Jeanne's story gradually unfolds. Dr. Kramer, with whom she has been meeting twice a week for five years, was a wonderful therapist until the impasse. He always understood what she was trying to say, not just the words, but also the feelings. He helped her comprehend her family dynamics and how they impact her work and her relationships with men. When I ask for some examples, Jeanne tells me that her father divorced her mother when Jeanne was four years old. He quickly remarried and fathered a son. During her childhood, Jeanne spent every other weekend and a good part of each summer vacation with her father and stepmother, but she could not compete with her half-brother for her father's affection and attention. His son was the apple of his eye. From her point of view, her father always took his son's side in any dispute. Even if her father did behave in a loving way toward her, making her feel special, she still had to leave him and return to her mother.

Jeanne first began therapy because she was unable to have a sustained relationship with a man. She had no trouble meeting men, but once involved, she would bump up against a brick wall of mistrust. For a long time, she told herself she just hadn't met the right person, but eventually, she saw that she was repeating a pattern. She knew the pattern was connected to her emotional conflicts with her father and her half-brother, and she hoped that, by working with a male therapist, she would encounter and resolve them. She was happy with her female friendships and was successful in her work as director of a shelter for battered women. But how would she ever trust a man? She believed she could trust Dr. Kramer, but now that belief seems like a naive and misguided idea. She becomes anxious at this statement, as if assessing whether or not I am going to take Dr. Kramer's side.

I ask her to tell me what happened in their last session. Jeanne sighs and leans forward, elbows on her knees, covering her face with her hands. After a pause, she takes a breath and sits up straight. She explains that she found Dr. Kramer's name from a list of referrals at her agency. She did not realize that he was also seeing a friend and coworker at her agency until recently, when Clare made a remark about beginning therapy. Without thinking about it, she asked Clare whom she was seeing. She was shocked at her immediate physical reaction to hearing Clare say Dr. Kramer's name. She could feel the blood drain out of her head, her heart started racing, and she came close to fainting. But she managed to pull herself together and did not tell Clare the reason for her physical distress.

Later, the more she thought about having to share Dr. Kramer with Clare, the more intolerable the idea seemed. She didn't feel able to wait two more days until her next appointment with Dr. Kramer, so she called him. When he returned her call, she told him she had learned that he was Clare's therapist and was having trouble accepting it. Did he have any time to meet with her before her next scheduled appointment? Unfortunately, he didn't. She waited for him to say something empathic or reassuring, but he was silent. Finally, she ended the silence by saying that she would see him at her regular time. She tried to reason with herself, tell herself that he would have given her a time if he had one, but some part of her found it unbearable that he didn't find a way to meet with her.

Listening to Jeanne, I think about the dual levels of trauma for patients when there is a rupture. The first level resides in the therapist's original upsetting action, and the second level in the therapist's subsequent failure to communicate a psychological understanding of why the action was upsetting, what primary vulnerability was activated in the patient, and that a primary vulnerability of the therapist might have been involved.

Jeanne, becoming visibly upset, describes the ensuing session with Dr. Kramer. She was angry when she began the session and felt out of control. She berated Dr. Kramer for taking Clare on as a patient when he was already working with her. She urged him to transfer Clare to a different therapist. She accused him of being unethical, of violating a boundary by taking on a coworker of a patient. Dr. Kramer did not respond in his usual calm, empathic way. He said, sounding angry, that he had not known Clare worked at the same agency when he accepted her into therapy. Therapists often work with individuals who know each other. This situation provides an opportunity to work with feelings of rivalry and envy.

Jeanne, who had won awards in debate in college, argued vigorously with him about his judgment. She told him she had enough opportunity to work on competition in childhood and needed less, not more. She said that Dr. Kramer stubbornly refused to consider her point of view. In what she thought was a hostile tone of voice, he told her that her wish for an exclusive relationship with her father could not come true in the real world. Shocked by his mean comment, Jeanne was speechless. She sat there for a moment not knowing what to do. Finally, she realized that she could not win the debate, nor could she locate the loving and empathic therapist he had been. Worse, she could not tolerate the intensity of her rage and hurt. Seeing no alternative but to leave an impossible situation, she announced she was leaving. She went home and waited for a telephone call from Dr. Kramer that never came. After a few days, she left him a message canceling her next appointment and then telephoned me.

As I listen to Jeanne, I too can feel angry at Dr. Kramer. Why did he participate in an argument only one of them could win? How could he miss the importance of Jeanne's expression of her hurt and angry feelings, the feelings she probably could not risk expressing to her father? I recognize my identification with Jeanne as the misunderstood patient, but from the consultant's vantage point, I can also identify with Dr. Kramer. I can easily appreciate how intimidating Jeanne must have been to him and how Dr. Kramer might have been knocked off-center by the force of her anger. Because I am in the role of a consultant, I am not directly caught up in their affects. Consequently, I am able to discern the transference matrix, apparent to me yet obscured for them. The capacity to regard both patient and therapist with a maximum of empathy and a minimum of judgment is available to a consultant but is often difficult to access in the role of patient or therapist.

As our session draws to a close, I am able to offer Jeanne a conceptual framework that makes sense of their impasse. Dr. Kramer unwittingly catapulted her into an area of primary vulnerability—abandonment and betrayal—shaped early on by the loss of her father and subsequent competition for his love. The wounding in her area of primary vulnerability was compounded by Dr. Kramer's inability to offer her an extra session and his failure to convey an understanding of the roots of the wounding (that he was activating the inaccessible and abandoning father complex). Her anger appears to have catapulted him into a defensive stance. Now her attachment bond to him is in jeopardy. I explain how, when significant attachment bonds are at risk, we experience anxiety, grief, and a lack of safety in the world. No wonder she is as upset as she is.

I ask if she thinks Dr. Kramer would be willing to participate in the consultation and, if so, whether she would want him to. We discuss the advantages and disadvantages of his participation. Right now, I am her ally, but if I meet with him, she may feel that I have taken his side, reenacting the experience of abandonment, becoming like a stepmother in the transference, but there is also the possibility that the three of us might find a way to work together cooperatively on her behalf. If we can work together cooperatively, she might have a new experience, one that was missing in childhood when her mother and father competed for her love just as she and her half-brother competed for attention from her father.

After some deliberation and discussion, Jeanne decides to sign a release and to contact Dr. Kramer, asking him to participate in the consultation with me. We schedule another appointment for the following week, hoping that I will have had some communication with Dr. Kramer by that time.

The consultation is now constructively underway. Regardless of whether Dr. Kramer meets with me, even though I am hopeful that he will, Jeanne has already altered the impasse, simply by taking the constructive action of enlisting my help. She has empowered herself in a way that was not possible when she was a dependent child. She is not responding only as the angry and hurt young daughter in the transference, but also as an adult who has enough hope of being understood and of working through the impasse with Dr. Kramer to bring in a consultant.

Dr. Kramer contacts me promptly. Although he has some reservations, he is willing to consult with me. I introduce myself, explain how impasse consultations work, and acknowledge the awkwardness of our working together without prior contact. We proceed to have an interesting discussion about the crisis in the therapeutic relationship. Initially, Dr. Kramer is convinced that Jeanne needs to tolerate his holding a different point of view. He cannot sustain the position of the yearned-for, empathic father. Jeanne needs to accept this reality and grieve the loss of her fantasy. Without disagreeing, I ask him to make some space to think about his response to her. Is there any part of his response that might be an enactment related to Jeanne's family? Is there anything in his reaction that feels personally familiar to him? Is there a way in which he may have lost his connection to her when she became so angry? Eventually, Dr. Kramer recalls how gratifying a patient Jeanne was when she adored him unambivalently, and how shocked he was when confronted unexpectedly with her rage. We wonder whether Jeanne's father and mother might have had a similar experience. Dr. Kramer's explorations then go beyond the transference matrix. He begins to consider his self-righteous stance regarding the legitimacy of working with Clare, and he realizes that aggressive self-righteousness has always served him well as a personal defensive style. As we consider these possibilities, a space for reflection opens up, and we both feel the deadlock loosen.

I ponder my role and function as a consultant to Jeanne and Dr. Kramer. I know that, for Jeanne, I am the strong ally she lacked as a child. I am providing the empathic understanding and the adult power to intervene that was absent from her mother or father. For Dr. Kramer, I am providing a qualitatively different reflective space than might be available to him in conventional consultation, in which the consultant only has indirect access to the patient through the therapist's perceptions and ideas. I have an experiential connection to both of them. Optimally, my empathic link to each of them can create a bridge that will enable the therapy to continue and Jeanne's experience of abandonment, betrayal, and rageful attack to be integrated into the therapeutic relationship. A rupture alone, without a conscious working through process, leads to the most damaging and negative experiences. An experience of rupture *and* repair, which appears likely to occur here, can be positive.

Providing the often essential third perspective of a consultant to patients and therapists who inevitably become tangled in transference–countertransference knots and in colliding personal primary vulnerabilities is extraordinarily gratifying for me. When the knots loosen, I have a reparative moment of understanding my negative experiences as a patient, in which the painful affects associated with them are contained by psychological understanding. I have also been in the position of the therapist enlisting the help of a consultant for an impasse with a patient. I felt remarkable relief at being understood and at the knowledge that someone else was helping me. In this case my patient had a similar experience, I have often wondered what might have transpired in my analyses if a consultant had been available to us.

CONCLUSION

If I had to choose the single most significant impact of my negative experiences as a patient, I would point to my heightened awareness of the significance of intersecting vulnerabilities and defenses of patient and therapist in understanding injurious or negative (and positive) experiences in analysis. Remaining in a fixed stance of judgment about who created the difficulties can block an opportunity to conceptualize the mutual and unconscious impact of patient and therapist (see Robbin, 1995). Whether the therapeutic relationship continues or terminates is ultimately less important than whether patient and therapist have a psychological understanding of what occurred. Psychological understanding contains painful affects and opens up the possibility of empathy and compassion for our human vulnerabilities and the defenses that we rely on to manage them.

REFERENCES

Elkind, S. (1992), *Resolving Impasses in Therapeutic Relationships*. New York: Guilford.
—— (1994), The consultant's role in resolving impasses in therapeutic relationships. *Amer. J. Psychoanal.*, 4:3–13.
—— (1995), The consultant's role when the analyst terminates therapy. *Amer. J. Psychoanal.*, 55:331–346.
Feldman, E. & de Paola, H. (1994), An investigation into the psychoanalytic concept of envy. *Internat. J. Psycho-Anal.*, 75(Part 2):217–234.
Leowald, H. (1980), On the therapeutic action of psychoanalysis. In: *Papers on Psychoanalysis*. New Haven, CT: Yale University Press, pp. 221–256.
Nathanson, S. (1989), *Soul-Crisis: One Woman's Journey Through Abortion to Renewal*. New York: New American Library.
Robbin, S. (1995), War games: Getting even or getting out. *Survivorship*, 7:1–3.
Winnicott, D. W. (1960), The theory of the parent–infant relationship. In: *Maturational Processes and the Facilitating Environment*. New York: International Universities Press, 1965, pp. 37–55.
—— (1971), The use of an object and relating through identifications. In: *Playing and Reality*. Middlesex, England: Penguin, pp. 101–111.

II

Childhood Life Crises and Identity Concerns of Therapists

11

The Effects of Sexual Trauma on the Self in Clinical Work

B. F. STEVENS

I was sexually violated by my older brother from the time I was six until I was 16. The forms of sexual violation included prolonged kissing, fondling my breasts and touching my genitals, and masturbating himself against me. When I was eight, I told my father. He punished my brother and told him that he would kill him if it happened again. My brother beat me severely for telling and told me he would kill me if I said anything again. My father told my mother, who said nothing to me. I didn't tell another adult until I was an adult. Neither of my parents comforted me; their philosophy was the less said, the better; it would be forgotten. I loved my brother, and I hated him. He was in love with me and envied and was jealous of me. He didn't understand, nor does he understand now, that making me do things I didn't want to do, touching me in ways I didn't want to be touched, trying to force me to give him something I had and he wanted, has had enduring consequences.

As a subject of the abuse that I read about in the literature, I have a unique perspective. I have lived within the shame and secrecy that the denial surrounding the sexual violation of children promotes. As a consequence, I am especially attuned to these characteristics in my clinical work. In this chapter, I discuss some of the themes that run through my work and the strengths and limitations that I see arising from my experience of sexual violation. I include case material from two patients, both of whom were sexually violated as children and with whom I have learned a good deal. While my experience and that of both patients are separate and unique, I believe that it is my experience of having been sexually violated that allows me to be helpful in the ways that I am.

WHO I AM AS A THERAPIST

Being violated sexually was horrible. There was and is nothing good about it. It has not made me a better person or a better therapist. I have learned some things from working through my experience, one of which is the willingness to look evil in the eye. I am writing about what comes naturally to me, not what I have learned from my training or from intellectual sources. I hear about sexual violation because I am open and willing to hear about it, and I convey this to patients. My clinical training is sometimes less helpful in working with sexual violation than my reading in women's studies and feminist research. Believing is not the problem for me that it is for many others (and not because I am incredulous or naive) because I grew up in a period (1965 to now) favorable to feminist interpretation. Using my own experience of sexual violation as a way to identify with patients allows me to believe what might seem unbelievable to the patient and to others.

Both my past and current constructions of myself relate to my strengths and weaknesses as a therapist. My own therapy and my training and clinical experience have eliminated some of the element of surprise from the exploration of transferential and countertransferential difficulties related to my history. My choice of therapeutic orientation has likely been influenced by my own historical experience. I have never been able to wholly embrace Freudian theory, in which the distinction was not clearly held between my own fantasies and wishes and the reality that someone else's fantasies were being enacted upon me. The schools of object-relations and developmental theory have been friendlier intellectual homes to me. I engage in therapy with the belief that thoughts and feelings can be put into words and not actions and that, through this process, relief and integration are possible. I acknowledge the efficacy and sometime necessity of other kinds of therapy (art and movement, for example) for people who have been severely traumatized, but I don't practice them. Words are what feel safest for me.

My interest is in how people make sense and learn not to make sense out of their own experiences. My goal in treatment is to help them learn more about themselves so they have more of themselves—so they have more choice-making abilities in the present. I see the work of therapy as requiring a necessary suspension of judgement; I am not, however, morally neutral about sexual violation. This is a tension that I often find difficult to hold. The framework of therapy requires a stance of neutrality, and I can take it. My ability to do so is what permits me the objectivity that I am able to offer patients. I see my work as being not about judging, but about my being able to see with increased complexity and clarity where and for what I stand.

The consequences of sexual abuse, especially that which is ongoing and within the family, are great. They take time to understand and to learn to live with in new ways. Change is constant, and we now know enough about traumatic experience to know that it is its unchanging quality that makes it continue to be traumatic. The reexperiencing that can happen during the course of treatment can be used to alter the traumatic course so that the material begins to change and can be made sense of in new ways, can be remembered. This means that one is able to have a different relationship to the content of the memories; perspective allows for some measure of control. Concomitantly, one comes to have a different relationship to one's internal life and to others in the world. This is the real work of therapy, the process of creating different relationships with self and others than were possible before. This process tends to be gradual and, from my point of view, continues throughout the life span.

Some people are reluctant to accept the changes that remembering requires, fearing that the veracity of their experiences is lost in the process. These people know that some things are too horrible to be forgotten and fear that, if one can come to learn to live in a different relation to one's pain, one is in danger of forgetting the source or minimizing what happened. While I can appreciate this fear, it isn't my experience of healing, for myself or for others. This is one aspect of my own experience that I draw upon to give me patience and authority in my approach to "resistance." I know whence I speak, and I know I convey this to patients. Those who are most likely to forget or to minimize are those who were not violated: bystanders and perpetrators and even therapists whose feelings are not readily available to them.

I write this chapter because I believe that, through sharing information, we develop understanding, and our understanding of one another deepens. In general, I believe that secrecy, the keeping of a secret more than the secret itself, is what destroys trust and inhibits movement and intimacy. I write using a pseudonym because I value my privacy, which is a choice I have as an adult that I didn't have as a child. I write not to tell my story, but to demonstrate how I use my story on behalf of my patients.

INTRODUCING MR. A AND MS. D

Mr. A and Ms. D are two patients I've seen in treatment for several years. Mr. A came into treatment with concern about his sexual practices, which he linked directly to an incestuous relationship in his past. His initial awareness has not made the treatment any more straightforward for either of us. Ms. D came into treatment without any awareness of incest, and its emergence in the treatment was horrifying to her. Our work together has been easier, nevertheless, in many respects. I account for this in a very basic way: I empathize and fail to empathize with different aspects of these clients' experiences of themselves. What follows is a short presentation of each patient and an exploration of how my history contributes to this process and affects their treatment.

Mr. A

I have chosen to write about my work with this man because this is work in which I feel especially vulnerable on many levels. Mr. A is a single, heterosexual man in his late twenties whom I have seen in treatment once a week for three years. Mr. A initially sought treatment for incest, which he continues to find very difficult to address with me. He specifically requested a woman, having come from a year of counseling with a man whom he found helpful but with whom he was reluctant to speak about incest.

Bright, insightful, and sensitive, Mr. A holds a master's degree in Fine Arts and works in a halfway house for the mentally ill. Although he is artistically inclined and trained, Mr. A does not seriously pursue a career in his field. Until very recently, he evidenced contempt for "white middle-class values" when the matter of career was raised. Raised in an upper middle-class family, he now lives a socially and economically marginal life. He defends this as a choice based on social consciousness and says he wants to live as dissimilar a life to his parents as possible.

An only child, Mr. A spent long periods of time in the care of a maternal aunt who was psychotic at times, seeing him as her sexual partner and not as a child. Business endeavors took his father away on long trips and his mother often accompanied him. The aunt lived in the household from the time he was four years old and took care of Mr. A while his parents were gone, often for extended periods of time.

Mr. A describes his parents' relationship as "fake" and full of pretense. He remembers his father behaving "like a child" in the face of conflict and says there was every effort to avoid conflict. His mother was emotionally absent, spending a lot of time on her appearance and social connections. His aunt he describes as "very smart and very crazy." She seems to have provided him with emotional warmth and a sense of playfulness that his parents could not. The family atmosphere was formal and distant most of the time, and Mr. A describes himself as a lonely child who, in early adolescence, often thought about dying.

Mr. A is both highly motivated in the treatment and highly anxious. The anxiety inhibits his movement in treatment and in his life, and while it is real, it serves as a resistance to knowing what he feels. He has pursued short-term cognitive therapy and psychopharmacology for help with his anxiety. He is increasingly aware that he has a self that is separate from his anxiety: he is not only his anxiety when he is anxious.

Over the course of the three years, Mr. A has made many changes. He has become fully employed, following a period during which he lived on general relief when he was disabled and new to the area. This was a very debilitating experience that he finds almost unbearably painful to recall. During this period, he began to frequent nude bars to watch the dancers, and his enjoyment of his sadistic fantasies began to trouble him. When he first came to see me, he reported that, while he enjoyed having sex with different women, he couldn't sleep with any woman. He is now living with a woman and feels secure in her love for him. He is uncertain if this is the woman he will marry, and our current focus in treatment is on the many ways he distances himself in his relationships with women and why.

In the beginning of treatment, Mr. A was unable to maintain any eye contact with me. He is now able to look at me, even when he is telling me he will miss me during a vacation. He is able to sit facing me and doesn't worry about his ability to maintain control of himself as he once did. During the same time, I have come to appreciate his sense of humor and can play more easily with words with him. I have become more relaxed in the face of his desire for reassurance and am able to convey this to him.

Mr. A's abstract abilities are highly developed and he is quite creative, but his ability to envision a future for himself is in stark contrast to his ability to visualize three-dimensional designs. He has a hard time believing that he is loved and is worthy of love. He has difficulty holding onto a conception of himself over time. His aunt's impingement upon him during his childhood, against a backdrop of well-to-do neglect, continues to have a profound effect on him now. For him, a core sense of unworthiness and compromised selfhood continues to predominate and shine dully through every effort to change.

Ms. D

I've chosen to write about my work with Ms. D because she is a client with whom I feel a good deal of identification. While our life circumstances are and have been very different, Ms. D's experience of her therapy is one for which I have a lot of empathy.

Ms. D came with an initial request for help with issues about body image and eating patterns. Ms. D found herself either overeating or dieting in a way that she experienced as "out of control." A strikingly beautiful woman of 20, she told me that she'd had no therapy, wanted to see me two times weekly, and said that payment would be no problem. She had graduated the previous year from college and had embarked upon a graduate degree. She was living at home with her parents. She had resumed a relationship with a boyfriend, with whom she had broken up the year before, and things seemed to be going well. She had one woman friend with whom she thought she might like to be closer.

The middle of three children, Ms. D excelled in academic studies and was supported by both parents in this area. What she studied, however, was jointly "agreed upon," and in spite of her ambition and level of achievement, "their" aspirations for her did not extend beyond teaching in a private school. Her parents are prominent leaders in a conservative Greek community, and though affiliated with extended family members, her nuclear family isolated itself from the larger social context. Both sets of grandparents were involved in the brutal tensions on Cypress between Greeks and Turks. The family retains a strong sense of cultural identity, and Ms. D's adolescent exploration of American culture was severely punished. Initially, her sole objection to familial interference in her life was with regard to the privacy of her bedroom.

During the first year, our work revolved around separation issues. Ms. D moved out of the parental home and into a house with others. For the first time, she was reluctant to use her parents' connections and, over the months following her graduation, obtained a job on her own in a business.

During the summer, Ms. D decided she might want to become an analyst and, without saying anything to me, decided to quit treatment to enter analysis. At the session she intended to make her final one with me, she arrived early as usual. When I went to get her from the waiting room, I saw that she looked like a much older woman wearing a long black dress. My association was to her grandmother in Cypress. I was surprised and angry with her lack of communication with me about her plan to terminate and was puzzled by the dress, which was unlike anything I'd ever seen her wear. Towards the middle of the hour, she became silent and said she'd had a dream that was too horrible to tell me. She thought she was going crazy, and she didn't want me to know anything about the dream because I would think she was disgusting. She was too ashamed. At the end of the hour, I encouraged her to keep her analytic consult as a learning experience and to continue therapy with me while we explored what was going on. She agreed to the proposal, and we are now entering the fifth year of therapy.

Subsequently, a brutal and sadistic history of sexual violation by her father has emerged with enough detail to assure Ms. D that she isn't "surely crazy to have these thoughts." While she has continued to refuse to have any contact whatsoever with him or with her brothers, who have assaulted her in public for "lying" and smearing the family name, she is gradually reconnecting with other family members who, to her surprise, believe her. Her relationship to her mother continues to be a primary focus of treatment, with Ms. D mourning the loss of the mother she wants to have but doesn't.

Ms. D's worklife continues to serve as a focus for her ambition. She has quickly risen to a responsible, autonomous, and prestigious position in her company. She is aware that she has many talents and skills and is beginning to think seriously about what she wants to do for a career. She pursues activities for the sake of enjoyment now, and while she continues to become irritable and frustrated when she doesn't have enough to do, her work is no longer the sole channel for her energies or sole source of self-esteem. Her friendships have increased in number and in depth over the course of treatment, and for the first time in her life, she is proud of her ability to be a good friend and to have good friends. Her relationship with her boyfriend has been through many ups and downs; both are uncertain about their future together. They are deeply connected, however, and have stood by each other through an important time in their lives.

THEMES IN THE TREATMENT

Some themes that run throughout my work have a unique meaning to me, given my particular history, and as such, they affect the work. These themes have several sides, which can be seen as strengths and limitations, depending on the context. In this section, I focus on the benefit to treatment that my heightened empathy brings and some of the drawbacks of such attunement. I am going to focus on dilemmas that I'm particularly vulnerable to, illustrated by moments and/or periods in the treatment where the interface in the present between my history and the patient's history is especially crucial.

I AM YOU AND YOU ARE ME

At times, identification is helpful, and at times, it is not helpful to the patient. Identification with another's experience can be an important source of empathy, and yet when there is too much identification, movement and creativity may cease. Differences and conflict can get submerged. If this happens, identification becomes overidentification and can be destructive.

Loss of Historical Family

A very painful point of identification with both Mr. A and Ms. D is in terms of the loss of historical family. At this time, I have contact with many family members, but this wasn't the case for several years. Both patients chose to cut ties with their families and did so with great anger and grief. When Ms. D was ready to reestablish ties with family members, my support came too quickly, perhaps out of the painfulness of my own loss. Again, while I truly know what a loss this is, using my experience to be helpful to her in this dimension was very confounded with my wanting a "good" or "happier" outcome for her. By this, I mean that some relationship is better than none. After several physical altercations, Ms. D again cut off contact with her family. Family members now take up less psychic space than they once did, and she has once again decided to have minimal contact with family members. She no longer pretends they're nonexistent, which for a long time was the most hurtful thing she could imagine doing.

Mr. A spent several excruciatingly lonely years seeing himself as unable to have more than superficial contact with others. This was especially poignant during the holiday season, when he worried about his ability to hold himself together. Early in our work together, he told me that his father had never wanted children and had often let him know this. His mother seems to have been equally disinterested, without saying anything directly to him. From her, he receives polite cards at the holidays and sometimes a small package. His aunt writes to him. He alternates between hating her and having great pity for her in her craziness. He is aware of a painful mix of both wanting and not wanting to hurt her.

It is very painful for me to sit with both patients through their struggles to accept their historical families as they are and to choose not to have contact with them. A part of me always protests, even in the face of bad behavior, that families aren't the people we choose: they're the ones we got. To me, there is something inhumane about refusing contact with family at the time of a birth or a death. I struggle to see my way between taking adequate care of myself in my historical, nuclear family (who deny the significance of my brother's admitted behavior) and living in accordance with my belief that I have a human obligation not to abandon.

Shame in the Transference

One of the major drawbacks to my sense of identification with both patients relates to shame and the working through of the shame in the transference. Working in the transference can be so shame-producing that it is avoided by both of us. It is so intimate and it is with such exposure that one's sense of being defective is revealed. While I may be a "good enough" therapist enough of the time, I privately shame myself about not working more in the transference with Ms. D. Drawing out her devaluation of and contempt for me has been a slow process. The complexity lies in the presence of both the narcissistic vulnerability that arises from the character structures of both sets of parents and the sense of shame that arises from having been sexually violated. In this realm, the client and I have almost too much in common for me to keep perspective on our separateness. There are moments when I forget to be curious about her experience and tend to assume that I know what she's feeling.

The experience of shame is more familiar to me and more tolerable than it used to be. It is considerably more tolerable for me than it is for Ms. D. I have learned that the experience of shame or its milder cousin, embarrassment, are normal experiences, and having such experiences is part of being human. This makes it possible for me to persist in the face of discouragement and to cheerfully encourage my patients to embrace foolishness. Once it is named and the initial shameful response is tolerated, we are able to continue working with this as another piece of information.

For Ms. D, sexual violation and shame for the sexual violation was first introduced in a dream. Her attempted retraction of the material appeared to have shame at its core, too. Shame came to permeate all the work, making it difficult to address. Here, my identification just as often muddies the waters. There is shame for having crazy thoughts, shame for what occurred, shame for continuing to be affected (I should be over this by now), and shame for the ways in which one is affected. For Ms. D, this includes her sexuality and her ability to be sexual. Her avoidance of sexuality is only now being confronted. There is shame for how one is treated, especially by men, and Ms. D's ability to defend herself is what she is proudest of and also most despairing about when she feels she fails.

What I am most aware of is how ashamed I can feel when I realize how I continue to be affected. I am clear that my experience is what I use as the source of my authority, and yet I find my saying "yes" or "no" in a variety of situations often has little meaning to me. I feel ashamed of this, especially when I expect myself to be competent and in charge. I connect this with the meaninglessness my "no" had in the face of my brother's stubbornness. How I say "yes" in the present is a consequence of how I learned in the past that my "yes" and "no" didn't really matter. I have to struggle to know my own desire, and to put my desire first before the other's is yet another struggle. Ms. D does not struggle with this in the way that I do, which is fortunate for both of us.

Individual Differences

Not being able to envision a future for myself, I have learned to live well in the present, to attend fully to where I am. This is a real strength. I am able to empathize with a broad range of people who find themselves in a position of not being where they want to be or where they thought they'd be. Seeing how things do come together gives me faith in the way people are organized and can grow and help themselves when given the occasion to reflect on who they are and what they want. I appreciate deeply the individuality of a life and the resiliency of people in the face of trauma. I try to use the different ways in which I identify with Mr. A and Ms. D to provide me with hope for them in the treatment and to convey to them a sense of hope and belief both in them and in the world.

I identify with Ms. D as being the only female in a sibling group and because of the real and perceived unfairness of treatment attributable to gender. The cultural value of education required her to be well-educated, and she was encouraged in this direction by her parents. However, her parents' vision of her future was to have a career that was expendable when she married and had children, and not one that mattered greatly to her. As the girl, she was responsible for taking care of her brothers, especially her younger one. In this relationship, she received nurturing through her nurturance of him, and so kept alive her sensitivity to others in relationships. This, too, is something for which I have deep empathy, my experience with a younger brother having been quite similar.

Since I am outside her ethnic network and I represent an alternative way of being in the world, I have been, on the whole, more idealized and depended upon than denigrated and resisted in the therapy. This is similar to my own treatment, in which my therapist has not been subject to most of the negative projections that others in my life have suffered from in the process of my work. In our work, what stands out for me is my admiration of Ms. D's determination and the work she has been willing to actively engage in. She committed herself to her treatment and has stuck with it. She has had to learn that she doesn't have to do everything on her own, and over the years, she has become able to trust that "work" is happening, even when she's not consciously doing it. She has gotten a lot of help and has used it well. I identify with this determination and hard work, having worked similarly in my own therapy.

I identify with Mr. A in his deep concern for what is right and wrong and his sensitivity to the suffering of others. His aesthetic sensibility is important to him and is a source of pleasure and self-esteem. He is easily touched by whimsy and takes delight in his own spontaneity. I also identify with Mr. A in the ways in which he gets blocked in his search for self-esteem in both love and work, with his sense of loneliness in the world, and with his genuine sense of surprise that anyone really cares for him.

An important difference between these patients that provides me with a greater sense of perspective lies in the context of violation. It may be that the circumstances of Ms. D's violation contributed to her less compromised sense of herself as a powerful woman. Her sense of entitlement can be joined to her ambition, and she will work to get what she wants. She completely dissociated her nighttime experience of rape, and it would seem that the father did as well. This absolute split may have allowed parts of her self-experience to continue to develop without compromise, so that she has a broader intact base of self-experience with good experiences of the world. The disruption of this self by traumatic experience is different than the disruption of a more neglected self who is asked from an early age to make sense on a daily basis out of great discrepancies in reality with and for a primary caretaker. This was the reality for Mr. A.

While both are quite sensitive and creative, Ms. D has a pragmatism and a "survivor's" skill that was passed along to her from both grandmothers. She is powerfully tied to a tradition of women surviving brutal assault by men. Mr. A received no such cultural message. His sense of the world's safety doesn't reside in "us versus them" as does Ms. D's, because from early on, the danger clearly resided within "us." His father, distant and removed from the realm of children, was unavailable to help his son negotiate learning the ways of the world, and Mr. A continues to struggle, feeling inadequate to the task of taking on his own authority and using it on his own behalf. He is able to use it when he is a part of a group but not for himself alone. Ms. D is able to use her own authority on her own behalf as well as on behalf of others.

BE HERE NOW: EMPATHY AND PRESENCE IN TREATMENT

Bearing Pain

I came to clinical work late in life with the sure knowledge that I knew something about bearing pain. I believe we're responsible to do something with what happens to us and that doing so gives our lives meaning. This pain is not fundamentally different from other sources of pain, and at the same time, there are unique aspects. The psychodynamics one is subject to are ones shared with others, luckily so, since too much specialness in treatment is no gift. While I have a special attunement to sexual violation, I am not necessarily a better therapist for someone who has been sexually abused than another who is willing to listen and to witness.

Winnicott (1965) has described the psyche-soma that comes into being in infancy. Sexual violation in childhood is always a violation of the self, not only of the body, but of the whole self. Young children's selves are their bodies. Working with childhood sexual abuse is working with violations of the self, then, and in this respect, such work is not unique. This is what a good deal of therapy in general is about. This, then, is the balance I am creating in this chapter: there are elements of working with the pain of sexual violation that are true of all kinds of pain, and there are some unique elements. As a therapist, I have sensitivities and empathy that arise from my experience of sexual violation, which are unique, yet I can also see that pain is pain.

I deeply enjoy life, and when I am in sync with myself, my "yes" to life is whole and without question. I like to laugh and laugh deeply. I take deep pleasure in being surprised and spontaneous, which is the essence of being alive and living in the present. I like this in myself. My ability to be present in the moment gives me great enjoyment and allows me to connect as quickly and deeply as I do. A little can go a long way for me, and this contributes to my resilience in the face of sorrow.

Bearing pain includes having the ability to trust in life in the face of despair and to move beyond despair. This requires perseverance, an abiding faith in God or Providence, and a deep love of life. I come from a long line of farmers and often attribute my perseverance to them. They cannot account for my perseverance in human relationships, however, for my

ancestors aren't remembered for the quality of their personal relationships. Getting what is good from another and abiding with another in
the face of adversity and conflict are strengths I've developed that relate
to having been violated. My capacity to trust is deep, and I'm more
willing to trust than mistrust. This is somewhat surprising to me, and it
is out of what I know in myself that I'm able to respond to others who
want to and are afraid to trust. Perseverance is important to the endeavor
of building, of creating, and since I have fashioned my life through taking
charge of myself and continuing to move forward, I appreciate what it
takes.

The ability that developed as I grew to "take in" and live in spite of
what was happening to me, I am now using consciously to help others
bear their pain and rage. To sit with a patient, I have to be willing to
explore my own pain and the defenses I used to protect myself from the
pain. What this means is containing both their and my feelings and experiences. The containing function I perform I see as the most basic and
most important thing I do throughout the therapy. Being able to explore
and contain my own feelings precedes being able to contain the feelings
of my patients. In some ways, I see containing as being the transformed
experience of having, as a child, to accept the projections and sadism of
the one who violated me.

Intimacy: Shame, Distance, and Closeness

Intimacy for me, as well as for these patients, can be confusing. Boundaries
must be and are clarified regularly, raising issues of shame and loss of
perspective. The boundary violations I experienced as a child affect the
ways I perceive and misperceive projected and attempted boundary violations in the treatment. I tend to believe in the historical reality of what
people tell me. I am also likely to believe that what they tell me about
myself in the treatment is true. Separating the internal reality from external
reality in the treatment is sometimes more confusing for me than it may
be for clinicians who haven't been violated.

Reenacted erotic transference comes loaded with anxiety for me given
the broken boundaries in the past. As with projective identification, when
I am aware of something in the room and haven't yet identified it, whether
they are feelings or a particular dynamic, I become anxious until I am
able to name and put into words what I'm feeling and what I think is
going on. This typically occurs with patients who have themselves been
sexually abused, who enact their feelings in the room for a long while
before they can put them into words. For these patients, the fantasies are
more real, and their belief often is that they will be enacted with me.
With patients who haven't been sexually violated, I am more able to be
curious about their experience, and the dynamic feels less murky.

As a clinician committed to verbal treatment, I have to struggle to stay in my chair and keep talking even when I don't want to hear what is being said to me. As a woman who was herself the recipient of acted-out fantasy, I have to contain for myself and the patient the distinction between fantasy and action, feelings and action, thoughts and action.

Shame for the self inhibits the development of intimacy. I know how small something can seem to be, yet feel overwhelmingly shameful. I know the pervasive sense of badness that can pervade the self. When identified as belonging to the experience of sexual violation, it begins to lift. Slightly different than narcissistic shame of the self, it is tied directly to the sexual violation. However, it is similar in its all-pervasiveness. It doesn't seem that this makes a difference in the process of working with the shame, but it does seem that there are more windows of opportunity for strengthening the self so it can continue growing. I try to meet my patients in those "windows."

While I do not identify with many of Ms. D's sexual difficulties, I do understand from whence they come. I empathize with the difficulty of trusting one's own sexual feelings and connecting sexual and loving feelings. Her insistence that sex of any kind is disgusting has proven itself to be a part of the power dynamic between her and her boyfriend, and she refused to work with this at all in therapy, even at the risk of losing the relationship with him. I felt myself at a loss at this point in the treatment. Initially, I thought her fears were only about her sexuality, and I didn't see the sadism involved; we both colluded to keep this aspect of her life out of the room. My caution about being intrusive upon her privacy prevented me from dealing with the sexuality and with the shame that promoted her disgust. The inhibition of intimacy between us paralleled the absence of intimacy between Ms. D and her boyfriend.

My concern about being overly intrusive sometimes prevents me from just being curious with Ms. D and allowing myself to be a real person in the room. I inhibit my use of myself in treatment in order not to overwhelm, intrude upon, or hurt. My effort not to be intrusive often causes me not to ask enough questions about what she says. I've learned over time and from experience of her feeling shamed that she doesn't want to speak when she feels ashamed. When I don't ask, the shame remains unexplored and grows bigger. Over time, we have learned to negotiate these moments, and I have become less inadvertently shaming of her. This process of negotiation has led to greater intimacy between us.

With Mr. A, I am required to be present and not to feel too deeply or visibly. He is easily frightened and experiences me as intrusive or in need of care if I am moved to tears. His concentration in himself is easily disrupted, and this, I now appreciate, is less a response to me than to his internal life. For a long time, I tried not to show much feeling, thinking this would be reassuring; it wasn't. I now concentrate on putting as much into words as I can of what is going on with me and what I imagine his emotional response might be. In working together, I've come to expect a retreat after an especially poignant or moving moment, or the session that follows an especially intimate one will be distant. For the first two years, he wouldn't show up the following week; now, in the third year, he spends the following session either telling me about a new treatment plan he's considering or speaking again about his overwhelming anxiety. This no longer seems to have to do as much with his fear of my power over him but, rather, with my closeness to him and his question about whether or not he can regulate the distance between us.

The confusion between fantasy and reality and internal and external reality is especially poignant for Mr. A. He is troubled by his fantasies about other women and worries that having these fantasies means he wants to act on them. This leads to fears that he will jeopardize his relationship with his girlfriend. For example, in the therapy, Mr. A speaks about what he considers a fantasy, revealing that he is responding to an actual woman's demonstrated interest in him. This interest is more disturbing than gratifying, and as we continue talking, he associates to how he felt as a late adolescent in his aunt's presence. As the feeling becomes real for him, he begins to withdraw with anxiety. I remind him that I am not his aunt, that we can work with the feeling in the room and learn more about what goes on for him. He tells me that he is afraid I will use what he says against him to trap him and that I just want to prove he's as bad as other men. I remind him of his prior experience with me, and he relaxes visibly. He goes on to describe how his aunt denigrated men, while holding him exempt because he wasn't yet a man, and tells me more about how she interpreted his thoughts and feelings to and for him. He is afraid I will do this, and I remind him that I haven't done this so far and tell him that I appreciate his fear given his experience of her. Mr. A went on to talk about his father, surprising himself a second time when he realized that his father, too, had a hard time fending off the "mind games" of the aunt and recalls the fits he saw his father throw in her presence. Mr. A's self-denigrating interpretation of his and his father's behavior as "childish" gives way to my suggestion that they both found ways to maintain their integrity. Several weeks after this, he says he is thinking about writing his father and mentions that, when I work with him on something very specific, he feels more trusting of me and feels safe letting me know more about him.

KNOWING AND NOT KNOWING

When bad things happen to you that affect you, there are ways you know it and ways you don't. I always knew that my older brother sexually violated

me, and I knew it had a big effect on me. I also didn't know. This is
the fundamental paradox that I faced as a child and that I continue to
face as an adult. While in some respects my history gives me a kind of
familiarity with the work required of patients who have been sexually
violated, the work also stretches me in ways that are perennially uncomfortable. When I am conscious and my anxiety is contained, knowing
and not knowing allows me to tolerate uncertainty. When I am caught in
anxiety and not aware of what is going on with me, knowing and not
knowing is one of the blind spots with which I work.

The problem of reality testing and denial in the moment is an old one:
is this happening, and what is it that is happening? The loss of perspective that I am subject to arises when I doubt the reality of my experience. This can happen when I am too much in the present and don't step
back and reflect on what is/has been happening. It can happen when I
become very anxious and when I'm frightened. Remembering that I am
not responsible for the thoughts, feelings, fantasies, and actions of others
is my task as therapist. I am especially sensitive to projective identification, having been the object of much of this defense in my historical
family. When I am afraid or confused, I tend to forget that defenses are
defenses. In the moment, things that I know not to be happening feel
real and true. I am subject to many of the same irrealities as the patient,
and even if this is primarily an internal experience for me, I am subject
to a loss of perspective that I usually count on in doing my work. *Am* I
being abusive as I'm accused of being? I can get just as caught as the
patient in these moments; it is very humbling.

Mr. A acknowledges that I am important to him and that he is fond
of me and that this is hard for him to let me know. He risks my taking
advantage of his admission to misuse him in some way. This extends to
his doing the work he is in therapy to do: I can get him to do it. He
doesn't want to do it; he is ashamed and fears that I will think poorly
of him. He separates me into Dr. S, whom he doesn't think means him
harm, and B, a woman who is not to be trusted for any reason. I can
sometimes be a woman who is desirable: he is very ashamed to admit
this. Or I can stand for his aunt and, as such, am an object of hatred
and fear: nothing would be too bad to subject me to in fantasy.

Holding onto these distinctions and playing with them brings Mr. A
close to experiencing disintegration. While he is able to do this in his
artwork and with ideas and words, he says he is too frightened to do this
in his work with me about his aunt. It is as if he takes on her psychotic
reality when words are the medium. This may be related to word games
having been an important sexualized connection between them as he got
older. This leaves him vulnerable to intelligent women who use language
well, something he finds important. He can experience women "getting
into his mind" as a literal experience and spends much time in our sessions

preventing me from taking over his mind. (What has been most astonishing for me in my work with Mr. A is how seemingly psychotic material is suddenly present, without warning, and then is gone. Some material
exists in dissociated states over which he has very little control.)

This has been an especially important endeavor in this past year because
his life is in better shape and there is less to focus on that is external.
Just letting me know that this is what he is doing gives me an edge that
he dreads because, to him, knowledge is power. As I press on, keeping
us both as uncomfortable as is tolerable, my intent is merely to level the
playing field, to bring us both into an area of uncertainty where something new might happen. There is something almost physical about this,
which I suspect is the level of tension and all that is contained in the
silence, in the absence of words. Words are only safe after the fact for
the purpose of describing what has happened between us in those moments.
I can speak about my experience when I am clear that I speak only for
me in my chair, and I am careful to describe what I experience internally that is me and what I see visually that is him, across from me.

There is another aspect to knowing and not knowing that has to do
with making meaning out of the whole of one's experiences. This seems
to be a basic problem of integration. Various capacities and domains of
the self's experience can remain separate and dissociated for those who
have been sexually violated. This can interfere with the maintenance of
a consistent sense of self-esteem. I have particular empathy for the struggles with self-esteem and efficacy that can hang on far beyond what would
seem to make sense in the face of contrary evidence. The internal experience of feeling oneself "worthy" or "good enough" over time and unin-
terrupted by chance occurrences can be hard to achieve and maintain.

The experience of not being able to see and to attribute accurate meaning
to what one does is very painful, for one is left feeling inadequate and
incompetent no matter what. The connections between who one is and
what one does get muddled and rigidified when sexual violation occurs.
Coming to make new distinctions that are both stable and flexible are an
important part of coming to see that abilities are transferable across
domains.

The cognitive rigidity that inhibits both the learning of new experience and the connecting of experiences is something with which I am
familiar from my own experience. For Mr. A, this is apparent in his attitude towards himself as a man in a relationship and a man at work. He
is currently involved in a loving relationship with a woman to whom he
feels equal in many respects and of whom he feels deserving. He can
imagine that, if things do not work out on the long run, he will be sad
but recover and be able to find another important relationship. He is
increasingly confident that what she sees in him is real and that his good
treatment of her is not just a fluke, that he really is a pretty nice guy.

He can let me know that I have been helpful, and he appreciates me. This belief in his basic goodness and worthiness with her and in the context of relationships does not carry over into his career pursuits, however. Though he has even more concrete evidence of his skills and his intelligence in his work, carrying over a basic sense of being "good enough" from one domain into another is inconceivable to him. When I mention such a cross-over, he is blank and uncomprehending. In the face of anything *new*, Mr. A's characteristic response is, "I can't." This gut response is at odds with his demonstrated persistence, intelligence, creativity, and real abilities in the world, and yet it is this *belief* that appears as an unexamined one every time he attempts something new. He is willing to take a chance and to be dependent enough on me to let me help him by talking in the session about what he is doing outside the session, but he can't really believe in what he is doing.

BLINDNESS TO PATHOLOGY

My understanding of pathology has two sides. I have a great tolerance for the variability of human motive and behavior and am quite nonjudgemental of what is pathological. I work well with very disturbed people, often because I see their pathology as "normal." Being able to see that we all share in having chaotic experiences and that there is great integrity in the craziest of symptoms is a strength for a therapist. However, I get into trouble in not recognizing and naming sickness outside of me, because I too readily assume the "burden of proof" for sickness. This arises from not having been able to acknowledge or know the meaning of the assaults on me, to say aloud and have it acknowledged that my brother was disturbed. The family fiction was that he was a "late bloomer," and I was "too fragile" and "too sensitive." In adolescence, I was called "hysterical" and "angry." As a child, I tried to protect myself against others' projections by "spacing out" and by taking care of others' feelings. The downside of containment of the others' feelings, when they are yet unable to contain and modulate their feelings on their own, is that I still take in too much for my own good. I err on the side of seeing the truth in the patient's projection and take it on as if it weren't also a projection.

A serious drawback to my sense of identification with Ms. D includes overidentifying in such a way as to minimize her disturbance of character. In part because I see us both as hard workers in therapy, I assume that it is longevity in treatment that makes the difference between us. In part because I tend to want to see others as they can be and not always as they are, I misjudge the depth of pathology. In my work with Ms. D, I followed her lead and focused on the sexual violation for a long time before beginning to deal with the narcissistic inheritance from both parents. In some ways, I think that I didn't want to see how relationally impaired she is because I didn't want to know how difficult the work ahead was going to be. I wanted to see her as she wanted to be seen, and this was protective for me. It did not necessarily help her.

Reenactment, Projective Identification, and Dissociation

I am deeply committed to people coming to know their own truth and being able to stand for and behind themselves. To this end, I put myself at the service of my patients. I am able to bear a good deal of pain, to call it up, to face it, and to contain it. I do not give up in despair in the face of evil, pain, and endless human travail. This translates in my work as a willingness to hear, to witness, and to contain whatever comes.

Putting these strengths into practice with patients who reenact rather than remember is a challenge. Reenactment, often a consequence of traumatic violation, is a way of showing what cannot be spoken. I do not always meet this challenge as adequately as I would like. I struggle with getting caught in projective identifications and other primitive defenses. One limitation of the stance that I should be able to contain whatever comes my way is that I can take insufficient care of myself. I can also find myself taking too much responsibility for the work of the patient out of a sense of overidentification.

One projective identification bind where I enact what the other feels, occurs when I withdraw out of fear in the face of what I feel to be toxic rage. I experience the rage as the only reality, and I don't recognize the fear behind it. I tend to forget that the patient's defenses are defenses when I'm really scared. Everything feels real and true in the moment. When I'm sensing the fear-rage coming from the other, I become immobilized. I use old and familiar defenses like minimizing, denying, or dissociating, for example, "This isn't really happening." However, once rage is recognizably out in the room and I can see it and name it, my fear usually disappears. I settle down and am present for the patient again. I get more comfortable as the boundaries get clearer, both within me and between the patient and me. Being able to put words to the experience makes being annihilated by the other tolerable: it is having a theoretical framework that makes sense out of *why* I am having this experience that makes the having of the experience *again* make sense.

Mr. A has great difficulty describing how he dissociates, unlike Ms. D who is clearer about it and has worked to stop it. One big difference between the two is that she fundamentally believes that I want to be helpful to her and that I will be. She doesn't believe I want to harm her. Mr. A believes I can and will harm him. The dissociation of both Mr. A and Ms. D arises because there has been a profound violation of spirit and body by someone who was trusted and upon whom, as children, both were entirely dependent. Mr. A's difficulties are with the fact of abuse, not with sex.

When sometimes in utter frustration I suggest he consider stopping therapy if he doesn't want to do the work he came to do, he feels scared that I will kick him out and acknowledges that he spends a lot of time "keeping me out" without looking at what this is about. In a curious way, he is carrying out the dominant–submissive fantasy with me, without the sexualized content. I feel used. He acknowledges having all the power and working to keep it, to keep me from realizing what he is doing. He gets a lot of satisfaction being able to "outsmart" me, especially since he believes me to be a very smart woman, as his aunt was. He enacts a ritual with me, a sado-masochistic fantasy without the sex. He says he has no sexual fantasies about me; however, when I bring up erotic feelings, I feel a lot of sexual energy in the room. We remain at this place, and as with Ms. D, the most fruitful point of entry seems to be through the terminology of "power dynamics." He freely admits to engaging in a power struggle; sadism is a bit harder as he becomes overcome with shame, and sexual or erotic feelings, towards me especially, are harder to speak about.

As with Ms. D, working in the transference in these moments is very difficult. The trust that is necessary to count on the boundaries between fantasy and reality staying in place seems to disappear, and Mr. A doesn't believe it's possible. His fear is that he is psychotic at a deep level he doesn't want me to know about, and it is less that I will hurt him than that I'll *see* him. See him as he is and then he'll be without hope, and he will have to leave.

Mr. A is afraid he is crazy and a bad man, and Ms. D is afraid she is damaged in a fundamental way that she can never recover from, that her sexual being is without hope. I have known all three beliefs and have worked through enough in my own treatment to know that they are beliefs and not facts and that beliefs have a lot of truth that may be as strong as fact. So I can say both that I know the way and know that I cannot know what lies ahead for them. It is a curious position to find oneself in, and it's where I spend most of my time during the working day, with greater or lesser appreciation at any given moment.

WORKING WITH SADISM: HEY DEVIL, OVER HERE!

Welcoming the Negative Transference

I increasingly feel more comfortable working with sadism. I think that this kind of work precedes the development of intimacy and that it is important work for me to be open to do. I don't always like it, even though I believe it's necessary. However, I find hatred and hostility most difficult when they remain hidden and indirect, and I now go to some lengths to bring these feelings into the open.

I am vulnerable to being devalued, and this often comes up most concretely around the fee. I am sensitive to being encroached upon, given my history. I am usually relieved that the power dynamic beneath the devaluation is becoming clear in the field between the patient and me, because I deal better with what is out in the open.

Mr. A is a patient for whom paying buys safety and clarity of boundaries and for whom being able to pay and paying reflect on his sense of himself as an adequate man. What is striking about Mr. A's relationship to money and paying for his own treatment is his integrity: he wants to pay for treatment, and he is very careful with the management of his funds so he can. He has gone from paying nothing to paying a negotiated reduced fee, which he is able to afford on a weekly basis because he is now working full-time. With the payment and the weekly sessions, the devaluation stopped. I have come to see his devaluation of me as a way of dealing with his fear of me.

He was initially seen at a clinic with a sliding-scale fee structure, and at the beginning of treatment, he paid nothing. This was deeply shameful for him, and in response, he tried to shame and humiliate me. As he became more dependent on me, his hostility towards me increased. He would look at me in silence and make sexual innuendoes, and his body posture and movements were sexualized in a manner that I found intimidating. His hostile questioning of the way I conducted therapy was both covert and overt, and I became defensive and doubtful of my judgement. The devaluation of me as a woman and a therapist were the same. The perennial question for me became, "Shouldn't he see a man?" because he worked to convince me that all women were untrustworthy.

I found the sexualizing particularly intimidating, in part because I was keenly aware of my own sense of vulnerability and had a difficult time appreciating his sense of vulnerability. I often find it easier to look at what I bring to the relationship rather than paying attention to how the patient defends. Rather than seeing his behavior as a defense, as an attempt to humiliate me so that I wouldn't humiliate him, and paying attention to his projection that I was being humiliating and hurtful, I found myself thinking that I was being overly sensitive given my experiences with my brother. My brother often humiliated me, belittling my logic and use of language. He expressed his rage in a covert manner that left me feeling sickened without knowing why. Within my historical family, men were considered smarter, more objective, and having better judgment than women. Mr. A's distancing of himself as he did meshed perfectly with my desire not to be experienced as hurtful and abusive, and my vulnerability to the indirect expression of hostility and rage was the perfect match for his covert rage.

Since he has seen me in private practice, where he pays a negotiated reduced fee, his shame is less as is his devaluation of the therapy. He is paying for his safety. As he works to bring into our relationship his feelings towards me, he is clearer about how he sees me as a therapist and what he projects upon me as a woman. The clarification of these boundaries and being more in touch with his feelings has further reduced the devaluation.

Ms. D constructs her relationships on a win–lose basis, and for a long while, I didn't see this because it didn't happen directly with me. The dynamic doesn't come up between us in quite the same way as it does outside treatment because of her wish to comply with and please me. Her identification with the aggressor in this case is with me, a helper, like herself, and this generally inhibits the expression of hatred in the room. During those times when I am seen as being like the mother, I am seen as holding unrealistically high standards with which I expect her to comply immediately. Her response is to become silent and angry and to "forget" to come to sessions and then to deny any possibility of her feelings and her actions having anything to do with me.

Hatred comes more obviously into the room when her overt sadism is present. This is rarely directed at me but, more typically, is directed at her father in fantasy and her fiancé in actuality. Her hurtfulness towards him has come out verbally in their fights and in her refusal to be sexual for many years. They take turns hurting each other so that each will know "what it's like" to hurt. Her attitude towards sex has been derogatory and dismissive, and she had little interest for a long time in looking at how this affected him.

It took until the fourth year of our work together for Ms. D to face her sadism. Her desire to hurt and the satisfaction she took in hurting were especially anathema to her when connected to her father's sadism. I continually and repeatedly pointed out the power dynamic she and her fiancé engaged in and how really hurtful each could be to the other. This proved to be a more fruitful way into a very powerful area than trying to use her relationship with her mother or with me. It took about a year for her to move from being very hurtful and denying any true desire to be hurtful, to beginning to accept that she wanted to hurt, followed by becoming interested in a dynamic in which she engaged. Seeing herself as sadistic is less frightening now than before, and she is able to take some pleasure in having a sadistic fantasy with the confidence that she won't enact it or even have the desire to enact it.

What transpired between us during the course of this fourth year was quite mixed. There was a big "No" to my suggestion that something was going on between us, which alternated with being very dependent on me as a source of reality testing and support for the work she was engaged in with her mother. I dropped all attempts at transferential work except with reference to stubbornness with mothers, which is the one thing that usually makes sense to her, given that she sees me as expecting almost too much from her. Until recently, working in the transference has been sporadic and seems to create more anxiety than has been helpful in the treatment. Being straightforward about her not wanting to work in the therapy, the unfairness of her situation, and the importance of resistance has worked. What has been important for me to learn is how much she does want to please me, how much she does on her own, and how important it has been to allow for this and not to insist that she work out everything with me in the room.

Sadistic Erotic Fantasy

Patients' sadistic erotic fantasies can be difficult for me to hear. I sometimes seem to get caught in the details of the fantasy and the in-between reality where fantasy takes place when it seems uncertain that the patient knows it is a fantasy. This state can feel uncanny, even psychotic, and I get frightened at these times. I trust patients to let me know what is going on for them. For patients who have been abused, however, their blind spots are often similar to mine. If they dissociate when they're frightened, they can't let me know what they're thinking and feeling. I may not notice if I am also defending with dissociation.

When Mr. A shares a sadistic sexual fantasy about me with me, he tends to perceive me as moving away in disgust or fear. He will then either retreat in shame and become inaccessible in a cloud of anxiety, or he will escalate the sadism in the fantasy and become agitated and excited. In the latter case especially, I can become anxious and afraid. This example contains both the place of fantasying that can feel psychotic, as when he becomes increasingly sadistic and excited in it, and my response of becoming rigid and unavailable psychically. When I become like a caricature of a teacher (a superego position I am familiar with), I have left the play space between us in a way that isn't helpful to Mr. A, out of my own fear for myself. What is important to note here is that I don't really believe Mr. A is going to hurt me, and he isn't someone whose reality testing I question. These are moments he leads me into so I can help him, and I sometimes disappoint him. This, too, is the point.

Sometimes I become frightened when I've let something go on too long and it's no longer contained in the play between us. This means that we have moved from "playing" to "not playing," or reenacting. This has happened in the course of Mr. A's verbal "banter," where I sometimes find myself "suddenly" mirroring with approval a sadistic comment directed towards me. Because I assume it is my job to receive whatever a patient brings in, I can be quite undone in these moments of uninhibited sadism Mr. A introduces. While this is unpleasant, it allows me to be in touch with Mr. A's fear.

Mr. A is both fond of me and wants very much to hurt me so I will understand how he has been hurt. He is exquisitely attuned to any hint of disapproval or dislike on my part and is very sensitive to shame and humiliation. Finding a distance between us that works has been a very slow process punctuated by long periods of withdrawal on his part. As he is becoming more able to say aloud in the moment what he dislikes about me and the way I work, the working distance between us is shifting, and with the shift, his anxiety gets aroused and he gets more vigilant. He is very adept with words and quite sarcastic and verbally humiliating. He learned to perfect this in word games he and his aunt played, during which she praised his intelligence while the two of them laughed. These were moments that were pleasurable, as well as sadistic towards others, and they were moments in which he and she were on the same side.

When he is anxious and feels I've humiliated him, he gets mean and directs this toward me. While on the other hand, it's important that he's able to do this in the treatment with me, it's also not acceptable to be abusive of me, for example, calling me names or threatening to really hurt me. And what is important is that we be able to speak about these occasions, which is what he feels unable to do without feeling humiliated by me again. What's called for is navigating a very narrow passageway between what he's there to work out in the treatment and his acting it out in a way that makes it too difficult for me to help.

For this patient, the struggle with authority that is most anxiety-producing is the sexualized one where he feels humiliated. He is reluctant to work with his fantasies with me, especially those that are about me. However, the repetitiveness of the pattern gives us something to look at together, and, slowly, we are exploring what goes on emotionally in the moments before everything seems to change suddenly. What is emerging is that, in these moments, I also become like his father to him. Putting this into words seems to be a relief to him and provides a movement in the work from the psychotic "mother" to the dismissive father. This moving in and out of contact with deep disturbance gives me increased empathy for the terror and bleakness he experienced as a child.

CONCLUSION

I bring to my work the certainty that life is worth living, regardless of the horrors of the past. However, I believe that choosing to live and how to live is up to the individual. I bring a deep love for life, which I know my patients take in no matter how "neutral" I try to remain. Humor slips in, and we share laughter. This is what I have to offer that is often the difference that makes a difference.

My work is healing for me. Many emotional experiences I have with clients I would not seek out on my own, yet I learn with each successive sharing that all things are bearable. I also come to this work with a predisposition to listen to and to witness intense pain-filled experiences, given my own. And because of the work I have done and continue to do with my own healing, I am able to be more helpful than if I hadn't suffered in certain ways. In doing therapy, my experience of suffering is transformed. In using my experiences to be helpful to others, my story acquires a meaning that is both mine and beyond mine. In this way, I participate in the larger social symphony, doing my part to create a new piece of music.

REFERENCE

Winnicott, D. W. (1965), *The Maturational Processes and the Facilitating Environment.* New York: International Universities Press.

12

The Loss of My Father in Adolescence

Its Impact on My Work as a Psychoanalyst

SUSAN C. WARSHAW

My father died when I was thirteen years old. He died suddenly, after a three-week illness. I cannot say whether I would have become a psychoanalyst had this not occurred, but I know that my life-long efforts to resolve issues that the loss of my father stimulated have profoundly influenced my clinical work.

I believe that analysts' personal experiences with early trauma have been insufficiently discussed as powerful forces in shaping their views about and management of the analytic process. A body of literature on what has come to be called "the wounded healer," while not focussing specifically on psychoanalysts, suggests that early trauma might have motivational impact on the choice of psychotherapy as a career (Grosbeck,1977; Holmes,1991; Sadowsky, 1996). While I am not aware of the incidence specifically of childhood or adolescent bereavement among practicing psychoanalysts, I have over the years, known several colleagues who had lost a parent during an early period in life. Many of these people had involved themselves in personal analysis as part of their efforts to integrate aspects of these early traumas and to better resolve the psychological sequelae of the trauma. Thus the importance of beginning a discourse about the impact on our work of early life traumas seems significant, not only from a purely personal perspective, but possibly as an important shaping influence upon the work of others in this field.

To this end, I will be writing about two related areas, the first being some specific issues that emerged for me personally and professionally as a result of my father's death. I will discuss some aspects of what I remember and what I have come to know about my attempts to reestablish stablity, to integrate, and to compensate for and move beyond this powerfully traumatic experience. Second, I will present clinical material from my work with two patients who experienced significant early trauma. Illustrating the ways in which my conceptualization of the clinical material was affected by my own experience, I will explore these patients' avoidance of the affective experience of trauma (including profound help-lessness and rage), the powerful desire for control that trauma stimulates, the yearning for and search for the lost and idealized parent, and the search for developmentally necessary surrogate parents, as played out in their analyses. One of the patients is a five-year-old child who had lost his father at the age of two, and the other is an adult patient who, while not experiencing actual permanent object loss, had had traumatic experiences with important figures in her family and intermittent emotional object loss. Then I will discuss how my ongoing work towards resolution of my own related issues impacted upon my evolving beliefs about the treatment process.

MY OWN EXPERIENCE

I remember my mom coming home from the hospital, looking awful. We sat on my bed, my sister on one side of her, I on the other. She told us daddy had died, and we all burst into tears. The shock was enormous. There had really been no preparation. He'd been ill for just a few weeks, and I had not expected it to be terminal. Though my parents had become aware of that possibility, neither had shared it with us, for a variety of reasons. Almost forty years later, the power of that first moment causes me to shudder. I realize how rarely I've actually thought about it. "How can we live?" I had asked. "How will we live?" It felt like there would be no way to survive or to tolerate what had occurred. I worried about money; with mom working part-time and with limited insurance money, we were, in truth, in serious financial difficulty. I was, however, even more terrified of the idea of death and dying—not just the finality of it all, not just missing my father, whom, I adored, but the gruesome, terrifying image and odor of decay. At the funeral, I wanted to look at him in the casket and to kiss him goodbye, but the actuality of it was horrifying. I had never before seen a dead person. Though I had lost a grandmother at the age of five, I had not seen her in her final days. My memories of her death were olfactory, the odor of decaying food in the refrigerator of her apartment, which we had gone to clean out. The odor of death that had permeated the hospital room during my last visit to my father, similarly, was to stay with me forever. Bodily decomposition, however, was too terrifying a thought for a thirteen-year-old. Obsessive worrying about money, rooted in a concrete reality, though awful, was more tolerable. Here was something I could control. Here was a way I could contribute, identifying with my father in his provider role. I began to work to earn money, literally stashing away as much as possible.

Life changed in some subtle and many powerfully significant ways. We were never again to be a family with two parents and two children, singing silly songs on long car trips to New England. My mother took a new job and handled the financial burdens that had already been there but had usually been more manageable with my father's income. She decided to go to college to prepare for a career as a teacher, realizing a childhood dream. Friends praised her competence and self-sufficiency, talking about her as some sort of heroine, which, indeed, she seemed to be in the 1950s. I worried about her health, assisted her by helping around the house, identifying with and assuming a parental and caretaking function. I was an attentive therapist in the making. I was furious with her as well, focusing my anger at the time on the fact that she began to date during my first year in high school, unfairly moving into my arena, "competing" for and assuming my role. Years later, I came to understand another source of my anger, the overwhelming sense of helplessness and despair that is turned upon the surviving parent, whose role was to have been to assure security.

We all moved on, yet as I later understood, there were some ways in which we didn't. I wanted desperately to have nothing change, ever again, and worked actively to have that happen. I entered my first analysis concurrent with my mother's remarriage, not quite seven years after my father's death. I was in my junior year of college and, in some ways, still felt as unprepared for the wider world as I had in seventh grade. I wanted desperately to find a safe place, a predeath home. My first therapist was quite senior as a training analyst at the time we began to work together. He died several years after I left treatment with him. He was an aging gentleman who, despite a warm and kindly manner, had a grandiose air that, early on, made me uneasy. Unfortunately, I soon dismissed this awareness because he embraced me emotionally and had a powerful need to create the emotional home I wished for. Unknown to me until sometime later were the numerous and tragic personal losses he had sustained, both in adolescence and adulthood. When I did learn of these losses however, I felt closer to him, rather than worried. I was touched by a sense of shared tragedy. To fill the void in his life, he gathered his patients around him, and rarely did they leave. It took me many years to do so.

Paradoxically, an aspect of what was important in that treatment was also part of its flaw: the total lack of pressure to do anything about moving on with my life and the timeless quality that the womblike ambience created. Feeling I had lost my home too early, I could imagine that this was a home that would never be destroyed. I fantasized that the leaving would not be precipitated by external forces. It was to be totally within my control. I felt I had found a devoted, constantly attuned parent surrogate, a very maternal father who calmed my fears and created a sense that all was safe when I was within his orbit. I believe I grew to feel more secure that the world would not collapse around me, less panicky, and somewhat more courageous. In this treatment, however, there was much holding and very little analyzing of the transference, in fact with little discussion of its powerful presence. The holding, which had for a long time helped me feel that I could move at my own pace, eventually became insufficient. The failure to understand my need to have nothing change, to come to know that which was being warded off, in all its complexity, was an obstacle to further growth. I left that analysis with anger and difficulty, but propelled by what I believe was a developmental desire to move beyond what was being offered. To his credit, an awareness of that desire had been rekindled during that treatment.

My second analysis, beginning while I was in analytic training in my mid-thirties, was an additional stimulus to an enormous amount of personal and professional growth. A central theme of that treatment was my overwhelming desire and search for a father surrogate. However it proved not to be the comforting "daddy" of my childhood for whom I searched with greatest tenacity, but rather a replacement for the missing father of my adolescence and my adulthood. It seemed to be easier to work through my defensive clinging to the "daddy" of my earlier childhood than to relinquish the idealized lost father of my adolescence or adulthood, the father whom I wished to have known and befriended as I moved forward into adulthood. This was the father with whom I needed to become gradually disillusioned. It was not until many years subsequent to the ending of the analysis that I could fully appreciate the extent to which I had clung defensively to an idealized version of that relationship. The intensity of my father hunger was enormous, of the sort I have come to recognize in bereaved children whom I have treated.

As an analyst in training, the power of my attachment to my analyst "father" was further sustained by the expectation of professional contact into the future. The commingling of the healthy and neurotic aspects of this attachment were extremely difficult to sort out. My desire for my analyst as a figure for identification and as a mentor, while important to the development of my professional as well as personal identity, had a problematic edge to it. Without an understanding and a resolution of my wish for a relationship with an *idealized* version of the father of my adolescence and adulthood, I could not complete that which had been left incomplete in adolescence. I believe however, that I could not have permitted myself to tolerate experiencing the pain associated with the loss of my idealized father had I not experienced the powerful presence of a warm and available father figure in my analysis.

THE IMPACT ON MY WORK

I have highlighted just a few of the issues that emerged for me as a result of the death of my father, a primary one being the powerful need to restore a sense of security and stability once the illusion of safety had been shattered. My response to the overwhelming sense of helplessness and loss included a desire to forestall change and thereby control many aspects of life in order to reestablish an illusory safety. I discussed my eager search for a surrogate parent, which was motivated both by a healthy need for a fathering person and a defensive need to idealize him. The idealization served many purposes, one of which was to recreate, through attachment to an idealized other, an illusion of safety in a world whose dangers had intruded too early with shattering intensity. Through the use of clinical material, I would like to trace these related themes as they were recognized by me as present in the symptomatology and analytic treatment of two patients, one of whom was a young boy working through issues related to the death of his father and the other of whom was an adult woman whose childhood, while not including parental death, was in many ways traumatic. In each of these cases, I will discuss some thoughts I have had about the impact of my own struggle to resolve issues related to my father's death upon my conceptualization of the material and my approach to the treatment.

Control, Stability, and the Illusion of Safety: The Role of Actual Parents

The desire for contol in order to defend against the terror of utter helplessness, the need to reestablish stability, and the wish to recreate a childhood illusion of safety are all powerfully present in the psychic world of the person who has experienced trauma. Observing the impact on the functioning of close friends and relatives who have recently experienced traumatic losses, I am reminded, as I am writing this, of the terror that overwhelms one when persons upon whom we depend are lost. One friend who recently experienced the death of her adult sister finds herself panicked when an expected call from her parents does not occur. My mother, in her later years, dealing with the loss of siblings and friends, uncharacteristically checks upon my whereabouts on an almost daily basis. Disaster lurks behind every corner. Those who remain need to be held close. Each of us, in our own way, struggles with these issues and copes in our own idiosyncratic fashion.

For children and adolescents whose personality development is in process and dependent upon the presence of primary caregivers, the actual loss of a parent can have powerful lifelong consequences impacting upon the total structure of the personality. The search for the lost parent, whose presence serves such vital developmental functions, can become a lifetime preoccupation. The traumatic experience of the loss and the attempts at defense against the affects associated with overwhelming disillusionment and helplessness become incorporated into the personality.

Robbie, whose father died suddenly when he was two years old, was brought to treatment by his mother when he was turning five. He had for the past several months become increasingly difficult for his mother to manage. He was arrogant, willful, and commanding, grandiosely proclaiming himself "The Boss of the World." A series of housekeepers had quit abruptly, finding Robbie disobedient and disrespectful. He had adopted a macho style that, at times, seemed an imitation of various tough guys he had seen on television. In fact, he frequently "acquired" the personality characteristics of older male figures, including a much adored neighbor. In a multidetermined way, Robbie appeared to be dealing with integrating the loss of his father and filling the void in his life through forms of identification that were primarily rooted in relationships with fantasy figures. Idealized for their toughness and invulnerability, Robbie's identifications with these powerful figures reflected his need to deny his own vulnerable little boyness. His fantasy play reflected both his desire to be a heroic rescuer, as well as his powerful identification with the bad guys who seemed to personify the badness he himself felt, and the anger he could in no way express towards the father whose actual vulnerability was so terrifying and whose "abandonment" was incomprehensible.

A grandiosely controlling approach towards women in general, and his mother in particular, reflected his rage towards her for failing to keep things safe, as well as for her emotional withdrawal during the grieving period. In addition, his mother had recently ended a relationship with a man Robbie had become fond of, and he was confronted again with the loss of an important father figure. His desire to control her thus served multiple purposes, one primarily being to forestall any possibility of further abandonment and to decrease his powerful sense of endangerment. A second related to increased anxiety regarding his intensified longing for his mother as his "woman" and reflected his need to create a certain amount of distance from her, albeit controllable distance, a distance that would not lead to abandonment.

For a period of time, mother had become all bad, a woman to be attacked, ridiculed, and manipulated. These themes emerged clearly within the play and dominated the transference. Certainly, the developmental level Robbie was at when his father died, a barely verbal toddler, significantly shaped his adaptation. His defenses reflected an early level of object relations, with a tendency towards primitive idealization alternating with rageful denigration. His fascination with money, which he hoarded, as I had after my father's death, while having an unmistakenly anal cast to it, could also be understood as his attempted adaptation to feared and actual changed economic circumstances in his family. Most importantly, I believe, Robbie's desire to acquire money seemed to serve the purpose of concretely incorporating an aspect of his lost father, father as breadwinner. Through his acquisition of money he bolstered his fantasied image of himself as a powerful provider, a big man.

In order to understand his presenting symptoms, it was also important to understand the recent precipitating events and Robbie's developmental conflicts at the time of the referral at age five. Simply stated, it was important to be clear about the conflicts generated and the new demands being placed on him to resolve old issues, as his mother began to date other men, stimulating envy and competition, as well as renewed fears of abandonment. Robbie was terrified and retreated from the social world of after school-playdates. He preferred to spend spare time engaged in fantasy play in his room, not wishing to leave the safety of his home. Robbie's overwhelming need to control others, and the world around him evoked memories of my own vulnerability and my early attempts at adaptation through withdrawal and control.

How was Robbie helped in treatment to achieve a better adaptation? To what extent did the interpretive work we did around his defensive grandiosity facilitate the very rapid diminishing of Robbie's symptoms? An eager and bright patient, Robbie readily understood my interpretations of his play and seemed relieved to begin to discuss his previously hidden beliefs and childhood confusions about his father's death.

Equally potent as a force in his development, however, was the successful work that occurred with his mother, resulting in major changes in her engagement with and management of Robbie. A psychologically sophisticated woman who was able to hear and understand what Robbie needed from her, his mother, with support from me, began to feel more capable of attuning to his needs, as well as firmly disciplining him. Robbie desperately needed to experience the strength of his mother's responses in order to confront the limitations of his imagined powers. Of considerable importance also were the powerful shifts that took place when Robbie's mother later remarried a man whom Robbie genuinely liked. Knowing there were caretaking and powerful parents around, Robbie began to feel safe enough to resume his role as a little boy in the family and gradually began to relinquish his grandiose stance. Facilitating changes in real-life circumstances, recreating an experience of safety and stability, and the potency of gratifying external relationships seemed to play as important a role in Robbie's resumption of more appropriate development as did the work that took place within our sessions. His poignant eagerness to establish a relationship with the new man in his life had the quality of desire that has been noted by numerous therapists working with affectively deprived youngsters. The availability of an actually present man with whom to identify, to compete, to work through his fears, and to test out his illusions seemed significant both in resolution of symptomatology and in facilitation of development of this child's identity. My own quest for missing parenting that had resulted from my father's death reinforced my beliefs regarding the necessity for active parent work in this situation. I paid a great deal of attention to assisting Robbie's mother in creating a more appropriate response to her son's defensive grandiosity. This resulted in a healthier adaptation. Robbie ended his treatment at his request, with the support of his mother who was pleased with the delightful boy he had become. We were all aware that despite significant symptomatic relief and the major developmental strides he was clearly making, Robbie still carried within him residual issues that might require treatment subsequent to his requested termination. One such issue became apparent some time later when, on the anniversary of his father's death, he asked to return to therapy. Upon his return, he anxiously inquired whether I ate my fruits and vegetables, clearly worrying about how I cared for myself physically, wondering whether I was a responsible adult. He also seemed to need to check out whether I had survived both his departure and his still present anger at doctors, as well as mothers, who failed to save his father's life. Caretaking adults, while desperately needed, were still vulnerable to destruction and were potentially disappointing, perhaps as a result of their inadequacies or perhaps as a result of his hostile thoughts. Despite my countertransferential wish that the restitution of good parenting would resolve all his problems, there was still some important analytic work to be done.

It is fairly easy to accept the necessity of parent work as a significant component of child treatment. Parents are, after all, the most important persons in the lives of their children. There is little question regarding the necessity of parents as figures with whom children need to identify, as well as people whose differences and failings must eventually require acknowledgement and acceptance by the growing youngster. We also intuitively acknowledge the importance of parental figures as those who provide safety and security, so that life's dangers can be experienced gradually and adapted to slowly. Our counseling is geared to support the parent in supplying the appropriately facilitating environment.

With our adult patients, however, we rarely work with those in the environment to make changes that will enhance development. Resolutions of problems related to missed and/or wished for parental provision hopefully occur within the course of analysis. We assume that personality growth within a good-enough treatment situation will then enhance the capacity of the adult to seek out developmentally facilitating opportunities with others, including with the parents of their adulthood. But what are those factors that are most important in order to facilitate resumption of healthy development in adults who have had traumatic life experiences? To what extent can we or should we strive to recreate the illusion of safety that the parents of childhood provide? In what way does disillusionment fit into the process of growth? To what extent do we or can we become surrogate providers of unmet developmental needs, and how do we determine the essential versus the defensive aspects of the pull to meet those expressed needs? These are issues with which the profession has struggled throughout its history and ones with which I have personally grappled.

Control, Stability, and the Illusion of Safety:
The Adult's Search for the Idealized Parent

Altschul (1988) suggests that we can use our understanding of reactions to situations of traumatic loss to enhance our understanding of reactions to a wide range of important events that occur throughout the lifespan. "It seems crucial to develop a dynamic understanding of gradations of reactions to important events such as death, divorce, family disruption and other disasters and to fit them into a usable, dynamic schema of trauma and its derivatives" (Altschul, 1988, p. 6). Experiences, other than parental death, that arouse powerful feelings of helplessness and rage can stimulate similar attempts at adaptation. One young woman named Carol, whose childhood family life was seriously disrupted by the presence of a severely handicapped brother, shared some similar conflicts, anxieties, and defenses with my young patient Robbie, as well as with myself.

In our final session of a lengthy psychoanalysis, Carol and I talked about the meaning of our work to her. "Patience," she said, "I think the most important thing to me has always been your patience. I guess," said Carol, "I've needed to feel that I could do things in my own time, for me, not for my mom, nor my dad, and not because of or for Louis." Louis was her seriously handicapped, neurologically impaired, older brother. "I guess," she said, "I take my time about everything." We both laughed, thinking about her eight-year courtship with her husband, the apartment they'd just moved from that had been hers for ten years, and the corporation for which she'd worked for the same length of time. None of this would seem out of place for a person ten to fifteen years older, but so much seeming "stability" in a woman in her early thirties was, I think, symptomatic of her approach to life. She moved slowly in her personal life, despite the fact that she is a highly competitive woman who has a senior management position in a major corporation. Within the treatment, however, she often needed to hide her competitiveness, indeed much of her competence, and maintained her position as my frightened, at times whiny, little girl. For years, she had tried to make time stop, to keep things under control, to nest in her tiny apartment, which she referred to as her private safe place. I wondered if she would ever leave therapy, which had become another "safe" nest, and after more than a decade of our work together, feeling that she had accomplished a great deal and that she "should" be getting ready, I began to ask her if she could ever imagine such an event occurring. To some extent, my queries reflected my own concerns that I not collude with her in her desire to nest, as I was well aware of my own tendency in that direction. After angrily enjoining me not to rush her, feeling I ought to know better, she confidently assured me that she would leave treatment after she'd had a healthy baby. Following some further working through, that is precisely what happened.

My reaction to Carol's pronouncement was ambivalent. I was pleased that she was at least contemplating the conditions under which she might feel capable of leaving therapy, though it was with some degree of disbelief, sadness and admiration for her courage that I contemplated saying goodbye. Goodbyes have never been my forte. I was also delighted that she was capable of imagining herself as nondamaged enough to dare to try to conceive and mother a hopefully nondamaged child. Before me sat a lively young woman who was now able to forcefully put me in my place, rather than resort to tears or her historical presentation as a little girl. I was struck, however, by her still present need to test out the illusory power with which she wished to endow me—the power to insure safe passage. She could dare to take this developmental step if I stayed with her, simultaneously assuring her that I believed in her nondamagedness, in her essential competence, and would not enviously spoil or steal from her the child she was to conceive. For multiple reasons, being near me was supposed to assure her that she was safe enough to take the risk. Carol's fantasy that closeness to me would insure safety for all of us had been playing a significant role in her avoidance of termination. Having been forced by life circumstances to confront and resolve my own wishes for an omnipotent, protective analyst, I recognized and identified with her desire to endow me with such power. I was determined not to collude with her.

Carol is today, and in many ways has been for a long time, a well functioning woman in significant areas of her life. She genuinely feels quite pleased with the outcome of our years of work. She describes herself as feeling "real," a feeling of transient unreality having been a chronic complaint in the early years. When she began treatment, she described herself as feeling like "the organ grinder's monkey," who performed on command when the music began, whose purpose was to delight the crowd and whose reward was their cheers. She had feared that this was not simply a metaphor for her experience, but worried that, in fact, she was subhuman, perhaps like Louis, whose odd handicap she could never quite grasp and about whom she still held the theories she had developed in her early childhood. Carol felt that she herself had grown up as a cute plaything of others, with no freedom of movement, her most important value to her parents having been her performance, which was to be the family remedy for Louis's defectiveness.

Some background follows: Carol is the younger of two children of a successful professional couple. Her older brother Louis was born six years prior to her and had sustained a serious birth injury, which left him partially paralyzed and with many of the behavioral peculiarities associated with significant neurological dysfunction. While not globally mentally retarded, he had some specific cognitive deficits that caused him to become frequently confused; for example, he had difficulty following directions and seeing cause–effect relationships. He tended to be perseverative and was given to rageful tirades, stimulated by events that often seemed insignificant to the casual observer. He was experienced by my patient as both her loving older brother, who nurtured her in the emotional and physical absence of their mother and father, and her unpredictably "crazy" brother, who terrified her and caused her to feel great shame. As she grew older and began to surpass Louis in many ways, Carol felt pressure from within herself and from her parents to treat him carefully, to watch out for him, and to understand and not be angry with him for his limitations. She felt profoundly helpless regarding the irrationality she encountered.

Carol's mother apparently became extremely depressed in reaction to the birth of her handicapped son, and while she reveled in her daughter's precociousness, she alternated between intense educative engagement with her and long periods of withdrawal, which we came to understand were manifestations of her longstanding depression.

Carol's father, an accomplished author and a somewhat schizoid man, withdrew into his work, spending long hours in his home office. Carol reports feeling that she never knew him, finding it impossible to determine what he was feeling about important matters and finding him noncommunicative about his work, which he failed to share with his daughter. She frequently experienced his lack of communication as a belief that she was too stupid to speak with and obviously damaged like her brother.

The most emotionally related person in her family was her brother, and as she grew older and realized that something was not right with him, she developed conflicts about loving and hating him, as well as intense survivor's guilt, which resulted in anxiety about having more than Louis. She feared that her own growth and success had been and would be damaging to him. She also strongly identified with him and, in many ways, yearned to be like him because she at least did not feel lonely in the relationship. She feared that, if she lost control, she would become irrational and rageful in the ways that Louis did. She was never quite sure that she wasn't damaged like her brother. Thus, she monitored herself carefully. To further reinforce her anxieties about her own growth, she felt that all her developmental achievements would be stolen by her parents, who needed so desperately to have her succeed. Her achievements, she believed, were for them, not for her. She did not want to give that to them because she felt robbed in the process.

As a way of salvaging herself in an environment that Carol experienced as traumatic, she developed a literal and metaphoric private safe place in which to hide. Like my young patient Robbie, as a child she had often retreated to her bedroom, spending long hours talking to her pets, her real and stuffed animals. Despite subsequently obtaining a graduate degree from a top university, Carol remained, in part, the little girl who had retreated to her safe place with her magical theories about the causes of her brother's damage and her deep fears about her own subhuman status.

These factors created some important treatment issues, which I believe contributed to the length of our work. One issue was Carol's clearly articulated need for my "patience" and for my permission for her to do things in her own time, as well as her related fear of my intrusion with the possibility that I might take her over. A second issue was Carol's extreme reluctance to give up her private "safe" place, where, since childhood, she had gone to magically avoid the dangers of the world. The analysis had become such a safe place. Her need to create a timeless experience was evidenced in her seeming lack of awareness, for many years, that this treatment should ever come to an end. Her wish to be in absolute control of the extent of our engagement, as well as the pace of our work, began to yield gradually over time. Carol had always felt that she lived in everyone else's time and space, except of course in her private place, and, reluctantly, and somewhat oppositionally, she was determined not to be intruded upon by anyone else's agenda. In this way, she also identified with each of her parents, who responded in a similar fashion. I believe that she did profit from my attempts to interpret her dilemma, but I believe that she may have profited as much, if not more, from our joint effort to develop a good balance of involvement.

As a youngster, Carol had lived in a world of fearsome, dehumanized monsters. Struggling to find ways to make the world feel safe, she sought protection from cuddly teddy bears and rabbits. She did not experience her parents as reliable buffers that could provide security from the dangers of the world. In fact, she had secretly feared that they were the perpetrators of the heinous crime that had damaged her brother. In this way, Carol was similar to Robbie in his fearful attribution of the cause of disaster to the all-powerful and disappointingly powerless parent. We explored this scary world within the relative safety of our frame. I believed that Carol's need to endow me with the omnipotent power to protect her from the dangers of the world masked her fear that I might fail her in the ways she believed her parents had and that the family badness that she feared was part of her, would be perpetuated by her. Until the end of our work, she reassured herself of and clung to the safety of our relationship, using it as a protective shield as she tested out the possibilities that she could really be nondamaged and hope to have a nondamaged child and that I would support and not enviously spoil or steal from her that which she had attained.

Carol's difficulty in leaving treatment was also related to her desire to maintain a supportive relationship with me as she moved into her new role as a mother. This desire reflected realistic anxieties and healthy needs for a maternal mentor, as well as an idealized image of what our relationship might bring. Angry and disappointed as she was, not only with the parents of her childhood, but with the parents of her adulthood as well, she worried about her capacity to parent her child in nontoxic ways and felt the lack of healthy role models, as well as the lack of appropriate contemporary support from her parents. She wished that she could stay in treatment with me forever, having me become an idealized mother to her adult mothering self. I worried, however, that for Carol to remain in treatment at that point in her life would have infantalized her, as well as deprived her of the opportunity to grow as a mother in her own right, deriving support from her husband and friends and struggling with her less than ideal, but real, parents. In addition, I had no illusions regarding my capacity to provide her with the degree of protection for which she wished. I took a position in favor of her terminating, and we ended having explored these issues. For a considerable period of time, however, I wondered about the aftermath of our work. Had I prematurely pushed her out as a result of my own needs to deidealize the power of the analyst? Had I accurately assessed her strengths?

During the course of writing this chapter, I contacted Carol, both to obtain her permission to use this material and also to see how she was doing. It was a pleasure to learn that she was flourishing, enjoying being a mother, and managing her parents and her sibling with humor and perspective. "We have our own family now," said Carol, referring to her husband and child, "and that becomes most important. I worry about Louis and dealing with his problems, and we see my parents a lot, but it's fine." She related that her child adored seeing her grandparents and that she felt a great deal of pleasure in sharing anecdotes regarding her child with them and with her mother in particular.

SUMMARY

Throughout the years of my work, I have been fascinated by developmental theory. In my early years as an analyst, I was much influenced by the work of the object relations theorists, both British and American. What most interested me was the delineation of the role of the environmental parents in the facilitation of the growth of the self and the parallels drawn to the role of the analyst. The analyst as a provider of important developmentally facilitating functions was, however, most usually likened to the mother of earliest childhood, reflecting the primacy given to the earliest period in genesis of both health and pathology. The holding, soothing, mirroring, and containing functions were those most frequently talked about as the noninterpretive relational factors in the treatment. During a post-traumatic period in my life, I eagerly sought the comfort of a soothing, nonintrusive therapeutic relationship, from which I profited in significant ways. As noted above, my experience in my first treatment had a significant shaping effect upon my early work as an analyst, as I believe my work with Carol reflected. It was that experience that taught me the value of analytic patience and the restorative power of a soothing containing relationship. Undoubtedly, my fascination with theory that supported that work was an outgrowth of my deeply felt need for missed parenting, as well as the more positive aspects of my first treatment experience. However, after a lengthy period of time, it also had become apparent to me that the environment of my first analysis had not been conducive to the resolution of numerous issues that were essentially adolescent in nature. For example, I believe that my analyst's emphasis upon early mothering issues rendered him less able to note the manifestations of and defenses against my adolescent father transference in the work. (I hope I have made clear that I also felt that there was an insufficiency of the interpretive aspect of the analytic work as well.) The search for restitution of a relationship that has been lost, and/or traumatic in other ways, can occur at various developmental levels, not only at the earliest. While soothing and holding are important parental functions, so too are limit setting, confrontation, and the capacity to survive the process of deidealization. The pull for provision of wished for parental functions is certainly a constant occurrence in analysis with adults, with enactments of parent/child interactions occurring from all developmental levels, including the most mature.

Recently, I have been particularly interested in understanding the nature of appropriate developmental provision for adults in analysis. My experiences in attempting to resolve the residue of adolescent trauma have taught me that a broad range of parental functions are solicited from the analyst during the course of treatment and that too heavy a focus on the containing and soothing functions, while useful in facilitating the resolution of some aspects of trauma, can obscure defenses against, as well as needs for, other parental involvement. The lack of actual appropriate parental provision during adolescence and into adulthood can create a powerful pull in the treatment of adults, with a transference into the treatment of conflicted and wished for relationships from these later developmental stages as well. My own life experience had taught me this, and my work with Carol and other patients has confirmed this.

Most significantly, I have come to understand an important paradox inherent in the provision of an analytic environment in which a variety of important developmental needs are met. That is, while adult patients may benefit from relationships with analysts as providers of certain adult developmental needs, in particular as significant persons in their lives with whom to interact and identify, at some point it is important that the illusion of safety that the analysis provides be relinquished. Much as the preadolescent and adolescent youngster needs to go through a period of disillusionment with the parent in order to resolve earlier idealizations and leave home, so too does the patient. Without such a shift, analysis may become interminable. In situations where trauma has been extensive and where very severe gaps in parenting have existed, sorting out what is actually needed from what is wished for for the purposes of creating an illusory safety is not easy. Relinquishing the illusion of safety that the analysis provides can be one of the most difficult tasks of all.

REFERENCES

Altschul, S. (1988), Trauma, mourning and adaptation: A dynamic point of view. In: *Childhood Bereavement and Its Aftermath*, ed. S. Altschul & G. Pollock. Madison, CT: International Universities Press, pp. 3–15.

Grosbeck, C. G. (1977), The psychiatrist as a wounded physician. *Amer. J. Psychoanal.*, 37:131–139.

Holmes, C. A. (1991), The wounded healer. *Soc. Psychoanal. Psychother. Bull.*, 6:33–36.

Sadowsky, G. (1996), Career Choice and Early Experience. Unpublished manuscript, Ferkauf Graduate School of Psychology, Yeshiva University.

13

Psychoanalysis In and Out of the Closet

MARK J. BLECHNER

I would like to do a number of things in this chapter. First, I wish to summarize my own growing awareness of my homosexual feelings, their role in my development, and the integration of my own homosexuality into my personal and professional life. This indulgence in autobiography is not so common in psychoanalytic writing. I do so here, not because I find my life so fascinating, but because it shows some of the major psychological hurdles faced by a gay or lesbian person growing up in our society. It is my hope that I can sensitize and educate heterosexual readers to the special problems gay people face. In all of my training, I was never once taught about such issues—neither in coursework nor in supervision—and this may be true of many readers. A lack of such knowledge may lead therapists to be unhelpful or even destructive to their gay patients, as Isay (1991) has noted. I would also like to consider how the mores of society have changed over the last four decades and the effect of that change on psychoanalytic practice. Finally, I would like to address how these changes in society and my own personal development can interact with patient dynamics and affect the course and outcome of clinical work.

I would like to start with a fact that may seem so obvious that it can be taken for granted. All of us need role models, which allow us to form goals and ideals that guide our lives. The heterosexual world is so filled with role models that people can pick out models that are most conducive to them. For gay people, it has not been so easy. The tyranny of the closet is that it hides, from young lesbian and gay people, the broad range of lesbian and gay adults who have led fulfilling lives. When I was 15, I had my first summer job in Manhattan. It was at a data processing company, and I was becoming gradually more aware of my attraction to men. At the company, there was one obviously gay person. He was loud and nasty and would refer to men with women's names. He had a clerical job that was going nowhere, and he was bitter. I remember thinking, is this what life is like if you are gay? Unfortunately, at that time, people did not talk frankly to teenagers about homosexuality; there were usually only furtive remarks, usually with a tone of disdain, statements like, "All homosexuals are hairdressers or interior decorators." Since I had no talent in either area, what would become of me?

In the mid-1960s, I had dear friends in high school with whom I shared many interests and who, I now know, were gay, too, but we never spoke about it. But others saw it. My close friend Roger and I were inseparable. One day, the biology teacher threw something at us during class, and said, "Blechner, do you go home and wash Roger's back at night?" The meaning was obvious, but dissociation being what it is, I only vaguely apprehended that he was suggesting Roger and I were having a physical affair. And since we weren't, surely we weren't gay. After all, we only loved being with each other every moment of the day.

Some of my friends of that time who turned out to be gay managed the difficulties well, but a few suffered seriously from their closetedness. One became extremely obese and spent most of his adult life living with his mother. Two of them dropped out of college and "disappeared," although one of those turned out to have moved to another part of the country where he felt he could live life as a gay man without constant exposure to the disdain of his family.

Each of us had to struggle to "come out." Some excellent articles have been written on the coming-out process, and psychoanalysts should become familiar with them (e.g., Martin, 1991; Troiden, 1988). But I think we should also look at the need for "coming out" as a sign of social pathology. Society will be cured of this pathology only when there is *no more need for coming out*. When homosexuality is not something publicly condemned, but merely acknowledged as one of the acceptable variants of human development, then children and teenagers will be free to discover the vagaries of their own sexuality openly and without fear. It will still be a difficult process. Adolescence and the discovery of the self are always difficult tasks, but at least the need for secrecy and shame will have been removed or reduced, as well as the hiddenness, the excessive emphasis on sexual acts over loving acts, and the lack of preparatory rituals, like open dating, that will allow young gays and lesbians the opportunity to test out their social, romantic yearnings.[1]

In the current world, because of widespread anti-homosexual prejudice and the resultant secrecy surrounding homosexuality, there is often a conflict between a gay person's self-concept and public opprobrium of gay people. How does one deal with this discordance between what one knows of oneself and the images that one receives from society? Often, without guidance, one can try identification with the aggressor. One can start to feel contemptuous of gay people and give others the impression that, "I'm certainly not like that." I did this on a limited scale. In high school, we read *The Devil's Advocate*, which, if I remember correctly, had a sinister homosexual character in it who tries to seduce a young

---

[1] Society puts a great deal of pressure on adolescents not to become homosexual, and it is a popular view that such pressure discourages homosexuality. I have seen a number of cases where the opposite is true. People who had the potential for romantic involvement with either sex are sometimes pushed into declaring their identities, prematurely, as gay or straight, and this may foreclose an open understanding of their sexual and affectional make-up.

man, and we made jokes about people in the class who were like that young man. Fortunately, we never went beyond that, but I can see how, under different cultural circumstances, a budding gay adolescent may try to deny his homosexuality by beating up openly gay people.

When I got to college at the University of Chicago, I immediately formed an extremely close friendship with Dan Kozloff. We met in the music practice room of our dormitory. We were both pianists, and we started to explore the section of the library where four-hand piano music was stored. In this way, we could study together huge amounts of the symphonic and chamber repertory. I loved the time I spent with him, and we were nearly inseparable, but I was also dating women and did not call myself homosexual.

After nine months of this life, Dan came to my room one day and said, "I have something important I want to discuss with you. Can we talk openly?" I said, "Of course," and he said that what he had to say was difficult, and it would be easier if we had the lights off. I agreed to that, too. We both sat on the bed, and he told me that he loved me and was very attracted to me. I was stunned, but also intrigued. I said, "I need three days to decide." So we spent the next three days in endless discussion. What did it mean to be in love with another man? What would this mean for our futures? Was it normal? Despite all the abstraction, I realized that I loved Dan, too, and so we would see. And we did.

What does a young man in conflict, who has strong academic leanings, do when faced with a difficult issue? He goes to the library. I went straight to the card index and looked up homosexuality. I looked up every book and journal article I could find on the subject, and of course, I took every detail, no matter how silly, with deadly seriousness. I remember one study of what homosexuals were like. It said that they prefer impressionistic music. I remember thinking, "Dan really likes Ravel and Debussy, while I am not such a great fan of theirs. Does that mean that he is more homosexual than I am?"

There were books on the *Boys of Boise* and *The Tearoom Trade,* which painted a sleazy picture of promiscuous sex in bathrooms. This wasn't part of my life, but books seemed so authoritative, I worried terribly that that was where my life would end up. And then, of course, there was the dreadful Edmund Bergler, whose titles leaped out at me from the card catalogue: *Homosexuality: Disease or Way of Life?* All the psychiatric texts in those days were discussing how to treat the disease called homosexuality. And yet I was having the most glorious times with Dan. I was in love with him, and we were learning and teaching each other all sorts of new things. We argued about "life" in the way adolescents do and were constantly inspired and prodded by each other to grand plans and less grand achievements. How did this all fit together with the view that our relationship was diseased?

I began to scrutinize how life was being lived by other gay people. The picture was mixed. There were a number of homosexuals on campus whose suffering was quite public. There was the campus carillonneur, a man who was flamboyant and supposedly had wild parties. He killed himself. There was one eternal student, a man who attended the same courses year after year, with no apparent goal in life. What was wrong with him? He was very conflicted about his homosexuality and apparently went from one psychiatric consultation to another and from one treatment to another but was never "cured." Unfortunately, the psycho-analysts were attempting to cure his homosexuality, instead of curing his internalized homophobia and his general self-hatred.

Gradually, I discovered that there were alternatives. One pair of professors, Roger Weiss and Howard Brown, lived together as a couple on campus and were apparently accepted, since they kept their sexuality relatively discreet.[2] There was a man who was rumored to be the next Nobel Prize winner, who was secretly gay. I got to know him and was impressed, at the time, by how he managed to make his personal life seem completely irrelevant to his work, which seemed easier perhaps in the hard sciences, but he lived alone and seemed quite lonely.

Gradually, this "research" became integrated with my academic work. I took a course on Rorschach testing with Samuel Beck and discovered the extensive literature on the "signs" on the Rorschach of homosexu-ality. Why anyone needed such "signs" wasn't exactly clear. Was it mere abstract interest, was it to help clinical assessment, or were they trying to find ways of weeding out homosexuals from situations in which they were prohibited, like the military? Many of the studies were done during the McCarthy era and seemed tainted by it. When it came time to do a term paper, "The Rorschach and Homosexuality" was my topic. I found that many of the studies claiming to find different signs contradicted each other. Evelyn Hooker (1957) finally put this area to rest with her land-mark study, in which she sent Rorschach protocols to acknowledged experts, and they were unable to distinguish the protocols of gay men from straight men.

That paper was my first step out of the closet professionally. I real-ized that some might ask, why is he so interested in this topic? No one did so to my face, and I went ahead with the project.

Dan and I read André Gide's *Corydon,* which was one of the more gay-positive tracts around, but still had the tone of an apologia. Today, I think, "What was there to apologize for?"—but in those days, the oppro-brium of society was not something I could shrug off. And then there

---

[2]Their story of their relationship will be told in detail in a book being written by Thomas Jacobs, entitled *The Marriage of Howard Brown and Roger Weiss.*

was Gide's *L'Immoraliste,* that moving tale of bisexual torment. Gide's diaries became regular nighttime reading. There was a feeling of constant sleuthing: Where are the homosexuals of our culture hiding?

For example, when I was in high school, I fell in love with the works of Thomas Mann. It started with *Buddenbrooks,* the great novel of a German family (that had astonishing resemblances to my own family). By the time I had finished high school, I had read every work of fiction Mann had written. Besides my interest in his insights into my family and the genius of his writing, there was the prevalent homoerotic element: the crush between schoolboys in "Tonio Kröger," the thrilling tragic kiss between Mario and the Magician, and, most of all, *Death in Venice.* It was odd that in those days, it was considered inappropriate to speak of *Death in Venice* as a novella about suppressed homosexual desires. I did so in a paper, and the professor (who I know now was gay) called it grotesque. Mann's work was supposed to be about aesthetic love, or so we were told, and anyone who saw it having to do with suppressed homosexuality was a vulgarian.

Vulgarian that I was, I persisted in trying to discover if Mann himself had homoerotic interests and felt vindicated when Mann's letters were published (Winston, 1971), and I found this in a letter to André Gide on August 22, 1924: "I received and studied [*Corydon*] with extraordinary pleasure: the spiritual apology for an area of feeling which I too hold can be despised and condemned only by barbarians and ignoramuses."

Later, in the 1980s, I heard Mann's son Golo give a talk at Columbia University's Deutches Haus, which included a documentary by a man in California who told of taking Mann to see Muscle Beach, "and how he stared!"

But in the era before Stonewall, duplicity about homosexuality was the prevalent ethic—proper manners meant that gays should not identify themselves as such, and straights were considered ill-mannered if they spoke overtly about someone's homosexuality. Certain code words were devised instead and were even used by psychoanalysts. Clara Thompson (1964) put it quite bluntly: "Moreover, we of this Institute [the White Institute] maintain that a man's capacity as a therapist will be adequately revealed in his work with patients, so that his supervisors will be able to judge. The reply to this statement is that there is no way of knowing whether a man is a psychopath—by which, I think, is usually meant a homosexual—because psychopaths are often good therapists" (pp. 58–59). This tradition allowed prejudice against gays without open acknowledgment—"the prejudice that dare not speak its name"—a phenomenon still very much alive today.

For someone gay, this crazy tradition is a constant challenge to know what is really going on; it turned me and many others into devotees of a kind of counterespionage. Who were the secret, influential homosexuals, and where, how, and why were they hiding? I learned about J. Edgar Hoover's longstanding love affair with Clyde Tolson, which went on while they persecuted gays in America. Roy Cohn was doing the same thing, and so were many others (see von Hoffman, 1988). It is an odd fact that people who are the victims of prejudice often become the purveyors of that prejudice and persecute their own people.[3] It is as if they identify with the aggressor and end up doing the dirty work for their persecutors. We have seen this not only with gays but often among blacks (the Anita Hill investigation, where all the traditional hypersexualized stereotypes about black men and women were dragged out) and among Jews (the case of Otto Weininger, a Jewish psychoanalyst who converted to Christianity and wrote damning, prejudicial things about Jews [Weininger, 1903]).

I was very lucky to have begun my gay life with Dan, a relationship that integrated sexual, loving, and intellectual aspects of my self. For many gay men, romantic life can begin quite differently. Their first sexual experiences may be just furtive sexual acts, not coordinated with an ongoing relationship, and this may set up a pattern of a separation between sex and emotional connection that can be problematic in later life. This is made more likely by the necessity for secrecy in a hostile world and by the lack of social supports to adolescent gays and lesbians to help them in dating. So many of the institutions of the heterosexual world—dances, proms, and other social functions—are not hospitable to gays and lesbians. It is difficult to gauge how important such rituals are to adolescent development, but for gays and lesbians, dances and proms are often a painful experience of either exclusion or false-self development.

Dan went off to California after college, and our relationship ended. I began graduate school at Yale and met John Silberman, whom I quickly decided would be the man with whom I would spend the rest of my life. (It turned out to be 14 years.) He was in school in the Boston area, and so we had to commute to see each other every weekend. During graduate school, most people did not ask many questions about one's sexuality, and life, mostly in the closet, seemed easy and enjoyable. Some people asked why I was going to Boston so often, and one person told everyone she had figured it out: I was having an affair with a married woman, and so I didn't want to tell anyone.

John and I moved to New York, where we lived together and settled down to develop our lives. During my internship, I was also not usually asked about my sexuality, but I started to see the phenomenon of the closeted gay or lesbian psychiatrists and psychologists who diagnose homosexuality and its supposed pathology, partly to cover suspicion about their

---

[3] I am indebted to Dr. Kathleen White for this insight.

own lives. I also came to recognize how pervasive was the belief that homosexuals can and should be encouraged to change to heterosexuality. One particular internship experience stands out: I had a supervisor whom I considered quite sophisticated clinically. I was working with a gay man who was extremely detached and had developed an elaborate group of defenses to avoid connection with any human being. As the therapy relationship developed, he became quite anxious by the closeness of contact with me. One day, he reported a brief encounter with a woman friend, in which she gave him oral sex. I raised in supervision the idea that this was a case of "sexual acting out" (those were the terms we used in those days; I would not use such language today), in which he was trying to dispel his anxiety about the relationship to me. My supervisor said something I shall never forget: "You are probably right about the psychodynamics, but clinically, it has been my experience that whenever a homosexual patient shows any signs of heterosexuality, he should be encouraged in that direction." This was really my first contact with the way that clinical thinking was skewed by professional and societal homophobia.

I think such thinking is still very prevalent today, although it is becoming less ego-syntonic for some practitioners. Schafer writes (1995): "I believe that, by and large, it is still that way in the analytic treatment of the great majority of patients. Heterosexual tendencies are taken for granted; it is conflict over them that is to be examined, understood, and reduced. In contrast, homosexual tendencies are considered central to psychological problems, and it is the temptation to act on them in fact or fantasy that is to be examined, understood, and reduced." A survey of members of the American Psychoanalytic Association (MacIntosh, 1994) found that 97.6% do not believe that "homosexual patients can and should change to heterosexuality," yet 34.4% believe that "most other analysts think homosexual patients can and should change to heterosexuality." This statistic could be interpreted as a divergence between what psychoanalysts think and do; however, the letter that accompanied the survey was very directive in its implications and defensive of the profession against charges of prejudice, so it is hardly surprising that most respondents disavowed prejudice and a wish to change a patient's sexual orientation on their own part. But given the reality of psychoanalytic practice, it is not surprising, either, that many thought prejudice against homosexuality rampant among their colleagues.

In 1979, I was accepted by the William Alanson White Institute for psychoanalytic training. I wondered whether I ought to be open about my homosexuality during my training or not. During the summer, I met Dr. Ellis Perlswig, a gay psychiatrist from New Haven. About twenty years before, he began training at the New York Psychoanalytic Institute. His training analyst was Dr. Jacob Arlow. During his first session, Perlswig told Arlow that he was gay. Arlow reported it to the training committee of the New York Psychoanalytic, and Perlswig's standing as a candidate of the New York Psychoanalytic Institute was ended.

So Perlswig's advice to me was not to be open about my homosexuality at the White Institute until after I received my psychoanalytic certificate. But then he added, "Of course, the longer you wait and the more advanced you become, the more you will have to lose by coming out."

I took his advice and went through my psychoanalytic training in the closet for the most part. I told my analyst I was gay, of course. He was trying to be open-minded about it, but there were many signs of his entrenched heterosexism. When I referred to my lover, he asked what the term *lover* meant. To him, it had the connotations of an illicit paramour, as in "Madame Bovary took a lover." Of course, from an old-fashioned heterosexual standpoint, that was right, but it showed his vantage point. I gave him John Boswell's (1980) book *Christianity, Social Tolerance, and Homosexuality,* which was at the time a book of revolutionary gay scholarship, with the hope that it would teach him about the history of prejudice and the significance of gay love relationships.

When I mentioned that Sullivan was homosexual, he responded, "Do you know anyone who slept with him?" This was the first sign I observed of the tremendous dread that many Interpersonal analysts feel about Sullivan's homosexuality. Sullivan was a genius, and he was the theoretical and clinical mentor of the Interpersonalists, but many Interpersonalists prejudiced against homosexuals have great difficulty with Sullivan's sexuality. Some refuse to recognize Sullivan's adopted son, Jimmie, as anything other than an adopted son, although gay men who attended events at Sullivan's home have told me that there was no doubt that Harry and Jimmie Sullivan were lovers. The usual cover invoked is that Sullivan's sexuality was questionable. "We don't really know whether or not Sullivan was gay." A gay man told me his Interpersonal analyst said these very words to him in the spring of 1995. This is the fate of being in the closet. Others may see you as asexual or schizoid or simply mysterious. In the middle of the twentieth century, this was a common spectacle. People were called confirmed bachelors and surrounded themselves with rumors of possible marriages, thus quelling suspicion of homosexuality, which could damage your career. This was commonly done by men and women in all walks of public life, including show business and politics.

In the context of such obfuscation, the late Dr. Ralph Crowley was a breath of fresh air. He was able to talk candidly and nondefensively about Sullivan's homosexuality. Crowley directed me to an important book by Kenneth Chatelaine (1981), which includes interviews with mental health aides who worked on Sullivan's extraordinary ward for schizophrenics and who are unambiguous in their discussions of the relationship between Sullivan's homosexuality and his clinical work. Crowley also told me that he once attended a lecture of Sullivan's at a conference. At the end of the talk, Crowley went up to Sullivan to ask him some questions. Sullivan invited the young Crowley to continue the conversation in his room at the hotel where the conference was being held. "We went up to his room," Crowley told me, "and there were two single beds in the room. Sullivan lay on one bed, and I on the other, and we talked. I'm sure if I had been a little less square, he would have approached me."

Being in the closet during analytic training turned out to be increasingly difficult. My classmates and I were very close, and we socialized quite a bit. When people came to my house, it had to be arranged for a time when my lover John would not be at home. Analysts being the sort of people who are interested in other people's lives, they asked probing questions that I mostly finessed. Most people began to think of me as lonely and schizoid, with no intimate relationships. It was painful to be misperceived that way, but I stuck with my choice. It was especially difficult when there were weekend events to which everyone brought his or her spouse or significant other, and I attended alone. It also caused stresses in my relationship with John, although this way of living was mutual; I did not attend the social functions at his law firm.

Sometimes I slipped. One summer, a fellow candidate from the White Institute and her boyfriend visited me at my summer home. We were preparing lunch, and her boyfriend asked me, "Is there usually someone else here with you?" I asked him why he asked that. He replied, "Because you have set the table with four place settings, and there are only three of us here!"

My reaction to this slip was informative. I did not think, as I might have earlier in my life, "Oh, no! That was a terrible mistake!" Rather, I thought, "I wish I could simply reply, 'Yes, usually my lover John is here with me.'" It signaled to me that I would not put up with such hiding much longer.

I also came to realize how damaging it was to maintain secrecy. One of the problems with being in the closet for a long time is that you get used to it, and you start to lose awareness of how debilitating it is (see Sedgwick, 1990). Heterosexual analysts who work with gay and lesbian patients need to devote special efforts to appreciate this. If you want to understand the agony of being in the closet and of coming out, read first-person accounts of treatment histories, such as Martin Duberman's *Cures* (1991) or Paul Monette's *Becoming a Man* (1992) or the poignant account by Richard Socarides of coming out to his father, the psychoanalyst Charles Socarides (Nagourney, 1995). Also, if you are straight and married, try an experiment on yourself. For one month, do not ever mention your husband or wife or your children in conversation with anyone. When you describe an experience that you shared with your spouse, tell of it as if you did it alone. Always say "I," even when you mean "we." These things are all done by gay men and lesbians who must keep their homo-sexuality hidden. I know straight people who have gone through this exercise and been astonished at how debilitating it is—to one's sense of self, reality, integrity, honesty, and cohesion. We may ask, how is it that anyone who does this day in and day out—not for just one month, but for years, for a lifetime—how does such a person manage not to have a feeling of loss of self, of false self?

One of the most powerful antidotes to the loneliness of the closet is affiliation with others who are in the same predicament or who have found a solution to it. I certainly benefited from collegial discussions with other gay psychoanalysts, including Drs. Bertram Schaffner, Gerald Perlman, Jack Drescher, Richard Isay, and Martin Frommer. Several gay and lesbian colleagues and I founded the Association of Lesbian and Gay Psychoanalysts at the White Institute, a small group that has allowed us to compare our experiences and speak out on them with an official voice.

And then there was AIDS. It is impossible to describe in words the impact that the advent of AIDS has had on me personally and in my clinical work. I knew someone in 1980 who started to become strangely sick and was first diagnosed with Hodgkin's disease. It turned out to be AIDS. Now, fifteen years of constant death of friends, colleagues, and patients, most in the prime of life, have taken an intolerable toll, all the worse since there is no sign of the epidemic being stopped or the disease cured. Although I was lucky to be healthy, AIDS gave me a new sense of urgency to live life fully and honestly. Part of the psychology of being in the closet is tenacious procrastination. One thinks that, someday, the secrecy will stop. Someday, I will not worry about what others think of my romantic life. Someday, I will stand up against injustice and inequality. All of these "somedays" can extend into infinite delay. I was really jogged out of such procrastination by working with people with AIDS, whom I saw trying to fulfill long-postponed goals in a shortened life span. It forced me to realize that, someday, there would be no more days left, and no one could say when that time would come (Blechner, 1993b).

With Dr. Bertram Schaffner, I founded and directed the HIV Clinical Service at the White Institute, which provided psychotherapy for people with AIDS and those traumatized in other ways by the epidemic. Our monthly seminars also allowed remarkably free discussions of all aspects of sexuality. It also revealed that many of the younger generation of analysts were relatively free of the homophobia so common in the older generation.

In 1992, I organized and chaired a conference on "The Experience of Hating and Being Hated." It brought together six distinguished psycho-analysts, who had special identities by virtue of their race, sex, sexual orientation, or national and religious background, to speak openly about their own experiences of hating and being hated. Two black women spoke about racism and sexism, an ethnic German spoke about Nazi anti-Semitism and current attitudes in Germany to the Holocaust, and three gay analysts spoke about homophobia. One of them was Bertram Schaffner, who was an openly gay candidate at the White Institute from 1949 to 1953. It was the clinical custom of the time for an analyst to encourage a gay patient to pursue heterosexual relationships. Dr. Schaffner had planned to fly to Europe to become engaged to a woman he knew there. He feared that, otherwise, he would not be able to have a psychiatric practice, and he knew that his analyst was pleased. However, he had a dream in which he was in an airplane that had no roof and was flying upside down. He realized the dream's message and felt that his plans violated his core sense of being and mental health. He canceled the trip and changed psychiatrists (Schaffner, 1995).

The more I emerge from the closet, the more instances of homophobia within psychoanalytic organizations, which I had once tolerated, seem unacceptable. The great advantage of not being in the closet is that one can speak out publicly against such blatant prejudice. In 1992, I attended a conference on Psychoanalysis and Musical Biography. It was part of a series of conferences organized by the seminar on Psychoanalysis and Music of the American Psychoanalytic Association, which I had been attending for years. At this particular conference, held at the City University of New York, the moderator announced that a paper on the great British composer Benjamin Britten was to have been delivered by a musicologist, Professor Chip Whitesell, who was the head of the Gay and Lesbian Musicologists Association, "an organization that actually exists." (He actually said that.) He also said the musicologist could not attend but had sent his manuscript and that the manuscript could be read to the audience if they wished to hear it. Did anyone want to hear the paper? I replied, loudly and alone, "Yes." The speaker got ready to read it, but there was an interruption from the chairman, and it was not read. When I protested, I was ignored. I left the conference. I since have received a copy of Professor Whitesell's paper, entitled "Britten, Inside and Outside." It is an excellent piece of work and would have provided a much-needed balance to the stultifying pathologizing of Britten that occurred at the conference.

Prejudice continues. In the old days, one could be prejudiced against homosexuals with impunity. Now people are a bit more careful, but still, homosexuals are the one group in America about which openly prejudicial statements can be made with little or no repercussion. Congressman Dick Armey publicly referred to Congressman Barney Frank as Barney Fag. People made virulently antigay speeches at the Republican National Convention in 1992. States continue to attempt and, at times, succeed in passing laws that allow discrimination against gays to continue. The military continues to bar open homosexuals from serving. To all these aspects of discrimination, most psychoanalysts have been either silent or have actually supported such discrimination through pathologizing theories of homosexuality.

Certainly, there have been exceptions. Harry Stack Sullivan, as a psychiatrist for the military forces, attempted to remove homosexuality as a disqualifying factor for admission to military service, although he was eventually overruled by the military establishment (Bérubé, 1990). Judd Marmor was extremely helpful in combating the homophobia in organized psychiatry and continues to be a rational voice on the subject today.

In their practices, psychoanalysts must become aware of the traumatizing effects such pronouncements have on a gay person's sense of safety. It takes work for a heterosexual analyst to become sensitive and empathic with these issues, which are so much taken for granted in society (see O'Leary, 1995).

One of the most poignant spectacles of internalized homophobia is of a closeted gay analyst saying prejudicial things about gay people. During my psychoanalytic training, I remember one married teacher (whom I presumed to be bisexual and which I have now confirmed) discussing a patient who had a severe thought disorder. He asked, "Is his homosexuality treatable?" Besides the essential misguidedness and inherent prejudice of the question, this patient had much more important and fundamental issues to solve besides his homosexuality. I felt hopeful about the future when one of my fellow students stated this in blunt terms.

In psychoanalysis, things are changing, but the changes are quite a bit behind the progress of organized psychology and psychiatry (see Tabin, 1995; Blechner, 1995a). People who used to be openly prejudiced against gays now are more likely to say prejudicial things in private. In 1994, a colleague of mine had dinner with a senior analyst of the White Institute and his wife. This analyst had been very supportive of my work when he was my advisor and supervisor during my training, at a time when I was still closeted about my homosexuality. At the dinner, my colleague mentioned my name a few times during the discussion. The analyst's wife said, "Who is this Mark Blechner?" Her husband replied, "Oh, he is the White Institute's resident homosexual." So is one reduced.

CLINICAL WORK

I would like to discuss one case in which the issue of my sexual orientation was especially significant and which spanned my years of being in and out of the closet. I will not go into the entire details of the case but will stay focused primarily on those aspects having to do with sexuality and sexual orientation. Then I will consider further the effect of this change in my life on my clinical work in general.

In 1983, I began an analysis with a patient whom I shall call Rick. A man in his early thirties, he was suffering from a severe depression following the loss of his aunt, with whom he was extremely close. He was, at the start of analysis, lost in all areas of his life. Although he was extremely intelligent, he had a history of dropping out of various graduate programs and of a series of underpaid jobs for which he was overqualified.

His romantic life existed only in his fantasies. In his early twenties, he had had a number of relatively brief gay affairs, some of which he found to be very exciting sexually but which he found unacceptable because of severe internalized homophobia.

Rick had had a previous therapy experience in which the therapist had become directly involved in his life, so I found myself trying harder than usual to stick to an analytic, relatively anonymous stance. This had good and bad points. I never spoke to Rick about my own sexual orientation, nor did he ask me. He presumed I was heterosexual, yet the transference was extremely intense and highly eroticized. He fantasized my being on the couch with him and embracing him. The erotic fantasies were complex to analyze, since his father had been seductive with Rick (or so Rick perceived him).[4]

I devoted a great deal of attention to Rick's case and felt quite inspired by his devotion to the analysis and his progress. After 10 years of analysis, he achieved a prominent professional position and had made other significant gains in his life, but he was still extremely lonely. He had made an occasional attempt to date women at his place of work, but they seemed unappealing to him erotically (although he had some close platonic friendships with women). He was also not seeking out any romantic relationships with men. He would spend weekends and vacations mostly alone, and he would complain terribly about his loneliness.

The transference no longer had the passionate, yearning erotic quality that it did in the early years of our work together; however, while Rick was ruling out any romantic involvements with other men, he seemed perfectly comfortable saying things like: "Why don't the two of us run off together?" I gradually came to acknowledge to myself that there was

---

[4] This is a fundamental and important question. We know that gay men often feel that their fathers or other male figures were seductive with them, and it is easy for an analyst to jump to the conclusion that these adults had a secret homosexual attraction to the boy. However, it can also be true that relatively innocuous physical contact was experienced by the boy as erotic, and is so reported in his analysis as an adult. While it may be impossible to determine this definitively, it is important for the analyst to be aware of this special "confusion of tongues" (Ferenczi, 1933).

something false in our relationship. Rick was presuming I was straight and that I shared his internalized homophobia. When I interpreted his own homophobia, he felt that I was being patronizing. He was idealizing me as the competent male who was being accepting of his homosexual yearnings while maintaining his comfortably dominant position as a heterosexual. After a great deal of soul-searching, I decided to tell Rick that I was gay. This eventually took place in a session in which he was speaking in a way that presumed I was straight, and the miscommunication between us was growing.

His response to learning that I was gay was dramatic. He seemed genuinely surprised and relieved. He took my own homosexuality as a permission to explore his own feelings. He began to date and eventually developed a close attachment.

Rick was astonished at how my revelation to him had a significant effect. He was angry, too, that I had not told him sooner. Rick raised the question of how the analysis would have gone differently if he had known that I was gay earlier in the treatment. It is possible that he would never have worked with me, since his internalized homophobia and his general self-hatred were so intense when the analysis started. He wondered, though, if much of the mystification of the transference would have been done away with. Of course, there is also the question of why he saw my sexual life as so conventional and never questioned it, which may have to do with his wish to conventionalize an unconventional family history. So we have several factors interacting: 1) Rick's own personality development during the analysis; 2) my own changing stance with regard to my homosexuality and the psychoanalytic professional world; and 3) the changes in attitudes toward homosexuality in society and in the professions of psychiatry, psychology, and psychoanalysis. It is impossible to separate these factors, but it is unusual for all three to change so rapidly within a decade. (Something similar may have occurred with regard to feminism and the treatment of women.)

I would like to think that the timing of my revelation to Rick about my own sexual orientation was totally determined by clinical judgment and his own progress in the analysis, but that would be quite disingenuous. It was intricately connected to my own sense of openness in the outside world, especially in the psychoanalytic world. Five years before my revelation to him, I had begun to take decisive steps to being more open about, or at least not hiding, my involvement with my lover from the psychoanalytic professional world. I hardly need to state that I was terrified. I was warned by gay colleagues that if I "came out," many of my referral sources would stop referring to me, and, in any case, I would only receive referrals of gay patients. This has not turned out to be true for me, but I did not know that then. I decided, in any case, that the gain in personal integrity and freedom would be worth it. As I gained courage, I began also to speak and to publish about the antihomosexual bias that is still so rampant in organized psychoanalysis and that is distorting clinical work (Blechner, 1992, 1993a, 1994, 1995a, b, d; Blechner and Casden, 1994, 1995).

Some of my heterosexual patients came to know that I was gay during this time. Mostly, this was productive for the progress of their analyses, although there were often difficult times. One woman expressed her thoughts rather freely: Did my being gay mean that I hate women? Did it mean that I thought all women were bitches? Did it mean that I cared less for her than for my male patients? While all of these concerns had special personal significances for her, I found myself rather grateful for the candor with which she expressed these blatant and false stereotypes, for they gave me a view of the sorts of misconceptions held by many heterosexuals.

She also raised the question of what my relationship was like with the community. I really didn't know what she meant by the community, and it emerged that, by that, she meant the community at large, that is, from her viewpoint, the heterosexual community. This seemed a good example of what Moss (1992) has called the tyranny of the first-person plural. "We" means "we heterosexuals."

There were some quite surprising outcomes. One woman patient felt freed to tell me that she had pervasive fantasies about anal sex. Previously, she had felt too ashamed to admit this, but knowing that I was gay led her to assume that I would be more accepting of such wishes. Those who had the most trouble were those men whose behavioral lives were predominantly heterosexual, but who had strong currents of homosexual feelings with which they were not at peace.

Some people were able to explore areas of homosexual feeling and attitudes toward homosexuality in new ways. A woman patient had the following dream: "My boss, Elaine, wanted to marry me. She asked me. I didn't want to. I didn't know how to say it. An hour later, I told her, NO. I was so upset by it. It was not what I wanted for my life, to be tied to her."

The dream had obvious implications about being tied to her mother in an eroticized relationship that does not give her independence and the way she was reexperiencing that in her workplace and in the analysis. But, as is often the case, the dream was followed by an enactment of the dream (Blechner, 1995). The next session, she told me that she had not been able to tell me all her thoughts about the dream at the time. "She didn't know how to say it." But now, "an hour later" (i.e. a session later), she could tell me: she thought that being gay would be a fate worse than death.

How prevalent is her view in our society? We would have to surmise that it is quite prevalent, judging from the intensity with which some analysts cling to notions of homosexuality as pathology (see Tabin, 1995;

Blechner, 1995a). It shows the complex connection between societal norms and views of psychopathology, an area that has been explored far too little (see Hartmann, 1960; Wakefield, 1992). Psychoanalysts' views of what constitutes mental health are sharply colored by cultural standards and prejudices.

Not being in the closet has had a very healthful effect on all my clinical work. I don't bring up my sexual orientation and my domestic situation needlessly with patients. If patients ask, I may tell them, after suitable exploration of their own fantasies and motives, but even if the subject never comes up, the fact that I am not afraid if it does is certainly freeing. Some psychoanalysts adopt a position of not deliberately revealing personal information to patients; still, there is a great difference between whether one does that out of clinical conviction or because there are important things about oneself that one would really not like to be revealed. This principle applies to all aspects of an analyst's personality, not just social–sexual–familial factors. For me, to bring my true private self into alignment with my public self has given me much more freedom to work as an analyst, on any issue with any patient. Even if it has meant facing some ugly and painful discrimination, it has been worth it.

REFERENCES

Bérubé, A. (1990) *Coming Out Under Fire: The History of Gay Men and Women in World War II.* New York: Free Press.
Blechner, M. J. (1992), Psychoanalysis, homophobia, racism, and anti-Semitism: Introduction. Presented at the conference of the William Alanson White Society, The Experience of Hating and Being Hated, New York.
—— (1993a), Homophobia in psychoanalytic writing and practice. *Psychoanal. Dial.,* 3:627–637.
—— (1993b), Psychoanalysis and HIV disease. *Contemp. Psychoanal.,* 29:61–80.
—— (1994), Review of Darlene Ehrenberg's *The Intimate Edge. Psychoanal. Dial.,* 4:283–292.
—— (1995a), The interaction of societal prejudice with psychodiagnosis and treatment aims. *Round Robin,* 11:10–14.
—— (1995b), Homosexuality, homophobia, and clinical psychoanalysis. Presented to the Graduate Faculty, New School for Social Research, New York City.
—— (1995c), The patient's dreams and the countertransference. *Psychoanal. Dial.,* 5:1–25.
—— (1995d), The shaping of psychoanalytic theory and practice by cultural and personal biases about sexuality. In: *Disorienting Sexuality,* ed. T. Domenici & R. Lesser. New York: Routledge, pp. 265–288. An earlier version was presented at the conference, Perspectives on Homosexuality: An Open Dialogue, New York University, December 4, 1993.
—— & Casden, S. (1994), Special considerations in the psychoanalytic psychotherapy of gay men. Presented at the Connecticut Society of Psychoanalytic Psychologists, Hartford, CT.
—— & —— (1995), Further considerations in the psychoanalytic psychotherapy of gay men and lesbians. Presented at the Connecticut Psychological Association, Hartford, CT.

Boswell, J. E. (1980), *Christianity, Social Tolerance, and Homosexuality.* Chicago: University of Chicago Press.

Chatelaine, K. (1981), *Harry Stack Sullivan: The Formative Years.* Washington, DC: University Press of America.

Duberman, M. (1991), *Cures.* New York: Dutton.

Ferenczi, S. (1933), Confusion of tongues between adults and the child. In: *Final Contributions to the Problems and Methods of Psycho-Analysis,* ed. M. Balint. New York: Brunner/Mazel, 1980, pp. 156–167.

Hartmann, H. (1960), *Psychoanalysis and Moral Values.* New York: International Universities Press.

Hooker, E. (1957), The adjustment of the male overt homosexual. *J. Project. Tech.,* 21:18–31.

Isay, R. (1991), The homosexual analyst: Clinical considerations. *The Psychoanalytic Study of the Child,* 46:199–216, New Haven, CT: Yale University Press.

MacIntosh, H. (1994), Attitudes and experiences of psychoanalysts in analyzing homosexual patients. *J. Amer. Psychoanal. Assn.,* 42:1183–1207.

Martin, H. (1991), The coming-out process for homosexuals. *Hosp. & Commun. Psych.,* 42:158–162.

Monette, P. (1992), *Becoming a Man.* New York: Harcourt Brace Jovanovich.

Moss, D. (1992), Introductory thoughts: Hating in the first person plural: The example of homophobia. *Amer. Imago,* 49:277–291.

Nagourney, A. (1995), Father doesn't know best. *Out,* February, 75–115.

O'Leary, J. (1995), A heterosexual male therapist's journey of self discovery: Wearing a straight-jacket in a gay men's bereavement group. Paper presented at the HIV Clinical Service of the William Alanson White Institute, New York City, and at the conference Revisiting Sex and Gender: At the Threshold of the 21st Century, July 2, Paris, France.

Schafer, R. (1995), The evolution of my views on nonnormative sexual practices. In: *Disorienting Sexuality,* ed. T. Domenici & R. Lesser. New York: Routledge, pp. 187–202.

Schaffner, B. (1995), The difficulty of being a gay psychoanalyst during the last 50 years. In: *Disorienting Sexuality* ed. T. Domenici & R. Lesser. New York: Routledge, pp. 243–254.

Sedgwick, E. K. (1990), *Epistemology of the Closet.* Berkeley: University of California Press.

Tabin, J. K. (1995), A note on homosexuality. *Round Robin,* 11:1.

Thompson, C. (1964), A study of the emotional climate of psychoanalytic institutes. In: *Interpersonal Psychoanalysis: The Selected Papers of Clara M. Thompson,* ed. M. Green. New York: Basic Books, pp. 54–62.

Troiden, R. (1988), Homosexual identity development. *J. Adol. Health Care,* 9:105–113.

von Hoffman, N. (1988), *Citizen Cohn.* New York: Doubleday.

Wakefield, J. C. (1992), The concept of mental disorder: On the boundary between biological facts and social values. *Amer. Psychol.,* 47:373–388.

Weininger, O. (1903), *Sex and Character.* London: Heinemann.

Winston, R., ed. (1971), *Letters of Thomas Mann.* New York: Knopf.

14

Different Strokes, Different Folks

Meanings of Difference, Meaningful Differences

NAOMI RUCKER

As a young child, I hated my name. Unusual names were not fashionable in the 1950s and 1960s. None I knew had ever heard of the name Naomi and few could spell or pronounce it correctly. When some of the boys in my elementary school began to call me Wyoming, I decided something had to be done. So I began to spin fantasies of being named Cathy, Linda, or Susan, and I asked my parents to call me by the name I chose on a given day. They always complied, but in my heart I knew I was still Naomi, verging on Wyoming. My feelings about my name are one of my earliest recollections of having been aware that I felt very different from everyone around me. This sense of difference was to be a subtle, organizing force in many areas of my life, but in particular, to shape the professional path I would walk.

I am the only child of a biracial couple who married in the early 1940s. My mother is a Caucasian woman raised in the Midwest within a small, educated Catholic family of German–Irish ancestry. My father, now deceased, was the third of 12 children in a poor black family residing in Ohio. His mother was the child of a Cherokee woman and a white man, and his father was the child of a white slave master and a black slave. My father was born in Virginia as his parents were escaping from the South to the North. My paternal grandfather had retaliated for an assault on his wife by a white man—an event that placed the family in grave danger. My father remained in Virginia for the first few months of his life while his parents continued onwards to Ohio. He was brought to join them there as an infant.

My parents met in New York City in the late 1930s while they were both involved in the Leftist political movement. My father fought in the Abraham Lincoln Brigade during the Spanish Civil War and later was injured severely in WWII. He was blacklisted during the McCarthy era for his political involvement in Spain. Both my parents were educated, highly intelligent, and politically active people, although my father's injury and its sequelae marred his psychological, interpersonal, and professional well-being for the duration of his life.

I was born in the early 1950s unexpectedly, since one of the consequences of the treatments my father underwent for his war injury was sterility. My mother was approaching 40 at the time of my birth, which in those years was considered old for first motherhood. Our family was stable and warm, but fraught with the tension and psychological residuals of my father's difficult and painful life. Although my father could walk independently, he was noticeably handicapped and harbored deep resentment and anger for the racial and political discrimination he continually suffered.

Most of my childhood was spent in an integrated, middle- to upper-middle-class suburban community that was a victim of "white flight" in the late 1960s and subsequently deteriorated economically. For reasons of personal principle, my parents refused to leave this community, but we became more and more an anomaly as the neighborhood changed. My parents were significantly older, more educated, and had somewhat more financial resources than the parents of many of my peers. They also had different values and interests. As both my parents had abandoned their original religious affiliations and considered themselves atheists, I was never incorporated into any religion. As a family, we were at variance from the local community along class, racial, political, and religious dimensions. No one was like us and we were like no one with whom we interacted.

In the 1950s and early 1960s, during which I spent my childhood, there were very few biracial children, and virtually no awareness of biracial families existed among the general public. From my early elementary school years, I was aware of feeling different than my classmates and of yearning for a sense of belonging to a conventional family. I looked neither black nor white, and I had an unusual name; I lived in a working-class neighborhood within a family that valued education and intellectual pursuits less important to many other families in the neighborhood; my father was visibly handicapped, and my parents were noticeably older and held radical political views that were alien to the families of my peers. Although I had an exposure to cultural opportunities that many other children did not, my parents' notions of childrearing and the family policies they established often diverged significantly from the community norm. We looked different, acted different, and were different as a family in an era in which difference was not understood or well tolerated.

Although I felt dearly loved by both my parents, I felt very alone in my efforts to understand where I stood in relation to the larger world. I never knew how to answer questions about my race, nationality, or religion, nor how to deal with people's interest in my appearance. Any expressed hostility was beyond my capacities to digest. I loved my family but often felt ashamed of their unconventionality and then ashamed of my shame. I eventually became depressed by my isolation and by the experiences of rejection and twisted envy that I encountered, and silently endured. My parents did not seem to notice that my difference was causing me pain. Much of my childhood and adolescence was spent concealing and attempting to assimilate vague feelings of inadequacy that I could not articulate. Because no one gave voice to the possibility that the circumstances of my life might be difficult, my feelings seemed unacceptable. They only confirmed to me that something must be deeply wrong with me. In retrospect, as an adult, I am aware that class and racial issues were difficult and painful for my parents as well, and it was very hard to acknowledge their child's suffering. Unconsciously, they may have been invested in my ability to "integrate" within myself what the larger society has never been able to integrate.

At the age of 21, I began graduate school in a program where class, racial, and ethnic differences were obscured by a common newfound love of psychoanalysis. There I found the first community in which I felt that I belonged. By the time I completed analytic training, I felt I had made my peace with the reflections of difference that had been so painful to me in my childhood, adolescence, and early twenties. I was quite self-assured in most arenas and usually able to evade the troublesome ones. I was increasingly comfortable with myself and with the cards life had dealt me, and my earlier inner struggles seemed muted. Professionally, I had found my niche. At work, I was an analyst—interpersonally related, socially aware, but internally oriented. Unconsciously, I had designed my professsional demeanor to be innovative enough to be interesting, but conventional enough to be accepted with respect. Yet I found myself still unsettled by my patients' occasional questions about my nationality or religion. I reacted inwardly with feelings reminiscent of the shame and self-consciousness that I felt as a child and outwardly by retreating to a standard analytic nonresponse that was inconsistent with my overall clinical presence. As had happened with my parents, I found myself unable to discuss these anxieties with friends or colleagues or to incorporate sociocultural issues directly in my clinical work.

On one level, I was reluctant to address sociocultural issues with patients because I feared that to do so would somehow betray my psychoanalytic commitment to individual unconscious processes. On a deeper level, however, I was afraid to identify with my parents' political and philosophical perspectives, fearing that such a step either would entrap me or would estrange me from the one community within which I felt I belonged. Perhaps I was also afraid of blemishing my professional self with a resurgence of the bad feelings I had wanted for so long to expunge from my psychic life. Nevertheless, an awareness that I kept this facet of my experience outside of my office only by a closed door, so to speak, began to creep into my consciousness.

As I progressed in my professional life, I gradually have begun to feel dissatisfied with the limits imposed by the inner focus of psychoanalytic conceptualizations. I have become ideologically more like my parents, and I have begun to struggle anew with the very issues of individuality that I had sought refuge from in psychoanalysis. Once again, I find myself in uncomfortable territory vis-à-vis the outer world. All roads eventually lead back to Rome.

It is of interest that I did not begin to deal more actively with socio-cultural and existential issues directly in my work until my father became aged and infirm, nor to write of them at all until his death a few years ago. As my father's life faded, I became more able to identify with him as a person of principle, a man who tried continuously to live a life consistent with his beliefs, who made sacrifices of personal comfort and ease for what he saw as a greater social good and to take risks in order to do so. Upon his death, it was time to be my father's daughter, even if only in my own small, relatively protective (and protected) domain.

In recent years, I have come to appreciate the pervasiveness of the tension between individuality and belonging as common to patients from many walks of life, not just as my own personal nemesis. Interwoven among many threads of their internal and external lives, this struggle is often hidden from cursory observation. Often, the people we see as patients have felt painfully different within their families, their communities, the larger society, or among their peers. Until quite recently, there was little room in American society for recognition of, empathy towards, or even discourse about feelings of difference. Diversity was not valued. To be too different was shameful; to be set apart, if not ostracized, was consciously, or unconsciously, considered by many to be a just dessert for not being of the right kind.

Although it may carry some truth to say that everyone feels different in some way, such a statement is overly facile. For some people, being different is a dominant, relentless experience that isolates them from a sense of connection, while for others, it is only a circumscribed facet of their identity with limited, perhaps transitory, ramifications. For those for whom difference defines much of their lives, a sense of narcissistic injury and fragility can become embedded in their character and can structure the nucleus of their sense of self. For these persons, there are few, if any, places to which they feel they can turn for feelings of belonging and acceptance. Conformity, which many individuals choose as a remedy for inner woundedness, is not an available solace for those who are radically different. On this note, I would like now to turn to Anita, the first of four patients I have selected to discuss.

Anita is a young dancer who came to analysis in her late twenties. She had had one prior psychotherapy experience for about three years with a psychoanalytically oriented clinician whom she found helpful, but naggingly unfulfilling. She liked him and found his conceptualizations about her and her life to be plausible and even accurate, but somehow they "missed the mark." She terminated therapy with his approval, but left feeling unsatisfied and unsettled about the experience.

Anita is a beautiful, graceful woman with a gentle, unassertive, and self-effacing manner. She had been born in a rural area of Portugal and had come to the United States in late childhood. From humble, rural beginnings her father eventually became an engineer who worked at a series of jobs in a series of small southwestern towns. As the only girl in a large family of boys, Anita's role in the family was to be obedient, unobtrusive, and subservient to male authority. Her parents, having married in their late teens, were quite young when they began a family. The demands of supporting many children in isolation from a cultural community and extended family fostered chronic tension and periods of depression in both her parents.

Anita's mother had been a beauty contest winner in Portugal and Anita was always compared negatively to her mother in terms of physical appearance. Her brothers would tease her about her femininity, and her father would use her appearance to reminisce about the early years of his relationship with his wife. Although she is a genuinely beautiful woman, she grew up feeling like an ugly duckling. She felt out-of-place, a misfit, in both her family and her social milieu. Hours of her childhood were spent alone outside, dancing in the fields that often surrounded their homes. Here, her affinity for dance flowered, but her parents did not recognize her talent or cultivate her artistic interests. It was not until she went to college that she had the opportunity to be formally trained.

At the time I met Anita, she had been living for a number of years with a man, Ben, whom she loved, but whom she presented as controlling and self-centered. She often felt inadequate with him—less intelligent, less articulate, more troubled by neurosis than he. Her relationship with her family was close but somewhat conflictual, and he was highly critical of them and of her ongoing attachment to them. There was no place in her life where she felt free to be authentically herself. Anita absorbed Ben's interpretations of her and of events almost automatically, leading her often to feel depressed and discouraged. Her self-esteem had gradually eroded. Ben was relentlessly trying to pull her away from her parents and from their expectations for her in the guise of encouraging her to be independent and autonomous and more mature. Alternately, her family felt her to be the failed daughter—unmarried, childless, living with a man out of wedlock, not sufficiently involved with or responsible for them. They had little, if any, understanding of her pleasure in dance, seeing it as "teenage fantasy" that she should have outgrown, and they were barely acknowledging of her professional accomplishments.

The poles represented by Ben and her parents paralleled Anita's inner conflict between her identity as a contemporary American woman and her earlier sense of self structured around Portuguese values and expectations of women. She too felt that she was simultaneously far too dependent and far too autonomous. She should be standing on her own two feet with her own opinions and doing want she wants, as Ben wanted of her, and simultaneously be a wife and mother, functioning in a traditional female role in a traditional Portuguese family as her parents expected of her and as she expected of herself. Wherever she turned, she felt different, not better than or interesting in her difference, but destined never to belong.

The problems that Anita identified upon entering analysis reflected a common pattern among people for whom feelings of difference have been chronic. The feelings attendant upon being different accumulate quietly over time. They are part of everyday life, tingeing experience with painful affect that may not clearly correspond to life events and thus cannot be readily identified or articulated. Often, themes of difference are couched in interpersonal difficulties.

Anita, as do many others, unwittingly colluded with the societal and interpersonal blindness to the impact of difference. Her primary concerns revolved around her relationship with Ben, and she conceptualized her psychological life around interpersonal dynamics. She expressed no awareness of the centrality that feeling different had and was having in her life. In this regard, I was perplexed. The ongoing experience of feeling different had had such a direct impact in my life that I was perhaps more sensitized than others might have been to its potential for insidious stress. I found her obliviousness to this aspect of her self more glaring and less syntonic than I otherwise might.

Furthermore, Anita was inclined to look inward for answers to her problems, a tendency furthered by her earlier years of therapy, but despite her introspection, the answers she produced were never satisfactory. Repeatedly, her feelings of inadequacy were reinforced by these efforts at self-reflection. Early in her analysis with me, she came to view her previous therapy as fostering the same process, leaving her feeling stuck, circling around the same material, but never attaining an understanding that felt comforting or adequately meaningful.

Our attempts to examine her memories of her childhood similarly met with frustrated disquietude. Anita would recant many things about her life, sharing her emotions candidly. Clearly, there were contributions to her injured narcissism and depressive pulls from family dynamics and developmental circumstances, but the connections we were able to establish did not seem to change very much of what she felt. At one point, Anita inadvertently heard outside of the analysis that I was from a mixed racial background. When questioned about this by her, I answered candidly. For the first time, Anita began to talk animatedly about her experience as an outsider in California. I commented on how painful it must be to feel so different from everyone around her. For many subsequent sessions, she discussed her mixed feelings about her national origin, her despair that she would never find a balance between her American identity and her rural Portuguese background, her resentment that Ben had no compassion for the relational style or values of her family. She has since told me that the interchanges between us around feeling different were a decisive turning point in her relationship with me, her understanding of how she became who she is, and in her feelings about herself.

At the moment in which I acknowledged my mixed racial background to Anita, it seemed to be a very natural thing to do, and I did so almost without thinking. In retrospect, I realize that to have done otherwise would have been an enactment of the hidden nature of cultural issues within myself, within Anita, and within our work together. Although being of an unusual background was a prominent feature of my inner experience, as a child I could never speak of it directly; such a topic seemed taboo. A part of me held onto the knowledge of my difference, while another part of me denied it. It was always in the background of my life, but in the forefront of my private experience. Thus, in those years, I never felt authentic within myself or in relation to those around me. The disclosure I shared with Anita dissipated the semi-dissociation of the issue of cultural differences, which was inherent in both of us, and we were able to shift away from our shared collusion in keeping it out of the analytic foreground.

Caroline, a businesswoman in her mid-thirties, captures the theme of difference from another angle. She is a very successful, poised, articulate woman with a formidable intellect. Frankly, she is one of very few patients with whom I have worked that I feel has a greater intellectual endowment than I do. Caroline is also a modest individual of impeccable integrity whose high personal standards parallel an emotional rigidity that has become problematic in her life. Yet, despite her striking intelligence and her professional achievements, she is quite naive about the workings of the world. She is caring and considerate of others and approaches people and situations with high expectations for competence, responsibility, and sincerity. She has not been able to appreciate that the workings of the world are generally much more mediocre than she demands. She is frequently frustrated and disappointed by the failures of others to comprehend what seems obvious to her, to work with the level of competence, efficiency, and responsibility that seem natural to her, and she has blamed herself for their shortcomings.

In contrast to Anita, Caroline is from an affluent, stable family that did seem to recognize and support her individual assets. However, scant attention was paid by her parents or by other adults around her to the ramifications of these assets on her relationships with others. Rather than become critical of others, she became highly critical of herself. Early in my experience with her, I recognized that it required extensive intellectual energy for me to keep up with the speed and range of her thinking. I generally felt like I was running breathlessly to keep up with her. Caroline is a generally well integrated individual with warmth and sensitivity, and I did not feel that I was reacting to any disorganization in her thought processes. Rather, I seemed to be responding to a level of brilliance in this tall, self-assured woman that I found intimidating. I next wondered that, if I found this off-putting, what must it be like for her to interact with others and how must she feel in relation to them? When I suggested to her that the world has different criteria and a different level of comprehension about things than she does, Caroline was clearly taken aback. Her initial response was to be critical of me for being superior and disrespectful of others, claiming that everyone has something special to offer and no one is better than anyone else. I responded that in a large sense that may be true, but that not everyone had the same things to offer and only some things matter in any given circumstance. I conveyed to her that I experienced her intellectual capacity to be formidable, that it seemed logical that others might as well, and that that experience might have some repercussion for the quality of her contact with them.

She began to speak of her school years when no one seemed to connect with her or understand her at home or in school. She would hide in her older brother's closet reading his books for comfort and connection with some world outside herself. She described a lifelong voraciousness for intellectual stimulation that seldom was met, leaving her in a constant state of low-grade frustration. As our work continues, it has become clearer that her feelings of difference are not linked only with her individual history or internalized representation of relational patterns within her family, but had origins in the insidious, cumulative experiences of feeling apart from those around her. Her reaction to me as being superior and disrespectful has come to be understood as a mechanism of dealing with her own sense of being different. She could not simultaneously belong and be so very different from the norm.

Caroline and I shared a sense that it was often "lonely at the top." This loneliness, for both of us, was a mixture of being intellectually apart from most people and finding a degree of safety and self-esteem in that distance. It served both to protect each of us from painful exposure and rejection and to leave us isolated. For me, intellectualism provided a connection to my parents, a retreat from those by whom I felt rejected and an arena of compensatory superiority. For Caroline, her intelligence gave her the tools to create a compensatory source of nurturance in a realm where she felt control and mastery. For us both, our intelligence represented a combination of self-protective strategies and the maturation of intellectual assets that developed into an anchor for our identities.

The third case I have chosen is that of Diana, a middle-aged woman whose life has revolved around music. Diana spent her childhood in a tumultuous family in which she got little attention. Her one brother, whom she felt was the favored child, was doted upon at her expense. She states that she always felt that she had to "introduce herself to her mother every morning" in order to be recognized. Diana now is a highly accomplished singer who is always taken aback by her success and by the reactions of others to her performances. Diana feels that she connects most fully with herself when she is performing, but she is always left feeling that her audience's praise of her is uncomprehensible. She feels herself to be a much more simple person than they seem to perceive her. Diana is an intelligent, deeply loving, and highly emotionally attuned woman with many friends, but with a history of troubled intimate relationships. With a humorous delivery, she will say that her soulmate is her dog, Suzy.

Recently, Diana has become involved with a man, Eli, with whom she deeply wishes to sustain a relationship. Yet she finds herself constantly frustrated by his inability to match her emotional intensity. She is pained, angered, and continually exasperated in their interactions, while he feels inadequate, guilty, and confused by her demands. He cannot understand why sometimes she can't just have fun without being so serious about everything. Her response to this, spoken in a sad, defeated voice, is, "This is just who I am." A joke between them that captures this disparity in their perspectives involves the scenario of going to a multiplex cinema together—Eli will walk into Theater 1 and see *Aladdin,* while Diana enters Theater 2 to see *The Sorrow and the Pity.* In fact, after eight months of a relationship, they have yet to be able to decide on a movie to see together. I, as well as Eli and others, experience Diana as unusually intense. Although I find this trait of hers stimulating and intriguing, I understand that, to many people, it would be bewildering and perhaps distancing. Diana attends and reacts to undercurrents in the environment that would just wash over most other people. As she once remarked in a statement condensing her musicality, emotionality, and solitude: "I live in a world of Salieri ... too many notes." Amidst her frustration and resentment, Diana recognizes that Eli is a sensitive, loving, and insightful individual who makes sincere efforts to understand what she needs and to respond to her feelings. Consequently, her resentment evokes guilt and confusion.

In one especially poignant session with Diana and Eli, it became clear to me that her frustration with Eli expressed a lifelong frustration and resentment that she had never fit in and no one had appreciated or understood her as completely as she yearned to be understood. Tearfully, she described herself to Eli as always having been the "gifted child who is out to lunch," never fitting in, always seeing and responding to a layer of things that no one else recognized. I commented that she desperately wanted Eli to see the nuances that were so clear to her. I further commented that the kind of connections and mutual vision that she yearned for in an intimate relationship might never happen, that this may be her personal form of existential aloneness, and that she has felt deep sorrow in it. Sobbing, she was able to tell Eli that she had been unfair to expect so much of him when he tried so hard, that no one had ever been able to fully meet her need for connection, and that it was unfair of her to expect that of him. She began to explain to Eli, who had been rather intolerant of her attachment to her dog, that Suzy (the dog) understood her more than people ever seemed able to. She said that that was why she had such trouble leaving Suzy, that Suzy attended to the subtleties of her emotional state to which the people around her always seemed oblivious.

Diana's connection to Suzy and her deeply felt aloneness reverberated with my childhood attachment to our family dog, Tassie, who I experienced as a dear, quasi-human friend, companion, and source of respite from my sense of aloneness for over a decade. Both in the childhood sense and the adult sense, I inwardly responded personally to the meaning and import of her existential plight.

Paul, a young history professor, captures a less usual manner of handling feelings of difference. Paul was one of seven boys in a family that spent much time in Third World countries. Paul's father was a university professor who had been born into a Jewish family in Germany that had emigrated to South America at the onset of the Nazi regime. Paul's father set aside his German-Jewish heritage and South American nationality early in life and considered himself, as did my father, to be an atheist and a "citizen of the world."

Although Paul's family was educationally middle-class, the size of the family meant that there were constant financial difficulties. Raised in a southern, rural, Christian town, Paul and his family were considered to be the "town weirdoes." Paul's father, who held Marxist political views, stood out in this conservative, anti-intellectual community. For many months out of many years, Paul and his whole family traveled to various Third World countries, some of which were war-torn environments, as part of his father's professional pursuits. Paul remembers his childhood as fraught with hostility and ostracism from the townspeople. He recalls making a conscious choice to be isolative and intellectually focused to escape the social anxieties the outside world imposed upon him. As was the case with Caroline, this scenario was very familiar to me from my own life.

Paul entered psychotherapy with his wife Christine because of growing tension between them. They presented as an affectionate, stable couple with expectations and disappointments in each other that were making certain things difficult between them. What is most germane to this chapter is not the interpersonal dynamics between them, but the evolution of a lifestyle that allowed Paul to disengage himself from his childhood feelings of difference and rejection. His relationship with Christine, however, was hampered by his inability to access and express deep feeling, which she experienced as false and withholding.

Paul had geographically distanced himself from his family, and while contact was maintained among them, it was superficial and unemotional. He had developed virtually no sense of national, religious, or ethnic identity. Christine, a teacher and writer, was from an affluent, conventional family. While she was attracted to the unconventional nature of his background, he found her family origins to signify security and acceptance into mainstream society. Each wanted the other to live up to their histories, but both were struggling for some connection to the opposite societal pole from where they came. Christine had radical political leanings and was eager to make active movement in her life towards unconventional aims. Conversely, Paul was quietly radical, but longed for stability, security, and the maintenance of distance from the lifestyle of his childhood.

Over the course of therapy, it became clear that Paul had erected a wall of compartmentalization between his past and present lives that was consonant with his overall defensive style of isolation. Initially, he spoke of his childhood with bland emotion. Without much feeling, he could recall experiences of rejection by his peers, the introduction to lives of poverty and violence in the Third World, and episodes of fearing for his family's safety in his rural hometown during the 1960s. He expressed a lack of impact of these experiences on his life. Paul seemed generally content, accepting, and genuinely puzzled by Christine's frustration that he did not have more feelings about things.

Many of the experiences Paul recalled resonated with similarities in my own background—in particular, the tension imposed by his father's radical politics and the rejection and hostility experienced at the hands of his peers. I could see readily that such experiences had to have impacted him, but I, as did Christine, found it very difficult to access his emotional responses about them. In contrast to Anita, Caroline, and Diana, Paul seemed to have made his peace with his differences without therapy and without much pain. Yet, over time, it became clear that Paul's isolative style left him with only a remote affective connection with himself as a child. This issue became the entrance into his need to create distance and separation from a childhood self that stimulated emotional disruption.

Paul had constructed a self of the present and future that shared only minimal links with his past. He had established a stable, relatively secure job in an esoteric area of history related to the far past and far removed from Third World concerns. He lived in a very conventional upper-middle-class housing community in which he was quite comfortable and, not surprisingly, had little interest in traveling. Interestingly, Paul enjoyed living next to, but not within, a foreign country. He wished to have a small family, imagining himself content to follow a conventional path.

However, as time went on, Paul began to express fears of being uprooted, a sense that he did not and never would fit neatly into the kind of social structure in which Christine moved with ease, and a chronic underlying feeling that economic security and social stability were never assured. As we explored these issues, feelings of being appalled by the poverty and war he saw in Africa and Asia as a young child, the insecurity and culture shock he experienced traveling from the United States to places so vastly different, the anxiety invoked when he returned to school for only a few months following one trip and preceding the next, and memories of his father walking rural southern streets wearing a "Free Cuba" T-shirt began to be integrated with his detached, even-tempered presentation. He came to his own realization that he never would feel quite like the professional affluent Americans that were his social cohorts, nor would he ever take for granted the conventional stability and identifications that they seldom questioned. His comfort zone required external securities, but internally he could not adhere to the sources of identity available to his peers. He wanted to be rooted in one place and to "fit in," but psychically he was also a "citizen of the world," linked to all, but allied with none.

Anita, Caroline, Diana, and Paul all illustrate that difference cannot be overcome only by the exploration of early parent–child relationships. Each of these individuals developed an association with his or her cultural surround that contributed to certain personality traits and modes of relatedness. These psychological characteristics had a primary sociocultural derivation that was not explicable by family dynamics alone.

Paul exemplifies a style of affective isolation disguised by a seeming acceptance and adjustment, which left him restricted in his capacities for intimacy and open exchange of emotion. Anita, Caroline, and Diana all had more overt anguish about their circumstances. With Anita, material about feeling different was most sequestered and thus emerged only with direct disclosure and engagement within the analytic relationship. Caroline, and Diana, in contrast, had more connection with their feelings of being different, although neither could articulate these feelings. Thus, the motif of difference could be accessed via extra-analytic relationships, before it became transferentially/countertransferentially apparent. With Paul, the dynamics of being different were segregated from the rest of his personality but could well have gone unnoticed were it not for the parallels between aspects of his family and mine. These parallels raised my skepticism about his adjustment to such an unusual background and enabled me to question, in my own mind and with him, the fate of his childhood self.

Difference goes beyond one's experiences within one's family to encompass one's relationship to and with the sociocultural enclave in which one develops. It is often rooted in some inherent and immutable characteristic of the individual that serves to distinguish him or her from their interpersonal environment. Who one is is not solely a psychological phenomenon, but is also a relational phenomenon. Who one is means who one is vis-à-vis others. These others are not only internal imagoes, but also are both actual others in the current environment and Other as represented by manifestations of sociocultural values. If the kernel of "who I am" does not intertwine with the psychosocial surround, there is no validation of its worth. The individual must then turn to nonrelational sources to express that part of his or her psyche, which results in isolation from human engagement.

Diana and Paul, in particular, exemplified this position. Paul's intellectual and somewhat solitary orientation allowed him to titrate the social ostracism that upset his psychological well-being at the expense of a fully developed capacity for intimacy, but with little overt distress. Diana felt more keenly the pain of choosing between pulls towards closeness and self-protective isolation. To be in an intimate relationship, she had to adapt to conditions that left an intrinsic part of herself isolated and untouched by the one with whom she strove to be intimate. In feeling authentic, she was alone. The opportunity to find easy comfort in relatedness with others may be seldom, if ever, available to those whose background or personal traits separate them from the crowd. This is the price to be paid for being too different.

I have come to view the tension between adaptation and personal distinctiveness as a dialectical struggle, rather than a problem for which there is a solution. Each individual must form his or her own compromise and this compromise will likely shift many times in the course of one's life span. The analytic therapist needs to be aware that themes of difference are existential difficulties that often cannot be overcome. While these motifs may have dynamic meaning, they may not be rooted in internalized patterns of interpersonal relatedness or internal conflicts, but based upon ongoing struggles between one's personhood and societal values and expectations. Frequently, the impact of difference can be mitigated by its recognition and appreciation by the analyst, as was the case with Diana in particular, but often, it must be endured.

In like fashion, the tension between conformity and the expression of individuality within the field of psychoanalysis also cannot be escaped. Antagonisms between individualism and conformity are endemic to the national culture of the United States and have become inherent in the tradition of American psychoanalysis. Issues of assimilation into the mainstream culture, intellectual climate, and scientific community; concepts of psychic adaptation to external reality; and themes of individuation, autonomy, and social adaptation permeate psychoanalytic life in this country. When societal submersion of difference coincides with the suppression of these motifs in psychoanalysis and in the individual psyches of patient and/or analyst, a collusion emerges that carries societal, interpersonal, and intra-psychic meanings.

Interestingly, as Bettelheim (1956) argues, much of Freud's life was spent striving for personal conventionality while simultaneously producing a theory that deviated radically from this conventionality. The English translation of Freud's theories, upon which much later psychoanalytic work was founded, promoted assimilation at the expense of meaning in a fashion that parallels the choice between estrangement and sacrifice of personhood that many individuals face. Bettelheim argues further that the internal orientation of Freudian theory represented an unconscious attempt on Freud's part to contend with the political upheaval in which he found himself at the turn of the century. By turning his intellectual focus inward, Freud retreated from the external threat posed by the events he was witnessing. This solution is not very different from the ones created by Anita, Caroline, Diana, or Paul, all of whom found solace in immersion in intellectual or creative endeavors that have an introspective, internal bent. It is also the path that I have chosen in becoming a psychoanalyst.

Anita, Caroline, Diana, and Paul are all especially meaningful to me. Each of them holds some characteristic of difference that I have felt in my life and about which I harbor a quiet loneliness and sorrow that never fully go away. In this way, we are the same. In the ironic fashion that is found so often in psychoanalytic work, this element of sameness in our difference fostered identification, understanding, and mutual affinity. Perhaps the meanings of difference and similarity can only be seen and appreciated from the vantage point of each other. If this is so and since we are all simultaneously both individuals and members of the human collective, perhaps we naturally are led to seek meaningful similarities in the realm of difference and meaningful differences in the realm of similarity. The undercurrent of familiarity and sameness within each of my relationships with Anita, Caroline, Diana, and Paul both underscored and contained their sense of being different. I believe all of us were left a little less isolated and a little less alone in our difference.

REFERENCE

Bettelheim, B. (1956), *Freud's Vienna*. New York: Knopf, 1989.

15

The Therapist's Body in Reality and Fantasy
A Perspective from an Overweight Therapist

JANE B. BURKA

In a first session with a 47-year-old woman, I was being interviewed and assessed. She had met with several therapists and did not want to talk about herself until she settled on the one she knew she would stay with, so she talked about me. Toward the end of the session, she gave me her decision. She liked me, she said, because I seemed both warm and smart, and I had a nice office, but she'd decided not to work with me. I was too young (I was 46) and "not Jungian enough." I asked her what else about our interaction was on her mind. "I feel embarrassed to talk about it," she said hesitantly. I encouraged her to continue. "I have a problem with your weight. I'm not overweight now, but I've gained and lost 20 pounds many times. It makes me anxious to be in the room with you. It makes me worry that I could slide back into it. It seems too risky." My response was mixed. I was somewhat disappointed (I like being chosen), somewhat relieved (she was probably going to be a difficult patient), and somewhat hurt (being overweight had cost me again). I knew that her experience of my body was not the only reason she could not reveal herself or begin psychotherapy with me, but it was an easy target for her ambivalence.

This exchange exemplifies the interaction between the reality of my body and the fantasies stirred up in a patient's unconscious. I am overweight, in the heavy/*zoftig*/earth-mother range, and my shape is sometimes an explicit subject of exploration with my patients, as it was with this woman. She reacted as if being overweight were a contagious disease that she could catch from me. I suppose that unconsciously she feared a primitive merger experience. Perhaps she had unconscious concerns about the stability of the personal and body boundaries between herself and another. Perhaps she was afraid of losing control of her own impulses and attributed to me a lack of control. Since I didn't work with her, I couldn't get to know all of the unconscious elements that so quickly reverberated to her perception of me, but I could see the manifestations of her anxieties: she reacted to my body by being afraid that her body would become like mine, and this fear reinforced her need to protect herself from me.

During the development of this chapter, many people contributed to my knowledge and my courage. I would like to thank especially Alice Abarbanel, Hilde Burton, Philip Cushman, Marc Glassman, Peter Goldberg, Dan Greenson, Kathy Mill, and Tom Ogden.

Earlier in my professional life, when I had fewer theoretical tools and very little of my own therapy, I was far less able to deal directly with patients on the issue of my being overweight, so I hoped that patients would not bring it up. Not surprisingly, most of them didn't, thanks to that special blend of patients' attunement to their therapists' vulnerabilities and their own need for compliance. And when the subject of my appearance did come up, I was never sure how to deal with it. One meeting, which I have never forgotten, occurred when I was still in graduate school, working at a university counseling center. A graduate student came for a first session, and he was the most difficult patient I'd encountered up to that time. He was extremely contemptuous of me in every way, and I felt paralyzed. Finally, in the ultimate dismissal, he said, "This has been a complete waste of time. I'd thought if it didn't work out for counseling I might want to date you, but even that isn't appealing." I felt devastated by his pointed hostility. I managed to say, "Are you aware of what you're trying to do to me?" He quieted, and finally said, "Yeah, I'm really a son of a bitch, aren't I?" Then the tone of the session changed as he began to reflect on his need to be cruel.

My words had come intuitively as an act of desperation. Fortunately, my supervisor at that time was able to put my spontaneous intervention into a theoretical perspective, pointing out that I had successfully engaged his observing ego. This knowledge gave me both more understanding and more courage to continue to deal with the issue of my appearance as a potentially useful subject in therapy with my patients.

I have gradually become better able to talk comfortably about patients' reactions to my body and to handle these reactions like other transference responses, as useful information for the therapy. I have found that the more I can tolerate having my body be a subject of discourse and the more flexibility I have thinking about this discourse theoretically as well as in terms of my own reactions and countertransference, the more useful it becomes as a meaningful element in the therapy.

In this chapter, I will discuss some of my own personal experiences as a therapist who is overweight, and try to place these experiences in the theoretical contexts that I have found helpful. The most traditional context involves my own countertransference, assuming that my anxieties about my body which occur during sessions are personal issues that I must deal with. That is certainly one avenue I have explored. But as the only avenue, it is very limiting. It puts the exclusive emphasis on me and my intrapsychic life and ignores the interactional contexts in which my reactions occur—the therapeutic context involving the specific patient with whom I'm relating and the broader cultural context that has assigned meaning to body size and appearance.

Much has been written about the patient's body. We have focused on the patient's body in psychosomatic illness, eating disorders, addictions, and basic identity boundaries. We have tried to understand the association or dissociation between mind and body and the significant dialectic of the psyche-soma. We have explored patients' fantasies about specific parts of the therapist's body—the erogenous part-objects represented by the penis, breast, vagina, womb, and anus. Some therapists have written about their bodies in the context of the clinical impact of unusual physical circumstances that have disrupted the course of therapy, such as the therapist's pregnancy (Gerson, 1994) or the therapist's illness (Schwartz and Silver, 1990). Recently, there has been more writing, both self-revealing and theoretical, about the therapist's erotic countertransference (Symposium on Passion in the Countertransference, 1994). Yet very little has been written about the therapist's actual body.

Contemporary psychoanalytic theory acknowledges that each therapist is not an interchangeable blank screen, because the unique aspects of a particular therapist influence, limit, and allow the patient's development—for example, the therapist's personality, theory, or style of intervention. The therapist's body is also a significant part of his or her unique contribution to the therapy.

Talking about the therapist's actual real-life body as an ongoing aspect of the unconscious exchange between patient and therapist may be challenging a taboo, but every therapist has a body, and this particular physical presence is a significant aspect of the reality of the therapist that forms the context in which all of psychotherapy occurs. "The analytic situation," according to Andre Green (1975, p. 9), "is the totality of the elements making up the analytic relationship," and one of these elements is the therapist's body.

I believe that I have become sensitized to this ubiquitous background aspect of every psychotherapy because my own body size is outside the average range and, in that way, is immediately noticeable to my patients. But every patient is in the room with a therapist's body, and any therapist can be aware of the impact of his or her particular physical stature on each patient, can pay attention to whether or not it is talked about in the therapy, and can notice how the therapist's body becomes an element in the unconscious life of the therapy.

THE CULTURAL CONTEXT

Any aspect of the therapist can stimulate fantasies or can be used for defensive purposes by a patient at any time during the course of therapy, and this includes the seemingly objective fact of the therapist's body. But a seemingly "objective" fact is never exclusively objective, certainly not from the perspective of post-modern psychoanalytic psychotherapy. The patient's perception of the therapist's body is heavily influenced by fantasy, even if the fantasies generated about the therapist's body are spun from the physical reality. In addition, the patient's perception of the "fact" of the therapist's body (as well as the therapist's own body image) is significantly influenced by the current cultural meanings attributed to the appearance of the body.

Social constructionists believe that all "reality" is constructed, and feminists point to a compelling example in the definition of attractiveness, which has changed markedly from one historical era to another (Fast, 1984; Wolf, 1991). In our era, attractiveness for women is equated with being thin and fit, with as little obtruding body fat as possible. Bordo (1993) suggests that heavy people represent a threat because they embody a pervasive fear that underlies our culture: the loss of self-control. Heavy women are considered lazy and self-indulgent, lacking self-regulation. They have given into their impulses instead of restricting them. They have not harnessed themselves to moderation. We live in an era in which greed is supposed to be expressed through ambition, not indulgence; in which we are led toward excessive consumption of products and services, not food. The standards for what is or is not attractive become equated with what is good or bad, right or wrong, and so matters of appearance become confused with issues of morality.

All of us, patients and therapists, are subjected to these current cultural pressures about attractiveness and goodness, and some people are more susceptible to the socially constructed notions of beauty than others. Several of my male patients have equated attractiveness with sexuality and then have been surprised by my comfort discussing sexual matters. Some women use me as a role model for feeling less compelled to strive to meet the prevailing standards of beauty.

On the other hand, one of my patients was a beautiful single female lawyer in her twenties who searched for a plastic surgeon to remove the wrinkles she saw developing on her thighs, only to be turned down by each surgeon she consulted. Robin's preoccupation with maintaining or improving her attractiveness was intense, and she viewed my questions about this preoccupation as coming from my own physical limitations or from my jealousy. She held rigidly to the cultural norms of beauty and used the fact that I did not fit myself into the mainstream as a reason not to take my interpretations seriously.

Although we had a basically good working alliance, the transference/countertransference dynamic was very competitive. Robin treated me as the useless mother she didn't have to need or respect. She created a contest between us over who better understood relationships between men and women and then made me the loser, by definition, because of my weight. As I examined my own emotional responses to her, I found myself envying her ability to attract men easily, but on occasion I would have the mean-spirited thought that she couldn't keep men once she got them. Her competitive dismissal of me, ostensibly because of my body size, stirred up my competitive feelings, and I responded by equalizing the relationship through finding fault in her, in the very arena that caused her pain. We were reenacting the competitive relationship between her and her mother, which had been largely unconscious for her until we examined the competitive transference in the therapy. But, in addition, we were two women eyeing each other, comparing bodies: one large, rounded, and culturally devalued; one slim, angular, and culturally idealized. Our unconscious experiences of each other were influenced not only by the repetition of an unconscious dynamic between her and her mother, but also by the culturally defined ways that we have learned to evaluate each other's bodies. In the transference/countertransference interplay, cultural codes interacted with her psychological need to use me as a devalued object.

THE THERAPIST'S BODY AS MOTHER

At the beginning of therapy, my patients typically experience my body as a maternal object, and they usually establish a maternal transference fairly quickly. I believe that my size recreates for my patients the experience of being a child with the mother, who is a large figure for any young child. I think that because my body concretely replicates one aspect of childhood—the experience of being with a large woman—there is initially and continually a regressive pull toward early mother/child experiences in the transference for my patients. This regressive longing may be expressed directly, or it may be defended against or acted out. I think that primitive wishes for merger with the mother's body, along with coexisting fears of being swallowed up by the mother's body, are more readily activated with me than some other basic unconscious fantasies—for example, fears of hard penetration, which might be more quickly activated with an angular male therapist.

For my patients, my shape defines the particular physical context for their transference experiences. For every patient, the therapist's body is the shape of the background supporting object in that therapy. As a background object, the therapist functions for the patient as a "Skin Ego," "a containing, unifying envelope for the Self" (Anzieu, 1989, p. 98). Like the sense of security internalized via the ministrations of a good enough mother, the Skin Ego function of the therapist "maintains the psyche" (Anzieu, 1989). The therapist offers the possibility of a "primary identification with a supporting object," satisfying the "clinging or attachment drive" (Anzieu, 1989, p. 99). The shape of the therapist's body is the shape of the supporting object. Therefore, the therapist's body is both a concrete contour and the symbolic container of the holding and supporting environment.

My physical outline happens to match the cultural stereotype of the earth mother and therefore pulls quickly for maternal transferences and their vicissitudes. But from a theoretical perspective, the physical outline of *any* therapist is the symbolic outline of the womb for each patient (Ferenczi, 1924; Grunberger, 1956). When a patient encounters a therapist for the first time, the physical body of that therapist is already becoming the embodiment of the symbolic mother, because every therapist of whatever physical stature or gender is symbolically a mother to the patient. Chasseguet-Smirgel describes "the femininity of the analyst" in both men and women (1986, pp. 29–44). She points out that every analyst fulfills traditionally maternal functions: in establishing the patient within the analytic situation, in being a "receptacle" for the patient's inner contents, in being interested in the "internal life" of patients, and in the quiet capacity to wait and watch a relationship develop. All of these functions are traditionally defined as feminine and maternal. She states that this "maternal aptitude" is the "backcloth" to the work, whether the therapist is male or female. At the same time, every analyst also fulfills traditionally male functions, by establishing the laws of the therapy and by making penetrating interpretations that name the process and therefore break into the nonverbal union with the holding object. According to Chasseguet-Smirgel, the voice is male.

If the therapist's voice (man's or woman's) is the father, then the therapist's body (man's or woman's) is the mother. Because my body outline triggers maternal associations, both longings and defenses, I usually become involved in the maternal object relations drama of the patient from the beginning of therapy. Wrye and Welles (1994) have identified the "erotic maternal transference," which occurs and can be explored in any intensive therapy if it is not unconsciously defended against by either patient or therapist, female or male. They note how the process of therapy, with its mutual flow of words and feelings, evokes the early erotic experiences of mother and infant whose mutual pleasure involves "the earliest, most primitively based hungers, impulses, and longings oriented toward the mother's voluptuous and sensually experienced body" (p. xvi).

While the maternal transference is usually established quickly with me, patients are not very likely to bring up the subject of my body and their fantasies about it. That task is usually left to me. I try to notice when their experience of my body is becoming meaningful in the therapy and when I might try to address it. I am guided not only by the material they provide, but also by my own countertransference.

One of my patients, Madeline, was an unusually attractive woman in her thirties who suffered from claustrophobia. Though she was beautiful, she felt old and unattractive, especially compared to her younger days, when she had lived in France. The discrepancy between how she looked and how she experienced her looks was immense. I was intrigued by this: I envied her beauty and thought that if I looked like that, I'd feel gorgeous. Over the years, I have come to understand that a person does not have to have a body distorted by too much weight or too little weight to have a distorted body image, and I wondered what in her history and her internal experience was preventing her from feeling beautiful. I really wanted to help her feel pretty again, but this was not a pressing priority for her. For two years, as we worked on the fears and anxieties that kept her out of theaters, elevators, and crowded rooms, we talked a lot about her body: her somatic experiences of anxiety, her experience of physical vulnerability, her sexual inhibitions. We were discussing her body as if it were a separate entity, and we did not directly address her body vis-à-vis my body.

The first inroad to discussing explicitly the unconscious relationship of our bodies came via the issue of competition. (This was after she had largely overcome her claustrophobia and was working and socializing more comfortably.) In the session from which I will quote, she was talking about her fear of being competitive with people, and especially with me. It had occurred to her that she might want to study psychology, she said, but there was a big problem because psychology was my field. I inquired why that was such a problem.

P. You're smarter, you're more experienced. This reminds me of my sister. My sister was the smart one, I was the pretty one. OK, I'm smart too but I know you're really smart.

T. You talk about only one-half of the comparison—the part where you put me on top, but not about the other half, where you're prettier than I am.

P. (She is moved; she cries.) I can't believe you'd let me be that, let me be prettier.

T. It's not a case of "let." It's a case of acknowledging that by most standards, you are prettier.

P. (crying) But how can you let us talk about that? That's extraordinary. I don't know your self-image, but what if this is something you feel bad about? You never know what goes on underneath. My self-image is so rocky. What if this is an area that causes you pain, but still you're willing for us to talk about it. That's amazing. That puts you right at the top of human beings.

T. Even as we both acknowledge a way that you're better than I am, at the same time you put me "at the top of human beings"?

P. You think that's defensive? So I don't feel so great? So you're still a better person than I am?

T. I think you can't enjoy the feeling that you're prettier if you think it's my area of vulnerability.

P. That's right. Who lets you do that? The very best of friends, a therapist if you're lucky, or . . . parents.

Madeline then went on to talk about her mother's depression and how Madeline believed that her prettiness as a child had made her mother feel old and unattractive.

This introduction to the subject of her body vis-à-vis my body enabled her to become more conscious of my body and allowed us to engage openly in discourse that included her fantasies about our bodies in relation to each other. As she talked about her terror of competing with me, she reviewed the contentious relationship she and her mother had had as two very attractive women. Then she began to explore the developmentally more primitive terrain of her body and her mother's body. Madeline had slept in bed with her mother until she was eight (which had a lot to do with her claustrophobic anxieties and her sexual inhibitions), so that talking about her body in relation to my body in the transference was essential to her treatment. Her primordial fantasies about my body began to emerge as a longing to be held inside my maternal womb. Madeline's longings to be inside my body first appeared in a dream: "There was a fish swimming in a bowl, and the fish didn't have enough water, and somehow this was my fault. It was dying. So I gave it some water and it seemed to revive."

Madeline's associations to the dream went to how the therapy was enlivening her. She said, "I've talked myself to life." In the dream, she was able to rejuvenate the dying fish, and this healing took place in the bowl, inside my maternal therapist's holding/womb/body. Together, between the container (me) and the rescuer (her), we saved the fish (fetus) from death. In this dream, I think Madeline was expressing the hope that within our relation-ship, we were helping her to be reborn. The dream can be interpreted as representing a transformative wish that, through the creative use of my maternal body, she will resuscitate her own deadened self.

This type of dream is not unusual in an intensive therapy. Wrye and Welles, writing about the maternal erotic transference, describe the wish for transformation via the therapist/mother: "At this point in the transference, it is the baby who is making the mother into a whole object, and the mother/analyst is often dreamed of as a container" (1994, p. 40). Many writers have talked about the universal fantasy of fusion with the mother (Ferenczi, 1924; Freud, 1926; Chasseguet-Smirgel, 1986; McDougall, 1989). In the transference, when a patient imagines fusing with the mother's body, he or she is longing for union with a *representation* of a particular therapist's body as it stands for the mother. The body representation of the mother may not even resemble the therapist (i.e., patients who want to be held in the womb of male therapists), but these fantasies are nevertheless directed in the transference toward a particular therapist with a particular body and are reacted to in the countertransference by a therapist with particular feelings about his or her internal spaces and contents.

My being a large woman does not necessarily make it likely that my patients will wish for transformation through my body more than other therapists' patients want to be reborn through their bodies. But I do think that bringing my body into the interpretive discourse helps my patients make conscious their unconscious interests in the inner contents of my body. And when they do, they have the idea, unconsciously, that there's room for them in there.

THE THERAPIST'S BODY AS A CO-CREATION

I have been addressing the relatively common unconscious reaction that my patients have to the shape of my body: the early maternal transference. However, in my work I have also been struck by the remarkable range of differences in patients' observations about my appearance and also by the great variability of my own experiences of my body as I work with patients.

The intimacy of therapy is not only emotional but is also physical. In psychotherapy, patient and therapist sit together repeatedly in the same relatively small space, body to body (and therefore visually face to face, belly to belly, pelvis to pelvis, and toe to toe). In psychoanalysis, the patient and analyst are in even closer physical proximity, back to front. The analyst observes the patient's body fully stretched out, while the patient grasps the presence of the analyst's body through hearing, not seeing, sensing the body through the analyst's voice, breathing, writing, or shifting. Since the patient is not able to see the analyst visually while on the couch, fantasies about the analyst's body are perhaps more clearly recognized as fantasies. However, most of my patients are in face-to-face psychotherapy, and the fact that they are looking directly at the physical dimensions of my body does not at all determine how realistically they experience me physically or how they use my body unconsciously.

Consciously and unconsciously, different patients have talked about the reality of my body in very different ways, from a preoccupation with worrying about my health or mental health, to admiration that I am well dressed and seem comfortable with myself, to an eroticized fascination with my amplitude, to a denial that I am overweight. And I too have very different experiences of my body at different times with different patients. I have noticed changes in my body image, sometimes dumpy and self-conscious, sometimes voluptuous and racy, sometimes motherly and nurturing, sometimes shriveled and empty. My same body can seem frail in relation to a large man or monumental in relation a petite woman. With two bodies present and two unconsciouses at play, any experience is possible.

The Body as an Analytic Object

One concept that has helped me understand the inconsistent and change-able ways I have experienced my body as a therapist is Andre Green's (1975) notion of the "analytic object." The therapist's body can simultaneously be a concrete object and an analytic object. An analytic object is neither strictly internal, that is, part of the patient's internal object relations, nor strictly external, that is, an object in reality. An analytic object exists in the mutual in-between unconscious space between therapist and patient. Green writes, "But in the end the real analytic object is neither on the patient's side nor on the analyst's, but in the meeting of these two communications in the potential space which lies between them, limited by the setting which is broken at each separation and reconstituted at each new meeting" (Green, 1975, p. 12). Thus, the therapist's body belongs to both the therapist and the patient. The physical reality of the therapist's body is measured in pounds and inches, but the psychical reality of the therapist's body cannot be seen, measured, or separated out from the physical and psychological context of a particular patient/therapist pair.

The therapist's body is always present in the room, but it is not always an analytic object. It becomes an analytic object if, at a particular moment in the therapy, it is "a carrier of psychological meanings that had not existed prior to that moment" (Ogden, 1994, p. 75). The therapist's body can become an analytic object at a certain point in a session, as demonstrated in the opening vignette of this chapter which described a potential patient's unconscious reactions to my body in an initial meeting. In that therapy, my body was an analytic object, a "carrier of meanings" right from the beginning. Or the therapist's body might serve as an analytic object (or as several different types of analytic objects) at other times in the treatment. For example, at the beginning of therapy with Madeline, her body was the subject of our mutual attention, and my body was not functioning as an analytic object. Later, when her presenting phobic anxieties decreased and we could explore other dynamics, my body became an analytic object—a relatively less attractive woman's figure which she had to defensively ignore or deny, as protection against dangerous maternal competition. In a subsequent phase of our work, my body became an analytic object of another dimension, the good mothering environment revealed in her fishbowl dream. Working through her issues and levels of defenses over time meant that my body, as an analytic object, carried different meanings as the therapy progressed.

If both the therapist and the patient participate in creating the analytic object as something new, something that has never existed before, something that can only exist at this time between these two people, then both therapist and patient co-create their experiences of the therapist's body. At first, this seems like an odd idea.

I had been accustomed to thinking of my body as *my* body, a relatively stable presentation, which might fluctuate by a few pounds gained or lost, by a good clothes day or a bad clothes day. I knew that how I felt about my body could change drastically, depending on factors like my mood, my level of self-criticism, my intake of food, or the recent use of my body in exercise or sex. But there is another dimension that contributes to how I feel about my body at a particular time, and that is the experience of a relationship with another person. If I think about how I feel about my body when it is being evaluated by a critical eye (oh, just take my mother as a random example) versus how I feel about my body when it is being appreciated by an admiring eye (an ardent lover springs to mind), then it is easier to understand how in therapy the specific transference/countertransference relationship generates the shared (-unconscious) experience of the therapist's body.

For example, I worked for five years with Rick, a handsome, seductive man in his forties. During the entire course of the therapy, he was very focused on my body; therefore, my own awareness of my body was very prominent within me. The therapy with Rick helped me realize that body image is indeed a fantasy, because I had vastly different experiences of my own body as I worked with him over time. In the beginning of his treatment, I felt unusually frumpy. I began to dress up on the days when I would see him, and I was self-conscious as I observed him studying my body, looking me over as if evaluating the merchandise. On one occasion, soon after therapy began, as we entered my office and I was going to sit down, I became so flustered at his blatantly evaluative staring that I actually missed my chair and fell slightly before catching myself! Later that day, when I could think about it, I sensed that my body anxiety might be a countertransference clue to his dynamics. I thought that perhaps he was using his frank sexualized appraisals to try to gain control of our relationship. He found a seductive and sadistic way to counteract his own vulnerability about beginning therapy with a woman. My self-effacing need to dress up was my unconscious countertransference response to his defensive depreciation. Consciously, I had started to feel sweetly nurturing toward this maternally deprived man.

In retrospect I think that the two of us were colluding unconsciously to create a dowdy therapist for him. I think that together we unconsciously retreated from the hostile sexualization he usually used to gain control in all his relations with women. We unwittingly sidestepped the nonverbal sadomasochism at play in the beginning and shifted, instead, to a dowdy mother/fair-haired boy transference/countertransference matrix, which lasted for some time. I don't want to represent this as a conscious or theoretical choice; instead, I think it occurred as a mutually designed unconscious escape from aggression to love, transforming my body as an analytic object from clumsy fatgirl to nurturing mother. Perhaps we had to establish a comfortable mother/infant experience before we could tackle the sadistic misuse of sexuality.

The initial sexual charge was relegated to the background, but did not disappear, of course. As I felt less need to protect myself from his sexual energy, he was able to express his sexual fantasies more directly, and I was able to experience sexuality more explicitly in the countertransference.

Countertransference feelings can signal the presence of an analytic object and can provide a clue about the therapist's participation in the patient's internal object relations dynamics. After two years with Rick, my countertransference was less maternal and more sexual. Rick was reporting dreams of having intercourse with me and lying afterward with his cheek on my soft stomach. His use of my body at this time, in fantasy and in dreams, was for a regressive erotic merger with a welcoming woman whom he could safely enter and then blissfully unite with.

During this time, my own body image shifted. I was no longer lumpy, but voluptuous, ripely seductive, and curvaceous. At this point in the therapy, my body had become a different kind of analytic object: the idealized sexual mother. I experienced erotic feelings in the sessions as he described his attraction to me, and I even had two dreams of potential sexual encounters with Rick, though I was relieved that in each dream I stopped short of sexual contact because I was his therapist. In my own unconscious life, which was influenced by Rick and his unconscious life, I was struggling to maintain some boundaries in my role, because my body boundaries did not feel secure. I had become part of a sexual union without ever leaving my chair.

Later in the therapy, as the defensive idealization in the transference and countertransference subsided, Rick bumped up against a crucial stumbling block—whether he was really going to depend on me as a separate, whole, important other human being. He could not. Rick demanded that I change my way of working as a therapist and either do hypnotherapy with him or have an affair with him. Threatening to quit therapy, he said, "If you want to talk about being a mistress *and* a therapist, then maybe we've got a deal." I had the image of myself as an over-the-hill streetwalker who had run out of options, reduced to a sordid sexual business arrangement. My maternal body no longer existed, and my erotic body no longer existed, because of the predominantly controlling, coercive, and perverse transference at that time in the therapy. Rick had recycled back to the initial perverse scenario in which he defended himself against experiencing his dependency on me by turning his sadomasochistic sexuality against me. But at this point in the therapy, years beyond the uncertain beginning, we could deal explicitly with these issues that had always been there but could not previously be elaborated in the transference/countertransference or brought directly into the discourse.

In this therapy with Rick, my body often became an analytic object, which took on different and new meanings as our relationship progressed.

In a way, my body did not remain only mine, because Rick strongly influenced my experience of my body and appropriated that experience for his own psychological purposes. In the sequence of his defenses, first, he protected me from his sadistic sexuality by denying my sexuality, and I colluded by feeling frumpy; then he began to long for a transformative union with my idealized maternal body, and I participated by feeling generously voluptuous; then he retreated from these longings by demeaning me sexually, and I indeed felt sexually degraded.

Working with Rick was often confusing: I was so unusually aware of my body and had so many different body images throughout the therapy. In trying to understand how my experiences of my body in relation to Rick could be so variable, it has been helpful to think in a postmodern context. Then I can see that my experience of my body is not only mine, which of course it is, but is also a mutual creation of Rick's and mine at each point in the therapy.

The Postmodern Body

For most of the history of psychoanalysis, the focus of attention and analysis was on the unconscious life of the patient: a one-person psychology. From this perspective, only the patient's unconscious material is welcomed into the therapy; the emergence of the therapist's countertransference indicates an intrusion of his or her unresolved unconscious conflicts. In modern psychoanalysis, the focus of therapeutic attention has broadened to include inquiry and curiosity about the unconscious life of the therapist as well, as a response to the patient: a two-person psychology. In this paradigm, countertransference feelings are viewed as providing useful or even necessary information about the patient's unconscious life and about the nature of the unconscious relationship the therapist is being invited into. The therapist's unconscious is reacting to these unspoken messages that are emanating from the patient, like a tuning instrument vibrating in response to a particular chord being struck.

In postmodern psychoanalysis, both patient and therapist contribute mutually to unconscious communication, each one continuously influenced by being in relationship with the other. The two participants jointly create a third psychology—the unconscious life of the therapy. This third unconscious is mutually created. It draws from each person, yet is more than the sum of two parts. The third unconscious is like the group unconscious, which develops beyond the sum of individual unconscious lives of group members. The therapist and the patient can be seen as belonging to a two-person group, and the unconscious life of the therapy, like the group unconscious, has a life of its own. The intersubjective unconscious co-creation of therapist and patient has been named the "analytic third" by Ogden (1994, pp. 61–95). The analytic third is an unconscious process, which Ogden describes as "the intersubjectively generated experience of the analytic pair" (Ogden, 1994, p. 94). Each person in the pair retains an individual subjectivity and, at the same time, participates in a jointly created ongoing intersubjectivity. This joint unconscious creating is the ongoing unconscious life of the therapy. It operates simultaneously with (in dialectic tension with) the separate unconscious worlds of the two individuals.

Bodies are significant elements in the unconscious life of the therapy—the therapist's intersubjectively created body; the patient's intersubjectively created body; and the creation of one body for two, the body that represents the shared unconscious life of the therapist/patient pair. I have described an example of the intersubjectively created therapist's body when I discussed how my body image fluctuated in Rick's therapy. Now I would like to talk about my recognition of the patient's co-created body and then my experience of "our" body.

I came to an awareness of the patient's intersubjectively created body as I have thought about my reactions to women patients who are quite attractive. With all of them, to some extent I envy them, I admire them, I wonder, how do they do that? But I have found that my envy and curiosity take on a particular idiosyncratic form with each patient which turns out to be very telling about our unconscious relationship.

For example, with Elaine, a pretty woman who is both short and slim, I found myself wondering, "Where does she fit all of her organs?" Later, I learned that Elaine is quite terrified of her internal bodily experiences, and she exerts control over everything that goes into her body (food), as well as attempting control of everything that occurs inside her (feelings). My fantasy about her conjured up a body so small that it could not be correctly human, holding every organ in the right place. Elaine has since told me, with flat affect and no psychological interest, about some serious physical problems with her body during her birth and just after she was born. While she cannot yet consciously recognize that she feels she was not born "properly and whole" (Wrye and Welles, 1994), she had managed to communicate this feeling to me unconsciously. Together, unconsciously, we have both participated in creating a defective minuscule baby's body, which represents her "basic fault" (Balint, 1968). And together we have both created a concerned mother who may help her transform herself into a whole intact body.

With Teresa, a dramatic-looking, tall, slender, athletic woman, I found myself thinking, "I wonder what she eats?" Teresa is very efficient and ambitious and is the caretaker of everyone in her large family. But Teresa cannot nurture herself, and she counts on me for the only maternal provisions she gets. That my countertransference interest in her body focused on how she feeds herself was, I think, an example of my participating in her unconscious object relations, with me in the role of the nurturing mother. At the point in the therapy when I wondered what she eats, her body had become an analytic object, the carrier of unconscious meaning about the transference/countertransference. On the surface, I was thinking about how she organizes her diet to stay thin, but in the unconscious translation, I was saying, "Eat, bubeleh, eat."

My associations to patients' bodies can also tell us something about the intersubjectively created common fantasy body shared by patient and therapist. I became aware of this mutually shared body through my experience with Madeline, whom I mentioned earlier, and her inventive way with clothes.

In the four years I've seen her, Madeline has never worn the same outfit twice. I've seen the same pieces reappear a few times, but always put together differently and imaginatively. One day, she came in wearing a new raincoat, and I noticed as she draped it behind her on her chair that it was exactly the same raincoat that I'd recently bought. I felt very pleased with myself that I'd picked out the same coat that this very stylish woman would wear. Then I became curious about the size of her coat. Trying to be discreet, I leaned forward slightly as she was speaking, so that I might read the size on her coat label, which was visible to me. I had to look twice to believe it: size 2 Petite. I didn't know such a size existed. I thought to myself, what would my life be like if I had my brain and my personality and her body?

If I view this thought as just plain envy, I could take it as a self-reproach: I should be thinner, I should look like that. But that one-dimensional view of my countertransference does not add to my understanding of the therapy relationship or forward the analytic process. Instead, if I view my question to myself as countertransference-in-context, meaningful as a mutually created moment in this therapy, then perhaps I can learn something about her and about our work. I believe that, in thinking about my brain and my personality residing in her body, I was imagining a mixture of the two of us, a new entity made up of parts of each of us. I was creating a therapist/patient merged body.

At this time in the therapy, Madeline was certainly not consciously expressing any wish for merger with me. She was adamant that I was not serving as a mother to her, but was more like a sister or a best friend, the person with whom she shared her most intimate secrets.

Madeline, as I have mentioned, slept in the same bed with her mother until she was eight. Presumably, she experienced that much physical contact with her mother's body as both comforting and overstimulating, and she remained terrified of repeating these conflicted and threatening longings with me. Wrye and Welles, following Kumin (1985), refer to the patient's avoidance of the maternal erotic transference as "erotic horror," and it is manifest in therapy as "fear of the patient's consuming wish to invade the analyst's body" (Wrye and Welles, 1994, p. 65). Madeline could not allow herself to become conscious of her wish to join up with my body, but I became aware of this unspoken aspect of her transference through my countertransference fantasy of wanting to combine our bodies.

My envious musings about these attractive women used to concern me. I felt guilty and worried that I was lost in countertransference when I should have been listening. Wondering where Elaine put her organs, how Teresa knew what to eat, and what size raincoat Madeline wore seemed at first to come exclusively from my own envy and curiosity and did not obviously contain significance about the patient or our experience together. But I have come to feel differently about such "wandering" thoughts. I think that these countertransference responses helped me to understand something significant about the "analytic third" I had unconsciously participated in co-creating with each of these patients.

Ogden suggests that one possibility of becoming aware of the particular dynamic character of an analytic third unconscious process is to pay attention to the therapist's internal "reverie," the stream of associations including both responses to the patient and seemingly random or mundane ruminations by the therapist (Ogden, 1994, p. 74). My reveries revealed countertransference reactions to these attractive women that were in my own mind, yet they were not created exclusively by me. They occurred in the context of my being in relationship with each of these patients. I was simultaneously an overweight woman thinking about slender women and also a therapist being created by each of them in a unique object relationship as Elaine's transformational mother, as Teresa's nurturing mother, or as Madeline's merged mother. I find that, when the countertransference involves my body and my weight, an issue that is usually important and intense for me, it is especially helpful to realize that "we must continually reground the concept [of countertransference] in the dialectic of the analyst as a separate entity and the analyst as a creation of the analytic intersubjectivity" (Ogden, 1994, p. 74).

I have also been alerted to the mutual intersubjective process involving my body through patients' dreams, the unconscious form of reverie. Patients often represent the therapist's body in dreams, for wishful, fearful, or defensive purposes. I have already described how Rick dreamed of union with my soft, idealized, maternal/sexual body, and how Madeline dreamed of being reborn within my bowl-shaped body. One patient frequently dreamed of me being very fat when she was furious with me and then dreamed of me being quite thin when she wanted to go on a diet but did not want to risk separation from me.

A patient's dream representation of my body can also be a clue to the unconscious mutual process going on in the therapy at a certain time. A patient can communicate a description of the analytic third through dream symbols.

For example, Diane was a middle-aged woman who was somewhat overweight. As the child of an anxious mother, who was a nurse, and a physician father, Diane was very much preoccupied with the inner contents and the workings of her body and suffered from many illnesses, some seemingly organic and some clearly psychogenic. In relation to Diane, I felt robustly healthy. Although I was more overweight than she, in our work together, my body was experienced by both of us as reliable, whereas hers was always going wrong.

Diane had a dream in which she created a symbol for my body, which I think showed us an image of the mutually created unconscious relationship in our therapy at the time of the dream. Diane had this dream in the third year of therapy when she was wanting to cut down from three sessions a week to twice a week, but she wasn't sure if this desire came from practical time constraints, resentment against her dependency on me, or fear of something she was avoiding.

> I'm in a remote area where the road is steep and there's a ditch. I get out of my car, I'm on all four's trying to climb up this embankment. I'm too weak, I'm in the process of giving up. I end up back in the bottom of the ditch. I can't see what's on the road. I crawl up, out of the ditch and see a car and pull myself onto it. It's a big old car, like the ones when we were kids. The car starts moving—no one's in the driver's seat. I'm perplexed. I don't want to drive, someone will think I stole it. But if I don't drive, it will crash. I have no choice so I drive it. I don't know if the motor is on, but it works. I'm in mainstream fast traffic and have to keep up with it. I end up in a business district, where I turn around. The road is wider in the more civilized area, but I return to the more primitive area.

As she associated to the dream, Diane said that the car she used to pull herself up was a big red car. "Big Red" is one of her nicknames for me. (I have reddish hair.)

Diane's associations suggested that the big red car is me, is my body, and is the vehicle for our therapeutic journey together. As I listened to the dream and pictured the scene as she was describing it, I felt a strong sense of recognition and had the thought about the car, "That's us." Perhaps her dream is an unconscious representation of the analytic third process at that time in the therapy: our mutually created ongoing travels. Diane uses me to help pull herself out of her weakness; I am there as a containing presence, a big car without a driver, whose motor is silent and unnoticeable, like the good maternal environment. If she takes action and puts herself in the driver's seat, she will be thought stealing, because the power is not supposed to be hers. But if she does not, both she and the car will be destroyed. She is actually capable of taking charge and driving, and although she wants to escape the primitive areas, she and I together go back there. I am part of this car/therapy, and she is part of this car/therapy, and it is heading back to a primitive desolate area.

After Diane and I interpreted the dream in this way, she realized she was committed to returning to her own primitive area and decided to continue with therapy three times a week.

THE PERVERSE USE OF THE THERAPIST'S BODY

As I was writing this chapter and thinking about my body in relation to different patients, I realized that there was one clinical group of patients that made me most aware of my body and my weight. These are male patients with some degree of sexual perversion. By "perversion," I include not only patients with a developed sexual perversion like a fetish, but also patients who engage in perverse object relations, who have a "perverse structure," or "character perversions." Fogel, in his introduction to *Perversions and Near-Perversions in Clinical Practice*, asks "What special pressures, tensions, and blind spots exist for the therapist working with perverse material, and what are some ways to increase clinical competence and self-awareness?" (Fogel and Myers, 1991, p. 4).

One of the "special pressures" I have felt working with perverse patients is that my body is toyed with by the patient. My perverse patients are very intently focused on my body—consciously—and are playing controlling sadomasochistic games with my body—unconsciously.

I find that some of my most intense and disturbing reactions to perverse patients are registered *viscerally* first, only later (if I'm lucky) to be translated into an emotional experience or a cognitive idea that I can develop into an intervention or interpretation. Examples of these visceral reactions include an unexpected tightening of my stomach when I feel invaded by the patient against my will or a sudden feeling of being sickened when I'm asked to applaud behavior I think of as illicit or an unwilling recognition of an erotic charge when I have been seduced into sexual territory where I did not want to go. These immediate, spontaneous bodily signals can be indications to me that I'm being engaged in a controlling perverse scenario. The most succinct way I can describe how I feel in response to the body games played by perverse patients is, "Get out of my body!"

Betty Joseph has described the dynamics by which the perverse patient stimulates the therapist from within. "I have stressed especially the splitting and projective identification of sexual excitement, aimed not only to rid the patient of excitement which was too much fused with sadism, but particularly aimed at the destruction of calm and strength in his object, as an analytic feeding breast" (Joseph, 1971, p. 449). My visceral disturbances with perverse patients feel like attacks on my analytic calm.

For example, a 45-year-old male patient came to therapy because of marital problems. Jerry's homemaker wife wanted him to take more responsibility in the running of the household and the management of their three children. Her demands and his reluctance led to many arguments, and he was worried about losing her.

Jerry was intelligent, hard-working, and charming. He was also dedicated to leading a life in which he got his way as much as possible, and he expected to be taken care of and provided for. His child-like relationship with his wife did not bother him, but his fear of losing her terrified him.

In therapy, Jerry engaged in a perverse relationship with my body. He teased me if I gained or lost a couple of pounds. He noticed my clothes and guessed where I was going after work based on what I was wearing. He told sexual jokes, spoke in sexual innuendos, and was intent on eliciting a sexual reaction from me. For example, he said that it wasn't fair that when men became sexually aroused it was obvious, but when women were aroused it was invisible. So he wanted to invent a "wetometer" to see if I was responding to him. Intellectually, I could see that this was a statement of the perverse dilemma—women had something sexual he couldn't see, and he was defending himself against the anxiety of sexual differences by an invention that would make us the same. But, emotionally, his fantasy was disturbing to me—I felt impaled by his "wetometer" and wanted to close myself to his invasion.

In different ways, Jerry kept trying to recreate with me the erotized maternal environment he maintained with his wife, which was an extension of the overstimulating symbiosis he'd shared with his mother. He made my weight a repeated topic of conversation, the object of his barely covered sadism. The emotional effects of these sexual tactics on me were to disempower me as a therapist and dehumanize me as a woman, temporarily destroying the "analytic feeding breast."

Most of the time with Jerry, I was glad for my large size as a protection against his invasiveness, as if my layers gave me more of a boundary against his persistent intrusiveness. I was relieved that I did not fit the description of the type of women he found most attractive.

CONCLUSION

All through the history of psychoanalysis, there has been an understanding that the body is basic. Freud recognized that the ego was first a body ego (Freud, 1923) and that bodily experiences are the basis for the developing ego. Winnicott shifted the emphasis to remind us that bodily experiences occur within the maternal caretaking environment and are the basis for the developing self (Winnicott, 1949). The infant's ability to experience aliveness and vitality depends on an unrecognized confidence in its body "going on being." Considering the earliest infant experience of the psyche-soma, Winnicott says, "I suppose the word psyche here means the *imaginative elaboration of somatic parts, feelings, and functions,* that is, of physical aliveness" (p. 244). In other words, the psyche is an elaboration of the aliveness of the body.

The first reality is the reality of the body, and this reality is created by both the infant with its physiological needs and satisfactions and by the mother with her physical handling and caretaking. The mother's body first is experienced as an extension of the infant's body and then helps define the infant's body. "The mother's hands outline and define the original boundary of the body's surface: they describe a shape of which there was no previous sense" (Krueger, 1989, p. 5).

The mother's body is also the infant's first object, first transitional object, and first symbol. The mother's body exists both as a separate entity and simultaneously as a mutual creation of the mother/infant pair. Therapists have long recognized certain parallels between the mother/infant dyad and the psychotherapy relationship, in which the therapist/mother creates a maternal environment for the patient/child, and the two partners interact in the potential space between them. Perhaps, in addition, there is another parallel between the the mother/infant experience and the psychotherapy relationship that involves the maternal/therapist's body. That is, the therapist's body has great significance for the patient, and the therapist's actual and symbolic physicality plays a very important role in the patient's experience of aliveness and in the vitality of the therapy.

If my body is present and significant for me and for my patients, but remains outside the discourse of the therapy, what kind of taboo have my patients and I created? What deadness is insured and what vitality is precluded? Will the therapy have to take a skewed direction in order to protect my anxieties as the therapist, just as the infant learns to develop a pathological way to cope with a mother's anxieties? For example, are we agreeing that they must not attack a visible vulnerability of mine because that would be too dangerous? (I might be too fragile, or I might retaliate or withdraw from them.) Are they submitting to my power to set the limits for our discourse, silently signifying that certain topics are unspeakable? These collusions deaden the therapy and prevent an important object, the therapist's body, from becoming a verbalized issue that can be elaborated and understood.

Over a period of many years, I have gone from being unable to tolerate in psychotherapy the topic of my overweight body to being rather matter-of-factly curious about how my weight plays a part in the therapy with each of my patients. When I was unable to allow patients to talk about my being overweight, I was interfering with the spontaneity of our work. Now that I am more comfortable with myself and with my body as a subject between us, there is a larger space for the therapy to become more authentic and more alive.

REFERENCES

Anzieu, D. (1989), *The Skin Ego*. New Haven, CT: Yale University Press.

Balint, M. (1968), *The Basic Fault*. London: Tavistock.

Bordo, S. (1993), *Unbearable Weight: Feminism, Western Culture and the Body*. Berkeley: University of California Press.

Chasseguet-Smirgel, J. (1986), *Sexuality and Mind*. New York: New York University Press.

Fast, I. (1984), *Gender Identity*. Hillsdale, NJ: The Analytic Press.

Ferenczi, S. (1924), Thalassa: A theory on genitality. *The Psychoanal. Quart.*, 1938.

Fogel, G. & Myers, W. (1991), *Perversions and Near-Perversions in Clinical Practice*. New Haven, CT: Yale University Press.

Freud, S. (1923), The ego and the id. *Standard Edition*, 19:12–59. London: Hogarth Press, 1961.

—— (1926), Inhibitions, symptoms and anxiety. *Standard Edition*, 20:87–172. London: Hogarth Press, 1959.

Gerson, B. (1994), An analyst's pregnancy loss and its effect on treatment: Disruption and growth. *Psychoanal. Dial.*, 4:1–17.

Green, A. (1975), The analyst, symbolization and absence in the analytic setting. *Internat. J. Psycho-Anal.*, 56:1–22.

Grunberger, B. (1956), The analytic situation and the dynamics of the healing process. In: *Narcissism: Psychoanalytic Essays*. New York: International Universities Press, pp. 35–89, 1979.

Joseph, B. (1971), A clinical contribution to the analysis of a perversion. *Internat. J. Psycho-Anal.*, 52:441–449.

Kreuger, D. (1989), *Body Self and Psychological Self*. New York: Bruner/Mazel.

Kumin, I. (1985), Erotic horror: Desire and resistance in the psychoanalytic situation. *Internat. J. Psychoanal. Psychother.*, 11:3–20.

McDougall, J. (1989), *Theaters of the Body*. New York: Norton.

Ogden, T. (1994), The analytic third: Working with intersubjective clinical facts. In: *Subjects of Analysis*. Northvale, NJ: Aronson, pp. 61–95.

Schwartz, H. & Silver, A. L. (1990), *Illness in the Analyst*. New York: International Universities Press.

Symposium on Passion in the Countertransference (1994), *Psychoanal. Dial.*, 4:139–152.

Winnicott, D. (1949), Mind and its relation to the psyche-soma. In: *Through Paediatrics to Psycho-analysis*. London: Hogarth Press, 1977.

Wolf, N. (1991), *The Beauty Myth*. New York: Morrow.

Wrye, H. & Welles, J. (1994), *The Narration of Desire*. Hillsdale, NJ: The Analytic Press.

16

Working as an Elder Analyst

HELEN MAY STRAUSS

I will be 80, or perhaps even 81, in my sixth decade as an aspiring psychologist/analyst, by the time this book is published. I was born and have lived in the New York–New Jersey metropolitan area all my life, and my formal education took place there as well. I am a widow of 22 years, after 30 years of marriage, mother of five, and grandmother of eleven. A first-generation American, I stem from a middle-class German- and Austrian-Jewish background and practice as a psychoanalyst/psychotherapist in suburban New Jersey.

That is who I am today. But the odyssey that brought me to this day was fraught, in younger years, with agonizing embarrassment and self-doubt. My father was an assimilationist, a Jewish-born man who Christianized his children to save them from the rife anti-Semitism that suffused society in those years and, he feared, would diminish his children's life chances in crucial ways. And so we were enjoined, without any explanation, to conceal our Jewish origins and to attend a Presbyterian Sunday School.

Neither parent ever entered the doors of that little suburban church or attempted to conceal *their* origins. In fact, Father would regularly ask, at our weekly Sunday roast beef dinner, what we had learned in Sunday School that day. "Nonsense, mystical superstitious nonsense," was his characteristic response to our replies, which, naturally, were couched in the traditional Calvinistic belief system. While he believed he was thinking rationally and acting in the best interests of his children, he was actually planting a corrosive sense of shame in me, as I understood only that who we truly were was something one should hide. The occasional anti-Semitic remarks made by folks in that almost wholly Wasp suburb, who thought I was as Presbyterian as they, did little to relieve me of that shame. I have that early pain to thank for my awareness of the importance for patients when family secrets generate shame. I am thankful, too, that during undergraduate years I was determined and able to "come out of the closet" and acknowledge my Jewish origins.

To give Father his due on the positive side, he was a loving and lovable man equipped with a work ethic equalled only by my mother's. Seared in my memory is his intermittently asked question, "What did you do today, to justify your existence?" The salience of that question in motivating my early interests and later career choice is clear to me, for I knew that what he wanted to hear in response was, not only that I had worked hard, but that I had done something helpful to others. What all of this has to do with my sense of myself as an aged therapist should be obvious to all colleagues who work psychodynamically. "What the mother says to you in the cradle remains with you to the coffin," to quote Harriett Beecher Stowe. And that goes for the father, too.

I had always wanted to be a psychologist—from high school through college years, to graduate school, never wavering, to this day. Mother adamantly opposed that wish, yearning for a daughter who would willingly wear white gloves and toy with the piano until "Mr. Right" came along and whisked her away. However, rebellious adolescence was firmly in place at that time. Mother's prudishness fueled my already strong resolve to study psychology. Not even the considerable professional obstacles could deter me. Nothing but psychophysics was taught in the graduate school at Columbia in those years, nothing for an aspiring therapist, and "Freud" was a dirty word.

My first very brief job was as research assistant (and translator from German) to Franz Kallmann, a psychiatrist at New York State Psychiatric Institute. Kallmann had recently emigrated from Berlin. He was reestablishing his investigation of familial factors in schizophrenia, begun fifteen years earlier. The study, "The Genetics of Schizophrenia," published in 1938, was groundbreaking at the time, because it was the first voice to speak in America against the dominant environmentalist climate of the time. I quit after three months, disaffected by Kallmann's authoritarian manner, as well as by my mother's insistence that I would be permanently scarred if I continued to work in a mental hospital. Kallmann's ways had put me too much in mind of the downside of my otherwise loving feelings toward my German-born, often authoritarian father, so that I yielded to her pressure without too much regret.

My first real job, in 1938, was as a psychologist-intern at a state institution for retarded girls. Later, I was a teaching assistant in the psychology department of an Ivy League women's college. And still later, I joined the Navy in WWII and became classification and selection officer at the "boot camp" for WAVES, as the women in the Navy were called then.

Let me proceed with the thoughts, feelings, and transference–countertransference experiences that I have committed myself to relate. It has been a searing, yet rewarding, self-examination. My selfhood has avoided seeing myself as a maven of anything at all, certainly not of being elderly, despite the objective evidence that I am. Aside from the genetic good health that has permitted this blatant denial of reality to persist, the myriad interests that dominate my waking life have helped to shove it under the rug.

As analysts, we would be presumptuous to assume that we are immune to the fears and anxieties that sound a muted obbligato to the daily lives of many of our patients. Denial and avoidance are our most useful (and as often, overused) defenses. In my thirties at the time of my first analysis, aging was not addressed at all and was, indeed, irrelevant to the burning issues of that period of my life. At the time of my second, however, it was central to me, but anxiety-provoking to my analyst (or so I, at least, sensed it, maybe rightly, maybe wrongly). So, we colluded in avoiding/denying, a choreography that was ego-syntonic to us both. Serving under the same flag is my resistance to going back to her as my issues having to do with my advancing age begin to flare. Nor do I seek another analyst. Denial/avoidance are still in the saddle, for better or worse.

CRISIS: 7/24/94

This day gives me pause. My only sibling, a brother two years my senior, celebrated his 81st birthday today, the same day that my daughter marked her 44th. Who am I, kid sister or aging parent? To be kid sister feels fine now, though the feeling was once dismissive.

The many memories of those early days have become an inside joke to my brother and myself, as we comment acidly to each other about our aging selves—but, God forbid that we should relinquish the competing and one-upping that suffused our relationship in days of yore. Gone are those innocent days of childish "sibling stuff." And gone is the society that we, idealizing the past as elders are wont to do, remember as a homey place where "good" and "bad" were easily distinguishable. No wonder we use humor as a defense in our "papering over" of the depressing irreversibility of our aging.

How do elder therapists integrate the rapid, dramatic changes in society, mores, sexual freedom, and so on—or can they? And what are the effects on transference and countertransference of the subtle or not-so-subtle messages sent by unconsciously held biases that transmit a judgmental attitude? My mother's Victorian attitude toward any mention of sex-related behavior or even natural phenomena such as menstruation was extreme; the mere thought that I may have introjected some of that is anathema!

Often, I experience an uncomfortable sense that a younger patient hesitates to talk about his/her sexual life or about feelings of hatred for mother or grandmother. "How should I use my discomfort?" has been a question I've often asked myself as I quell the impulse to say, "Come on, now. Out with it! I may seem like a puritanical/nonunderstanding old lady to you, but I was there once and I haven't forgotten." Instead, of course, I dutifully probe for transferential material. My discomfort at the thought that my unconscious identification with Mama's prudishness may be "showing" is a bit surprising, as hers was not so far "to the right" of the dominant mores of my youth. The dean of the college I attended, Virginia Gildersleeve, was noted as a feminist before her time, but her attitudes toward sexual matters were not much different than my mother's and were generally accepted by the students of the early 1930s. Students were more concerned with being able to get through college financially in those Depression years and to be able to pursue the careers of their choice in a chauvinistic world than with sexual freedom.

The difficulties of my work with Frieda, a colleague much younger than I, is a case in point. With her, I felt the transference–countertransference choreography bounce around uncomfortably from the start, for the two and a half years that we worked together. Frieda and her mother still played out a love–hate relationship begun in Frieda's childhood. In the transference, I felt tempest-tossed between the two poles of her intense, unresolved feelings toward that mother. I was loved because I "was," transferentially, the nonjudgmental role model who turned a blind eye from the flamboyant sexual acting out that Frieda had begun in her early adolescence. Even more seductively gratifying, I was respected as a professional older woman, like her mother, whom she described as a widely recognized lawyer and political force in their community.

Frieda had emulated her mother's ambitiousness and had indeed rivaled her victoriously by completing her medical education and establishing a successful practice in a wealthy suburb. I had to be better than her mother, though, by not disapproving of her sexual acting out while applauding her professional success. But, then, I had to be hated because I had other patients besides herself, to whom I surely devoted myself more lovingly than to her. Again, I was "Mother," the mother who had filled Frieda's childhood home with a constantly shifting group of foster children, most carrying court records of delinquent behavior, children drawn from the most poverty-stricken parts of the metropolitan area in which they lived. These kids were expert in their ability to devise ingenious tortures for Frieda, whom they hated because she was the mother's "real" child whom they yearned to eliminate, in trying to fill the black holes of their own neediness. Frieda's childhood pain has lived on, and I caught some unmistakably venomous glances that she bestowed on other patients whom she occasionally encountered when coming to or leaving my office.

In the end, hate won out. I was dismissed, ostensibly because I refused her request that I become her five-year-old daughter's therapist, instead of continuing our work together. I sensed her need to find the "good mother" she never had, for little Laura, in me, as well as her feelings about herself, not *wanting* motherhood. Her ambivalence, both loving and hating her child and her role in life, could be relieved if only I would take over the mothering. Thinly disguised, I felt, was her live feeling that I disapproved of her still-flamboyant sexual acting out. I knew that she was right. The truly judgmental coloration of my countertransference shone through, despite my wish to be perceived as wholly empathic. I could not disguise the assault on my not entirely unconscious moralistic inclinations by her ever more lurid accounts of her current sexual exploits. Were my judgmental countertransferential reactions a function of my elderliness, identified as I unconsciously may have been with my prudish,

Victorian mother and of the era of my own youth, or were they an ordinary 1990s response anyone of any age might have had to such lurid goings-on? In my metropolitan professional community, gossip about Frieda did trickle down to my ears and mostly from folks much younger than myself.

Frieda wanted me to be the "good mother," displaced to Laura, so that she wouldn't have to change and become a "good girl" by giving up her way of enjoying sex. She had tapped into my feelings of hopelessness and judgmental countertransference that nothing could change her entrenched pattern of living, that is, being sexually involved with one man for a brief period, while already searching for a new one who might promise greater excitement or challenge. So much for the "crisis" of the moralistic, judgmental underpinnings of my countertransference. It had been fostered by Frieda's unconscious projective identification of her unresolved need to provoke her mother's rejection of herself, and her rejection of her own daughter, onto me. Her unconscious recognized that I was, in reality, available to play out that dynamic with her.

A "crisis" feeling of my own making builds when I perceive similarities, particularly of age and life experiences, with patients. To contain myself from remarking on them at salient times is something I have struggled with, not always successfully. In the case of Maura, whose obsessive need to accumulate, but never to throw away, has troubled her for at least fifteen years, I have been singularly unsuccessful in curbing the impulse to share our commonalities of age, professional status, and obsessively tinged difficulty with throwing away useless objects.

Maura was my age-mate in her sixties when she started treatment in 1976. She was inconsolable because of her youngest son's drowning death the previous year. He, a college freshman, had disappeared while swimming from a jetty on the Atlantic coast. She reported that she scanned the newspapers daily for news of his body being washed ashore and searched every young man's face she passed on the street, out of her inability to believe that he had actually died. She told, with equal sadness and agitation, that her husband of thirty years had left her shortly after their son's death.

As she unfolded the story of their marriage, she described her husband as a profligate alcoholic whom she hated venomously but loved desperately. Such were Maura's dramatic skills that both feelings were convincingly depicted. But where was the compromise formation that would enable Maura to invoke reality and to accept, albeit neurotically, the death of her son and the abandonment by her husband?

Maura's resolution took the form of an enactment that defined the parameters of her private life. She became unable to touch any object in her home, let mail pile up on the dining room table without examining it, newspapers likewise, à la Collier brothers, until only a narrow pathway allowed her to move from the kitchen to her bedroom upstairs. No one was allowed to enter the house, and she experienced painful shame when plumbing and heating emergencies forced her to call for help. Bargain shopping binges provided Maura with transitory "highs," but once the parcels were brought into the house, they were thrown atop a growing heap in the sun-parlor, never to be opened.

Jumping ahead to the present, pack-rat tendencies that I recognize in myself and have shared with Maura have generated a fruitful transference-countertransference choreography, almost from the beginning to the present, fifteen years later. I've empathized with her inability to throw anything away and have confessed that I have often found myself enmired in ton-weights of paper, clothing, and miscellaneous useless possessions that cry out to me to finally be "thrown." This I am able to do with gusto, when I finally reach my own idiosyncratic level of "intolerance." The difference between us has become an "inside joke," as we acknowledge that her inability to "throw" has its origins in tragic experiences of loss far more traumatic than any I can claim. Self-disclosure such as this sharing of the troubling pack-rat syndrome is far from a usual technique for me and can validly be critiqued as transgressing boundaries. Knowing this makes me a bit uneasy, but not uneasy enough to stop, as I observe Maura feeling new hope that she too may reach her own level of "intolerance" and find the strength to "throw." She is beginning to entertain the possibility that she may one day master the fears and the rage that have held her paralyzed. Transferentially, she sees me as an idealized colleague/grandmother, admiring my neat working environment, the like of which no longer seems unattainable to her.

Currently, she yearns to be able to invite her grandchildren to her home, gratifying their wish to see the house her older son grew up in, his room and furniture. The result of my self-disclosure, now intensified by her fervent wish to be able to open her house to her grandchildren may, finally, break the log-jam created by the massive losses that she had been unable to integrate. And I confess to the equally fervent wish to be successful in cheering her on, no holds barred.

The sharing of our being age-mates, first, then of loss, then of professional strivings and successes, and finally, of the pack-rat flaw have fueled in herself hope that she, too, can energize herself to "throw" and thereby become the true grandmother that she yearns to be.

Meanwhile, as the years have passed, talk of her younger son's death have wound down. However, she still shrieks her rage with ever-increasing decibels when she thinks of her ex-husband's defection and remarriage and of her two remaining adult children who had "betrayed" her by attending his wedding. "I was livid" is her favored introductory phrase to the compulsively driven recounting of each vignette that reinforces her sense of their betrayal. Her children seem, indeed, driven to provoke her rage by reporting to her chapter and verse of each much enjoyed meeting with their father and his new wife (whom she contemptuously referred to as "the bride"). Meanwhile, the hoarding behavior and the shopping binges have significantly diminished, and, in their place, the hope grows, tacitly, that the ability to "throw" will follow.

Surprisingly, none of Maura's neurotic enactments are reflected in her public presentation. She is always impeccably groomed and dresses with such taste that a cursory glance would suggest that her clothes were of the most expensive kind. Not so. She knows how to feign the current "look" perfectly, using clothes hoarded from earlier years. At the start of treatment, it was a different story. Her ex-husband's worn thermal underwear, unmended but clean, were her standbys for nightly wear. Was it her fantasy that she could bring him back to bed by wearing his underwear? Not unlikely, as Maura had frequently alluded to her enjoyment of their sexual relationship while despising him for every other aspect of his behavior toward her.

"He would throw his pants pocket's collection of change on the floor to me, as all that I was entitled to, to feed the kids and take care of the house. I never knew when, or how much, to expect and I learned, almost gleefully, to make ends meet, no matter what." Thus, Maura turned her husband's sadism into victory for herself.

Frugality had been built into her character from early years because of her mother's almost despotic demand that the family present as a prosperous one, although the father's income was small. In Maura's marriage, that frugality and the role model that her mother had provided served her in good stead. I understood this very well, harking back to my own mother, who had mastered the same skills and had unwittingly passed them on to me via oft-repeated, fascinating tales of her own youth as an immigrant adolescent in a large family.

Just as surprising were Maura's professional status and functioning level. She had earned an MSW degree after her husband's departure and holds the top position today at the agency where she was hired ten years ago, after graduation from social work school. Her pride in having achieved her degree resonated countertransferentially as I thought—and felt—back to my own academic history. After an intermission of 17 years and after having married during the war and having my five kids, they were all, finally, in school. I went back to graduate school and completed my degree in social psychology in 1966. Then, seven years later, my husband died, he who had encouraged me to return to school and finish my Ph.D. Though my own unresolved grief had little of the ambivalence that Maura expressed, her crying sense of loss echoed with an intensity that enhanced our working alliance.

As Maura's treatment progressed, there were significant changes. *Some* repairs on the deteriorating structure of her house were made; *some* trash bags were filled with papers accumulated over the years and placed at the curb. Binge shopping ceased, and some of the unopened bags were examined. The positive features of her relationship with the "disloyal" children reappeared.

Treatment stopped ostensibly because Maura's insurance coverage ran out. Now she calls me periodically just to chat, but particularly to tell me of some momentous happening such as her ex-husband's death. Hoarding behavior is never mentioned. Maura had occasionally acknowledged, over the years, her fantasy that the drowned son and ex-husband might come back, so long as she kept everything in the house unchanged, and it was my sense that we both knew the insurance issue was a cover-up for her fear that, if she continued to gain emotional strength in therapy, she would finally have to relinquish the fantasy.

My 20-year working relationship with Will is different in every way from that with Maura, except for a similar crisis feeling of my own creation, when treatment continues year after year and the gains, though palpable, have required so many years to come about. How to reconcile more than *20 years* of treating the same person, with self-imposed, but admittedly unattainable, standards of being Dr. Super-therapist? "If I leave it to him, we will go on forever. I may want to retire before Will is ready to retire me." Thus mutters my sometimes tyrannical super-ego, as I ruminate over the fact that he and I began our work together when I was in training. He was the perplexing patient I brought into supervision those many years ago. Then, I felt inadequate to treat this person, years younger than myself, who could engender such a tidal wave of anxiety.

I approached each hour with Will as a potential crisis. I waited, muscles tense, for the critical, cynical, intrusive observations with which he invariably started every hour. The saving grace, reducing my anxiety to a tolerable level at that earlier time in my career, was that he would "dissolve," as he put it, never more than ten minutes into the hour, sinking to the floor. From that position, for the rest of the hour, would come quite different messages, spoken softly. There was desperation, a recital of failures, and verbal and gestural attempts to describe his sense of inner chaos. I could empathize with that, recognizing my own tendency to "dissolve" and feel weak and hopeless when things I cared about didn't go right. A bit guiltily, I realized that I felt more comfortable and free of the anxiety with which I reacted to Will's critical sallies, when he was indicating his deep-rooted insecurities. I wondered where this narcissistic, unempathic countertransference might lead the treatment. Certainly not in a positive direction.

Most difficult, for me, was Will's ritual "parting shot" in those early days. At the end of the session, as I would rise to leave, the arrangement of the doors necessitated my passing the chair he sat in. He, instead of rising, would remain seated and reach out his hand in a surreptitious gesture, with the obvious intent that I should grasp it. I never acceded and, just as ritualistically as his entreaty/invitation, would counter with regret that we couldn't discuss his behavior now, since our time was up but must do so next time. At the beginning of the next hour, discussion of hand-holding was often relegated to the back burner because more urgent needs seized precedence.

The years pass, my confidence grows, anxiety diminishes. Transferentially, I feel myself less and less the hated parent. "Aging has its advantages," I say to myself, as it is my less anxious reactions that seem to have quelled Will's impulses to utter his wounding criticisms. We enter a phase in which a part of each hour is devoted to problem solving, at his request, because here-and-now dilemmas have loomed. This new way of my being "there" for him has unveiled some windows of understanding not visible before, anent his feelings of newly owning a self and of his relationships, at home with his lover and his children or in the workplace with colleagues and bosses. There is no grimacing or outreaching hand, wanting to be held. Sitting in the chair is the preferred posture during problem-solving times, with feet on the floor, both literally and figuratively.

Will's marriage was floundering, his children were contemptuous of him, and he felt unable to focus on any one of the many career lines that offered themselves to him. He had many gifts: music, art, science, writing—any academic field he would elect to focus on with his multifaceted intelligence. Fragmented, he dashed from one project to another. Each time, there was the promise of success at first, but each time, he failed to complete the venture. Another interest would intrude, offering irresistible fascination. And I, inexperienced and anxious, was breathing hard to cope "therapeutically." How could I contain the roller-coaster countertransferential feelings when he projected into me the hated bad parent and the loved good parent, antiphonally, in the space of minutes, with chameleon-like ease?

Most anxiety-provoking of all was his habitual parting gesture of holding out his hand sidewise, that surreptitious enactment that, no doubt because of my sense of powerlessness to control or to make use of in the treatment, persisted for many months. Regardless of the fact that I never grasped his hand or of the number of times that I asked him to talk about the feelings he wanted to express by way of the gesture, he seemed unable to give it up. "My needy stuff," he called it and showed extreme embarrassment when I pressed for discussion, rather than enactment. Discussion and understanding *did* ensue, finally, though his embarrassment at trying to put his feelings into words endures to this day.

But for me, "crisis" feelings rise again, changed in nature, but not in intensity. "How long can this go on?" was the searing question to myself, as we entered our eighteenth year. What was worse, the "needy stuff" that had whipped up my anxiety level in the early days was coming back. He wanted to hold my hand, and he wanted to sit on the floor next to my chair. "The needy stuff" takes center stage again, as Will points out with intense embarrassment that he must confront it or he will never get well.

Only this time around, there is an important change. I'm not anxious. I decide to try taking his hand. I let him know that where he sits is his choice. We talk about it all, not easily for him, but still more talking than gesturing and grimacing. He seems able to hear me when I keep saying that I want to understand what he is feeling and when I throw out some hypotheses (a.k.a. genetic interpretations) about early experiences of trauma, which might underlie his current painful feelings. We can speculate about what he is yearning for in his feelings for me.

As for my countertransferential feelings and, consequently, my "therapist" behavior, I perceive the sea changes that have crept up on me in the 20 years of work with Will and search myself for understanding of the changes. Was it the mellowing that, granted, inevitably comes with age? That's descriptive but not explanatory.

Do patients' transference manifestations change as the therapist ages? And, conversely, do differences emerge in the countertransferential feelings that one had experienced in earlier years of work? Clearly, the answer is "yes" to both questions. Issues of separation, of death and dying, and of the unpredictability of life become increasingly salient, emotionally and realistically, as both analyst and patient age. Dramatic changes have taken place in the lives of both Will and another patient of mine, Jodie—changes wished for, as well as those reflecting increases in anxiety, as the termination of the relationships between themselves and myself became inexorably closer. Would I be the agent of that termination for reasons of personal decision or, perish the thought, because of my illness or death? Or would they take control and make conscious plans for termination, with or without my participation in the planning? Imponderables, but clearly present in the flow of associations coming from the couch.

As I write, my eye travels to some newly typed pages that I was given an hour ago. Interesting point–counterpoint: the disheveled, fragmented Will of twenty years ago whom I have been describing just handed me the abstract of his Ph.D. dissertation. He is still the same person, but no longer disheveled, and eminently able to on focus tasks, complete them, and relate to peers and authority figures with enough effectiveness and presence to put him near to the completion of his Ph.D. and to be in the running for three university teaching positions. Many of my own memories of the seven years of foot-slogging that it took to finish my Ph.D. and then, the seven years more of post-doctoral training, were with me again. Maybe Will and I won't have to go on to the 21st century after all, but I'll miss him when he "graduates."

A clutching, seemingly uncontrollable need for me, to see me, to be reassured that I care for them has suffused my work with both Will and Jodie, an African-American patient whom I have been seeing for the past ten years. My aging has introduced an ever-increasing component of fear, fear that I am ill, that I will die, that I will stop working. Will's aging, as well as mine, has worked its own effects on the twenty years of our work. But how can I separate those reality-based outcomes from those of other fortuitous life circumstances and from the therapy itself? Impossible.

Will still yearns for me to fill the "black hole" of his need for the loving mother he never had, for the bodily closeness of infant–mother intensity. He fears the unacceptable sexual overtones of these feelings almost as much as he fears that I will die or leave him because he is "repulsive" to me and has hurt me beyond my endurance.

Pre-oedipal issues focussing on their early significant relationships are the dynamics that underlie Will's and Jodie's difficulties. Will had given graphic evidence of having been rejected by his mother as far back as his excellent memory had taken him and even more graphic accounts of an older sibling being preferred.

Jodie is just as afraid that I will die, but the dynamics are very different. Her mother would have been the same age as I, had she not died 20 years ago. Such were Jodie's conflicting feelings for the mother that she felt unable to enter the room as her mother was breathing her last. Afterwards, she searched fruitlessly, over and over, among her mother's things for some message that her mother had loved her. I sensed my ardent countertransferential wish for Jodie that she had been able to repair her relationship with her mother before her death and reexperienced my feelings at the time of my own mother's death, when our feelings for each other had come full circle to the loving closeness that had existed during my latency years.

"You're *allowed* to love her." This is what I felt like saying to Jodie. After monumental efforts spanning all ten years of our work together, to help her work through her hateful feelings toward her mother, she was finally able to whisper, "But I loved her." With that, she quietly recalled memories of good times, never before mentioned, when her mother had read poetry to her, had taken her shopping, and more, which told of the benign side of the relationship. And my feelings, sensing the striking turnabout in her? A kaleidoscope of gladness that she was finally able to contain and express her loving feelings, changing to anxiety as I antic-ipated the long-awaited negative transference. How would I handle her

inevitable anger directed at me—I, who in eighty years of life have struggled against a seemingly unquenchable need to be liked. Would my unconscious, "sneaky" ways of undercutting others' anger be so powerful that
they would derail Jodie's progress toward health, signalled by the eventual resolution of her transference neurosis? A crisis is building in the
current stages of the treatment.

Again, echoes of myself and Mother ricocheted against the walls of
memory for me, as I reexperienced the delights of travel, theater, concerts,
opera, and the like when I was boon companion to the adventuresome
"joi de vivre" mother–self that she was in the days of my childhood.
Only later, in adolescence, was I to feel the anger toward her when she,
with thin-lipped disapproval, tried to derail my aspirations to become a
psychologist.

I remembered vividly my amazement one particular day when I was
a college freshman. Mother had said, as she left the house very early
that morning, "This is the day Aunt Margaret and I are going out to
Long Island to visit Old Lady Bernays." I was accustomed to this yearly
event and had never inquired how this unknown old lady fitted into her
life until Mother came home that evening with a granny-square afghan
draped over her arm.

"What's that?" I asked.

"Old Lady Bernays made it for me," was the answer.

"And who is this Old Lady Bernays, anyway?"

"Oh, she was Professor Freud's sister, and we got to know her on the
boat when we came over from Vienna."

"What!" I shrieked. "Freud's *sister?*"

With disdain came the response: "Yes, Professor Freud. He destroyed
the age of innocence."

It was this exchange with my prudish mother that came to mind when
I experienced the haughtily scientific anti-Freudian attitudes in my early
student years. The loving, but overprotective and possessive, sense of
herself as a mother determined a peaceful, harmonious relationship between
us through the latency years. Then came adolescence, when those same
qualities created the battleground for my own struggles to individuate.
The dividend for my development as a therapist was a deep understanding
of the centrality of the quality and nuances of the mother relationship.

Jodie had me helplessly locked into the "good mother," only rarely—
and then indirectly—expressing her positive feelings and intense loyalty
to that devaluing, critical, insensitive mother whom she had hated. I feared
that I had fostered treatment impasses time and again by failing to focus
earlier on her compulsive need to tell of any instance in her day-to-day
life when she had received praise or had been given evidence of being
liked by anyone. The other side of that coin was an equally persistent
need to "undo." She felt inadequate, fraudulent. She knew nothing. How

could she pretend to be an aspiring therapist? How often have I, too, had feelings of inadequacy, incompetence, blundering? Empathic countertransference pressures me to reassure; holding back is not easy.

Jodie's mother had rarely, if ever, praised her, as she remembered her childhood. But often, her mother had indicated that she suffered from exhaustion because of the grueling daily grind of teaching third-grade classes, a job she needed desperately as a single black parent and lone breadwinner. I, too, remembered an "exhausted" mother who could not be disturbed when she took her ritual afternoon nap, but she, unlike the mother of Jodie's first ten years of life, was equal in partnership with my benign father in creating a successful business. I bathed in countertransferential joy when Jodie described the positive change in her own life when her mother remarried, having found a man who fathered Jodie as lovingly as mine had dealt with me; however, Jodie still persisted in relating in minute detail every bit of positive feedback she herself received.

Finally, in a recent session, I had evidently "had it," countertransferentially, and had remarked on this need of hers, as I had done many times, but this time with a new, more urgent voice. Her response was equally urgent, joining me in asking "why," as though she was hearing the question for the first time and hadn't a clue as to the answer. From this, after a brief silence, came an avowal of her feelings of being disloyal, of betraying her mother when she spoke critically, angrily, or hatefully of her. After another pause, she gave an accounting of the good times, spoken with the somewhat hesitant voice that evoked from me, "You're *allowed* to love her."

And so it transpired that she was finally enabled to say, "But I loved her," by my irritable inflection. Now, looking back, I sense that my irritation stemmed not only from Jodie's manifest behavior of needing to "show and tell" every indication of her goodness. Underneath, I was irritated at her because she wasn't as "good" as I in realizing how much she loved, as well as hated, her mother *before* she died, as had I. However, I was relieved and gratified that I had restrained myself from self-disclosing, to the end result that she was able to do the work of uncovering her positive feelings for her mother unaided.

It gradually came clear to me that, when I asked why she always seemed to have to tell of every experience of being praised, my voice had conveyed irritation, ergo Jodie's ability to access her "guilt" at having badmouthed her mother to me again and again over the years. Something ineffable had taken place in the interpersonal and intersubjective space between us that was enabling. The "splitting" between myself, the transferential "good mother" and the real mother's "badness," could begin to be healed, and it was the countertransferential irritation that my voice conveyed that made it happen.

Another aspect of Jodie's feelings came to mind as I pondered all of this, namely its meaning in the transference—her thinly disguised feelings of envy and rivalry with my daughter, whom she had found out about in the "small world" in which I conduct a suburban practice. It became suddenly clear that her apparent compulsivity in having to relate even the seemingly most trivial feedback that she was good, bright, or competent had a "sibling rivalry" connotation. She had shown that she yearned to be my daughter many times in many ways. Telling me how good she was, how well-seen by others, served her need to say, "Please love me more than you love that daughter of yours." Often, I sensed an angry tone of voice when the jealousy was expressed, particularly when she had found out that my daughter was visiting. "*She* can take care of you now." The dividend for the analysis was that the negative transference was fueled by her anger, signalling a break in the thick "ozone layer" of her "good mother" transference neurosis.

The crisis that is aging is not sudden. It creeps up on you or, better said, comes full circle at you, gradually. I had worked with Hannah ten years ago, when she, a widow in her mid-seventies, had come for help in making crucial decisions. Should she sell the comfortable home and office combination that she had lived and worked in, as wife and as her physician-husband's lab assistant and office factotum? Should she move to a mid-western city, to be with her only close relative, a sister who urged her to do so and who, she felt, needed her? Having no children, she was free to choose. Or thought she was.

Hannah was an intellectually and artistically gifted woman who generated enormous feelings of discomfort in me, as she circled endlessly around and around, debating the pros and cons of the issues that she insisted, demanded quick decisions. A classic example of projective identification perhaps? Cold comfort, I moaned then, as I helplessly struggled with my countertransferential discomfort while she enjoyed yet another trip around the track of indecision. Finally, she decided to visit her sister in Kansas City. The sense of anomie and dislocation there was all she needed to come to a firm decision to return to New Jersey, which she could then acknowledge as her real home.

As Hannah unself-consciously enacted her inbred "Viennese-ness," she generated an overpowering countertransference stemming from the anti-Viennese-ness of my own Viennese mother. My mother abhorred the thought of being identified as one of "them," with their superficiality, insincerity, and manipulativeness (as she characterized "them"). Her accent, when speaking faultless English, was easily identified as European, but not as Viennese or German. This was an example par excellence of my mother's determination *not* to be identified as Viennese. American is what she wanted to be, with very little acknowledgment that any part of her identity was lost by denying the value of the past.

Meanwhile, I, firmly designated by her to be her constant companion and helper, became the parentified child who took care of her as she coped with the physical (very probably psychosomatic) ailments that signalled the price she paid for her denial of the past. The wisdom of hindsight tells me that the early loss of her mother, when she was 16, newly immigrated, and faced with the imperative to become a wage-earning adult, generated the neurotic need in her to tie me to her side. Her fantasy, as I piece it together from many things she said, was that, if only she had been constantly at her mother's side and had taken care of her, her mother would not have died. And so, consequently, I was elected to the office of doing and being where she had failed, so that she might succeed in staying alive.

Fast-forward to the present: Hannah, now in her mid-eighties, calls me and wants help as she faces crucial decisions. This time, they revolve again around a multi-faceted issue: a serious heart ailment undermines her confidence in living alone. She has already experienced the terror of suffering a heart attack and finding herself on the floor after an indeterminate period of unconsciousness. Should she, can she, remain alone in her beloved apartment, ailing as she is and fearful, not only because of her illness, but also because of the dangers that threaten outside her door? The apartment house in which she lives, once the most luxurious, now sits isolated in a high-crime, inner-city neighborhood. 'Round and 'round she circles once more, around the track of indecision, and once again, I moan with the pain of feeling compelled to trot right alongside her as she circles.

I find that working with Hannah requires constant vigilance for me, lest I be seduced into taking care of her: driving her to inspect various retirement communities, having dinner with her, intervening with friends who treated her badly. Again, my "parentified" relationship with my mother fuels wariness, negativity, and anger as I squirm out of unprofessional entanglements. Underneath the pain, I sense intimations of my own mortality, the excruciatingly painful decisions I, too, may be forced to make.

A very different relationship developed between myself and another age-mate patient, Lucie. She, also a European woman and a professional musician, had endured losses as traumatic to her as Hannah's. The recent loss of her husband and mother, almost simultaneously, were the issues that brought her to my office. The crying spells, insomnia, and general dysphoria from which she suffered diminished and then disappeared as she worked through her disabling grief.

However, she made no move to terminate and willingly answered when I asked if there might be other issues she wanted to explore. What then transpired was her candid revelation that she yearned for a new sexual relationship that would be more gratifying than the one she had endured with her husband, with whom she had often felt somewhat martyred because of his disinterest in sex. Sexual feelings were very much alive despite her age, she said, shooting me a mischievous twinkle. As we discussed the realities, both of her sexual "aliveness" and of the probabilities of her finding the relationship that would fulfill her yearnings, I found myself experiencing intense empathy. We exchanged grins as we realized that sexual feelings were alive and well, despite our age. Memories of events from a few years earlier in my life, as well as the knowledge that I shared her yearnings, flooded into the forefront of consciousness. I had written an account of that period, which occurred a few years after my own husband's death.

I had started to work with a new patient who had been referred by a colleague with whom I was not personally acquainted. The patient turned out to be the colleague's father. Depression, bordering on clinical depth, had been exacerbated, three years after his wife's death, by his felt need to sell his large suburban house in which he now "rattled around" alone and to close his laboratory and retire from an active professional life.

I had felt myself react positively as I ushered a tall, nice-looking, well-spoken gentleman from my waiting room into the office. "Hm, not bad, and he seems to be about my age," I muttered to myself.

After the third session, I recognized my discomfort at the situation. The sessions had been going well, too well. I caught myself indulging in fantasies and waking from a few dreams that told me unmistakably that my hormones were not dead. My patient acknowledged similar feelings, and it was agreed that patient–therapist work was *not* going to "work." There ensued a romantic flurry, which rapidly went downhill. I had come to resent his intimations that I was "too independent" and his tacit agreement when I suggested that he wished for a nurse more than a partner. So the final coup de grace was delivered with regrets but not despair, and the relationship ended.

Lucie's story developed very differently than mine—an almost Class C "Boy Meets Girl" movie ending. She met her knight in shining armor; he adored her on sight; they were married within a few months, and his sexual expertise was dreamily satisfying. Countertransferentially, as I followed the idyllic course of Lucie's romance, I heard the words "hope can spring eternal" running through my head. And after those words, "If at first you don't succeed, try, try again."

As I hear these words, other not-so-wee-small voices overtalk them in my head. "Would I really want to give up the lifestyle that I've become comfortable with?" Over the 20-plus years since my husband died, I've had myself alone to take care of. Being alone did not necessarily connote loneliness. On the contrary, children, grandchildren, friends and, above all, career demands readily filled days and evenings. Narcissistic proclivities were nourished by the fact that I did have only myself to take care of. Men who were interested in women my age became scarcer and scarcer. Those who *were* out there seemed to need nursing more than companionship. "Thanks—but no thanks" rings in my head now. I'll stay with the memories of the husband-friend and forget about scanning the scenery for a replacement. And what happened to the still-live sexual energies? They seem to have faded before the urgency of all the other fulfilling contributors to my emotional life.

Our work together has ended, though Lucie still calls occasionally to fill me in on her life and to show that she values keeping our relationship alive. I am also cognizant of the value I received from our work together, which enabled me to reexperience my later-life romantic episode and lay it peacefully to rest.

I am old. I am not even a member of the young-old by today's classifications that differentiate elders as they occupy one or another of the three categories of young-old, middle-aged-old, and old-old. That is the truth that I seem endlessly able to deny to myself, but frequently, I am ready to acknowledge that "my youngers are my betters." Many that I rub shoulders with are, to me, "my betters" and would be role models to me in one aspect of life or another, were they younger or older.

Reality must break through, finally. I am painfully aware that, even in the writing of this account, I am dependent on the competence of three younger women to keep me "on track": first, my own daughter's best friend from earliest years, who is today a teacher of writing; second, my daughter herself, whose insights are rapier sharp; and third, the editor of this volume, an analyst herself. Were it not for these three, would I be able to organize my thoughts in logical sequence enough to be readable? Would I be able to muster the objectivity I need to focus aspects of myself that are essential to the narrative truth of my writing? And, finally, could I restrain myself from the endless, garrulous digressions that are, stereotypically, a characteristic of aging? Not likely, is the answer. My dependency on "youngers and betters" grows with my years, clearly. Dependency is a thought I abhor, and yet I bask in it, knowing well that the other side of the coin is that, with it, I can continue to function as independently as I do.

Denial may again be responsible, as I realize that I have left the impending crises most salient to the aging analyst for the end of this chapter, namely, separation, loss, and death. Major issues related to the inevitabilities of life pervade my work. No week goes by without engagement of one or all. They have become increasingly manifest, as my own aging has become more visible. Countertransferentially, I have become more sensitively attuned to indirectly expressed, latent content and affect arising out of these issues, coping as best I can with my own defensive efforts to deny their importance, if not their centrality.

Often, the anxiety generated by patients' emerging awareness of the urgency of these issues is palpable, both with respect to their own histories and, in the patient–therapist dyad, their fear of hurting me by expressing these anxieties anent my own obvious age. Witness the sometimes laughable reactions of patients if I so much as cough or clear my throat. In tones of anxiety they ask, "Are you OK?" Cancelled sessions and vacations, when announced by me, are circuitously inquired into, in ways different from earlier years, to seek reassurance that I am not ill. As much as these occurrences generate "grist for the mill," they also position me face to face with my own anxieties about the inevitable diminishing of my abilities of sensitively attending and of cognitive functioning. Referrals diminish, but, even if they didn't, could I, in good conscience, accept patients whose issues and potential suggest long-term analysis? Do they even seek me out? And if they don't, is it my age, or the recession, or managed care, or all of the above?

I recognize that I was able to come full circle as I finally achieved my original goal, training in psychoanalysis, in the NYU postdoctoral program in psychoanalysis and psychotherapy. What did I care that one of the admissions interviewers told me that he would not have recommended my acceptance if there had been a larger number of applicants to the program? His reason, stated bluntly, was that it was of dubious value to invest so much training in an individual who had so few years left to practice the learnings. (I was 58 at the time.) Did he notice that my nostrils flared as I tried to appear smilingly impassive while taking in his message? Now, more than 20 years later, I am still happily anticipating the improvements in my work to come.

Afterword

STEPHEN A. MITCHELL

This is an extraordinary collection of papers that constitutes an important first step in filling a central gap in the psychoanalytic literature.

The traditional, one-person model of psychoanalysis portrays the analyst as a technician. The significant content of the analytic process was viewed as, in its entirety, generated from the mind of the patient. The analyst observed "strict" technical procedures based on a triad of principles that was designed essentially to keep the person of the analyst out of the way: neutrality, anonymity, and abstinence. The process, once begun and properly maintained, proceeded on its own psychodynamic momentum, as the patient's central conflicts and infantile neurosis unfolded. As long as the analyst was competent, he or she was a generic factor, like a skilled operator of an x-ray, cat-scan, or, in this case, a sort of time machine.

With the sweeping shift from a one-person to a two-person framework in psychoanalysis over the past two decades, this model of clinical process has become rapidly anachronistic. The very fact that there are now so many models and approaches to doing analytic work suggests that it is no longer possible to even imagine *the* generic psychoanalyst. Even in her or his choice of analytic model, the personality, the subjectivity, and the life experience of the analyst come to have a crucial impact on the process. And we have a burgeoning literature cataloging the forms through which countertransference—the enormous range of ways in which the analyst participates in and responds to the analytic process—plays a central role.

But there has been little written so far addressing the impact on the analytic process of major past and present crises and traumas in the analyst's life. Unlike Dorothy, we are beginning to pay more attention to the "man behind the curtain," and this collection of papers makes important strides in beginning to fill out the personhood of the analyst.

One striking feature about these essays is how different they are. Each clinician struggles with his or her situation and life experiences in his or her particular fashion. And that, one comes to feel, is inevitable. Just as there is no generic analyst, there is also no generic way to deal with crises and traumas in the analyst's life. If one gives up belief in the magic cloak of invisibility provided by classical theory of technique, there are enormous numbers of complex choices to be made: what to listen for? what to speak about? how much to tell? how to judge one's own manner of participation? There are certainly *wrong* decisions, where patients are hurt and treatments damaged, but there is no *right* decision in the sense of a singularly correct choice. This collection of essays demonstrates how many different ways psychoanalysts struggle to bring their own experience to bear constructively on their work with their patients, often in a different way with each patient.

We are becoming increasingly aware of how complex and how idiosyncratic is the development of an analytic clinician. Each of us finds our own way of working, our own way of bringing our life experience to the analytic process, in our own fashion. We cannot learn how to do it from someone else, because how he or she does it cannot work for us, except through crude (and distinctly nonanalytic) imitation. But we can learn a great deal from each other. In sharing their experiences with us, these authors have given us a great deal to think about, to puzzle through, to agree with and feel inspired by, to disagree and argue with. And this is how analysts, like analysands, grow.

Index

S

Sacks, O., 121n, 122n, *139*
Sadism, 201, 203, 273
  erotic fantasies and, 204–205
Sadowsky, G., 207, *221*
Sayres Van Niel, M., xvi, *xxiii*
Schafer, R., 129, *139*, 142, *157*, 229,
  239
Schaffner, B., 232, 233, *239*
Schiff, H., 6, *20*
Schoolman, J., xiii, *xxiii*, 56, *68*
Schwartz, H., xvi, *xxiii*, 56, 63, *68*, 145,
  157, 257, *275*
Searles, H., 90, 91, *99*
Sedgwick, E., 231, *239*
Self-concept, homosexuality and,
  224–225
Self-disclosure, 16–18, 23, 24, 56, 107,
  141–142, 246, 282. *see also*
  Childbearing issues; Divorce;
  Homosexuality; Personal distinc-
  tiveness
  analytic process and, 36–37
  associative processes and, 37
  clinical work and, 16–18, 23, 24, 25,
    55–57, 64, 141–142
  countertransference and, 37
  enforced disclosure and, 41–42, 53
  guilt and, 25–26
  transference and, 42
Self-esteem, 145, 146
Self-experience, 23
Self-state, 43
Sensory processing, 133, 134
Separation anxiety, 111–113, 160
Sexual perversion, 272
Sexual trauma, clinical work and, clinical
  material, 185–189. *see also*
  Childhood trauma; Sadism
  bearing pain and, 193–194
  and boundaries, intimacy and, 194–196,
    201–202
  empathy and, 185, 189, 193, 195
  individual differences and, 191–192
  loss of historical family, identification
    and, 189–190
  pathology and, blindness to, 199–201
  separation issues, 188
  shame and, 183, 194–195, 201
    in the transference, identification and,
    190–191
  transference and, erotic, 194, 201
  uncertainty and, 196–199

Shame. *see* Sexual trauma
Shapiro, D., xix, *xxiii*, 123, *139*
Silver, A., xvi, *xxiii*, 23, *40*, 56, 257,
  275
Simon, B., xvi, *xxii*, 56, *68*, 152, *157*
Singer, E., xvi, *xxiii*, 23, 24, 26, 36, 39,
  40, 56, *68*, 153, *157*
Social constructivism, 84, 258
Sociocultural issues. *see* Divorce; Personal
  distinctiveness; Therapist's age
Spitz, R., 97, *99*
Stern, D., *139*
Stokoe, W., 121n, *139*
Stolorow, R., 43, 51, *54*
Stricker, G., xv, *xxiii*
Sullivan, H., 39, *40*, 127, *139*
  homosexuality and, 230–231, 234
Symposium on Passion in the
  Countertransferance, 257, *275*

T

Tabin, J., 237, *239*
Therapeutic alliance, 137
  analytic process and, 36, 39
Therapeutic relationship. *see also* Clinical
  related topics; Therapist's *related
  topics*
  countertransference and, 94, 95–96
  and developmental needs, childhood
    trauma and, 219–220
  dream analysis and, 11–12
  enforced disclosure and, 41–42, 53
  envy and, 171–172
  impasse consultations and, 177–178
  interpersonal exchanges and, 36
  intersubjective field and, 51
  mutual influence in, 27
  psychotherapy and, 15–16
  "real" relationship, 207
  unconscious. *see* Therapist's body
Therapist's age. *see also* Therapist's body
  aging and, 290, 293–294
  background, 277–279
  clinical material, transference/counter-
    transference and, 280–293
  social issues and, 279, 280
Therapist's body, 263–267, 293
Thompson, C., xviii, *xxiii*, 227, *239*
Thompson, P., 43, 44, *54*
Transference, 11, 34, 160, 162–164,
  166–167. *see also*
  Countertransference; Sexual trauma